Let Us C

21st Edition

Yashavant Kanetkar

www.bpbonline.com

Twenty First Edition 2025
FIRST EDITION 2007

ISBN: 978-93-6589-968-9

Distributors:

BPB PUBLICATIONS
20, Ansari Road, Darya Ganj
New Delhi-110002
Ph: 23254990/23254991

DECCAN AGENCIES
4-3-329, Bank Street,
Hyderabad-500195
Ph: 24756967/24756400

MICRO MEDIA
Shop No. 5, Mahendra Chambers,
150 DN Rd. Next to Capital Cinema,
V.T. (C.S.T.) Station, MUMBAI-400 001
Ph: 22078296/22078297

Published by Manish Jain for BPB Publications, 20 Ansari Road, Darya Ganj, New Delhi-110002 and Printed at Akash Press, New Delhi

www.bpbonline.com

Dedicated to baba,

who could not be here to see this day...

About Yashavant Kanetkar

Through his books and online courses on C, C++, Data Structures, VC++, .NET, etc. Yashavant Kanetkar has created, molded and groomed lacs of IT careers in the last three decades. Yashavant's books and online courses have made a significant contribution in creating top-notch IT workforce in India and abroad.

Yashavant's books are globally recognized, and millions of students / professionals have benefited from them. His books have been translated into Hindi, Gujarati, Japanese, Korean, Russian and Chinese languages. Many of his books are published in India, USA, Japan, Singapore, Korea, Russia and China.

Yashavant is a much sought-after speaker in the IT field and has conducted seminars/workshops at TedEx, IITs, NITs, IIITs and global software companies.

Yashavant has been honored with the prestigious "Distinguished Alumnus Award" by IIT Kanpur for his entrepreneurial, professional and academic excellence. This award was given to top 50 alumni of IIT Kanpur who have made significant contributions towards their profession and betterment of society in the last 50 years.

In recognition of his immense contribution to IT education in India, he has been awarded the "Best .NET Technical Contributor" and "Most Valuable Professional" awards by Microsoft for 5 successive years.

Yashavant holds a BE from VJTI Mumbai and M. Tech. from IIT Kanpur. His current affiliations include being the Director of KICIT Pvt. Ltd. He can be reached at kanetkar@kicit.com or through www.ykanetkar.com.

1 Getting Started

"Well begun is half done..."

You cannot be great at the start, but you must start to be great. So, making a beginning is important. This chapter will help you wet your feet, before beginning a more arduous C journey...

Contents

Before we can begin to write programs in C, it would be interesting to find out what really is C, how it came into existence and how does it compare with other programming languages. In this chapter, we would briefly outline these issues.

Four important aspects of any language are—the way it stores data, the way it operates upon this data, how it accomplishes input and output, and how it lets you control the sequence of execution of instructions in a program. We would discuss the first three of these building blocks in this chapter.

What is C?

C is a programming language developed at AT & T's Bell Laboratories of USA in 1972 by Dennis Ritchie. C became popular because it is simple and easy to use. An opinion that is often heard today is—"C has been already superseded by languages like C++, C# and Java, so why bother to learn C today". I seriously beg to differ with this opinion. There are several reasons for this. These are as follows:

(a) C++, C# or Java make use of a principle called Object Oriented Programming (OOP) to organize programs which offers many advantages. While using OOP, you need basic programming skills. So, it makes more sense to first learn C and then migrate to C++, C# or Java. Though this two-step learning process may take more time, but at the end of it, you will find it worth the trouble.

(b) Major parts of popular operating systems like Windows, UNIX, Linux and Android are written in C. Moreover, if one is to extend the operating system to work with new devices, one needs to write device driver programs. These programs are written exclusively in C.

(c) Common consumer devices like microwave ovens, washing machines and digital cameras are getting smarter by the day. This smartness comes from a microprocessor, an operating system and a program embedded in these devices. These programs must run fast and work in limited amount of memory. C is the language of choice while building such operating systems and programs.

(d) You must have seen several computer games where the user navigates some object, like say a spaceship and fires bullets at invaders. The essence of all such games is speed. To match this expectation of speed, the game must react fast to the user inputs. The popular gaming frameworks (like DirectX) that are used for creating such games are written in C.

I hope that these are very convincing reasons why you should adopt C as the first step in your quest for learning programming.

Which C are we Learning?

Brian Kernighan and Dennis Ritchie published the official description of C programming language in 1978. It is commonly referred as K&R. In 1983, the American National Standards Institute formed a committee, X3J11, to establish a standard specification of C. The ANSI standard was completed in 1989 and ratified as ANSI X3.159-1989 "Programming Language C." This version of the language is referred to as ANSI C or C89.

In 1990, the ANSI C Standard was adopted unchanged by a joint committee of the International Organization for Standardization (ISO) and the International Electrotechnical Commission (IEC). Multiple editions of the C Standard have been published in years 1990, 1999, 2011 and 2018. These editions are known as C90, C99, C11 and C17 respectively. A new major revision is under development by ISO/IEC which is expected to be released in 2023 and would therefore become C23.

Getting Started with C

There is a close analogy between learning English language and learning C language. This is illustrated in the Figure 1.1.

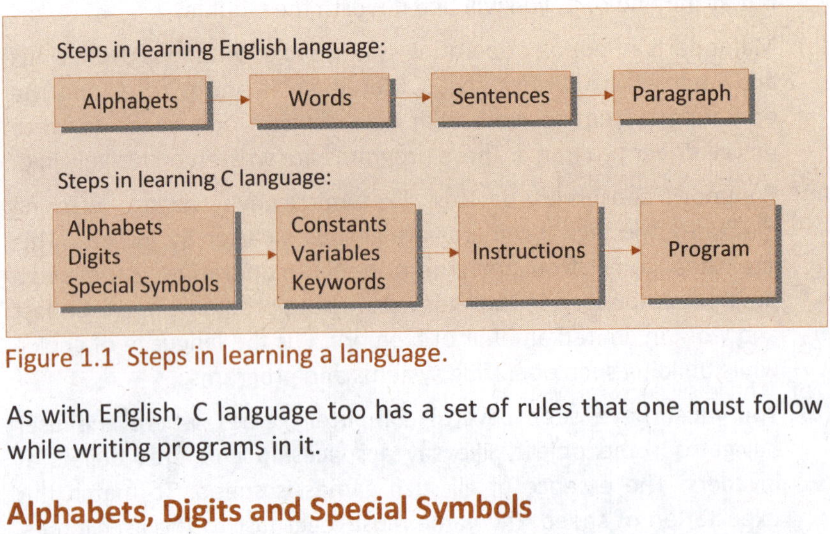

Figure 1.1 Steps in learning a language.

As with English, C language too has a set of rules that one must follow while writing programs in it.

Alphabets, Digits and Special Symbols

Figure 1.2 shows the valid alphabets, numbers and special symbols allowed in C.

<table>
<tr><td>Alphabets</td><td>A, B, ..., Y, Z
a, b,......, y, z</td></tr>
<tr><td>Digits</td><td>0, 1, 2, 3, 4, 5, 6, 7, 8, 9</td></tr>
<tr><td>Special symbols</td><td>~ ‘ ! @ # % ^ & * ( ) _ - + = | \ { } [ ] : ; " ' < > , . ? / $</td></tr>
</table>

Figure 1.2 Alphabets, digits, special symbols used in C.

Constants, Variables and Keywords

The alphabets, digits and special symbols when properly combined form constants, variables and keywords. A constant is an entity that doesn't change, whereas, a variable is an entity that may change. A keyword is a word that carries special meaning. In programming languages, constants are often called literals, whereas variables are called identifiers. Let us now see what different types of constants and variables exist in C.

Types of C Constants

Constants in C can be divided into two major categories:

(a) Primary Constants – Integer, Real, Character

(b) Secondary Constants – Pointer, Array, String, Structure, Union, Enum

At this stage, we would restrict our discussion to only Primary constants, namely, Integer, Real and Character constants. Following Rules have been laid down for constructing these different types of constants:

Rules for Constructing Integer Constants

(a) An integer constant must contain at least one digit.

(b) It must not contain a decimal point.

(c) Its value can be zero, positive or negative. If no sign precedes an integer constant, it is assumed to be positive.

(d) Commas or blanks are not allowed within an integer constant.

(e) The allowable range for integer constants is -2147483648 to +2147483647.

Ex.: 426 +782 -8000 -7605

Truly speaking, the range of an Integer constant depends upon the compiler. For compilers like Visual Studio, GCC, it is -2147483648 to +2147483647, whereas for compilers like Turbo C or Turbo C++, the range is -32768 to +32767.

Rules for Constructing Real Constants

Real constants are often called Floating Point constants. Real constants could be written in two forms—Fractional form and Exponential form. Following rules must be observed while constructing real constants expressed in fractional form:

(a) A real constant must contain at least one digit.

(b) It must contain a decimal point.

(c) It can be zero, positive or negative. Default sign is positive.

(d) Commas or blanks are not allowed within a real constant.

Ex.: +325.34 426.0 -32.76 -48.5792

The exponential form is usually used if the value of the constant is either too small or too large. It, however, does not restrict us from using exponential form for other real constants.

In exponential form, the real constant is represented in two parts. The part appearing before 'e' is called mantissa, whereas the part following 'e' is called exponent. Thus 0.000342 can be written in exponential form as 3.42e-4 (which in normal arithmetic means 3.42×10^{-4}).

Following rules must be observed while constructing real constants expressed in exponential form:

(a) A letter e or E. should separate the mantissa part and the exponential part

(b) The mantissa part may have a positive or negative sign. Default sign is positive.

(c) The exponent must have at least one digit, which may be a positive or negative integer. Default sign is positive.

(d) Range of real constants expressed in exponential form is -3.4e38 to +3.4e38.

Ex.: +3.2e-5 4.1e8 -0.2E+3 -3.2e-5

Rules for Constructing Character Constants

(a) A character constant is a *single* alphabet, digit or special symbol enclosed within single inverted commas.

(b) Both the single inverted commas should point to the left. For example, 'A' is a valid character constant, whereas 'A' is not.

```
Ex.: 'A'     'I'     '5'     '='
```

Types of C Variables

A particular type of variable can store only the same type of constant. For example, an integer variable can store only an integer constant, a real variable can store only a real constant and a character variable can store only a character constant. Hence there are as many types of variables in C, as the types of constants in it.

In any C program many calculations are done. The results of these calculations are stored in some cells (locations) of computer's memory. To make the retrieval and usage of these values easy, the memory cells are given names. Since the value stored in each location may change, the names given to these locations are called variable names.

The rules for constructing different types of constants are different. However, for constructing variable names of all types, the same set of rules applies. These rules are given below.

Rules for Constructing Variable Names

(a) A variable name is any combination of 1 to 31 alphabets, digits or underscores. Some compilers allow variable names whose length could be up to 247 characters. However, you should not create unnecessarily long variable names as it adds to your typing effort.

(b) The first character in the variable name must be an alphabet or underscore (_).

```
Ex.: si_int pop_e_89     avg     basic_salary
```

We should always create meaningful variable names. For example, while calculating simple interest, we should construct variable names like **prin**, **roi**, **noy** to represent Principle, Rate of interest and Number of years, rather than arbitrary variables like **a**, **b**, **c**.

Rules for creating variable names remain same for all the types of primary and secondary variables. So, to help differentiate between variables, it is compulsory to declare the type of any variable that we wish to use in a program. This type declaration is done as shown below.

```
Ex.: int   si, m_hra ;
     float bassal ;
     char  code ;
```

C Keywords

Keywords are the words whose meaning has already been explained to the C compiler (or in a broad sense to the computer). There are only 32 keywords available in C. Figure 1.3 gives a list of these keywords.

auto	double	int	struct
break	else	long	switch
case	enum	register	typedef
char	extern	return	union
const	float	short	unsigned
continue	for	signed	void
default	goto	sizeof	volatile
do	if	static	while

Figure 1.3 C keywords.

The keywords should not be used as variable names. However, some C compilers allow you to construct variable names that exactly resemble the keywords.

Compiler vendors provide additional keywords apart from the ones given in Figure 1.3. Though it has been suggested by the ANSI committee that every such compiler-specific keyword should be preceded by two underscores (as in **__asm**), not every vendor follows this rule.

The First C Program

Once armed with the knowledge of variables, constants and keywords, the next logical step is to combine them to form instructions. However, instead of this, we would write our first C program now. Once we have done that, we would see in detail the instructions that it made use of.

The first program is very simple. It calculates simple interest for a set of values representing principal, number of years and rate of interest.

```
/* Calculation of simple interest */
/* Author: gekay  Date: 25/06/2023 */
# include <stdio.h>
int main( )
{
    int  p, n ;
    float  r, si ;
    p = 1000 ;
    n = 3 ;
    r = 8.5 ;
    /* formula for simple interest */
    si = p * n * r / 100 ;
    printf ( "%f\n" , si ) ;
    return 0 ;
}
```

Let us now understand this program in detail.

Form of a C Program

Form of a C program indicates how it must be written. Though C is free-form language, there are certain rules about the form of a C program that are applicable to all C programs. These are as under:

(a) Each instruction in a C program is written as a separate statement.

(b) The statements in a program must appear in the same order in which we wish them to be executed.

(c) Blank spaces may be inserted between two words to improve the readability of the statement.

(d) All statements should be in lower case letters.

(e) Every C statement must end with a semicolon (;). Thus, ; acts as a statement terminator.

(f) Usually, each line contains one statement. However, you can write multiple statements in one line, provided each statement is terminated with a ;.

Comments in a C Program

Comments are used in a C program to clarify either the purpose of the program or the purpose of some statement in the program. It is a good practice to begin a program with a comment indicating the purpose of the program, its author and the date on which the program is written.

Here are a few tips for writing comments in a C program:

(a) Comments can be in small case, capital or a combination. They should be enclosed within /* */. Thus, the first two statements in our program are comments.

(b) Sometimes it is not obvious as to what a particular statement in a program accomplishes. At such times, a comment can be used to mention the purpose of the statement(s). For example,

```
/* formula for simple interest */
si = p * n * r / 100 ;
```

(c) Any number of comments can be written at any place in the program. So, a comment can be written before the statement, after the statement or within the statement as shown below.

```
/* formula */ si = p * n * r / 100 ;
si = p * n * r / 100 ; /* formula */
si = p * n * r / /* formula */ 100 ;
```

(d) Comments cannot be nested. This means one comment cannot be written inside another comment. So, following comment is invalid.

```
/* Cal of SI /* Author: gekay date: 25/06/2023 */ */
```

(e) A comment can be split over more than one line, as in,

```
/* This comment has
   three lines
   in it */
```

(f) ANSI C permits comments to be written in another way as follows:

```
// Calculation of simple interest
// Formula
```

What is *main( )*?

main( ) forms a crucial part of any C program. Let us understand its purpose as well as its intricacies.

(a) **main( )** is a function. It is a container for a set of statements. A C program may have multiple functions. If it contains only one function its name has to be **main( )**. All statements that belong to **main( )** are enclosed within a pair of braces { }.

(b) Like functions in a calculator, functions in C also return a value. **main( )** function always returns an integer value, hence there is an **int** before **main( )**. It is known as return type of the function. The integer value that we are returning is 0. 0 indicates success. If statements in **main( )** fail to do their intended work, we can return a non-zero number from **main( )**. This would indicate failure.

(c) The way to watch the value returned by **main( )** varies from one compiler to another, as shown below.

```
Turbo C, Turbo C++ - Alt C | Information
Visual Studio - $ReturnValue in Watch Window of Debugger
Linux - echo $? at command prompt after execution of the program
```

(d) Some compilers like Turbo C/C++ even permit us to return nothing from **main( )**. In such a case we should precede it with the keyword **void**. But this is the non-standard way of writing the **main( )** function. We would discuss functions and their working in detail in Chapter 8.

Variables and their Usage

Let us understand the significance of constants and variables with reference to our program.

(a) Any variable used in the program must be declared before it is used. For example,

```
int  p, n ;              /* declaration */
float  r, si ;           /* declaration */
si = p * n * r / 100 ;   /* usage */
```

(b) In the statement,

```
si = p * n * r / 100 ;
```

***** and **/** are the arithmetic operators. The arithmetic operators available in C are **+**, **-**, *****, **/** and **%**.

printf( ) and its Purpose

C does not contain any keyword to display output on the screen. All output to screen is achieved using readymade library functions like **printf( )**. Let us understand this function with respect to our program.

(a) Once the value of **si** is calculated it needs to be displayed on the screen. We have used **printf( )** to do so.

(b) To be able to use the **printf( )** function, it is necessary to use **#include <stdio.h>** at the beginning of the program. **#include** is a preprocessor directive. Its purpose will be clarified in Chapter 12.

(c) The general form of **printf( )** function is,

```
printf ( "<format string>", <list of variables> ) ;
```

<format string> can contain,

```
%f for printing real values
%d for printing integer values
%c for printing character values
```

In addition to format specifiers like **%f**, **%d** and **%c**, the format string may also contain any other characters. These characters are printed as they are when **printf( )** is executed.

(d) Given below are some more examples of usage of **printf( )** function:

```
printf ( "%f", si ) ;
printf ( "%d %d %f %f", p, n, r, si ) ;
printf ( "Simple interest = Rs. %f", si ) ;
printf ( "Principal = %d\nRate = %f", p, r ) ;
```

The output of the last statement would look like this...

```
Principal = 1000
Rate = 8.500000
```

The output is split over two lines because of newline character '\n'. It sends the cursor to next line. It is one of the several Escape Sequences available in C. These are discussed in detail in Chapter 18.

(e) **printf( )** can print values of variables as well as result of an expressions like 3, 3 + 2, c and a + b * c - d as shown below.

```
printf ( "%d %d %d %d", 3, 3 + 2, c, a + b * c – d ) ;
```

Note that **3** and **c** also represent valid expressions.

Compilation and Execution

Once you have written the program, you need to type it and instruct the machine to execute it. Two other programs are needed to do this—Editor and Compiler. Editor lets us type our program, whereas Compiler converts our program into machine language program. This conversion is necessary, since machine understands only machine language.

Apart from these two, there are other programs which you may need to improve your programming efficiency—Preprocessor, Linker and Debugger. Working with each one of them individually is a tedious job. Hence, often all these are bundled together with a layer of GUI on top of them. GUI makes using these programs easier for you. This bundle is often called Integrated Development Environment (IDE).

There are many IDEs available. Each IDE is targeted towards a particular operating system + microprocessor combination. This combination is known as a platform. A compiler created for one platform does not work with other platforms. Details of which IDE to use, from where to download it, how to install and use it are given in Appendix A. Instead of installing an IDE, there are online options available for compiling and executing programs. These are also discussed in Appendix A.

Receiving Input

In our first C program we assumed the values of **p**, **n** and **r** to be 1000, 3 and 8.5. Every time we run the program; we would get the same value for simple interest. If we want to calculate simple interest for some other set of values then we are required to incorporate these values in the program, and again compile and execute it. This means that our program is not general enough to calculate simple interest for any set of values without being required to make changes in the program. This is not a good practice.

To make the program general, the program itself should ask the user to supply the values of **p**, **n** and **r** through the keyboard during execution. This can be achieved using a function called **scanf( )**. It helps us receive input values them from the keyboard. This is illustrated in the program given below.

```
/* Calculation of simple interest */
/* Author gekay Date 25/06/2023 */
# include <stdio.h>
int main( )
{
    int  p, n ;
    float  r, si ;
    printf ( "Enter values of p, n, r" ) ;
    scanf ( "%d %d %f", &p, &n, &r ) ;
    si = p * n * r / 100 ;
    printf ( "%f\n" , si ) ;
    return 0 ;
}
```

The first **printf( )** outputs the message 'Enter values of p, n, r' on the screen. Here we have not used any expression in **printf( )** which means that using expressions in **printf( )** is optional.

Note the use of ampersand (**&**) before the variables in the **scanf( )** function is necessary. **&** is the 'Address of' operator. It gives the location number (address) used by the variable in memory. When we say **&a**, we are telling **scanf( )** at which memory location should it store the value supplied by the user from the keyboard. The detailed working of the **&** operator would be taken up in Chapter 9.

Note that a blank, a tab or a new line must separate the values supplied to **scanf( )**. A blank is created using a spacebar, tab using the Tab key and new line using the Enter key. This is shown below.

Ex.: Three values separated by blank:

```
1000 5 15.5
```

Ex.: Three values separated by tab:

```
1000	5	15.5
```

Ex.: Three values separated by newline:

```
1000
5
15.5
```

P</> Programs

Problem 1.1

Ramesh's basic salary is input through the keyboard. His dearness allowance is 40% of basic salary, and house rent allowance is 20% of basic salary. Write a program to calculate his gross salary.

Program

```
/* Calculate Ramesh's gross salary */
# include <stdio.h>
int main( )
{
    float  bp, da, hra, grpay ;
    printf ( "\nEnter Basic Salary of Ramesh: " ) ;
    scanf ( "%f", &bp ) ;
    da = 0.4 * bp ;
    hra = 0.2 * bp ;
    grpay = bp + da + hra ;
    printf ( "Basic Salary of Ramesh = %f\n", bp ) ;
    printf ( "Dearness Allowance = %f\n", da ) ;
    printf ( "House Rent Allowance = %f\n", hra ) ;
    printf ( "Gross Pay of Ramesh is %f\n", grpay ) ;
    return 0 ;
}
```

Output

```
Enter Basic Salary of Ramesh: 1200
Basic Salary of Ramesh = 1200.000000
Dearness Allowance = 480.000000
House Rent Allowance = 240.000000
Gross Pay of Ramesh is 1920.000000
```

Problem 1.2

The distance between two cities (in kilometers) is input through the keyboard. Write a program to convert and print this distance in meters, feet, inches and centimeters.

Program

```
/* Conversion of distance */
# include <stdio.h>
int main( )
{
    float  km, m , cm, ft, inch ;
    printf ( "\nEnter the distance in Kilometers: " ) ;
    scanf ( "%f", &km ) ;
    m = km * 1000 ;
    cm = m * 100 ;
    inch = cm / 2.54 ;
    ft = inch / 12 ;
    printf ( "Distance in meters = %f\n", m ) ;
    printf ( "Distance in centimeter = %f\n", cm ) ;
    printf ( "Distance in feet = %f\n", ft ) ;
    printf ( "Distance in inches = %f\n", inch ) ;
    return 0 ;
}
```

Output

```
Enter the distance in Kilometers: 3
Distance in meters = 3000.000000
Distance in centimeter = 300000.000
Distance in feet = 9842.519531
Distance in inches = 118110.234375
```

Problem 1.3

If the marks obtained by a student in five different subjects are input through the keyboard, write a program to find out the aggregate marks and percentage marks obtained by the student. Assume that the maximum marks that can be obtained by a student in each subject is 100.

Program

```
/* Calculation of aggregate & percentage marks */
# include <stdio.h>
int main( )
```

```
{
    int  m1, m2, m3, m4, m5, aggr ;
    float  per ;
    printf ( "\nEnter marks in 5 subjects: " ) ;
    scanf ( "%d %d %d %d %d", &m1, &m2, &m3, &m4, &m5 ) ;
    aggr = m1 + m2 + m3 + m4 + m5 ;
    per = aggr / 5 ;
    printf ( "Aggregate Marks = %d\n", aggr ) ;
    printf ( "Percentage Marks = %f\n", per ) ;
    return 0 ;
}
```

Output

```
Enter marks in 5 subjects: 85 75 60 72 56
Aggregate Marks = 348
Percentage Marks = 69.000000
```

Exercises

[A] Which of the following are invalid C constants and why?

'3.15'	35,550	3.25e2
2e-3	'eLearning'	"show"
'Quest'	2^3	4 6 5 2

[B] Which of the following are invalid variable names and why?

B'day	int	$hello
#HASH	dot.	number
totalArea	_main( )	temp_in_Deg
total%	1st	stack-queue
variable name	%name%	salary

[C] State whether the following statements are True or False:

(a) C language was developed by Dennis Ritchie.

(b) Operating systems like Windows, UNIX, Linux and Android are written in C.

(c) C language programs can easily interact with hardware of a PC / Laptop.

(d) A real constant in C can be expressed in both Fractional and Exponential forms.

(e) A character variable can at a time store only one character.

(f) The maximum value that an integer constant can have varies from one compiler to another.

(g) Usually, all C statements are written in small case letters.

(h) Spaces may be inserted between two words in a C statement.

(i) Spaces cannot be present within a variable name.

(j) C programs are converted into machine language with the help of a program called Editor.

(k) Most development environments provide an Editor to type a C program and a Compiler to convert it into machine language.

(l) int, char, float, real, integer, character, char, main, printf and scanf are keywords.

[D] Match the following pairs:

(a) \n	(1) Literal
(b) 3.145	(2) Statement terminator
(c) -6513	(3) Character constant
(d) 'D'	(4) Escape sequence
(e) 4.25e-3	(5) Input function
(f) main( )	(6) Function
(g) %f, %d, %c	(7) Integer constant
(h) ;	(8) Address of operator
(i) Constant	(9) Output function
(j) Variable	(10) Format specifier
(k) &	(11) Exponential form
(l) printf( )	(12) Real constant
(m) scanf( )	(13) Identifier

[E] Point out the errors, if any, in the following programs:

(a)
```
int main( )
{
    int a ; float b ; int c ;
    a = 25 ; b = 3.24 ; c = a + b * b – 35 ;
}
```

(b)
```
#include <stdio.h>
int main( )
```

```
{
    int a = 35 ; float b = 3.24 ;
    printf ( "%d %f %d", a, b + 1.5, 235 ) ;
}
```

(c)
```
#include <stdio.h>
int main( )
{
    int a, b, c ;
    scanf ( "%d %d %d", a, b, c ) ;
}
```

(d)
```
#include <stdio.h>
int main( )
{
    int m1, m2, m3
    printf ( "Enter values of marks in 3 subjects" )
    scanf ( "%d %d %d", &m1, &m2, &m3 )
    printf ( "You entered %d %d %d", m1, m2, m3 )
}
```

[F] Attempt the following questions:

(a) Temperature of a city in Fahrenheit degrees is input through the keyboard. Write a program to convert this temperature into Centigrade degrees.

(b) The length and breadth of a rectangle and radius of a circle are input through the keyboard. Write a program to calculate the area and perimeter of the rectangle, and the area and circumference of the circle.

(c) Paper of size A0 has dimensions 1189 mm x 841 mm. Each subsequent size A(n) is defined as A(n-1) cut in half, parallel to its shorter sides. Thus, paper of size A1 would have dimensions 841 mm x 594 mm. Write a program to calculate and print paper sizes A0, A1, A2, ... A8.

KanNotes

- 3 top reasons for learning C :
  - Good base for learning C++, C# or Java later
  - Unix, Linux, Windows, Gaming frameworks are written in C

- Embedded systems programs are written in C

- Constants = Literals -> Cannot change

  Variables = Identifiers -> May change

- Types of variables and constants : 1) Primary 2) Secondary

- 3 types in Primary : 1) Integer 2) Real (float) 3) Character

- Ranges :

  1) 2-byte integers : -32768 to +32767
  2) 4-byte integers : -2147483648 to +2147483647
  3) floats : -3.4×10^{38} to $+3.4 \times 10^{38}$

- In a char constant, both quotes must slant to the left, like 'A'

- Variable has two meanings :

  1) It is an entity whose value can change
  2) It is a name given to a location in memory

- Variable names are case-sensitive and must begin with an alphabet

- Total keywords = 32. Example char, int, float, etc.

- printf() is a function that can print multiple constants and variables

- Format specifiers in printf(), scanf() : int - %i, float - %f, char - %c

- main() is a function that must always return an integer value :

  0 - if it meets success, 1 - if it encounters failure

- void main() is wrong. Correct form is int main()

- Use /* ..... */ or // for a comment in a program

- & is 'address of' operator and must be used before a variable in scanf()

2 C Instructions

"On your mark, get set, go..."

Captain of a Cricket team is as good as his team. If the team is not good enough, captain alone cannot do much. Same is the case with C programming. Unless you know the instructions that it offers, you can hardly write a good program. This chapter discusses these instructions...

C Contents

- Types of Instructions
- Type Declaration Instruction
- Arithmetic Instruction
- Integer and Float Conversions
- Type Conversion in Assignment
- Hierarchy of Operations
- Associativity of Operators
- Control Instructions
- Programs
- Exercises
- KanNotes

A program is nothing but a set of instructions. Different instructions help us achieve different tasks in a program. In the last chapter we saw how to write simple C programs by using different instructions. In this chapter we would explore the instructions that we used in these programs.

Types of Instructions

There are three types of instructions in C:

(a) Type Declaration Instruction – This instruction is used to declare the types of variables used in a C program.

(b) Arithmetic Instruction – This instruction is used to perform arithmetic operations on constants and variables.

(c) Control Instruction – This instruction is used to control the sequence of execution of various statements in a C program.

Let us now take a closer look at these instructions.

Type Declaration Instruction

This instruction is used to declare the types of variables being used in the program. The type declaration instruction is written at the beginning of **main( )** function. A few examples are shown below.

```
int  bas ;
float  rs, grosssal ;
char  name, code ;
```

Here are a few subtle variations of the type declaration instruction...

(a) While declaring the type of a variable, we can also initialize it as shown below.

```
int  i = 10, j = 25 ;
float  a = 1.5, b = 1.99 + 2.4 * 1.44 ;
```

(b) A variable must stand defined before using it. The following statement is illegal since we are using variable **a** before defining it.

```
float  b = a + 3.1, a = 1.5 ;
```

(c) The following statements would work:

```
int a, b, c, d ;
a = b = c = 10 ;  /* each variable would be assigned a value 10 */
```

However, the following statement would not work:

```
int a = b = c = d = 10 ;
```

The error is we are trying to use **b** (to assign to **a**) before defining it.

Arithmetic Instruction

An arithmetic instruction in C consists of a variable name on the left-hand side of = and variable names and constants connected using operators on the right-hand side of =.

```
Ex.:  int  ad ;
      float  kot, deta, alpha, beta, gamma ;
      ad = 3200 ;
      kot = 0.0056 ;
      deta = alpha * beta / gamma + 3.2 * 2 / 5 ;
```

Here,

***, /, -, +** are the arithmetic operators.

= is an assignment operator.

2, 5 and 3200 are integer constants.

3.2 and 0.0056 are real constants.

ad is an integer variable.

kot, deta, alpha, beta, gamma are real variables.

The variables and constants together are called 'operands'. While executing an arithmetic statement, the operands on right hand side are operated upon by the 'arithmetic operators' and the result is assigned, using an assignment operator, to the variable on left-hand side.

An arithmetic statement in C could be of three types. These are as follows:

(a) Integer mode arithmetic statement – In this statement, all operands are either integer variables or integer constants.

```
Ex.:  int  i, king, issac, noteit ;
      i = i + 1 ;
```

```
king = issac * 234 + noteit - 7689 ;
```

(b) Real mode arithmetic statement – In this statement, all operands are either real constants or real variables.

```
Ex.: float  qbee, antink, si, prin, anoy, roi ;
     qbee = antink + 23.123 / 4.5 * 0.3442 ;
     si = prin * anoy * roi / 100.0 ;
```

(c) Mixed mode arithmetic statement – In this statement, some operands are integers and some operands are real.

```
Ex.: float  si, prin, anoy, roi, avg ;
     int  a, b, c, num ;
     si = prin * anoy * roi / 100.0 ;
     avg = ( a + b + c + num ) / 4 ;
```

Note the following points about Arithmetic instructions carefully:

(a) C allows only one variable on left-hand side of =. That is, **z = k * l** is legal, whereas **k * l = z** is illegal.

(b) In addition to the division operator, C also provides a **modular division** operator. This operator returns the remainder on dividing one integer with another. Thus, the expression 10 / 2 yields 5, whereas, 10 % 2 yields 0.

Note that the modulus operator (**%**) cannot be used with floats. Also note that on using %, sign of the remainder is always same as the sign of the numerator. Thus -5 % 2 yields -1, whereas, 5 % -2 yields 1.

(c) Arithmetic operations can be performed on **ints**, **floats** and **chars**. Thus, the following statements are valid.

```
char  x = 'a', y = 'b' ;
int  z = x + y ;
```

ASCII codes are used to represent any character in memory. ASCII codes of 'a' and 'b' are 01100001 and 01100010. Their decimal equivalents are 97 and 98. The addition is performed on these decimal values and not on characters themselves.

(d) No operator is assumed to be present. It must be written explicitly. In the following example, the multiplication operator after **b** must be explicitly written.

```
a = c.d.b(xy)                usual arithmetic statement
a = c * d * b * ( x * y )    C statement
```

(e) There is no operator in C to perform exponentiation operation. Exponentiation has to be carried out as shown below:

```
float a ;
a = pow ( 3.0, 2.0 ) ;
printf ( "%f", a ) ;
```

Here **pow( )** function is a standard library function. It is being used to raise 3.0 to the power of 2.0. The **pow( )** function works only with real numbers, hence we have used 3.0 and 2.0.

Note that for **pow( )** to work, it is necessary to **#include <math.h>**. **#include** is a preprocessor directive. We would learn more about standard library functions in Chapter 8 and about preprocessor in Chapter 12.

You can explore other mathematical functions like **abs( )**, **sqrt( )**, **sin( )**, **cos( )**, **tan( )**, etc., declared in **math.h** on your own.

Integer and Float Conversions

To effectively develop C programs, it is necessary to understand the rules used for implicit conversion of floating point and integer values. These are mentioned below. Note them carefully.

(a) An arithmetic operation between an integer and integer always yields an integer result.

(b) An operation between a real and real always yields a real result.

(c) An operation between an integer and real always yields a real result. In this operation, the integer is first promoted to a real and then the operation is performed. Hence the result is real.

I think a few practical examples shown in Figure 2.1 would put the issue beyond doubt.

Operation	Result	Operation	Result
5 / 2	2	2 / 5	0
5.0 / 2	2.5	2.0 / 5	0.4
5 / 2.0	2.5	2 / 5.0	0.4
5.0 / 2.0	2.5	2.0 / 5.0	0.4

Figure 2.1 Integer and float conversion.

Type Conversion in Assignments

If types of expressions on RHS and LHS of = are not same then the value of the expression on RHS is promoted or demoted depending on the type of the variable on left-hand side of =. For example, consider the following assignment statements:

```
int  i ;
float  b ;
i = 3.5 ;
b = 30 ;
```

Here though 3.5 is a **float**, it cannot be stored in **i** since it is an **int**. Hence 3.5 (**float**) is demoted to 3 (**int**) and then stored in **i**. Opposite happens in the next statement. Here, 30 is promoted to 30.0 and then stored in **b**, since **b** being a **float** variable cannot hold anything except a **float** value.

Instead of a simple expression used in the above examples, if a complex expression is used, still the same rules apply. For example, consider the following program fragment.

```
float  a, b, c ; int  s ;
s = a * b * c / 100 + 32 / 4 - 3 * 1.1 ;
```

Here, in the assignment statement, some operands are **int**s whereas others are **float**s. As we know, during evaluation of the expression, the **int**s would be promoted to **float**s and the result of the expression would be a **float**. But when this **float** value is assigned to **s**, it is again demoted to an **int** and then stored in **s**.

Observe the results of the arithmetic statements shown in Figure 2.2. It has been assumed that **k** is an integer variable and **a** is a real variable.

Arithmetic Instruction	Result	Arithmetic Instruction	Result
k = 2 / 9	0	a = 2 / 9	0.0
k = 2.0 / 9	0	a = 2.0 / 9	0.222222
k = 2 / 9.0	0	a = 2 / 9.0	0.222222
k = 2.0 / 9.0	0	a = 2.0 / 9.0	0.222222
k = 9 / 2	4	a = 9 / 2	4.0
k = 9.0 / 2	4	a = 9.0 / 2	4.5
k = 9 / 2.0	4	a = 9 / 2.0	4.5
k = 9.0 / 2.0	4	a = 9.0 / 2.0	4.5

Figure 2.2 Type conversion in assignments.

Note that though the following statements give the same result, 0, the results are obtained differently.

```
k = 2 / 9 ;
k = 2.0 / 9 ;
```

In the first statement, since both 2 and 9 are integers, the result is an integer, i.e., 0. This 0 is then assigned to **k**. In the second statement 9 is promoted to 9.0 and then the division is performed. Division yields 0.222222. However, this cannot be stored in **k**, **k** being an **int**. Hence it is demoted to 0 and then stored in **k**.

Hierarchy of Operations

While evaluating an arithmetic statement, some issues may crop up. For example, does the expression 2 * x - 3 * y correspond to (2x)-(3y) or to 2(x-3y)? Similarly, does A / B * C correspond to A / (B * C) or to (A / B) * C? To answer these questions satisfactorily, one must understand the 'hierarchy' of operations. The priority or precedence in which the operations are performed is called the hierarchy of operations. The hierarchy of commonly used operators is shown in Figure 2.3.

Priority	Operators	Description
1st	* / %	Multiplication, Division, Modular division
2nd	+ -	Addition, Subtraction
3rd	=	Assignment

Figure 2.3 Hierarchy of operators.

Within parentheses the same hierarchy as mentioned in Figure 2.3 is operative. Also, if there are more than one set of parentheses, the operations within the innermost parentheses would be performed first, followed by the operations within the second innermost pair and so on.

A few examples would clarify the issue further.

Example 2.1: Determine the hierarchy of operations and evaluate the following expression, assuming that **i** is an integer variable:

```
i = 2 * 3 / 4 + 4 / 4 + 8 - 2 + 5 / 8
```

Stepwise evaluation of this expression is shown below:

```
i = 2 * 3 / 4 + 4 / 4 + 8 - 2 + 5 / 8
i = 6 / 4 + 4 / 4 + 8 - 2 + 5 / 8        operation: *
i = 1 + 4 / 4 + 8 - 2 + 5 / 8            operation: /
i = 1 + 1+ 8 - 2 + 5 / 8                 operation: /
i = 1 + 1 + 8 - 2 + 0                    operation: /
i = 2 + 8 - 2 + 0                        operation: +
i = 10 - 2 + 0                           operation: +
i = 8 + 0                                operation : -
i = 8                                    operation: +
```

Note that 6 / 4 gives 1 and not 1.5. This so happens because 6 and 4 both are integers and therefore 6 / 4 must evaluate to an integer. Similarly, 5 / 8 evaluates to zero, since 5 and 8 are integers and hence 5 / 8 must return an integer value.

Example 2.2: Determine the hierarchy of operations and evaluate the following expression, assuming that **k** is a float variable:

```
k = 3 / 2 * 4 + 3 / 8
```

Stepwise evaluation of this expression is shown below:

```
k = 3 / 2 * 4 + 3 / 8
k = 1 * 4 + 3 / 8                operation: /
k = 4 + 3 / 8                    operation: *
k = 4 + 0                        operation: /
k = 4                            operation: +
```

Note that 3 / 8 gives zero, again for the same reason mentioned in the previous example.

All the 45 operators in C are ranked according to their precedence. We have not encountered many of these operators, so we will not pursue the subject of precedence any further here. A full-fledged list of all operators and their precedence is given in Appendix B.

So far, we have seen how arithmetic statements written in C are evaluated. But our knowledge would be incomplete unless we know how to convert a general algebraic expression to a C statement. Some examples of algebraic expressions and their equivalent C expressions are shown in Figure 2.4.

Algebraic Expression	C Expression
a x b - c x d	a * b - c * d
(m + n) (a + b)	(m + n) * (a + b)
$3x^2 + 2x + 5$	3 * x * x + 2 * x + 5
$\frac{a+b+c}{d+e}$	(a + b + c) / (d + e)
$\left[\frac{2BY}{d+1} - \frac{x}{3(z+y)}\right]$	2 * b * y / (d + 1) - x / (3 * (z + y))

Figure 2.4 Algebraic expressions and their C equivalent.

Associativity of Operators

When an expression contains two operators of equal priority, the tie between them is settled using associativity of operators. All operators in C either have Left to Right associativity or Right to Left associativity. Let us understand this with the help of a few examples.

Consider the expression a = 3 / 2 * 5 ;

Here there is a tie between operators of same priority, that is between / and *. This tie is settled using the associativity of / and *. Both enjoy Left to Right associativity. Therefore firstly / operation is done followed by *.

Consider one more expression.

```
a = b = 3 ;
```

Here, both assignment operators have the same priority. So, order of operations is decided using associativity of = operator. = associates from Right to Left. Therefore, second = is performed earlier than first =.

Consider yet another expression.

```
z = a * b + c / d ;
```

Here * and / enjoy same priority and same associativity (Left to Right). In such cases Compiler is free to perform * or / operation as per its convenience, since no matter which is performed earlier, the result would be the same.

Appendix B gives associativity of all the operators available in C. Note that the precedence and associativity of all operators is predetermined and we cannot change it.

Control Instructions

Control Instructions control the order in which the instructions in a program get executed. In other words, the control instructions determine the 'flow of control' in a program. There are four types of control instructions in C. They are:

(a) Sequence Control Instruction
(b) Selection or Decision Control Instruction
(c) Repetition or Loop Control Instruction
(d) Case Control Instruction

The Sequence control instruction ensures that the instructions are executed in the same order in which they appear in the program. Decision and Case control instructions allow the computer to take a decision as to which instruction is to be executed next. The Loop control instruction helps execute a group of statements repeatedly. In the following chapters, we are going to discuss these instructions in detail.

P</> Programs

Problem 2.1

If lengths of three sides of a triangle are input through the keyboard, write a program to find the area of the triangle.

Program

```
/* Find area of a triangle, given its sides */
# include <stdio.h>
# include <math.h>      /* for sqrt( ) */
```

```
int main( )
{
    float a, b, c, sp, area ;
    printf ( "\nEnter sides of a triangle: " ) ;
    scanf ( "%f %f %f", &a, &b, &c ) ;
    sp = ( a + b + c ) / 2 ;
    area = sqrt ( sp * ( sp - a ) * ( sp - b ) * ( sp - c ) ) ;
    printf ( "Area of triangle = %f\n", area ) ;
    return 0 ;
}
```

Output

```
Enter sides of a triangle: 4 5 6
Area of triangle = 9.921567
```

Problem 2.2

If a five-digit number is input through the keyboard, write a program to reverse the number.

Program

```
/* Reverse digits of a 5-digit number */
# include <stdio.h>
int main( )
{
    int n, d5, d4, d3, d2, d1 ;
    long int revnum ;  /* offers a bigger range of integers */
    printf ( "\nEnter a five digit number (less than 32767): " ) ;
    scanf ( "%d", &n ) ;
    d5 = n % 10 ;       /* 5th digit */
    n = n / 10 ;        /* remaining digits */
    d4 = n % 10 ;       /* 4th digit */
    n = n / 10 ;        /* remaining digits */
    d3 = n % 10 ;       /* 3rd digit */
    n = n / 10 ;        /* remaining digits */
    d2 = n % 10 ;       /* 2nd digit */
    n = n / 10 ;        /* remaining digits */
    d1 = n % 10 ;       /* 1st digit */
    revnum = d5 * 10000 + d4 * 1000 + d3 * 100 + d2 * 10 + d1 ;
```

```
    /* specifier %ld is used for printing a long integer */
    printf ( "The reversed number is %ld\n", revnum ) ;
    return 0 ;
}
```

Output

```
Enter a five digit number (less than 32767): 12345
The reversed number is 54321
```

Problem 2.3

Consider a currency system in which there are notes of six denominations, namely, Re. 1, Rs. 2, Rs. 5, Rs. 10, Rs. 50, Rs. 100. If a sum of Rs. N is entered through the keyboard, write a program to compute the smallest number of notes that will combine to give Rs. N.

Program

```
#include <stdio.h>
int main( )
{
    int amount, nohun, nofifty, noten, nofive, notwo, noone, total ;
    printf ( "Enter the amount: " ) ;
    scanf ( "%d", &amount ) ;
    nohun = amount / 100 ;
    amount = amount % 100 ;
    nofifty = amount / 50 ;
    amount = amount % 50 ;
    noten = amount / 10 ;
    amount = amount % 10 ;
    nofive = amount / 5 ;
    amount = amount % 5 ;
    notwo = amount / 2 ;
    amount = amount % 2 ;
    noone = amount / 1 ;
    amount = amount % 1 ;
    total = nohun + nofifty + noten + nofive + notwo + noone ;
    printf ( "Smallest number of notes = %d\n", total ) ;
    return 0 ;
}
```

Output

```
Enter the amount: 570
Smallest number of notes = 8
```

Exercises

[A] Point out the errors, if any, in the following C statements:

(a) x = (y + 3) ;

(b) cir = 2 * 3.141593 * r ;

(c) char = '3' ;

(d) 4 / 3 * 3.14 * r * r * r = vol_of_sphere ;

(e) volume = a^3 ;

(f) area = 1 / 2 * base * height ;

(g) si = p * r * n / 100 ;

(h) area of circle = 3.14 * r * r ;

(i) peri_of_tri = a + b + c ;

(j) slope = (y2 - y1) ÷ (x2 - x1) ;

(k) 3 = b = 4 = a ;

(l) count = count + 1 ;

(m) char ch = '25 Apr 12' ;

[B] Evaluate the following expressions and show their hierarchy.

(a) ans = 5 * b * b * x - 3 * a * y * y - 8 * b * b * x + 10 * a * y ;
(a = 3, b = 2, x = 5, y = 4 assume **ans** to be an int)

(b) res = 4 * a * y / c - a * y / c ;
(a = 4, y = 1, c = 3, assume **res** to be an int)

(c) s = c + a * y * y / b ;
(a = 2.2, b = 0.0, c = 4.1, y = 3.0, assume **s** to be a float)

(d) R = x * x + 2 * x + 1 / 2 * x * x + x + 1 ;
(x = 3.5, assume **R** to be a float)

[C] Indicate the order in which the following expressions would be evaluated:

(a) g = 10 / 5 /2 / 1 ;

(b) b = 3 / 2 + 5 * 4 / 3 ;

(c) a = b = c = 3 + 4 ;

(d) x = 2 - 3 + 5 * 2 / 8 % 3 ;

(e) z = 5 % 3 / 8 * 3 + 4

(f) y = z = -3 % -8 / 2 + 7 ;

[D] What will be the output of the following programs?

(a)
```
# include <stdio.h>
int main( )
{
    int  i = 2, j = 3, k, l ;
    float  a, b ;
    k = i / j * j ;
    l = j / i * i ;
    a = i / j * j ;
    b = j / i * i ;
    printf ( "%d %d %f %f\n", k, l, a, b ) ;
    return 0 ;
}
```

(b)
```
# include <stdio.h>
int main( )
{
    int  a, b, c, d ;
    a = 2 % 5 ;
    b = -2 % 5 ;
    c = 2 % -5 ;
    d = -2 % -5 ;
    printf ( "a = %d b = %d c = %d d = %d\n", a, b, c, d ) ;
    return 0 ;
}
```

(c)
```
# include <stdio.h>
int main( )
{
    float a = 5,  b = 2 ;
    int c, d ;
    c = a % b ;
```

```
    d = a / 2 ;
    printf ( "%d\n", d ) ;
    return 0 ;
}
```

(d)
```
# include <stdio.h>
int main( )
{
    printf ( "nn \n\n nn\n" ) ;
    printf ( "nn /n/n nn/n" ) ;
    return 0 ;
}
```

(e)
```
# include <stdio.h>
int main( )
{
    int a, b ;
    printf ( "Enter values of a and b" ) ;
    scanf ( "  %d %d  ", &a, &b ) ;
    printf ( "a  = %d b = %d", a, b ) ;
    return 0 ;
}
```

[E] State whether the following statements are True or False:

(a) * or /, + or - represents the correct hierarchy of arithmetic operators in C.

(b) [ ] and { } can be used in Arithmetic instructions.

(c) Hierarchy decides which operator is used first.

(d) In C, Arithmetic instruction cannot contain constants on left side of =.

(e) In C ** operator is used for exponentiation operation.

(f) % operator cannot be used with floats.

[F] Fill in the blanks:

(a) In y = 10 * x / 2 + z ; ___ operation will be performed first.

(b) If **a** is an integer variable, a = 11 / 2 would store ___ in **a**.

(c) The expression, a = 22 / 7 * 5 / 3 would evaluate to ______.

(d) The expression x = -7 % 2 - 8 would evaluate to ____.

(e) If **d** is a **float** the operation d = 2 / 7.0 would store ____ in **d**.

[G] Attempt the following questions:

(a) If a five-digit number is input through the keyboard, write a program to calculate the sum of its digits. (Hint: Use the modulus operator **%**)

(b) Write a program to receive Cartesian co-ordinates (x, y) of a point and convert them into polar co-ordinates (r, φ).

Hint: $r = sqrt (x^2 + y^2)$ and $\varphi = \tan^{-1} (y / x)$

(c) Write a program to receive values of latitude (L1, L2) and longitude (G1, G2), in degrees, of two places on the earth and output the distance (D) between them in nautical miles. The formula for distance in nautical miles is:

$D = 3963 \cos^{-1} (\sin L1 \sin L2 + \cos L1 \cos L2 * \cos (G2 – G1))$

(d) Wind-chill factor is the felt air temperature on exposed skin due to wind. The wind-chill temperature is always lower than the air temperature, and is calculated as per the following formula:

$wcf = 35.74 + 0.6215t + (0.4275t - 35.75) * v^{0.16}$

where **t** is temperature and **v** is wind velocity. Write a program to receive values of **t** and **v** and calculate wind-chill factor (wcf).

(e) If value of an angle is input through the keyboard, write a program to print all its Trigonometric ratios.

(f) Two numbers are input through the keyboard into two locations C and D. Write a program to interchange the contents of C and D.

KanNotes

- Standard steps in interchanging contents of two variables :

  t = a ; a = b ; b = t ;

- / gives quotient, % gives remainder. While taking %, sign of remainder is same as sign of numerator. % doesn't work with floats

- C offers 3 types of instructions :

1) Type declaration 2) Arithmetic 3) Control

- Declaration and assignment can be combined. Ex. : int a = 5 ;
- 3 types of Arithmetic instructions:
  1) Integer mode 2) Real mode 3) Mixed mode
- Rules for arithmetic instructions :
  - If one operand is float, result is a float
  - Result is int only if both operands are ints
- a = pow (2, 5) ; would store 2^5 in a. Remember to #include <math.h>
- Every operator has 1) Priority 2) Associativity
- Priority is * / %, + -, =. Priority can be changed using ()
- Associativity comes into play when priority cannot decide which operation to perform first. Associativity is either L to R or R to L. +, -, *, /, % has L to R, = has R to L associativity
- Format string of printf() can contain :
  1) Format specifiers - %c, %d, %f
  2) Escape sequences : \n, \t, many others
  3) Any other character
- Format string of scanf() can contain only format specifiers
- Control instructions control the sequence of execution of instructions in a program
- 4 types of control instructions :
  1) Sequence 2) Decision 3) Repetition 4) Case

3 Decision Control Instruction

"Indecision cost > Wrong decision cost"

As we lead our life, we have to take decisions. Similarly, as we make progress in C programming and try to implement complicated logics, our program has to take decisions. But how? Well, this chapter has the answer...

Contents

We all need to alter our actions in face of changing circumstances. If the weather is fine, then I would go for a stroll. If the highway is busy, I would take a diversion. If you join our WhatsApp group, I would send you interesting videos. You can notice that all these decisions depend on some condition being met.

In C programs too, we must be able to perform different sets of actions depending on the circumstances. In the programs written in Chapters 1 and 2, we used sequence control instruction in which the various statements got executed sequentially, i.e., in the same order in which they appeared in the program. In many programming situations, we want one set of instructions to be executed in one situation, and a different set in another situation. In C programming, such situations are dealt with using a decision control instruction.

The *if - else* Statement

C uses the keywords **if** and **else** to implement the decision control instruction. The general form of this statement looks like this:

```
if ( this condition is true )
    statement1 ;
else
    statement2 ;
```

The condition following the keyword **if** is always enclosed within a pair of parentheses. If the condition is true, then statement1 is executed. If the condition is not true, then statement2 is executed. The condition is expressed using 'relational' operators. These operators allow us to compare two values. Figure 3.1 shows how they look and how they are evaluated in C.

this expression	is true if
x == y	x is equal to y
x != y	x is not equal to y
x < y	x is less than y
x > y	x is greater than y
x <= y	x is less than or equal to y
x >= y	x is greater than or equal to y

Figure 3.1 Relational expressions and their meaning.

Here == is the equality operator and, != is the inequality operator. Note that = is used for assignment, whereas, == is used for comparison of two quantities. Let us now understand with the help of an example how **if - else** and the relational operators are used in a program.

Example 3.1: While purchasing certain items, a discount of 10% is offered if the quantity purchased is more than 1000. If quantity and price per item are input through the keyboard, write a program to calculate the total expenses.

Given below is a program that implements this logic.

```
/* Calculation of total expenses */
# include <stdio.h>
int main( )
{
    int  qty, dis ;
    float  rate, tot ;
    printf ( "Enter quantity and rate " ) ;
    scanf ( "%d %f", &qty, &rate) ;
    if ( qty > 1000 )
        dis = 10 ;
    else
        dis = 0 ;
    tot = ( qty * rate ) - ( qty * rate * dis / 100 ) ;
    printf ( "Total expenses = Rs. %f\n", tot ) ;
    return 0 ;
}
```

Here is some sample interaction with the program.

```
Enter quantity and rate 1200 15.50
Total expenses = Rs. 16740.000000
```

```
Enter quantity and rate 200 15.50
Total expenses = Rs. 3100.000000
```

In the first run of the program, the condition evaluates to true, as 1200 (value of **qty**) is greater than 1000. Therefore, the variable **dis** gets a value 10. Using this new value, total expenses are calculated and printed.

In the second run, the condition evaluates to false, as 200 (the value of **qty**) isn't greater than 1000. Thus, **dis**, this time gets a value 0. Hence the expression after the minus sign evaluates to zero, thereby offering no discount.

Note how the statements after **if** and after **else** are indented using tab. We would adopt this style throughout this book. Also note that if we do not wish to do anything when the condition fails, we can drop the **else** and the statement belonging to it.

Multiple Statements within *if - else*

It may so happen that in a program we want more than one statement to be executed when the expression following **if** is satisfied. If such multiple statements are to be executed, then they must be placed within a pair of braces, as illustrated in the following example:

Example 3.2: In a company an employee is paid as under:

If his basic salary is less than Rs. 1500, then HRA = 10% of basic salary and DA = 90% of basic salary. If his salary is either equal to or above Rs. 1500, then HRA = Rs. 500 and DA = 98% of basic salary. If the employee's salary is input through the keyboard write a program to find his gross salary.

The program that implements this logic is given below.

```
/* Calculation of gross salary */
# include <stdio.h>
int main( )
{
    float   bs, gs, da, hra ;
    printf ( "Enter basic salary " ) ;
    scanf ( "%f", &bs ) ;
    if ( bs < 1500 )
    {
        hra = bs * 10 / 100 ;
        da = bs * 90 / 100 ;
    }
    else
    {
        hra = 500 ;
        da = bs * 98 / 100 ;
    }
```

```
    gs = bs + hra + da ;
    printf ( "gross salary = Rs. %f\n", gs ) ;
    return 0 ;
}
```

Figure 3.2 would help you understand the flow of control in the program.

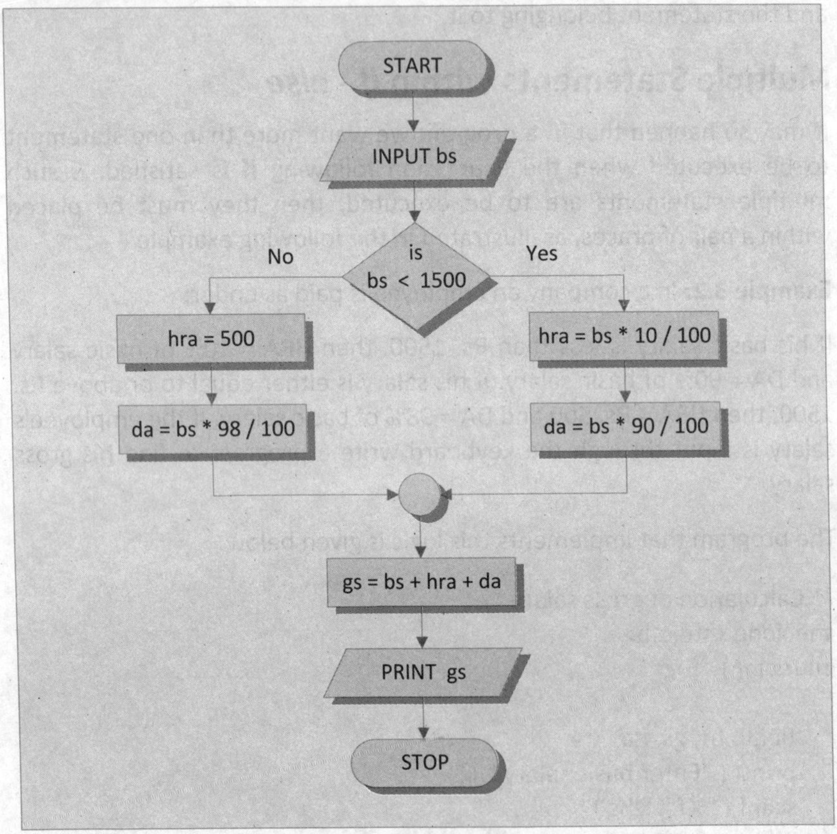

Figure 3.2 Flowchart for Example 3.2.

A few points worth noting about the program...

(a) The group of statements after the **if** up to and not including the **else** is called an 'if block'. Similarly, the statements after the **else** form the 'else block'.

(b) Notice that the **else** is written exactly below the **if**. The statements in the if block and those in the else block have been indented to the right. This formatting convention is followed throughout the book to enable you to understand the working of the program better.

(c) Had there been only one statement to be executed in the if block and only one statement in the else block, we could have dropped the pair of braces.

(d) The default scope of **if** as well as **else** is the statement immediately after them. To override this default scope, a pair of braces, as shown in the above example, must be used.

Nested *if-elses*

It is perfectly alright if we write another **if-else** construct within either the **if** block or the **else** block. This is called 'nesting' and is shown in the following code fragment:

```
if ( i == 1 )
    printf ( "More questions you ask, more you know!\n" ) ;
else
{
    if ( i == 2 )
        printf ( "If you ask a question you are a fool for some time!\n" ) ;
    else
        printf ( "If you don't ask a que you are fool for a lifetime!\n" ) ;
}
```

Note that the second **if-else** construct is nested in the first **else** block. If the condition in the first **if** is false, then the condition in the second **if** is checked. If it is false as well, then the second **else** is executed.

You can observe how each time an **if-else** construct is nested within another **if-else** construct, it is also indented to add clarity to the program. Inculcate this habit of indentation; otherwise, you would end up writing programs which nobody (you included) can understand easily later. Note that whether we indent or do not indent the program, it does not alter the flow of execution of instructions in the program.

In the above program, an **if-else** occurs within the '**else** block' of the first **if** statement. Similarly, in some other program, an **if-else** may occur in the '**if** block' as well. Depending upon the demands of the logic at hand, we may have deeply nested **if**s and **else**s.

A Word of Caution

Though usually a condition is used in **if** statement, any valid expression will also do. Thus, all the following **if** statements are valid.

```
if ( 3 + 2 % 5 )
    printf ( "This works" ) ;
if ( a = 10 )
    printf ( "Even this works" ) ;
if ( -5 )
    printf ( "Surprisingly even this works" ) ;
```

Note that in C a non-zero value is considered to be true, whereas 0 is considered to be false. In the first **if**, the expression evaluates to **5** and since **5** is non-zero it is considered to be true. Hence the first **printf( )** gets executed.

In the second **if**, 10 gets assigned to **a** so the **if** is now reduced to **if (a)** or **if (10)**. Since 10 is non-zero, it is true hence again **printf( )** goes to work.

In the third **if**, -5 is a non-zero number, hence true. So again **printf( )** goes to work. In place of -5 even if a float like 3.14 were used, it would be considered to be true. So, the issue is not whether the number is integer or float, or whether it is positive or negative. Issue is whether it is zero or non-zero.

A common mistake while using **if** statement is to write a semicolon (;) after the condition, as shown below.

```
scanf ( "%d", &i ) ;
if ( i == 5 ) ;
    printf ( "You entered 5\n" ) ;
```

The ; makes the compiler to interpret the statement as if you have written it in following manner:

```
if ( i == 5 )
    ;
printf ( "You entered 5\n" ) ;
```

Here, if the condition evaluates to true, the ; (null statement, which does nothing on execution) gets executed, following which **printf( )** gets executed. If the condition fails, then straightaway **printf( )** gets executed. So irrespective of whether the condition evaluates to true or false, **printf( )** is bound to get executed. Remember that compiler would not point out this as an error, since as far as the syntax is concerned, nothing has gone wrong but the logic has certainly gone awry.

P</> Programs

Problem 3.1

If cost price and selling price of an item is input through the keyboard, write a program to determine whether the seller has made profit or incurred loss. Also determine how much profit he made or loss he incurred.

Program

```
/* Calculate profit or loss */
# include <stdio.h>
int main( )
{
    float  cp, sp, p, l ;
    printf ( "\nEnter cost price and selling price: " ) ;
    scanf ( "%f %f", &cp, &sp ) ;
    p = sp - cp ;
    l = cp - sp ;
    if ( p > 0 )
        printf ( "The seller made a profit of Rs. %f\n", p ) ;
    if ( l > 0 )
        printf ( "The seller incurred loss of Rs. %f\n", l ) ;
    if ( p == 0 )
        printf ( "There is no loss, no profit\n" ) ;
    return 0 ;
}
```

Output

```
Enter cost price and selling price: 25 15
The seller incurred loss of Rs. 10.000000
```

Problem 3.2

Any integer is input through the keyboard. Write a program to find out whether it is an odd number or even number.

Program

```
/* Check whether a number is even or odd */
# include <stdio.h>
int main( )
{
    int n ;
    printf ( "\nEnter any number: " ) ;
    scanf ( "%d", &n ) ;
    if ( n % 2 == 0 )
        printf ( "The number is even\n" ) ;
    else
        printf ( "The number is odd\n" ) ;
    return 0 ;
}
```

Output

```
Enter any number: 45
The number is odd
```

Problem 3.3

Any year is input through the keyboard. Write a program to determine whether the year is a leap year or not.

Program

```
/* Check whether a year is leap or not */
# include <stdio.h>
int main( )
{
    int yr ;
    printf ( "\nEnter a year: " ) ;
    scanf ( "%d", &yr ) ;
    if ( yr % 100 == 0 )
    {
```

```
        if ( yr % 400 == 0 )
            printf ( "Leap year\n" ) ;
        else
            printf ( "Not a Leap year\n" ) ;
    }
    else
    {
        if ( yr % 4 == 0 )
            printf ( "Leap year\n" ) ;
        else
            printf ( "Not a leap year\n" ) ;
    }
    return 0 ;
}
```

Output

```
Enter a year: 2020
Leap year
```

Exercises

[A] What will be the output of the following programs?

(a)
```
# include <stdio.h>
int main( )
{
    int  a = 300, b, c ;
    if ( a >= 400 )
        b = 300 ;
    c = 200 ;
    printf ( "%d %d\n", b, c ) ;
    return 0 ;
}
```

(b)
```
# include <stdio.h>
int main( )
{
    int  x = 10, y = 20 ;
    if ( x == y ) ;
        printf ( "%d %d\n", x, y ) ;
```

```
    return 0 ;
}
```

(c)
```
# include <stdio.h>
int main( )
{
    int  x = 3 ;
    float  y = 3.0 ;
    if ( x == y )
        printf ( "x and y are equal\n" ) ;
    else
        printf ( "x and y are not equal\n" ) ;
    return 0 ;
}
```

(d)
```
# include <stdio.h>
int main( )
{
    int  x = 3, y, z ;
    y = x = 10 ;
    z = x < 10 ;
    printf ( "x = %d y = %d z = %d\n", x, y, z ) ;
    return 0 ;
}
```

(e)
```
# include <stdio.h>
int main( )
{
    int i = 65 ;
    char j = 'A' ;
    if ( i == j )
        printf ( "C is WOW\n" ) ;
    else
        printf ( "C is a headache\n" ) ;
    return 0 ;
}
```

[B] Point out the errors, if any, in the following programs:

(a)
```
# include <stdio.h>
int main( )
{
    float  a = 12.25, b = 12.52 ;
```

```
    if ( a = b )
        printf ( "a and b are equal\n" ) ;
    return 0 ;
}
```

(b)
```
# include <stdio.h>
int main( )
{
    int  j = 10, k = 12 ;
    if ( k >= j )
    {
        {
            k = j ;
            j = k ;
        }
    }
    return 0 ;
}
```

(c)
```
# include <stdio.h>
int main( )
{
    if ( 'X' < 'x' )
        printf ( "ascii value of X is smaller than that of x\n" ) ;
}
```

(d)
```
# include <stdio.h>
int main( )
{
    int  x = 10 ;
    if ( x >= 2 ) then
        printf ( "%d\n", x ) ;
    return 0 ;
}
```

(e)
```
# include <stdio.h>
int main( )
{
    int  x = 10, y = 15 ;
    if ( x % 2 = y % 3 )
        printf ( "Carpathians\n" ) ;
}
```

(f)
```
# include <stdio.h>
```

```
int main( )
{
    int a, b ;
    scanf ( "%d %d", a, b ) ;
    if ( a > b ) ;
        printf ( "This is a game\n" ) ;
    else
        printf ( "You have to play it\n" ) ;
    return 0 ;
}
```

[C] State whether the following statements are True or False:

(a) ; is a valid statement.

(b) Ifs can be nested.

(c) If there are multiple statements in if or else block, they should be enclosed within a pair of { }.

(d) If can occur within an if block but not in the else block.

(e) By default, there is only one statement in if block and only one in the else block.

(f) Nothing happens on execution of a null statement.

[D] Match the following pairs:

(a) Multiples statements	(1) Assignment operator
(b) else block	(2) Comparison operator
(c) ;	(3) Relational operators
(d) < > <= >= == !=	(4) optional
(e) ==	(5) { }
(f) + - * / %	(6) Arithmetic operators
(g) =	(7) Null statement
(h) Default control instruction	(8) if - else
(i) Decision control instruction	(9) Sequence

[E] Which of the following are valid ifs?

(a) if (-25)

(b) if (3.14)

(c) if (a)

(d) if (a + b)

(e) if (a >= b)

[F] Attempt the following questions:

(a) A five-digit number is entered through the keyboard. Write a program to obtain the reversed number and to determine whether the original and reversed numbers are equal or not.

(b) If ages of Ram, Shyam and Ajay are input through the keyboard, write a program to determine the youngest of the three.

(c) Write a program to check whether a triangle is valid or not, if three angles of the triangle are entered through the keyboard. A triangle is valid if the sum of all the three angles is equal to 180 degrees.

(d) Write a program to find the absolute value of a number entered through the keyboard.

(e) Given the length and breadth of a rectangle, write a program to find whether the area of the rectangle is greater than its perimeter. For example, the area of the rectangle with length = 5 and breadth = 4 is greater than its perimeter.

(f) Given three points **(x1, y1)**, **(x2, y2)** and **(x3, y3)**, write a program to check if the three points fall on one straight line.

(g) Given the coordinates **(x, y)** of center of a circle and its radius, write a program that will determine whether a point lies inside the circle, on the circle or outside the circle. (Hint: Use **sqrt( )** and **pow( )** functions)

(h) Given a point **(x, y)**, write a program to find out if it lies on X-axis, Y-axis or origin.

(i) According to Gregorian calendar, it was Monday on the date 01/01/01. If any year is input through the keyboard write a program to find out what is the day on 1st January of this year.

KanNotes

- General form of decision control instruction :

```
if ( condition )
    statement1 ;
else
    statement2 ;
```

- If there are several statements in if and else blocks, they must be enclosed within { }

```
if ( condition )
{
    statement1 ; statement2 ;
}
else
{
    statement3 ; statement4 ;
}
```

- The default scope of if and else statement is only the next statement. So, to execute multiple statements they must be written in a pair of braces.
- Condition is built using relation operators <, >, <=, >=, ==, !=
- An if need not always be associated with an else. However, an else must always be associated with an if
- An if-else statement can be nested inside another if-else statement
- a = b is assignment. a == b is comparison
- In if (a == b == c) result of a == b is compared with c
- If a condition is true it is replaced by 1, if it false it is replaced by 0
- Any non-zero number is true, 0 is false
- ; is a null statement. It does not do anything on execution

4 More Complex Decision Making

"Life is complex, so are decisions in life..."

If I get good marks in my final year and if my GRE and TOEFL scores are good and if I get good recommendations or if I do not get a job with good prospects and if my family conditions permit me, then I would think of doing MS in US. How can such complex decision making be implemented in C? This chapter will show you how...

Contents

We all face situations where the action that we carry out is based on multiple conditions. For example, I will join a company if the company allocates a metro location, gives me a good pay package and permits a joining period of 4 weeks. In programming too, action performed may be based on the result of multiple conditions. Such programming situations can be handled elegantly using Logical Operators. This chapter explores the use of logical operators and one more type of operators called conditional operators.

Use of Logical Operators - Checking Ranges

C allows usage of three logical operators, namely, &&, || and !. These should be read as 'AND', 'OR' and 'NOT' respectively. Of these, **&&** and **||** operators allow two or more conditions to be. Let us see how they are used in programs. Consider the following example:

Example 4.1: The marks obtained by a student in 5 different subjects are input through the keyboard. The student gets a division as per the following rules:

Percentage above or equal to 60 - First division
Percentage between 50 and 59 - Second division
Percentage between 40 and 49 - Third division
Percentage less than 40 - Fail

Write a program to calculate the division obtained by the student.

There are two ways in which we can write a program for this example. These methods are given below.

```
/* Method – I */
# include <stdio.h>
int main( )
{
    int  m1, m2, m3, m4, m5, per ;
    printf ( "Enter marks in five subjects " ) ;
    scanf ( "%d %d %d %d %d", &m1, &m2, &m3, &m4, &m5 ) ;
    per = ( m1 + m2 + m3 + m4 + m5 ) / 5 ;
    if ( per >= 60 )
        printf ( "First division\n" ) ;
    else
    {
        if ( per >= 50 )
            printf ( "Second division\n" ) ;
```

```
        else
        {
            if ( per >= 40 )
                printf ( "Third division\n" ) ;
            else
                printf ( "Fail\n" ) ;
        }
    }
    return 0 ;
}
```

This is a straight-forward program. Observe that the program uses nested **if-else**s. Though the program works fine, it has three disadvantages:

(a) As the number of conditions go on increasing the level of indentation also goes on increasing. As a result, the whole program creeps to the right. So much so, that entire program is not visible on the screen. So, if something goes wrong with the program, locating what is wrong where becomes difficult.

(b) It is difficult to match the corresponding **if**s and **else**s.

(c) It is difficult to match the corresponding pair of braces.

All these three problems can be eliminated by usage of 'Logical Operators'. The following program illustrates this:

```
/* Method – II */
# include <stdio.h>
int main( )
{
    int m1, m2, m3, m4, m5, per ;
    printf ( "Enter marks in five subjects " ) ;
    scanf ( "%d %d %d %d %d", &m1, &m2, &m3, &m4, &m5 ) ;
    per = ( m1 + m2 + m3 + m4 + m5 ) / 5 ;
    if ( per >= 60 )
        printf ( "First division\n" ) ;
    if ( ( per >= 50 ) && ( per < 60 ) )
        printf ( "Second division\n" ) ;
    if ( ( per >= 40 ) && ( per < 50 ) )
        printf ( "Third division\n" ) ;
    if ( per < 40 )
        printf ( "Fail\n" ) ;
```

```
    return 0 ;
}
```

In the second **if** statement, the **&&** operator is used to combine two conditions. ‘Second division’ gets printed only if both the conditions evaluate to true.

All the three disadvantages cited above have been overcome in this program. However, there is a negative side to the program too. Even if the first condition turns out to be true, all other conditions are still checked. This will increase the time of execution of the program. This can be avoided using the **else if** clause discussed in the next section.

The *else if* Clause

Let us now rewrite program for Example 4.1 using **else if** blocks.

```
/* else if ladder demo */
if ( per >= 60 )
    printf ( "First division\n" ) ;
else if ( per >= 50 )
    printf ( "Second division\n" ) ;
else if ( per >= 40 )
    printf ( "Third division\n" ) ;
else
    printf ( "fail\n" ) ;
```

Using **if - else if - else** reduces the indentation of the statements. Here the last **else** goes to work only if all conditions fail. Thus, the last **else** handles the 'none of the above' case.

Also, if a condition is satisfied, other conditions below it are not checked. If there is no explicit action to be taken if all conditions fail then else statement can be omitted.

Use of Logical Operators - Yes / No Problem

Another place where logical operators are useful is when we want to write programs for complicated logics that ultimately boil down to only two answers—yes or no. The following example illustrates this:

Example 4.2: A company insures its drivers in the following cases:

- If the driver is married.
- If the driver is unmarried, male & above 30 years of age.

– If the driver is unmarried, female & above 25 years of age.

In all other cases, the driver is not insured. If the marital status, sex and age of the driver are the inputs, write a program to determine whether the driver should be insured or not.

The outcome of the program would be—either the driver should be insured or the driver should not be insured. So, the program can be conveniently written using logical operators. For this let us first identify those cases in which the driver is insured. They are—Driver is married, Driver is an unmarried male above 30 years of age, and Driver is an unmarried female above 25 years of age. Since all these cases lead to the driver being insured, they can be combined using **&&** and **||** as shown in the program below.

```
/* Insurance of driver - using logical operators */
# include <stdio.h>
int main( )
{
    char  sex, ms ;
    int  age ;
    printf ( "Enter age, sex, marital status " ) ;
    scanf ( "%d %c %c", &age, &sex, &ms ) ;
    if ( ( ms == 'M') || ( ms == 'U' && sex == 'M' && age > 30 ) ||
                ( ms == 'U' && sex == 'F' && age > 25 ) )
        printf ( "Driver should be insured\n" ) ;
    else
        printf ( "Driver should not be insured\n" ) ;

    return 0 ;
}
```

In this program, it is important to note that:

- The driver will be insured only if one of the conditions enclosed in parentheses evaluates to true.
- For the expression in second pair of parentheses to evaluate to true, each condition in the expression separated by && must evaluate to true.
- Even if one of the conditions in the second parentheses evaluates to false, then the whole expression evaluates to false.
- The last two of the above arguments apply to third pair of parentheses as well.

In some programs we may combine the usage of **if—else if—else** and logical operators. This is demonstrated in the following program.

Example 4.3: Write a program to calculate the salary as per the following table:

Gender	Years of Service	Qualifications	Salary
Male	>= 10	Post-Graduate	11000
	>= 10	Graduate	10000
	< 10	Post-Graduate	10000
	< 10	Graduate	7000
Female	>= 10	Post-Graduate	12000
	>= 10	Graduate	9000
	< 10	Post-Graduate	10000
	< 10	Graduate	6000

Here is the program...

```
# include <stdio.h>
int main( )
{
    char  g ;
    int  yos, qual, sal = 0 ;
    printf ( "Enter Gender, Years of Service and
              Qualifications (0 = G, 1 = PG): " ) ;
    scanf ( "%c%d%d", &g, &yos, &qual ) ;
    if ( g == 'm' && yos >= 10 && qual == 1 )
        sal = 11000 ;
    else if ( ( g == 'm' && yos >= 10 && qual == 0 ) ||
        ( g == 'm' && yos < 10 && qual == 1 ) )
        sal = 10000 ;
    else if ( g == 'm' && yos < 10 && qual == 0 )
        sal = 7000 ;
    else if ( g == 'f' && yos >= 10 && qual == 1 )
        sal = 12000 ;
    else if ( g == 'f' && yos >= 10 && qual == 0 )
        sal = 9000 ;
    else if ( g == 'f' && yos < 10 && qual == 1 )
```

```
        sal = 10000 ;
    else if ( g == 'f' && yos < 10 && qual == 0 )
        sal = 6000 ;
    printf ( "\nSalary of Employee = %d\n", sal ) ;
    return 0 ;
}
```

I hope you can follow the implementation of this program on your own.

The ! Operator

The third logical operator is the NOT operator, written as **!**. This operator reverses the result of the expression it operates on. So if the expression evaluates to true, then applying **!** operator to it results into a false. Vice versa, if the expression evaluates to false, then applying **!** to it makes it true. Here is an example showing use of ! operator.

```
! ( y < 10 )
```

If **y** is less than 10, the result will be false, since **(y < 10)** is true.

The NOT operator is often used to reverse the logical value of a single variable, as in the expression

```
if ( ! flag )
```

This is another way of saying:

```
if ( flag == 0 )
```

Figure 4.1 summarizes the working of all the three logical operators.

Operands		Results			
x	**y**	**!x**	**!y**	**x && y**	**x || y**
False	False	True	True	False	False
False	True	True	False	False	True
True	False	False	True	False	True
True	True	False	False	True	True

Figure 4.1 Working of !, && and | |.

Hierarchy of Operators Revisited

Since we have now added the logical operators to the list of operators we know, it is time to review these operators and their priorities. Figure 4.2 summarizes the operators we have seen so far. The higher the position of an operator is in the table, higher is its priority. (A full-fledged precedence table of operators is given in Appendix B.)

Operators	Type
!	Logical NOT
* / %	Arithmetic and modulus
+ -	Arithmetic
< > <= >=	Relational
== !=	Relational
&&	Logical AND
||	Logical OR
=	Assignment

Figure 4.2 Hierarchy of operators.

The Conditional Operators

The conditional operators **?** and **:** are sometimes called ternary operators since they take three arguments. In fact, they form a kind of foreshortened if-then-else. Their general form is,

```
expression 1 ? expression 2 : expression 3
```

What this expression says is: "if **expression 1** is true, then the value returned will be **expression 2**, otherwise the value returned will be **expression 3**". Let us understand this with the help of a few examples.

(a)
```
int  x, y ;
scanf ( "%d", &x ) ;
y = ( x > 5 ? 3 : 4 ) ;
```

This statement will store 3 in **y** if **x** is greater than 5, otherwise it will store 4 in y.

(b)
```
char  a ;
int  y ;
scanf ( "%c", &a ) ;
y = ( a >= 65 && a <= 90 ? 1 : 0 ) ;
```

Here 1 would be assigned to **y** if **a >=65 && a <=90** evaluates to true, otherwise 0 would be assigned.

The following points may be noted about the conditional operators:

(a) It's not necessary that the statement after ? or : be only arithmetic statements. This is illustrated in the following examples:

```
Ex.:  int i ;
      scanf ( "%d", &i ) ;
      ( i == 1 ? printf ( "Amitabh" ) : printf ( "All and sundry" ) ) ;

Ex.:  char a = 'z' ;
      printf ( "%c", ( a >= 'a' ? a : '!' ) ) ;
```

(b) The conditional operators can be nested as shown below.

```
int big, a, b, c ;
big = ( a > b ? ( a > c ? 3: 4 ) : ( b > c ? 6: 8 ) ) ;
```

(c) Check out the following conditional expression:

```
a > b ? g = a : g = b ;
```

This will give you an error 'Lvalue Required'. The error can be overcome by enclosing the statement in the : part within a pair of parentheses. This is shown below.

```
a > b ? g = a : ( g = b ) ;
```

In absence of parentheses, the compiler believes that **b** is being assigned to the result of the expression to the left of second =. Hence it reports an error.

(d) The limitation of the conditional operators is that after the **?** or after the : , only one C statement can occur.

P</> Programs

Problem 4.1

A year is entered through the keyboard, write a program to determine whether the year is leap or not. Use the logical operators **&&** and **||**.

Program

```
/* Check whether a year is leap or not */
# include <stdio.h>
int main( )
{
    int year ;
    printf ( "\nEnter year: " ) ;
    scanf ( "%d", &year ) ;
    if ( year % 400 == 0 || year % 100 != 0 && year % 4 == 0 )
        printf ( "Leap year\n" ) ;
    else
        printf ( "Not a leap year\n" ) ;
    return 0 ;
}
```

Output

```
Enter year: 1900
Not a leap year
```

Problem 4.2

If a character is entered through the keyboard, write a program to determine whether the character is a capital letter, a small case letter, a digit or a special symbol.

The following table shows the range of ASCII values for various characters:

Characters	ASCII Values
A – Z	65 – 90
a – z	97 – 122
0 – 9	48 – 57
special symbols	0 - 47, 58 - 64, 91 - 96, 123 - 127

Program

```
/* Check type of character entered from the keyboard */
# include <stdio.h>
int main( )
{
    char ch ;
    printf ( "\nEnter a character from the keyboard: " ) ;
    scanf ( "%c", &ch ) ;
    if ( ch >= 65 && ch <= 90 )
        printf ( "The character is an uppercase letter\n" ) ;
    if ( ch >= 97 && ch <= 122 )
        printf ( "The character is a lowercase letter\n" ) ;
    if ( ch >= 48 && ch <= 57 )
        printf ( "The character is a digit\n" ) ;
    if ( ( ch >= 0 && ch < 48 ) || ( ch > 57 && ch < 65 )
        || ( ch > 90 && ch < 97 ) || ch > 122 )
        printf ( "The character is a special symbol\n" ) ;
    return 0 ;
}
```

Output

```
Enter a character from the keyboard: A
The character is an uppercase letter
```

Problem 4.3

If the lengths of three sides of a triangle are entered through the keyboard, write a program to check whether the triangle is valid or not. The triangle is valid if the sum of two sides is greater than the largest of the three sides.

Program

```
/* Check whether a triangle is valid or not */
# include <stdio.h>
int main( )
{
    int side1, side2, side3, largeside, sum ;
    printf ( "\nEnter three sides of the triangle: " ) ;
```

```
    scanf ( "%d %d %d", &side1, &side2, &side3 ) ;
    if ( side1 > side2 )
    {
        if ( side1 > side3 )
        {
            sum = side2 + side3 ; largeside = side1 ;
        }
        else
        {
            sum = side1 + side2 ; largeside = side3 ;
        }
    }
    else
    {
        if ( side2 > side3 )
        {
            sum = side1 + side3 ; largeside = side2 ;
        }
        else
        {
            sum = side1 + side2 ; largeside = side3 ;
        }
    }
    if ( sum > largeside )
        printf ( "The triangle is a valid triangle\n" ) ;
    else
        printf ( "The triangle is an invalid triangle\n" ) ;
    return 0 ;
}
```

Output

```
Enter three sides of the triangle: 3 4 5
The triangle is a valid triangle
```

Exercises

[A] If a = 10, b = 12, c = 0, find the values of the expressions in the following table:

Expression	Value
a != 6 && b > 5 a == 9 || b < 3 ! (a < 10) ! (a > 5 && c) 5 && c != 8 || !c	1

[B] What will be the output of the following programs?

(a)
```
# include <stdio.h>
int main( )
{
    int  i = 4, z = 12 ;
    if ( i = 5 || z > 50 )
        printf ( "Dean of students affairs\n" ) ;
    else
        printf ( "Dosa\n" ) ;
    return 0 ;
}
```

(b)
```
#include <stdio.h>
int main( )
{
    int  i = 4, j = -1, k = 0, w, x, y, z ;
    w = i || j || k ;
    x = i && j && k ;
    y = i || j && k ;
    z = i && j || k ;
    printf ( "w = %d x = %d y = %d z = %d\n", w, x, y, z ) ;
    return 0 ;
}
```

(c)
```
# include <stdio.h>
int main( )
{
    int x = 20, y = 40, z = 45 ;
    if ( x > y && x > z )
        printf ( "biggest = %d\n", x ) ;
```

```
    else if ( y > x && y > z )
        printf ( "biggest = %d\n", y ) ;
    else if ( z > x && z > y )
        printf ( "biggest = %d\n", z ) ;
    return 0 ;
}
```

(d)
```
# include <stdio.h>
int main( )
{
    int  i = -4, j, num ;
    j = ( num < 0 ? 0 : num * num ) ;
    printf ( "%d\n", j ) ;
    return 0 ;
}
```

(e)
```
# include <stdio.h>
int main( )
{
    int  k, num = 30 ;
    k = ( num > 5 ? ( num <= 10 ? 100 : 200 ) : 500 ) ;
    printf ( "%d\n", num ) ;
    return 0 ;
}
```

[C] Point out the errors, if any, in the following programs:

(a)
```
# include <stdio.h>
int main( )
{
    char  spy = 'a', password = 'z' ;
    if ( spy == 'a' or password == 'z' )
        printf ( "All the birds are safe in the nest\n" ) ;
    return 0 ;
}
```

(b)
```
# include <stdio.h>
int main( )
{
    int  i = 10, j = 20 ;
    if ( i = 5 ) && if ( j = 10 )
        printf ( "Have a nice day\n" ) ;
    return 0 ;
```

```
}
```

(c)
```
# include <stdio.h>
int main( )
{
    int  x = 10, y = 20 ;
    if ( x >= 2 and y <= 50 )
        printf ( "%d\n", x ) ;
    return 0 ;
}
```

(d)
```
# include <stdio.h>
int main( )
{
    int x = 2 ;
    if ( x == 2 && x != 0 ) ;
        printf ( "Hello\n" ) ;
    else
        printf ( "Bye\n" ) ;
    return 0 ;
}
```

(e)
```
# include <stdio.h>
int main( )
{
    int  j = 65 ;
    printf ( "j >= 65 ? %d : %c\n", j ) ;
    return 0 ;
}
```

(f)
```
# include <stdio.h>
int main( )
{
    int  i = 10, j ;
    i >= 5 ?  j = 10 : j = 15 ;
    printf ( "%d %d\n", i, j ) ;
    return 0 ;
}
```

(g)
```
# include <stdio.h>
int main( )
{
    int a = 5, b = 6 ;
    ( a == b ? printf ( "%d\n", a ) ) ;
```

```
    return 0 ;
}
```

(h)
```
# include <stdio.h>
int main( )
{
    int n = 9 ;
    ( n == 9 ? printf ( "Correct\n" ) ; : printf ( "Wrong\n" ) ; ) ;
    return 0 ;
}
```

[D] Attempt the following questions:

(a) If the lengths of three sides of a triangle are entered through the keyboard, write a program to check whether the triangle is an isosceles, an equilateral, a scalene or a right-angled triangle.

(b) In digital world colors are specified in Red-Green-Blue (RGB) format, with values of R, G, B varying on an integer scale from 0 to 255. In print publishing the colors are mentioned in Cyan-Magenta-Yellow-Black (CMYK) format, with values of C, M, Y, and K varying on a real scale from 0.0 to 1.0. Write a program that converts RGB color to CMYK color as per the following formulae:

$$White = Max(Red/255, Green/255, Blue/255)$$

$$Cyan = \left(\frac{White - Red/255}{White}\right)$$

$$Magenta = \left(\frac{White - Green/255}{White}\right)$$

$$Yellow = \left(\frac{White - Blue/255}{White}\right)$$

$$Black = 1 - White$$

Note that if the RGB values are all 0, then the CMY values are all 0 and the K value is 1.

(c) A certain grade of steel is graded according to the following conditions:

(i) Hardness must be greater than 50
(ii) Carbon content must be less than 0.7
(iii) Tensile strength must be greater than 5600

The grades are as follows:

Grade is 10 if all three conditions are met
Grade is 9 if conditions (i) and (ii) are met
Grade is 8 if conditions (ii) and (iii) are met
Grade is 7 if conditions (i) and (iii) are met
Grade is 6 if only one condition is met
Grade is 5 if none of the conditions are met

Write a program, which will require the user to give values of hardness, carbon content and tensile strength of the steel under consideration and output the grade of the steel.

(d) The Body Mass Index (BMI) is defined as ratio of the weight of a person (in kilograms) to the square of the height (in meters). Write a program that receives weight and height, calculates the BMI, and reports the BMI category as per the following table:

BMI Category	BMI
Starvation	< 15
Anorexic	15.1 to 17.5
Underweight	17.6 to 18.5
Ideal	18.6 to 24.9
Overweight	25 to 25.9
Obese	30 to 30.9
Morbidly Obese	>= 40

[E] Answer the following questions:

(a) Using conditional operators determine:

(1) Whether the character entered through the keyboard is a lower case alphabet or not.

(2) Whether a character entered through the keyboard is a special symbol or not.

(b) Write a program using conditional operators to determine whether a year entered through the keyboard is a leap year or not.

(c) Write a program to find the greatest of the three numbers entered through the keyboard. Use conditional operators.

(d) Write a program to receive value of an angle in degrees and check whether sum of squares of sine and cosine of this angle is equal to 1.

(e) Rewrite the following program using conditional operators.

```
# include <stdio.h>
int main( )
{
    float sal ;
    printf ( "Enter the salary" ) ;
    scanf ( "%f", &sal ) ;
    if ( sal >= 25000 && sal <= 40000 )
        printf ( "Manager\n" ) ;
    else
        if ( sal >= 15000 && sal < 25000 )
            printf ( "Accountant\n" ) ;
        else
            printf ( "Clerk\n" ) ;
    return 0 ;
}
```

KanNotes

- More complex decision making can be done using logical operators
- Logical operators are &&, || and !
- Logical operators are useful in 2 situations :
  1) Checking ranges 2) Solving yes/no problem
- One more form of decision control instruction is :

```
if ( condition1 )
    statement1 ;
else if ( condition2 )
    statement2 ;
else if ( condition3 )
    statement3 ;
else                    ← else goes to work if all 3 ifs fail
    statement4 ;
```

- Hierarchy :
  ! * / % + - < > <= >= && || =
- Unary operator - needs only 1 operand. Ex. ! sizeof
- Binary operator - needs 2 operands. Ex. + - * / % < > <= >= == != && ||
- sizeof is an operator. It gives number of bytes occupied by an entity
- Usage of sizeof operator :

  a = sizeof (int)
  b = sizeof (num) ;
- ! (a <= b) is same as (a > b). ! (a >= b) is same as (a < b)
- a = !b does not change value of b
- a = !a means, set a to 0 if it is 1 and set it to 1 if it is 0
- lvalue required error means something is wrong on LHS of =
- Conditional operators ? : are ternary operators. General form :

  expression1 ? expression2 : expression3
- ? : can have only 1 statement each
- ? : can be nested
- ? : always go together. : is not optional
- Always parenthesize assignment operation if used with ? :

5 Loop Control Instruction

"Merry go round..."

If you wish to find averages of 100 sets of three numbers, would you execute the program 100 times? Obviously not, there must be a better way out. This chapter will show you how to accomplish this...

Contents

The programs that we have developed so far used either a sequential or a decision control instruction. These programs performed the same series of actions, in the same way, exactly once. In programming, we frequently need to perform an action over and over, often with variations in the details each time. The mechanism which meets this need is the 'Loop Control Instruction', and loops are the subject of this chapter.

Loops

The versatility of computer lies in its ability to perform a set of instructions repeatedly. This involves repeating some portion of the program either a specified number of times or until a particular condition is satisfied. This repetitive operation is done through a loop control instruction. There are three ways to repeat a part of a program. They are:

(a) Using a **while** statement
(b) Using a **for** statement
(c) Using a **do-while** statement

Let us begin by understanding the **while** loop.

The *while* Loop

The **while** loop is ideally suited for situations where we wish to repeat some instructions till a condition remains true. Let us understand this with the help of an example. Suppose we wish to calculate simple interest for 3 sets of values of principal, number of years and rate of interest. Here is the program that can achieve this...

```
/* Calculation of simple interest for 3 sets of p, n and r */
# include <stdio.h>
int main( )
{
    int  p, n, count ;
    float  r, si ;
    count = 1 ;
    while ( count <= 3 )
    {
        printf ( "\nEnter values of p, n and r " ) ;
        scanf ( "%d %d %f", &p, &n, &r ) ;
        si = p * n * r / 100 ;
        printf ( "Simple interest = Rs. %\nf", si ) ;
```

```
        count = count + 1 ;
    }
    return 0 ;
}
```

Given below is the interaction with this program on its execution.

```
Enter values of p, n and r 1000 5 13.5
Simple interest = Rs. 675.000000
Enter values of p, n and r 2000 5 13.5
Simple interest = Rs. 1350.000000
Enter values of p, n and r 3500 5 3.5
Simple interest = Rs. 612.500000
```

The program executes all statements after the **while** 3 times. The logic for calculating the simple interest is written in these statements and they are enclosed within { }. These statements form the 'body' of the **while** loop. The parentheses after the **while** contain a condition. So long as this condition remains true, the statements in the body of the **while** loop keep getting executed repeatedly. To begin with, the variable **count** is initialized to 1 and every time the simple interest logic is executed, the value of **count** is incremented by one. The variable **count** is often called either a 'loop counter' or an 'index variable'.

The operation of the **while** loop is illustrated in Figure 5.1.

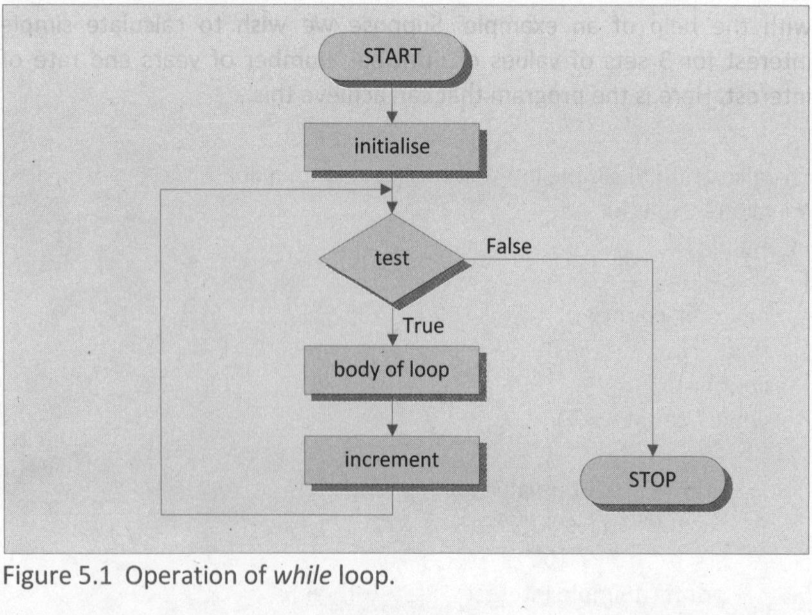

Figure 5.1 Operation of *while* loop.

Tips and Traps

Note the following points about **while**...

- The statements within the **while** loop would keep getting executed till the condition being tested remains true. When the condition becomes false, the control passes to the first statement that follows the body of the **while** loop.
- Almost always, the **while** must test a condition that will eventually become false, otherwise the loop would keep getting executed forever, indefinitely.

```
int  i = 1 ;
while ( i <= 10 )
    printf ( "%d\n", i ) ;
```

  This is an indefinite loop, since **i** always remains equal to 1. The correct form would increment **i** in the body of the loop.

- Instead of incrementing a loop counter, we can decrement it and still manage to get the body of the loop executed repeatedly. This is shown below.

```
int  i = 5 ;
while ( i >= 1 )
{
    printf ( "Make the computer literate!\n" ) ;
    i = i - 1 ;
}
```

- It is not necessary that a loop counter must only be an **int**. It can even be a **float**.

```
float  a = 10.0 ;
while ( a <= 10.5 )
{
    printf ( "Raindrops on roses..." ) ;
    printf ( "...and whiskers on kittens\n" ) ;
    a = a + 0.1 ;
}
```

– Even floating-point loop counters can be decremented. Once again, the increment and decrement could be by any suitable value, not necessarily 1.

– Multiple conditions can be used in the **while** loop by connecting them using logical operators as shown in the following examples:

```
while ( i >= 10 && j <= 15 )
while ( j > 10 && ( b < 15 || c < 20 ) )
```

– If there is only one statement within the loop then { } are optional.

– What will be the output of the following program?

```
# include <stdio.h>
int main( )
{
    int  i = 1 ;
    while ( i <= 10 ) ;
    {
        printf ( "%d\n", i ) ;
        i = i + 1 ;
    }
    return 0 ;
}
```

This is an indefinite loop, and it does not give any output at all. The reason is, we have carelessly put a **;** after the **while**. It would make the loop work like this...

```
while ( i <= 10 )
    ;
{
    printf ( "%d\n", i ) ;
    i = i + 1 ;
}
```

Since the value of **i** is not getting incremented, the control would keep rotating within the loop eternally. Note that enclosing **printf( )** and **i = i +1** within a pair of braces is not an error. In fact, we can put a pair of braces around any individual statement or set of statements without affecting the execution of the program.

More Operators

There are several operators that are frequently used with **while**. To illustrate their use, let us consider a problem wherein numbers from 1 to 10 are to be printed on the screen. The program for performing this task can be written using **while** in following different ways:

(a)
```
# include <stdio.h>
int main( )
{
    int  i = 1 ;
    while ( i <= 10 )
    {
        printf ( "%d\n", i ) ;
        i = i + 1 ;
    }
    return 0 ;
}
```

This is the most straight-forward way of printing numbers from 1 to 10.

(b)
```
# include <stdio.h>
int main( )
{
    int  i = 1 ;
    while ( i <= 10 )
    {
        printf ( "%d\n", i ) ;
        i++ ;
    }
    return 0 ;
}
```

Note that every time the statement **i++** gets executed the increment operator **++** increments the value of **i** by 1. Similarly, to reduce the value of a variable by 1, a decrement operator -- is also available.

However, never use **n+++** to increment the value of **n** by 2, since there doesn't exist an operator **+++** in C.

(c)
```
# include <stdio.h>
```

```
int main( )
{
    int  i = 1 ;
    while ( i <= 10 )
    {
        printf ( "%d\n", i ) ;
        i += 1 ;
    }
    return 0 ;
}
```

Note that **+=** is a compound assignment operator. It increments the value of **i** by 1. Similarly, **j = j + 10** can also be written as **j += 10**. Other compound assignment operators are **-=, *=, /** = and **%=**.

(d)
```
# include <stdio.h>
int main( )
{
    int  i = 0 ;
    while ( i++ < 10 )
        printf ( "%d\n", i ) ;
    return 0 ;
}
```

In the statement **while (i++ < 10)**, first the comparison of value of **i** with 10 is performed, and then the incrementation of **i** takes place. Since the incrementation of **i** happens after the comparison, here the **++** operator is called a post-incrementation operator. When the control reaches **printf( )**, **i** has already been incremented, hence **i** must be initialized to 0, not 1.

(e)
```
# include <stdio.h>
int main( )
{
    int  i = 0 ;
    while ( ++i <= 10 )
        printf ( "%d\n", i ) ;
    return 0 ;
}
```

In the statement **while (++i <= 10)**, first incrementation of **i** takes place, then the comparison of value of **i** with 10 is performed. Since the incrementation of **i** happens before the comparison, here the **++** operator is called a pre-incrementation operator.

P</> Programs

Problem 5.1

Write a program to calculate overtime pay of 10 employees. Overtime is paid at the rate of Rs. 120.00 per hour for every hour worked above 40 hours. Assume that employees do not work for fractional part of an hour.

Program

```
/* Determine overtime pay of 10 employees */
# include <stdio.h>
int main( )
{
    float otpay ;
    int hour, i = 1 ;
    while ( i <= 10 ) /* Loop for 10 employees */
    {
        printf ( "\nEnter no. of hours worked: " ) ;
        scanf ( "%d", &hour ) ;
        if ( hour >= 40 )
            otpay = ( hour - 40 ) * 120 ;
        else
            otpay = 0 ;
        printf ( "Hours = %d Overtime pay = Rs.%f\n", hour, otpay ) ;
        i++ ;
    }
    return 0 ;
}
```

Output

```
Enter no. of hours worked: 45
Hours = 45 Overtime pay = Rs.600.000000

Enter no. of hours worked: 50
Hours = 50 Overtime pay = Rs.1200.000000
```

```
Enter no. of hours worked: 20
Hours = 20 Overtime pay = Rs.0.000000
```

Problem 5.2

Write a program to find the factorial value of any number entered through the keyboard.

Program

```
/* Calculation of factorial value of a number */
# include <stdio.h>
int main( )
{
    int num, i, fact ;
    printf ( "Enter a number: " ) ;
    scanf ( "%d", &num ) ;
    fact = i = 1 ;
    while ( i <= num )
    {
        fact = fact * i ;
        i++ ;
    }
    printf ( "Factorial value of %d = %d\n", num, fact ) ;
    return 0 ;
}
```

Output

```
Enter a number: 7
Factorial value of 7 = 5040
```

Problem 5.3

Two numbers are entered through the keyboard. Write a program to find the value of one number raised to the power of another.

Program

```
/* Compute value of one number raised to another */
```

```
# include <stdio.h>
int main( )
{
    float x, power ;
    int  y, i ;
    printf ( "\nEnter two numbers: " ) ;
    scanf ( "%f %d", &x, &y ) ;
    power = i = 1 ;
    while ( i <= y )
    {
        power = power * x ;
        i++ ;
    }
    printf ( "%f to the power %d is %f\n", x, y, power ) ;
    return 0 ;
}
```

Output

```
Enter two numbers: 2.5 3
2.500000 to the power 3 is 15.625000
```

Exercises

[A] What will be the output of the following programs?

(a)
```
# include <stdio.h>
int main( )
{
    int  i = 1 ;
    while ( i <= 10 ) ;
    {
        printf ( "%d\n", i ) ;
        i++ ;
    }
    return 0 ;
}
```

(b)
```
# include <stdio.h>
int main( )
```

```
{
    int  x = 4, y, z ;
    y = --x ;
    z = x-- ;
    printf ( "%d %d %d\n", x, y, z ) ;
    return 0 ;
}
```

(c)
```
# include <stdio.h>
int main( )
{
    int  x = 4, y = 3, z ;
    z = x-- - y ;
    printf ( "%d %d %d\n", x, y, z ) ;
    return 0 ;
}
```

(d)
```
# include <stdio.h>
int main( )
{
    while ( 'a' < 'b' )
        printf ( "malayalam is a palindrome\n" ) ;
    return 0 ;
}
```

(e)
```
# include <stdio.h>
int main( )
{
    int  i ;
    while ( i = 10 )
    {
        printf ( "%d\n", i ) ;
        i = i + 1 ;
    }
    return 0 ;
}
```

(f)
```
# include <stdio.h>
int main( )
{
    float  x = 1.1 ;
    while ( x == 1.1 )
    {
```

```
        printf ( "%f\n", x ) ;
        x = x - 0.1 ;
    }
    return 0 ;
}
```

[B] Attempt the following questions:

(a) Write a program to print all the ASCII values and their equivalent characters using a while loop. The ASCII values vary from 0 to 255.

(b) Write a program to print out all Armstrong numbers between 100 and 500. If sum of cubes of each digit of the number is equal to the number itself, then the number is called an Armstrong number. For example, 153 = (1 * 1 * 1) + (5 * 5 * 5) + (3 * 3 * 3).

(c) Write a program for a matchstick game being played between the computer and a user. Your program should ensure that the computer always wins. Rules for the game are as follows:

- There are 21 matchsticks.
- The computer asks the player to pick 1, 2, 3, or 4 matchsticks.
- After the person picks, the computer does its picking.
- Whoever is forced to pick up the last matchstick loses the game.

(d) Write a program to enter numbers till the user wants. At the end it should display the count of positive, negative and zeros entered.

(e) Write a program to receive an integer and find its octal equivalent.

(Hint: To obtain octal equivalent of an integer, divide it continuously by 8 till dividend does not become zero, then write the remainders obtained in reverse direction.)

(f) Write a program to find the range of a set of numbers entered through the keyboard. Range is the difference between the smallest and biggest number in the list.

KanNotes

- Repetition control instruction is used to repeat a set of statements in a program.
- It is implemented using

  1) while loop

2) for loop
3) do - while loop

- General form of while:

```
i = 1 ; /* initialization of loop counter */
while ( i <= 10 ) /* testing of loop counter */
{
    statement1 ;
    statement2 ;
    i++ ; /* incrementation of loop counter */
}
```

- i++ increments vale by 1

  i-- decrements value of i by 1

  There are no **, // and %% operators
- The expressions i = i + 1, i++ and ++i are all same
- j = ++i ; first increments i, then assigns the incremented value to j
- j = i++ ; first assigns current value of i to j, then increments i
- while (++i < 10) first increments i, then checks condition
- while (i++ < 10) first checks condition, then increments i
- i = i + 5 is same as i += 5
- Compound assignment operators : +=, -=, *=, /= and %=
- Running sum and products are implemented using following :

```
s = 0 ;
p = 1 ;
while ( condition )
{
    /* calculate term */
    s = s + term ;
    p = p * term ;
}
```

6 More Complex Repetitions

"Run through the hoops..."

x takes values from 1 to 10. For every x, y takes values from 0.5 to 2.25 in steps of 0.5 and for every y, z goes from 100 to 55 in decrements of -2, and for every z, m increases in multiples of 4 starting with 4. Lost in the hoops? Well, this chapter will show you how such complex repetitions can be implemented in C...

Contents

The programs in the last chapter showed how instructions in a program can be repeated using a **while** loop. This chapter explores the other two loops—**for** and **do-while**. There is more to looping than just repeating instructions. For example, what if we wish to terminate the loop abruptly, or skip some instructions as the loop executes, or repeat something infinite times, unknown number of times or only once. All these scenarios are handled in this chapter.

The *for* Loop

The **for** loop allows us to specify three things about the loop in a single line:

(a) Setting a loop counter to an initial value.

(b) Testing the loop counter to determine whether its value has reached the number of repetitions desired.

(c) Increasing the value of loop counter each time the body of the loop has been executed.

The general form of **for** loop is as follows:

```
for ( initialize counter ; test counter ; increment counter )
{
    do this ;
    and this ;
}
```

Let us now write the simple interest program using **for**. Compare this program with the one that we wrote using **while** in Chapter 5.

```
/* Calculation of simple interest for 3 sets of p, n and r */
# include <stdio.h>
int main( )
{
    int p, n, count ;
    float r, si ;
    for ( count = 1 ; count <= 3 ; count = count + 1 )
    {
        printf ( "Enter values of p, n, and r " ) ;
        scanf ( "%d %d %f", &p, &n, &r ) ;
        si = p * n * r / 100 ;
        printf ( "Simple Interest = Rs.%f\n", si ) ;
    }
```

```
return 0 ;
}
```

You can observe that the three steps—initialization, testing and incrementation—required for the loop construct have now been incorporated in one single line in the **for** statement.

Let us now examine how the **for** statement gets executed:

- When **for** statement is executed for the first time, the value of **count** is set to an initial value 1.
- Next the condition **count <= 3** is tested. Since **count** is 1, the condition is satisfied and the body of the loop is executed for the first time.
- Upon reaching the closing brace of **for**, control is sent back to **for** statement, where the value of **count** gets incremented by 1.
- Again, the test is performed to check whether the new value of **count** is less than or equal to 3.
- If the value of **count** is less than or equal to 3, the statements within the braces of **for** are executed again.
- The body of **for** loop continues to get executed till **count** does not exceed the final value 3.
- When **count** reaches the value 4, the control exits from the loop and is transferred to the statement (if any) immediately after the body of **for**.

It is important to note that the initialization, testing and incrementation part of a **for** loop can be replaced by any valid expression. Thus, the following **for** loops are perfectly ok.

```
for ( i = 10 ; i ; i -- )
    printf ( "%d ", i ) ;
for ( i < 4 ; j = 5 ; j = 0 )
    printf ( "%d ", i ) ;
for ( i = 1; i <=10 ; printf ( "%d ", i++ ) )
    ;
for ( scanf ( "%d", &i ) ; i <= 10 ; i++ )
    printf ( "%d", i ) ;
```

Let us now write the program to print numbers from 1 to 10 in different ways. This time we would use a **for** loop instead of a **while** loop.

(a)
```
# include <stdio.h>
int main( )
{
    int  i ;
    for ( i = 1 ; i <= 10 ; i = i + 1 )
        printf ( "%d\n", i ) ;
    return 0 ;
}
```

Instead of **i = i + 1**, the statements **i++** or **i += 1** can also be used. Since there is only one statement in the body of the **for** loop, the pair of braces have been dropped. As with the **while**, the default scope of **for** is the immediately next statement after **for**.

(b)
```
# include <stdio.h>
int main( )
{
    int  i ;
    for ( i = 1 ; i <= 10 ; )
    {
        printf ( "%d\n", i ) ;
        i = i + 1 ;
    }
    return 0 ;
}
```

Here, the incrementation is done within the body of the **for** loop. In spite of this, the semicolon (;) after the condition is necessary.

(c)
```
# include <stdio.h>
int main( )
{
    int  i = 1 ;
    for ( ; i <= 10 ; i = i + 1 )
        printf ( "%d\n", i ) ;
    return 0 ;
}
```

Here the initialization is done in the declaration statement itself, but still the semicolon before the condition is necessary.

(d)
```
# include <stdio.h>
int main( )
{
    int  i = 1 ;
    for ( ; i <= 10 ; )
    {
        printf ( "%d\n", i ) ;
        i = i + 1 ;
    }
    return 0 ;
}
```

Here, neither the initialization nor the incrementation is done in the **for** statement, but still the two semicolons are necessary.

(e)
```
# include <stdio.h>
int main( )
{
    int  i ;
    for ( i = 0 ; i++ < 10 ; )
        printf ( "%d\n", i ) ;
    return 0 ;
}
```

Here, the comparison as well as the incrementation is done through the same expression, **i++ < 10**. Since the **++** operator comes after **i**, comparison is done first, followed by incrementation. Note that it is necessary to initialize **i** to 0.

(f)
```
# include <stdio.h>
int main( )
{
    int  i ;
    for ( i = 0 ; ++i <= 10 ; )
        printf ( "%d\n", i ) ;
    return 0 ;
}
```

Here again, both, the comparison and the incrementation are done through the same expression, **++i <= 10**. Since **++** precedes **i** firstly incrementation is done, followed by comparison. Note that it is necessary to initialize **i** to 0.

Nesting of Loops

The way **if** statements can be nested, similarly **while**s and **for**s can also be nested. The following program shows how nested loops work.

```
/* Demonstration of nested loops */
# include <stdio.h>
int main( )
{
    int  r, c, sum ;
    for ( r = 1 ; r <= 3 ; r++ )  /* outer loop */
    {
        for ( c = 1 ; c <= 2 ; c++ )  /* inner loop */
        {
            sum = r + c ;
            printf ( "r = %d c = %d sum = %d\n", r, c, sum ) ;
        }
    }
    return 0 ;
}
```

When you run this program, you will get the following output:

```
r = 1 c = 1 sum = 2
r = 1 c = 2 sum = 3
r = 2 c = 1 sum = 3
r = 2 c = 2 sum = 4
r = 3 c = 1 sum = 4
r = 3 c = 2 sum = 5
```

Here, for each value of **r**, the inner loop is cycled through twice, with the variable **c** taking values from 1 to 2. The inner loop terminates when the value of **c** exceeds 2, and the outer loop terminates when **r** exceeds 3.

As you can see, the body of the outer **for** loop is indented, and the body of the inner **for** loop is further indented. These multiple indentations make the program easier to understand.

Instead of using two statements, one to calculate **sum** and another to print it out, we can compact them into one single statement by saying:

```
printf ( "r = %d c = %d sum = %d\n", r, c, r + c ) ;
```

The way **for** loops have been nested here, similarly, two **while** loops can also be nested. Not only this, a **for** loop can occur within a **while** loop, or a **while** within a **for**.

Multiple Initializations in the *for* Loop

The initialization expression in the **for** loop can contain more than one statement separated by a comma. For example,

```
for ( i = 1, j = 2 ; j <= 10 ; j++ )
```

Multiple comma-separated incrementations can also be done in a **for** loop. Similarly, multiple conditions are allowed in the test expression. These conditions should be linked together using logical operators && and/or || as shown below.

```
for ( i = 1, j = 2 ; j <= 10  &&  i <= 15 ; j++, i = i + 2 )
```

The *do-while* Loop

The **do-while** loop looks like this:

```
do
{
    this ;
    and this ;
} while ( this condition is true ) ;
```

There is a minor difference between the working of **while** and **do-while** loops. This difference lies in the place where the condition is tested. The **while** tests the condition before executing any of the statements within the **while** loop. As against this, the **do-while** tests the condition after having executed the statements within the loop.

This means that **do-while** would execute its statements at least once, even if the condition fails for the first time. The **while**, on the other hand will not execute its statements if the condition fails for the first time. This difference is brought about more clearly by the following program:

```
# include <stdio.h>
int main( )
{
    while ( 4 < 1 )
        printf ( " Credit is yours, pleasure is mine \n" ) ;
```

```
    return 0 ;
}
```

Here, since the condition fails the first time itself, the **printf( )** will not get executed at all. Let us now write the same program using a **do-while** loop.

```
# include <stdio.h>
int main( )
{
    do
    {
        printf ( "Credit is yours, pleasure is mine\n" ) ;
    } while ( 4 < 1 ) ;
    return 0 ;
}
```

In this program, the **printf( )** would be executed once, since first the body of the loop is executed and then the condition is tested.

The *break* Statement

We often come across situations where we want to jump out of a loop instantly, without waiting to get back to the condition. The keyword **break** allows us to do this. When **break** is encountered inside a **while**, **for** or **do-while** loop, control automatically passes to the first statement after the loop. A **break** is usually associated with an **if**. Let us consider the following example to understand it:

Example 6.1: Write a program to determine whether a number is prime or not. A prime number is said to be prime if it is divisible only by 1 or itself.

All we must do to test whether a number is prime or not, is to divide it successively by all numbers from 2 to one less than itself. If remainder of any of these divisions is zero, the number is not a prime. If no division yields a zero then the number is a prime number. Following program implements this logic:

```
# include <stdio.h>
int main( )
{
    int num, i ;
    printf ( "Enter a number " ) ;
```

```
    scanf ( "%d", &num ) ;
    i = 2 ;
    while ( i <= num - 1 )
    {
        if ( num % i == 0 )
        {
            printf ( "Not a prime number\n" ) ;
            break ;
        }
        i++ ;
    }
    if ( i == num )
        printf ( "Prime number\n" ) ;
}
```

In this program, the moment **num % i** turns out to be zero, (i.e., **num** is exactly divisible by **i**), the message "Not a prime number" is printed and the control breaks out of the **while** loop. Why does the program require the **if** statement after the **while** loop at all? Well, there are two possibilities the control could have reached outside the **while** loop:

(a) It jumped out because **num** turned out to be not a prime.

(b) The loop came to an end because the value of **i** became equal to **num**.

When the loop terminates in the second case, it means that there was no number between 2 to **num - 1** that could exactly divide **num**. That is, **num** is indeed a prime. If this is true, the program should print out the message "Prime number".

The keyword **break**, breaks the control only from the **while** in which it is placed. Consider the following program, which illustrates this fact:

```
# include <stdio.h>
int main( )
{
    int i = 1 , j = 1 ;
    while ( i++ <= 100 )
    {
        while ( j++ <= 200 )
        {
            if ( j == 150 )
                break ;
```

```
            else
                printf ( "%d %d\n", i, j ) ;
        }
    }
    return 0 ;
}
```

In this program when **j** equals 150, **break** takes the control outside the inner **while** only, since it is placed inside the inner **while**.

The *continue* Statement

In some programming situations, we want to take the control to the beginning of the loop, bypassing the statements inside the loop, which have not yet been executed. The keyword **continue** allows us to do this. When **continue** is encountered inside a loop, control jumps to the beginning of the loop for performing next iteration.

A **continue** is usually associated with an **if**. As an example, let's consider the following program:

```
# include <stdio.h>
int main( )
{
    int  i, j ;
    for ( i = 1 ; i <= 2 ; i++ )
    {
        for ( j = 1 ; j <= 2 ; j++ )
        {
            if ( i == j )
                continue ;
            printf ( "%d %d\n", i, j ) ;
        }
    }
    return 0 ;
}
```

The output of the above program would be...

```
1 2
2 1
```

Note that when the value of **i** equals that of **j**, the **continue** statement takes the control to the incrementation part of the inner **for** loop bypassing the rest of the statements pending execution in the inner **for** loop.

A small quirk—when **continue** is encountered in a **while** or **do-while** control jumps to the condition, whereas in case of a **for** loop it takes the control to the incrementation part of the **for** loop.

The Odd Loop

The loops used so far executed the statements within them a finite number of times. However, at times one comes across a situation when it is not known beforehand, how many times the statements in the loop are to be executed. This situation can be programmed as shown below.

```
/* Execution of a loop an unknown number of times */
# include <stdio.h>
int main( )
{
    char another ;
    int num ;
    do
    {
        printf ( "Enter a number " ) ;
        scanf ( "%d", &num ) ;
        printf ( "square of %d is %d\n", num, num * num ) ;
        printf ( "Want to enter another number y/n " ) ;
        fflush ( stdin ) ;
        scanf ( "%c", &another ) ;
    } while ( another == 'y' ) ;
    return 0 ;
}
```

And here is the sample output...

```
Enter a number 5
square of 5 is 25
Want to enter another number y/n y
Enter a number 7
square of 7 is 49
Want to enter another number y/n n
```

In this program, the **do-while** loop would keep getting executed till the user continues to answer **y**. The moment user answers **n**, the loop terminates, since the condition (**another == 'y'**) fails. Note that this loop ensures that statements within it are executed at least once.

Though it is simpler to program such a requirement using a **do-while** loop, the same functionality, if required, can also be accomplished using **for** and **while** loops. You can try doing this as an exercise.

You must be wondering why have we used the function **fflush( )**. The reason is to get rid of a peculiarity of **scanf( )**. After supplying a number when we hit the Enter key, **scanf( )** assigns the number to variable **num** and keeps the Enter key unread in the keyboard buffer. So when it's time to supply y or n for the question 'Want to enter another number (y/n)', **scanf( )** will read the Enter key from the buffer thinking that user has entered the Enter key. To avoid this problem, we use the function **fflush( )**. It removes or 'flushes out' any data remaining in the buffer. The argument to **fflush( )** must be the buffer which we want to flush out. Here we have used 'stdin', which means buffer related with standard input device, i.e., keyboard.

P</> Programs

Problem 6.1

Write a program to print all prime numbers from 1 to 300.

Program

```
/* Generate all prime numbers from 1 to 300 */
# include <stdio.h>
int main( )
{
    int i, n = 1 ;
    printf ( "\nPrime numbers between 1 and 300 are :\n1\t" ) ;
    for ( n = 1 ; n <= 300 ; n++ )
    {
        i = 2 ;
        for ( i = 2 ; i < n ; i++ )
        {
            if ( n % i == 0 )
                break ;
```

```
    }
    if ( i == n )
        printf ( "%d\t", n ) ;
  }
  return 0 ;
}
```

Output

```
Prime numbers between 1 and 300 are :
1    2    3    5    7    11   13   17   19   23
29   31   37   41   43   47   53   59   61   67
71   73   79   83   89   97   101  103  107  109
113  127  131  137  139  149  151  157  163  167
173  179  181  191  193  197  199  211  223  227
229  233  239  241  251  257  263  269  271  277
281  283  293
```

Problem 6.2

Write a program to add first seven terms of the following series using a **for** loop.

$$\frac{1}{1!} + \frac{2}{2!} + \frac{3}{3!} + \ldots\ldots$$

Program

```
/* Sum of first seven terms of a series */
# include <stdio.h>
int main( )
{
    int i = 1, j ;
    float fact, sum = 0.0 ;
    for ( i = 1 ; i <= 7 ; i++ )
    {
        fact = 1.0 ;
        for ( j = 1 ; j <= i ; j++ )
            fact = fact * j ;
        sum = sum + i / fact ;
    }
```

```
    printf ( "Sum of series = %f\n", sum ) ;
    return 0 ;
}
```

Output

```
Sum of series = 2.718056
```

Problem 6.3

Write a program to generate all combinations of 1, 2 and 3 using for loop.

Program

```
/* Generate all possible combinations of 1 2 3 */
# include <stdio.h>
int main( )
{
    int i = 1, j = 1, k = 1 ;
    for ( i = 1 ; i <= 3 ; i++ )
    {
        for ( j = 1 ; j <= 3 ; j++ )
        {
            for ( k = 1 ; k <= 3 ; k++ )
                printf ( "%d %d %d\n", i , j , k ) ;
        }
    }
    return 0 ;
}
```

Output

```
1 1 1
1 1 2
..
..
2 1 1
..
..
2 3 3
```

```
3 1 1
..
..
3 3 3
```

Exercises

[A] Answer the following questions:

(a) The **break** statement is used to exit from:

1. An **if** statement
2. A **for** loop
3. A program
4. The **main( )** function

(b) A **do-while** loop is useful when we want that the statements within the loop must be executed:

1. Only once
2. At least once
3. More than once
4. None of the above

(c) In what sequence the initialization, testing and execution of body is done in a **do-while** loop?

1. Initialization, execution of body, testing
2. Execution of body, initialization, testing
3. Initialization, testing, execution of body
4. None of the above

(d) Which of the following is not an infinite loop?

1.
```
int i = 1 ;
while ( 1 )
{
    i++ ;
}
```

2.
```
for ( ; ; ) ;
```

3.
```
int t = 0, f ;
while ( t )
{
    f = 1 ;
}
```

4.
```
int y, x = 0 ;
do
{
    y = x ;
} while ( x == 0 ) ;
```

(e) Which of the following statements is true for the following program?

```
# include <stdio.h>
int main( )
{
    int x = 10, y = 100 % 90 ;
    for ( i = 1 ; i <= 10 ; i++ ) ;
        if ( x != y ) ;
            printf ( "x = %d y = %d\n", x, y ) ;
    return 0 ;
}
```

1. The **printf( )** function is called 10 times.
2. The program will produce the output x = 10 y = 10.
3. The ; after the **if (x != y)** will not produce an error.
4. The program will not produce any output.
5. The **printf( )** function is called infinite times.

(f) Which of the following statement is true about a **for** loop used in a C program?

1. **for** loop works faster than a **while** loop.
2. All things that can be done using a **for** loop can also be done using a **while** loop.
3. **for (; ;)** implements an infinite loop.
4. **for** loop can be used if we want statements in a loop to get executed at least once.
5. **for** loop works faster than a **do-while** loop.

[B] Attempt the following questions:

(a) Write a program to print the multiplication table of the number entered by the user. The table should get displayed in the following form:

29 * 1 = 29
29 * 2 = 58

...

(b) According to a study, the approximate level of intelligence of a person can be calculated using the following formula:

i = 2 + (y + 0.5 x)

Write a program that will produce a table of values of **i**, **y** and **x**, where **y** varies from 1 to 6, and, for each value of **y**, **x** varies from 5.5 to 12.5 in steps of 0.5.

(c) When interest compounds **q** times per year at an annual rate of **r** % for **n** years, the principal **p** compounds to an amount **a** as per the following formula

a = p (1 + r / q) ^{nq}

Write a program to read 10 sets of **p, r, n** & **q** and calculate the corresponding **a**s.

(d) The natural logarithm can be approximated by the following series.

$$\frac{x-1}{x}+\frac{1}{2}\left(\frac{x-1}{x}\right)^2+\frac{1}{2}\left(\frac{x-1}{x}\right)^3+\frac{1}{2}\left(\frac{x-1}{x}\right)^4+\ldots.$$

If **x** is input through the keyboard, write a program to calculate the sum of first seven terms of this series.

(e) Write a program to generate all Pythagorean Triplets with side length less than or equal to 30.

(f) Population of a town today is 100000. The population has increased steadily at the rate of 10% per year for last 10 years. Write a program to determine the population at the end of each year in the last decade.

(g) Ramanujan number (1729) is the smallest number that can be expressed as sum of two cubes in two different ways—1729 can be expressed as $1^3 + 12^3$ and $9^3 + 10^3$. Write a program to print all such numbers up to a reasonable limit.

(h) Write a program to print 24 hours of day with suitable suffixes like AM, PM, Noon and Midnight.

(i) Write a program to produce the following output:

```
            1
        2       3
    4       5       6
7       8       9       10
```

KanNotes

- 3 types of loops :

  1) while
  2) for
  3) do - while

- What can be done using one loop can always be done using the other two

- Usual usage :

  while - to repeat something an unknown number of times, i.e. when we do not know at the time of writing the program how many times the loop is going to be executed

  for - to repeat something a fixed number of times

  do - while - to repeat something at least once

- Equivalent forms :

```
i = 1 ;
while ( i <= 10 )
{
    statement1 ;
    statement2 ;
    i++ ;
}
```

```
for ( i = 1 ; i <= 10 ; i++ )
{
    statement1 ;
    statement2 ;
}
```

```
i = 1 ;
do
{
    statement1 ;
    statement2 ;
    i++ ;
} while ( i <= 10 ) ;
```

- for (; ;) is an infinite loop. while () results into an error

- Multiple initializations, conditions and incrementations in a for loop are acceptable. Ex. :

```
for ( i = 1 , j = 2 ; i <= 10 && j <= 24 ; i++, j += 3 )
{
    statement1 ;
    statement2 ;
}
```

- break - terminates the execution of the loop

  continue - abandons rest of the instructions in the loop and goes for the next iteration of the loop

- Usually break and continue are used in this form :

```
while ( condition1 )
{
    if ( condition2 )
        break ;
    statement1 ;
    statement2 ;
}
```

```
while ( condition1 )
{
    if ( condition2 )
        continue ;
    statement1 ;
    statement2 ;
}
```

7 Case Control Instruction

"The multi-point switch"

Choosing the right control instruction adds to the efficiency and speed of the program. So, even though a situation where different actions are to be carried out for 5 different values of variable x can be implemented using 5 ifs, it may not be a very efficient way of doing it. This chapter will show you how this can be done in a better and more efficient way...

Contents

In programming, we are often faced with situations where we are required to make a choice between a number of alternatives rather than only one or two. C provides a special control statement that allows us to handle such cases effectively; rather than using a series of **if** statements. This control instruction is the topic of this chapter. Towards the end of the chapter, we would also study a keyword called **goto** and understand why we should avoid its usage.

Decisions using *switch*

The control instruction that allows us to decide from the number of choices is called a **switch**, or more correctly a **switch-case-default**, since these three keywords go together to make up the control statement. They most often appear as follows:

```
switch ( integer expression )
{
    case constant 1 :
        do this ;
    case constant 2 :
        do this ;
    case constant 3 :
        do this ;
    default :
        do this ;
}
```

The integer expression following the keyword **switch** is any C expression that will yield an integer value. The keyword **case** is followed by an integer or a character constant. Constant used in each **case** must be different from those used in other cases. The "do this" lines in the above **switch** represent any valid C statement.

What happens when we run a program containing a **switch** statement? First, the integer expression following the keyword **switch** is evaluated. The value it gives is then matched, one-by-one, against the constant values that follow the **case** statements. When a match is found, the statements in that **case**, and those in all subsequent **case**s and **default** are executed. If no match is found with any of the **case** statements, the statements following the **default** case are executed. A few examples will show how this control instruction works.

Consider the following program:

```
# include <stdio.h>
int main( )
{
    int  i = 2 ;
    switch ( i )
    {
        case 1 :
            printf ( "I am in case 1 \n" ) ;
        case 2 :
            printf ( "I am in case 2 \n" ) ;
        case 3 :
            printf ( "I am in case 3 \n" ) ;
        default :
            printf ( "I am in default \n" ) ;
    }
    return 0 ;
}
```

The output of this program would be:

```
I am in case 2
I am in case 3
I am in default
```

The output is not what we expected! We did not expect the second and third lines in the above output. We got them because once the matching case is found all the statements in subsequent **case**s and **default** also get executed.

If you want that only case 2 should get executed, it is up to you to get out of the **switch** then and there by using a **break** statement. The following program shows how this is done. Note that there is no need for a **break** statement after the **default**, since on reaching the **default** case, the control comes out of the **switch** anyway.

```
# include <stdio.h>
int main( )
{
    int  i = 2 ;
    switch ( i )
    {
        case 1 :
```

```
            printf ( "I am in case 1 \n" ) ;
            break ;
        case 2 :
            printf ( "I am in case 2 \n" ) ;
            break ;
        case 3 :
            printf ( "I am in case 3 \n" ) ;
            break ;
        default :
            printf ( "I am in default \n" ) ;
    }
    return 0 ;
}
```

The output of this program would be:

```
I am in case 2
```

The Tips and Traps

Now let us understand a few tips about the usage of **switch** and a few pitfalls to be avoided.

(a) The program in the previous section may give you an impression that cases in a **switch** must be arranged in ascending order—1, 2, 3 and default. In fact, you can put the cases in any order you please.

(b) Even if there are multiple statements to be executed in each **case**, there is no need to enclose them within a pair of braces (unlike **if** and **else**).

(c) Every statement in a **switch** must belong to some **case** or the other.

(d) If we have no **default** case, and no case is satisfied, then the control exits the **switch** and continues with the next instruction (if any,) that follows the closing brace of **switch**.

(e) At times we may want to execute a common set of statements for multiple **case**s. The following example shows how this can be achieved:

```
# include <stdio.h>
int main( )
{
    char ch ;
```

```
    printf ( "Enter any one of the alphabets a, b, or c " ) ;
    scanf ( "%c", &ch ) ;
    switch ( ch )
    {
        case 'a' :
        case 'A' :
            printf ( "a as in apple\n" ) ;
            break ;
        case 'b' :
        case 'B' :
            printf ( "b as in brain\n" ) ;
            break ;
        case 'c' :
        case 'C' :
            printf ( "c as in cookie\n" ) ;
            break ;
        default :
            printf ( "wish you knew what are alphabets\n" ) ;
        return 0 ;
    }
}
```

Here, we are making use of the fact that once a **case** is satisfied; control simply falls through the **switch** till it does not encounter a **break** statement. That is why, if alphabet **a** is entered, **case 'a'** is satisfied and since there are no statements to be executed in this **case**, control automatically reaches the next **case**, i.e., **case 'A'** and executes all the statements in this **case**.

(f) Is **switch** a replacement for **if**? Yes and no. Yes, because it offers a better way of writing programs as compared to **if**, and no, because, in certain situations, we are left with no choice but to use **if**. The disadvantage of **switch** is that one cannot have a case in a **switch** which looks like:

```
case i <= 20 :
```

All that we can have after the case is an **int** constant or a **char** constant or an expression that evaluates to an int constant. Even a **float** is not allowed.

The advantage of **switch** over **if** is that it leads to a more structured program and the level of indentation is manageable, more so, if there are multiple statements within each **case** of a **switch**.

(g) We can check the value of any expression in a **switch**. Thus, the following **switch** statements are legal:

```
switch ( i + j * k )
switch ( 23 + 45 % 4 * k )
switch ( a < 4 && b > 7 )
```

Expressions can also be used in cases provided they are constant expressions. Thus, **case 3 + 7** is correct, however, **case a + b** is incorrect.

(h) The **break** statement when used in a **switch** takes the control outside the **switch**. However, use of **continue** does not take the control to the beginning of **switch**, as one is likely to believe.

(i) In principle, a **switch** may occur within another, but in practice, this is rarely done. Such statements would be called nested **switch** statements.

(j) The **switch** statement is very useful while writing menu driven programs. This aspect of **switch** is illustrated in Programs section of this chapter.

switch versus *if-else* Ladder

There are some things that you simply cannot do with a **switch**. These are:

(a) A float expression cannot be tested using a switch.

(b) Cases can never have variable expressions as in **case a + 3 :**.

(c) Multiple cases cannot use same expressions. Thus, the following switch is illegal:

```
switch ( a )
{
    case 3 :
        ...
    case 1 + 2 :
        ...
}
```

(a), (b) and (c) above may lead you to believe that these are obvious disadvantages with a **switch**, especially since there weren't any such limitations with **if-else**. Then why use a **switch** at all? For speed—**switch** works faster than an equivalent **if-else** ladder. This is because compiler generates a jump table for a **switch** during compilation. As a result, during execution, it simply refers the jump table to decide which case should be executed, rather than checking which case is satisfied. As against this, **if-else**s are slower because the conditions in them are evaluated at execution time. Note that a lookup in the jump table is faster than evaluation of a condition, especially if the condition is complex.

The *goto* Statement

The **goto** statement causes an unconditional jump to another statement in the same function. The destination of the jump is specified using a label following the **goto** keyword as shown below.

```
goto out ;
```

The label **out** is specified at a place in the program where we wish the control to be transferred to as shown below.

```
out :
```

Nothing special about **out**, you can use any other label instead. Labels serve only as destinations of **goto** statements, and have no effect at all if the labeled statement is reached in the normal course of sequential execution. Given below is a program that shows working of the **goto** statement.

```
# include <stdio.h>
# include <stdlib.h>

int main( )
{
    int goals ;
    printf ( "Enter the number of goals scored against India" ) ;
    scanf ( "%d", &goals ) ;
    if ( goals <= 5 )
        goto sos ;
    else
    {
```

```
        printf ( "About time soccer players learnt C\n" ) ;
        printf ( "and said goodbye to soccer\n" ) ;
        exit ( 1 ) ; /* terminates program execution */
    }
    sos :
        printf ( "To err is human!\n" ) ;
    return 0 ;
}
```

And here are two sample runs of the program...

```
Enter the number of goals scored against India 3
To err is human!
Enter the number of goals scored against India 7
About time soccer players learnt C
and said goodbye to soccer
```

A few remarks about the program would make its working clearer.

- If the condition is satisfied, **goto** statement transfers control to the label **sos**, causing **printf( )** following **sos** to be executed.
- The label can be on a separate line or on the same line as the statement following it, as in,

```
sos : printf ( "To err is human!\n" ) ;
```

- Any number of **goto**s can take the control to the same label.
- **exit( )** is a standard library function that terminates the execution of the program. It is necessary to use this function since we do not want the statement

```
printf ( "To err is human!\n" ) ;
```

  to get executed after execution of the **else** block.
- The argument 1 used in **exit( )** indicates the reason for termination. If there are multiple exit points in the program, this argument can be used to find which exit terminated the execution.
- For **exit( )** function to work, we need to **#include** the file 'stdlib.h'.

Avoid **goto** keyword! It obscures the flow of control and makes the program unreliable, unreadable, and hard to debug. In a difficult programming situation, it seems easy to use a **goto** to take the control where you want. However, almost always, there is a more elegant way of writing the same program using **if**, **for**, **while**, **do-while** and **switch**. These constructs are far more logical and easier to understand.

The only programming situation in favor of using **goto** is when we want to take the control out of the loop that is contained in several other loops. The following program illustrates this:

```
# include <stdio.h>
int main( )
{
    int i, j, k ;
    for ( i = 1 ; i <= 3 ; i++ )
    {
        for ( j = 1 ; j <= 3 ; j++ )
        {
            for ( k = 1 ; k <= 3 ; k++ )
            {
                if ( i == 3 && j == 3 && k == 3 )
                    goto out ;
                else
                    printf ( "%d %d %d\n", i, j, k ) ;
            }
        }
    }
    out :
        printf ( "Out of the loops at last!\n" ) ;
    return 0 ;
}
```

Go through the program carefully and find out how it works. Also write a program to implement the same logic without using **goto**.

P</> Programs

Problem 7.1

Write a menu driven program which has following options:

1. Factorial of a number
2. Prime or not

3. Odd or even
4. Exit

Once a menu item is selected the appropriate action should be taken and once this action is finished, the menu should reappear. Unless the user selects the 'Exit' option the program should continue to work.

Program

```
/* Menu driven program */
# include <stdio.h>
# include <stdlib.h>
int main( )
{
    int choice, num, i, fact ;
    while ( 1 )
    {
        printf ( "\n1. Factorial\n" ) ;
        printf ( "2. Prime\n" ) ;
        printf ( "3. Odd / Even\n" ) ;
        printf ( "4. Exit\n" ) ;
        printf ( "Your choice? " ) ;
        scanf ( "%d", &choice ) ;
        switch ( choice )
        {
            case 1 :
                printf ( "\nEnter number: " ) ;
                scanf ( "%d", &num ) ;
                fact = 1 ;
                for ( i = 1 ; i <= num ; i++ )
                    fact = fact * i ;
                printf ( "Factorial value = %d\n", fact ) ;
                break ;
            case 2 :
                printf ( "\nEnter number: " ) ;
                scanf ( "%d", &num ) ;
                for ( i = 2 ; i < num ; i++ )
                {
                    if ( num % i == 0 )
                    {
                        printf ( "Not a prime number\n" ) ;
                        break ;
```

```
                    }
                }
                if ( i == num )
                    printf ( "Prime number\n" ) ;
                break ;
            case 3 :
                printf ( "\nEnter number: " ) ;
                scanf ( "%d", &num ) ;
                if ( num % 2 == 0 )
                    printf ( "Even number\n" ) ;
                else
                    printf ( "Odd number\n" ) ;
                break ;
            case 4 :
                exit ( 0 ) ;  /* Terminates program execution */
            default :
                printf ( "Wrong choice!\a\n" ) ;
        }
    }
    return 0 ;
}
```

Output

```
1. Factorial
2. Prime
3. Odd / Even
4. Exit
Your choice?
1

Enter number: 5
Factorial value = 120

1. Factorial
2. Prime
3. Odd / Even
4. Exit
Your choice? 2

Enter number: 13
```

```
Prime number

1. Factorial
2. Prime
3. Odd / Even
4. Exit
Your choice? 3

Enter number: 13
Odd number

1. Factorial
2. Prime
3. Odd / Even
4. Exit
Your choice? 4
```

Exercises

[A] What will be the output of the following programs?

(a)
```
# include <stdio.h>
int main( )
{
    char suite = 3 ;
    switch ( suite )
    {
        case 1 :
            printf ( "Diamond\n" ) ;
        case 2 :
            printf ( "Spade\n" ) ;
        default :
            printf ( "Heart\n" ) ;
    }
    printf ( "I thought one wears a suite\n" ) ;
    return 0 ;
}
```

(b)
```
# include <stdio.h>
int main( )
{
```

```
    int c = 3 ;
    switch ( c )
    {
        case '3' :
            printf ( "You never win the silver prize\n" ) ;
            break ;
        case 3 :
            printf ( "You always lose the gold prize\n" ) ;
            break ;
        default :
            printf ( "Of course provided you win a prize\n" ) ;
    }
    return 0 ;
}
```

(c)
```
# include <stdio.h>
int main( )
{
    int i = 3 ;
    switch ( i )
    {
        case 0 :
            printf ( "Customers are dicey\n" ) ;
        case 1 + 2 :
            printf ( "Markets are pricey\n" ) ;
        case 4 / 2 :
            printf ( "Investors are moody\n" ) ;
    }
    return 0 ;
}
```

(d)
```
# include <stdio.h>
int main( )
{
    int k ;
    float j = 2.0 ;
    switch ( k = j + 1 )
    {
        case 3 :
            printf ( "Trapped\n" ) ;
            break ;
        default :
```

```
            printf ( "Caught!\n" ) ;
    }
    return 0 ;
}
```

(e)
```
# include <stdio.h>
int main( )
{
    int ch = 'a' + 'b' ;
    switch ( ch )
    {
        case 'a' :
        case 'b' :
            printf ( "Look at 10 ideas, 11th will occur to you\n" ) ;
        case 'A' :
            printf ( "If you have a good idea, project it\n" ) ;
        case 'b' + 'a' :
            printf ( "Have ideas, will fly\n" ) ;
    }
    return 0 ;
}
```

[B] Point out the errors, if any, in the following programs:

(a)
```
# include <stdio.h>
int main( )
{
    int suite = 1 ;
    switch ( suite ) ;
    {
        case 0 ;
            printf ( "Club\n" ) ;
        case 1 ;
            printf ( "Diamond\n" ) ;
    }
    return 0 ;
}
```

(b)
```
# include <stdio.h>
int main( )
{
    int temp ;
    scanf ( "%d", &temp ) ;
```

```
    switch ( temp )
    {
        case ( temp <= 20 ) :
            printf ( "Ooooooohhhh! Damn cool!\n" ) ;
        case ( temp > 20 && temp <= 30 ) :
            printf ( "Rain rain here again!\n" ) ;
        case ( temp > 30 && temp <= 40 ) :
            printf ( "Wish I am on Everest\n" ) ;
        default :
            printf ( "Good old Nagpur weather\n" ) ;
    }
    return 0 ;
}
```

(c)
```
# include <stdio.h>
int main( )
{
    float a = 3.5 ;
    switch ( a )
    {
        case 0.5 :
            printf ( "The art of C\n" ) ; break ;
        case 1.5 :
            printf ( "The spirit of C\n" ) ; break ;
        case 2.5 :
            printf ( "See through C\n" ) ; break ;
    }
    return 0 ;
}
```

(d)
```
# include <stdio.h>
int main( )
{
    int a = 3, b = 4, c ;
    c = b – a ;
    switch ( c )
    {
        case 1 || 2 :
            printf ( "God give me a chance to change things\n" ) ;
            break ;
        case a || b :
            printf ( "God give me a chance to run my show\n" ) ;
```

```
            break ;
    }
    return 0 ;
}
```

[C] Write a program to find the grace marks for a student using **switch**. The user should enter the class obtained by the student and the number of subjects he has failed in. Use the following logic:

- If the student gets first class and he fails in more than 3 subjects, he does not get any grace. Otherwise, he gets a grace of 5 marks per subject.
- If the student gets second class and he fails in more than 2 subjects, he does not get any grace. Otherwise, he gets a grace of 4 marks per subject.
- If the student gets third class and he fails in more than 1 subject, then he does not get any grace. Otherwise, he gets a grace of 5 marks.

KanNotes

- Three ways for taking decisions in a program :
  1) Using if-else statement
  2) Using conditional operators
  3) Using the switch statement
- switch should be used when we are to find out whether a variable or an expression has one of the several possible values
- switch should not be used for checking ranges or for a yes / no problem
- General form :

```
switch ( expression )                → use constant or variable expression
{
        case constant expression :   → use only constant expression
            ...
        case constant expression :
```

```
        ...
    default :
        ...
}
```

- If a case fails, control jumps to the next case
- If a case is satisfied, then all statements below it up to } of switch are executed
- Usually, a break is used at the end of statements in each case
- break takes the control out of the switch
- Continue DOES NOT take the control to the beginning of the switch
- Order in which cases are written does not matter
- Default case is optional
- cases in a switch must always be unique
- switch can be used with int, long int, char
- switch cannot be used with float, double
- switch works faster than a series of ifs
- switch is popularly used in menu driven programs to check which choice from the menu has been made by the user
- goto keyword can take the control from any place to any other place within the function
- goto should be used only in a situation where we wish to break out of the innermost loop in a nested loop system
- As far as possible, goto should be avoided since it is difficult to keep track of the control when multiple gotos are used
- exit( ) - function - Terminates program execution
- # include <stdlib.h> for exit() to work

8 Functions

"Think modern, think of functions..."

If you wish, you can write all the statements in a program within main( ). But that would be a stupid way of writing a program. Programming can be done more smartly using functions. How? Well, this chapter has the answer...

Contents

A computer program (except for the simplest one) cannot handle all the tasks by itself. Instead, it requests other program-like entities—called 'functions' in C—to get its tasks done. In this chapter, we will study these functions. We will look at a variety of features of these functions, starting with the simplest one and then working towards those that demonstrate the power of C functions.

What is a Function?

A function is a self-contained block of statements that performs a coherent task of some kind. Let us now look at a simple program that introduces us to the idea of a C function

```
# include <stdio.h>
void message( ) ; /* function prototype declaration */
int main( )
{
    message( ) ; /* function call */
    printf ( "Cry, and you stop the monotony!\n" ) ;
    return 0 ;
}
void message( ) /* function definition */
{
    printf ( "Smile, and the world smiles with you...\n" ) ;
}
```

And here's the output...

```
Smile, and the world smiles with you...
Cry, and you stop the monotony!
```

Here, we have defined two functions—**main( )** and **message( )**. In fact, we have used the word **message** at three places in the program. Let us understand the meaning of each.

The first is the function prototype declaration and is written as:

```
void message( ) ;
```

This prototype declaration indicates that **message( )** is a function which after completing its execution does not return any value. This 'does not return any value' is indicated using the keyword **void**. It is necessary to declare the prototype of every function that we intend to define in the program.

The second usage of **message** is...

```
void message( )
{
    printf ( "Smile, and the world smiles with you...\n" ) ;
}
```

This is the function definition. In this definition right now we are having only **printf( )**, but we can also use **if**, **for**, **while**, **switch**, etc., within it.

The third usage is...

```
message( ) ;
```

Here the function **message( )** is being called by **main( )**. When we call the **message( )** function, control passes to the function **message( )**. The activity of **main( )** is temporarily suspended; it falls asleep while the **message( )** function wakes up and goes to work. When the **message( )** function runs out of statements to execute, the control returns to **main( )**, which comes to life again and begins executing its code at the exact point where it left off. Thus, **main( )** becomes the 'calling' function, whereas **message( )** becomes the 'called' function.

If you have grasped the concept of 'calling' a function, you are prepared for a call to more than one function. Consider the following example:

```
# include <stdio.h>
void italy( ) ;
void brazil( ) ;
void argentina( ) ;
int main( )
{
    printf ( "I am in main\n" ) ;
    italy( ) ;
    brazil( ) ;
    argentina( ) ;
    return 0 ;
}
void italy( )
{
    printf ( "I am in italy\n" ) ;
}
void brazil( )
```

```
{
    printf ( "I am in brazil\n" ) ;
}
void argentina( )
{
    printf ( "I am in argentina\n" ) ;
}
```

The output of the above program when executed would be as under:

```
I am in main
I am in italy
I am in brazil
I am in argentina
```

Several conclusions can be drawn from this program:

- A C program is a collection of one or more functions.
- If a C program contains only one function, it must be **main( )**.
- If a C program contains more than one function, then one (and only one) of these functions must be **main( )**.
- Each function in a program is called in the sequence specified by the function calls in **main( )**.
- After each function has done its thing, control returns to **main( )**. When **main( )** runs out of statements and function calls, the program ends.

Given below are a few additional tips about functions.

(a) Program execution always begins with **main( )**. Except for this fact, all C functions enjoy a state of perfect equality. No precedence, no priorities, nobody is nobody's boss.

(b) Since program execution always begins with **main( )**, every function gets called directly or indirectly from **main( )**. In other words, the **main( )** function drives other functions.

(c) Any function can be called from any other function. Even **main( )** can be called from other functions.

(d) A function can be called multiple times.

(e) The order in which the functions are defined in a program and the order in which they get called need not necessarily be same.

However, it is advisable to define the functions in the same order in which they are called. This makes the program easier to understand.

(f) A function cannot be defined in another function. Thus, the following program would be wrong, since **argentina( )** is being defined inside another function, **main( )**:

```
int main( )
{
    printf ( "I am in main\n" ) ;
    void argentina( )
    {
        printf ( "I am in argentina\n" ) ;
    }
}
```

(g) There are basically two types of functions:

Library functions Ex. **printf( )**, **scanf( )**, etc.
User-defined functions Ex. **argentina( )**, **brazil( )**, etc.

Library functions are a collection of commonly required functions grouped together and stored in a Library file on the disk. This library of functions comes ready-made with development environments like Turbo C, Visual Studio, GCC, etc. The procedure for calling both types of functions is exactly same.

Why use Functions?

Why write separate functions at all? Why not squeeze the entire logic into one function, **main( )**? Well, for two reasons given below.

(a) Writing functions avoids rewriting the same code over and over and promotes code reuse. Suppose you have statements in your program that calculate area of a triangle. If later in the program, you want to calculate the area of a different triangle, it would be improper to write the same instructions again. Instead, you would prefer to jump to a function that calculates area and then jump back to the place from where you left off.

(b) If the operation of a program can be divided into separate activities, and each activity placed in a different function, then each could be written and checked independently. Separating the code into modular functions also makes the program easier to design and understand.

So, do not try to cram the entire logic in one function. Instead, break a program into small units and write functions for each of these isolated subdivisions. Do not hesitate to write functions that are called only once. What is important is that these functions perform some logically isolated tasks.

Communication between Functions

The functions that we have used so far weren't very flexible. We called them and they did what they were designed to do. Now we wish to communicate between the 'calling' and the 'called' functions.

Communication between functions is facilitated by arguments and return values. You have unknowingly used the arguments in the **printf( )** and **scanf( )** functions—the format string and the list of variables used inside the parentheses in these functions are arguments. The arguments are also called parameters.

Consider the following program. In this program, in **main( )** we receive the values of **a, b** and **c** through the keyboard and then output their sum. However, sum is calculated in the function **calsum( )**. So the values of **a, b** and **c** must be passed to **calsum( )**. Similarly, once the sum is calculated it must be returned back to **main( )**. That is communication in short.

```
/* Sending and receiving values between functions */
# include <stdio.h>
int calsum ( int x, int y, int z ) ;
int main( )
{
    int a, b, c, sum ;
    printf ( "Enter any three numbers " ) ;
    scanf ( "%d %d %d", &a, &b, &c ) ;
    sum = calsum ( a, b, c ) ;
    printf ( "Sum = %d\n", sum ) ;
    return 0 ;
}
int calsum ( int x, int y, int z )
{
    int d ;
    d = x + y + z ;
```

```
    return ( d ) ;
}
```

And here is the output of the program...

```
Enter any three numbers 10 20 30
Sum = 60
```

There are several things to note about this program:

(a) The values of **a**, **b** and **c** are passed from **main( )** to **calsum( )** by mentioning **a**, **b** and **c** in the parentheses while making the call.

```
sum = calsum ( a, b, c ) ;
```

In **calsum( )** these values are collected in three variables **x**, **y** and **z**:

```
int calsum ( int x, int y, int z )
```

Passing values of **a**, **b**, **c** is necessary, because variables are available only to the statements of a function in which they are defined.

(b) The variables **a**, **b** and **c** are called 'actual arguments', whereas the variables **x**, **y** and **z** are called 'formal arguments'. The type, order and number of the actual and formal arguments must always be same.

Instead of **x**, **y** and **z**, we could have used the same variable names **a**, **b** and **c**. But the compiler would still treat them as different variables since they are in different functions.

(c) Note the function prototype declaration of **calsum( )**. Instead of the usual **void**, we are using **int**. This indicates that **calsum( )** is going to return a value of the type **int**. It is not compulsory to use variable names in the prototype declaration. Hence, we could have written the prototype as:

```
int calsum ( int, int, int ) ;
```

In the definition of **calsum** too, **void** has been replaced by **int**.

(d) In the earlier programs, the moment closing brace (**}**) of the called function was encountered, the control returned to the calling function. No separate **return** statement was necessary to send back the control.

This approach is fine if the called function is not going to return any meaningful value to the calling function. In our program, however, we want to return the sum. Therefore, it is necessary to use the **return** statement. It serves two purposes:

(1) It transfers the control back to the calling function.
(2) It returns the value present in the parentheses (**d** in our program) after **return**, to the calling function.

(e) There is no restriction on the number of **return** statements that may be present in a function. Also, the **return** statement need not always be present at the end of the called function. The following function illustrates these facts:

```
int fun ( int n )
{
   if ( n <= 10 )
        return ( n * n  ) ;
   else
        return ( n * n * n ) ;
}
```

In this function, different **return** statements would be executed depending on value of **n**.

(f) When control returns from **calsum( )**, the returned value is collected in the variable **sum** through the statement

```
sum = calsum ( a, b, c ) ;
```

(g) All the following are valid **return** statements.

```
return ( a ) ;    /* or return a ; */
return ( 23 ) ; /* or return 23 ; */
return ;
```

In the last statement, only control is returned to the calling function. Note that, the parentheses after **return** are optional.

(h) A function can return only one value at a time. Thus, the following statements are invalid:

```
return ( a, b ) ;
```

```
return ( x, 12 ) ;
```

There is a way to get around this limitation, which would be discussed in Chapter 9.

(i) If the value of a formal argument is changed in the called function, the corresponding change does not take place in the calling function. For example,

```
# include <stdio.h>
void fun ( int ) ;
int main( )
{
    int a = 30 ;
    fun ( a ) ;
    printf ( "%d\n", a ) ;
    return 0 ;
}
void fun ( int b )
{
    b = 60 ;
    printf ( "%d\n", b ) ;
}
```

The output of the above program would be:

```
60
30
```

Thus, even though the value of **b** is changed in **fun( ),** the value of **a** in **main( )** remains unchanged. This means that when values are passed to a called function, copies of values in actual arguments are made into formal arguments.

Order of Passing Arguments

Consider the following function call:

```
fun (a, b, c, d ) ;
```

In this call, it does not matter whether the arguments are passed from left to right or from right to left. However, in some function calls, the order of passing arguments becomes an important consideration. For example:

```
int a = 1 ;
printf ( "%d %d %d\n", a, ++a, a++ ) ;
```

It appears that this **printf( )** would output 1 2 2.

This however is not the case. Surprisingly, it outputs 3 3 1. This is because, during a function call, the arguments are passed from right to left. That is, firstly 1 is passed through the expression **a++** and then **a** is incremented to 2. Then result of **++a** is passed. That is, **a** is incremented to 3 and then passed. Finally, latest value of **a**, i.e., 3, is passed. Thus, in right to left order, 1, 3, 3 get passed. Once **printf( )** collects them, it prints them in the order in which we have asked it to get them printed (and not the order in which they were passed). Thus 3 3 1 gets printed.

It is important to note that the order of passing arguments to a function is not specified by the language, and hence is compiler-dependent. Consequently, any code that is written disregarding this is bound to show unpredictable behavior. For instance, the **printf( )** example in question may give different outputs with different compilers.

Using Library Functions

Consider the following program:

```
# include <stdio.h>
# include <math.h>
int main( )
{
    float a = 0.5 ;
    float w, x, y, z ;
    w = sin ( a ) ;
    x = cos ( a ) ;
    y = tan ( a ) ;
    z = pow ( a, 2 ) ;
    printf ( "%f %f %f %f\n", w, x, y, z ) ;
    return 0 ;
}
```

Here we have called four standard library functions—**sin( )**, **cos( )**, **tan( )** and **pow( )**. As we know, before calling any function, we must declare its prototype. This helps the compiler in checking whether the values being passed and returned are as per the prototype declaration. But since we did not define the library functions (we merely called them), we do not know the prototype declarations of library functions. Hence, along with library functions a set of '.h' files are also provided. These header files contain the prototype declarations of library functions.

Library functions are divided into different groups and one header file is provided for each group. For example, prototypes of all input/output functions are provided in the file 'stdio.h', prototypes of all mathematical functions (like **sin( )**, **cos( )**, **tan( )** and **pow( )**) are provided in the file 'math.h', etc. If you open the header file 'math.h', the prototypes would appear as shown below.

```
double sin ( double ) ;
double cos ( double ) ;
double tan ( double ) ;
double pow ( double, double ) ;
```

Here **double** indicates a real number. We would learn more about **double** in Chapter 11.

Whenever we wish to call any library function, we must include the header file that contains its prototype declaration.

One Dicey Issue

Now consider the following program:

```
# include <stdio.h>
int main( )
{
    int i = 10, j = 20 ;
    printf ( "%d %d %d\n", i, j ) ;
    printf ( "%d\n", i, j ) ;
    return 0 ;
}
```

This program gets successfully compiled, even though there is a mismatch in the format specifiers and the variables in the list used in **printf( )**. This is because, **printf( )** accepts *variable* number of arguments —sometimes 2 arguments, sometimes 3 arguments, etc. Hence, even with the mismatch above, the call still matches with the prototype of **printf( )** present in 'stdio.h'. At run-time, when the first **printf( )** is executed, since there is no variable matching with the last specifier **%d**, a garbage integer gets printed. Similarly, in the second **printf( )**, since the format specifier for **j** has not been mentioned, its value does not get printed. How to define functions with variable number of arguments is discussed in Chapter 22.

Return Type of Function

Suppose we want to obtain square of a floating-point number using a function. This can be achieved through a simple program shown below.

```
# include <stdio.h>
float square ( float ) ;
int main( )
{
    float  a, b ;
    printf ( "Enter any number " ) ;
    scanf ( "%f", &a ) ;
    b = square ( a ) ;
    printf ( "Square of %f is %f\n", a, b ) ;
    return 0 ;
}
float square ( float  x )
{
    float  y ;
    y = x * x ;
    return ( y ) ;
}
```

And here are three sample runs of this program...

```
Enter any number 3
Square of 3 is 9.000000
Enter any number 1.5
Square of 1.5 is 2.250000
Enter any number 2.5
Square of 2.5 is 6.250000
```

Since we are returning a **float** value from this function, we have indicated the return type of the **square( )** function as **float** in the prototype declaration as well as in the function definition. Had we dropped **float** from the prototype and the definition, the compiler would have assumed that **square( )** is supposed to return an integer value. This is because, default return type of any function is **int**.

P</> Programs

Problem 8.1

Write a function to calculate the factorial value of any integer entered through the keyboard.

Program

```
/* Calculate factorial value of an integer using a function */
# include <stdio.h>
int fact ( int ) ;
int main( )
{
    int num ;
    int factorial ;
    printf ( "\nEnter a number: " ) ;
    scanf ( "%d", &num ) ;
    factorial = fact ( num ) ;
    printf ( "Factorial of %d = %ld\n", num, factorial ) ;
    return 0 ;
}
int fact ( int num )
{
    int i ;
    int factorial = 1 ;
    for ( i = 1 ; i <= num ; i++ )
        factorial = factorial * i ;
    return ( factorial ) ;
}
```

Output

```
Enter a number: 6
Factorial of 6 = 720
```

Problem 8.2

Write a function power (a, b), to calculate the value of a raised to b.

Program

```
/* Program to calculate power of a value */
# include <stdio.h>
float power ( float, int ) ;
int main( )
{
    float  x, pow ;
    int  y ;
    printf ( "\nEnter two numbers: " ) ;
    scanf ( "%f %d", &x, &y ) ;
    pow = power ( x , y ) ;
    printf ( "%f to the power %d = %f\n", x, y, pow ) ;
    return 0 ;
}
float power ( float x, int y )
{
    int  i ;
    float  p = 1 ;
    for ( i = 1 ; i <= y ; i++ )
        p = p * x ;
    return ( p ) ;
}
```

Output

```
Enter two numbers: 1.5 3
1.500000 to the power 3 = 3.375000
```

Problem 8.3

Define a function to convert any given year into its Roman equivalent. Use these Roman equivalents for decimal numbers: 1 – I, 5 – V, 10 – X, 50 – L, 100 – C, 500 – D, 1000 – M.

Example:
Roman equivalent of 1988 is mdcccclxxxviii.
Roman equivalent of 1525 is mdxxv.

Program

```
/* Convert given year into its roman equivalent */
# include <stdio.h>
int romanise ( int, int, char ) ;
int main( )
{
    int yr ;
    printf ( "\nEnter year: " ) ;
    scanf ( "%d", &yr ) ;
    yr = romanise ( yr, 1000, 'm' ) ;
    yr = romanise ( yr, 500, 'd' ) ;
    yr = romanise ( yr, 100, 'c' ) ;
    yr = romanise ( yr, 50, 'l' ) ;
    yr = romanise ( yr, 10, 'x' ) ;
    yr = romanise ( yr, 5, 'v' ) ;
    romanise ( yr, 1, 'i' ) ;
    return 0 ;
}
int romanise ( int y, int k, char ch )
{
    int i, j ;
    j = y / k ;
    for ( i = 1 ; i <= j ; i++ )
        printf ( "%c", ch ) ;
    return ( y % k ) ;
}
```

Output

```
Enter year: 1988
mdcccclxxxviii
```

Exercises

[A] Point out the errors, if any, in the following programs:

(a)
```
# include <stdio.h>
int addmult ( int, int )
```

```
int main( )
{
    int i = 3, j = 4, k, l ;
    k = addmult ( i, j ) ;
    l = addmult ( i, j ) ;
    printf ( "%d %d\n", k, l ) ;
    return 0 ;
}
int addmult ( int x, int y )
{
    int u, v ;
    u = x + y ;
    v = x * y ;
    return ( u, v ) ;
}
```

(b)
```
# include <stdio.h>
int main( )
{
    int a ;
    a = message( ) ;
    return 0 ;
}
void message( )
{
    printf ( "Learn from him online at ykanetkar.com\n" ) ;
    return ;
}
```

(c)
```
# include <stdio.h>
int main( )
{
    float a = 15.5 ;
    char ch = 'C' ;
    printit ( a, ch ) ;
    return 0 ;
}
printit ( a, ch )
{
    printf ( "%f %c\n", a, ch ) ;
}
```

(d)
```
# include <stdio.h>
int main( )
{
    let_us_c( )
    {
        printf ( "Learn C online...\n" ) ;
        printf ( "At ykanetkar.com\n" ) ;
    }
    return 0 ;
}
```

[B] State whether the following statements are True or False:

(a) Commonly used variables are available to all the functions in a program.

(b) To return the control back to the calling function we must use the keyword **return**.

(c) The same variable names can be used in different functions without any conflict.

(d) Every called function must contain a **return** statement.

(e) A function may contain more than one **return** statement.

(f) Each **return** statement in a function may return a different value.

(g) A function can still be useful even if you do not pass any arguments to it and the function does not return any value.

(h) Same names can be used for different functions without any conflict.

(i) A function may be called more than once from any other function.

[C] Answer the following questions:

(a) Any year is entered through the keyboard. Write a function to determine whether the year is a leap year or not.

(b) A positive integer is entered through the keyboard. Write a function to obtain the prime factors of this number.

For example, prime factors of 24 are 2, 2, 2 and 3, whereas prime factors of 35 are 5 and 7.

KanNotes

- Functions are a group of instructions achieving some goal
- Why create functions :

  1) Better complexity management - Easy to Design, Easy to Debug
  2) Provide reuse mechanism - Avoids rewriting same code repeatedly
- Types of functions :

  1) Library – printf(), scanf(), pow()
  2) User-defined – main()

  Rules for building both are same
- Three things should be done while creating a function :

  1) Function definition
  2) Function call
  3) Function prototype declaration
- General form :

```
return-type function-name ( type arg1, type arg2, type arg3 )
{
    statement1 ;   statement2 ;
    return (variable/constant/expression) ; → can return only 1 value
}
```

- A C program is a collection of one or more functions
- If a C program contains 1 function, its name is main()
- If it contains > 1 function, then one of them must be main()
- Execution of any C program always begins with main()
- Function names in a program must be unique
- Any function can call any other function

- Functions can be defined in any order
- More the function calls, slower the execution
- If values are passed to a function, the function must collect it while defining it
- Arguments passed to a function are called actual arguments
- Arguments received by a function are called formal arguments
- Actual & Formal arguments must match in Number, Order and Type
- Actual arguments can be constants / variables / expressions
- Formal arguments must be variables
- Nested calls are legal. Ex. : a = sin (cos (b)) ;
- Call within an expression is legal. Ex. : a = sin (b) + cos (c) ;
- The error "Unresolved external" usually means there is a mistake in the function name spelling
- return (s) ; - Returns control & value
- return ; - Returns only control
- If value is returned from a function, we can choose to ignore it
- To ensure that no value is returned from a function, use void as the return-type in function definition and its prototype declaration
- A function by default returns an integer value. If we do not specifically return an integer value then a garbage integer value would be returned
- A function can return a non-integer value. The type of value must be suitably mentioned in the function definition and its prototype declaration as in :

```
float area ( float r ) ;          /* function prototype declaration */
float area ( float r )  { .. }    /* function definition */
```

9 Pointers

"Know pointers, will travel..."

When you set out on a journey and reach an important milestone, you visit a temple and thank God. Pointer is such a milestone in your journey of learning C programming. Once you know it, it will open totally new vistas for you. This chapter will show you how...

C Contents

Which feature of C do beginners find most difficult to understand? The answer is easy: pointers. Other languages have pointers but few use them as frequently as C does. This chapter is devoted to pointers and their usage in function calls. Let us begin with the function calls.

Call by Value and Call by Reference

By now, we are well familiar with how to call functions. But, if you observe carefully, whenever we called a function and passed something to it, we always passed the 'values' of variables or expressions to the called function. Such function calls are called 'calls by value'. The examples of call by value are shown below:

```
sum = calsum ( a, b, c ) ;
f = factr ( a ) ;
```

Instead of passing the value of a variable, we can pass the location number (also called address) of the variable to a function. Such a call is known as 'call by reference'. To understand 'call by reference' and its utility, we must first equip ourselves with knowledge of a concept called 'pointers'.

An Introduction to Pointers

The difficulty beginners have with pointers has much to do with the pointer terminology than the actual concept. So, in our discussion of pointers, we will try to understand pointers in terms of programming concepts that we already know.

Consider the declaration,

```
int i = 3 ;
```

This declaration tells the C compiler to:

(a) Reserve space in memory to hold the integer value.
(b) Associate the name **i** with this memory location.
(c) Store the value 3 at this location.

We may represent **i**'s location in memory by the memory-map shown in Figure 9.1. We can see that the computer has selected memory location 65524 as the place to store the value 3. The location number 65524 is not a number to be relied upon, because some other time the computer may choose a different location for storing the value 3. The important point is, **i**'s address in memory is a number.

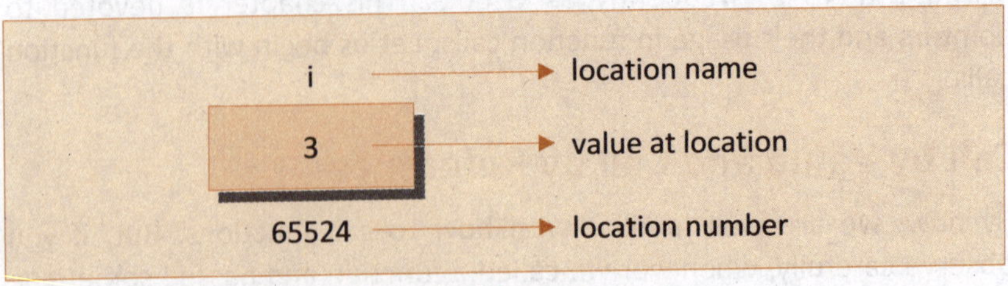

Figure 9.1 Memory-map of a variable.

We can print this address number through the following program:

```
# include <stdio.h>
int main( )
{
    int  i = 3 ;
    printf ( "Address of i = %u\n", &i ) ;
    printf ( "Value of i = %d\n", i ) ;
    printf ( "Value of i = %d\n", *( &i ) ) ;
    return 0 ;
}
```

The output of the above program would be:

```
Address of i = 65524
Value of i = 3
Value of i = 3
```

The '&' used in the first **printf( )** is 'address of' operator. The expression **&i** returns the address of the variable **i**, which in this case happens to be 65524. Since 65524 represents an address, there is no question of a sign being associated with it. Hence it is printed using **%u**, which is a format specifier for printing an unsigned integer.

65524 is a 16-bit address. If we execute this program on a 32-bit machine or a 64-bit machine we would get a 32-bit address or a 64-bit address respectively. A 32-bit address can be printed using **%lu** and a 64-bit address using **%llu**. Some compilers give a warning/error if we use **%u**, **%lu** or **%llu** to print addresses saying we are trying to treat an address as an unsigned integer. To avoid such situations, we can use the specifier **%p** which prints the address in hexadecimal format.

We have been using the '&' operator all the time in the **scanf( )** function. The other pointer operator available in C is **'*'**, called 'value at address' operator. It is being used in the third **printf( )**. It gives the value stored at an address 65524, which is 3. The 'value at address' operator is also called 'indirection' operator.

Note that printing the value of ***(&i)** is same as printing the value of **i**.

The expression **&i** gives the address of the variable **i**. This address can be collected in a variable, by saying,

```
j = &i ;
```

Figure 9.2 shows the memory-map of **i** and **j**.

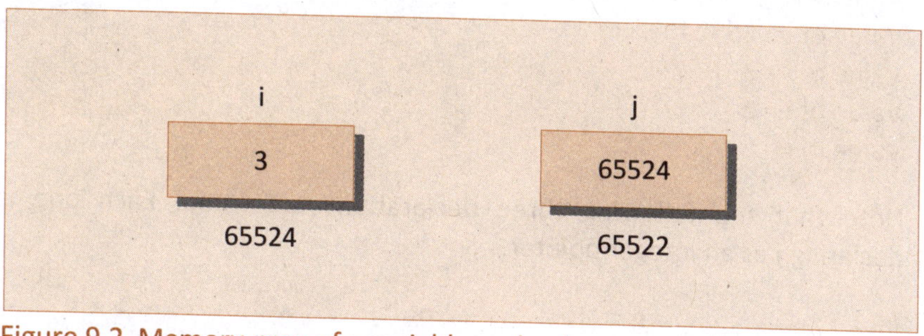

Figure 9.2 Memory-map of a variable and pointer variable.

As you can see, **i**'s value is 3 and **j**'s value is **i**'s address. Since **j** is a variable that contains the address of **i**, it is declared as,

```
int *j ;
```

This declaration tells the compiler that **j** will be used to store the address of an integer value. In other words, **j** points to an integer. How do we justify the usage of * in this declaration? For this, let us go by the meaning of *. It stands for 'value at address'. Thus, **int *j** would mean, the value at address stored in **j** is an **int**. Here is a program that demonstrates these relationships.

```
# include <stdio.h>
int main( )
{
    int i = 3 ;
    int *j ;
    j = &i ;
    printf ( "Address of i = %u\n", &i ) ;
```

```
    printf ( "Address of i = %u\n", j ) ;
    printf ( "Address of j = %u\n", &j ) ;
    printf ( "Value of j = %u\n", j ) ;
    printf ( "Value of i = %d\n", i ) ;
    printf ( "Value of i = %d\n", *( &i ) ) ;
    printf ( "Value of i = %d\n", *j ) ;
    return 0 ;
}
```

The output of the above program would be:

```
Address of i = 65524
Address of i = 65524
Address of j = 65522
Value of j = 65524
Value of i = 3
Value of i = 3
Value of i = 3
```

Note that the following three declarations are same. Each one is declaring **j** as an integer pointer.

```
int* j ;            int * j ;            int *j ;
```

Work through the above program carefully, taking help of the memory locations of **i** and **j** shown in Figure 9.2. This program summarizes everything that we have discussed so far. If you don't understand the program's output, or the meanings of **&i, &j, *j** and ***(&i)**, re-read the last few pages. Everything we say about pointers from here onwards will depend on your understanding these expressions thoroughly.

The concept of pointers has been further extended in the following program.

```
# include <stdio.h>
int main( )
{
    int i = 3, *j, **k ;
    j = &i ;
    k = &j ;
    printf ( "Address of i = %u\n", &i ) ;
    printf ( "Address of i = %u\n ", j ) ;
    printf ( "Address of i = %u\n ", *k ) ;
```

```
    printf ( "Address of j = %u\n ", &j ) ;
    printf ( "Address of j = %u\n ", k ) ;
    printf ( "Address of k = %u\n ", &k ) ;
    printf ( "Value of j  = %u\n ", j ) ;
    printf ( "Value of k  = %u\n ", k ) ;
    printf ( "Value of i  = %d\n ", i ) ;
    printf ( "Value of i  = %d\n ", * ( &i ) ) ;
    printf ( "Value of i  = %d\n ", *j ) ;
    printf ( "Value of i  = %d\n ", **k ) ;
    return 0 ;
}
```

The output of the above program would be:

```
Address of i = 65524
Address of i = 65524
Address of i = 65524
Address of j = 65522
Address of j = 65522
Address of k = 65520
Value of j  = 65524
Value of k  = 65522
Value of i  = 3
Value of i  = 3
Value of i  = 3
Value of i  = 3
```

Figure 9.3 would help you in tracing out how the program prints the above output.

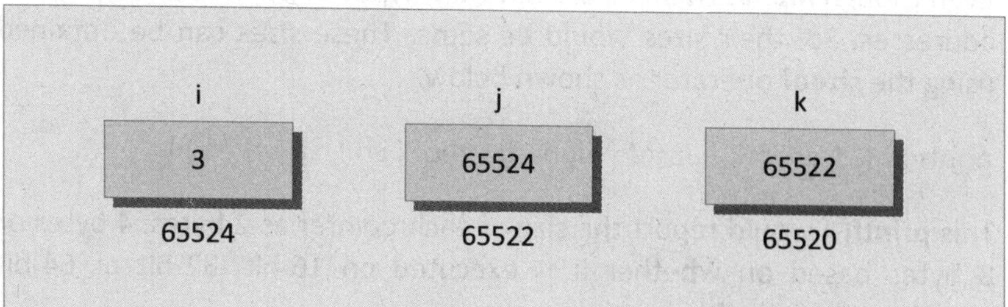

Figure 9.3 Memory-map of a variable and pointer variables.

Remember that when you run this program, the addresses that get printed might turn out to be something different than the ones shown in

Figure 9.3. However, for any addresses, the relationship between **i**, **j** and **k** would remain same.

Observe how the variables **j** and **k** have been declared,

```
int i, *j, **k ;
```

Here, **i** is an ordinary **int**, **j** is a pointer to an **int** (often called an integer pointer), whereas **k** is a pointer to an integer pointer.

We can extend the above program further by creating a pointer to a pointer to an integer pointer. Likewise, there can be a pointer to a pointer to a pointer to an integer pointer. There is no limit on how far can we go on extending this definition. Possibly, till the point we can comprehend it. And that point of comprehension is usually a pointer to a pointer. Beyond this, one rarely requires to extend the definition of a pointer. But just in case...

Pointer Types and their Sizes

Look at the following declarations:

```
int  *alpha ;
char  *ch ;
float  *s ;
```

Here, **alpha, ch** and **s** are declared as pointer variables, i.e., variables that hold addresses. The declaration **float *s** means that **s** is going to contain the address of a floating-point value. Similarly, **char *ch** means that **ch** is going to contain the address of a char value.

Even though **alpha**, **ch** and **s** are different types of pointers, they all hold addresses. So, their sizes would be same. These sizes can be obtained using the **sizeof** operator as shown below.

```
printf ( "%d %d %d", sizeof ( alpha ), sizeof ( ch ), sizeof ( s ) ) ;
```

This **printf( )** would report the size of each pointer as 2 bytes, 4 bytes or 8 bytes based on whether it is executed on 16-bit, 32-bit or 64-bit machine respectively.

Even though **alpha**, **ch** and **s** are different types of pointers, they all contain addresses (location nos.). Since addresses are always whole numbers, they contain whole numbers.

Back to Function Calls

Having had the first tryst with pointers, let us now get back to what we had originally set out to learn—the two types of function calls—call by value and call by reference.

In 'call by value' the 'value' of each actual argument in the call is copied into corresponding formal arguments of the called function. With this method, the changes made to the formal arguments in the called function have no effect on the values of actual arguments in the calling function. The following program illustrates the 'Call by Value':

```
# include <stdio.h>
void swapv ( int  x, int  y ) ;
int main( )
{
    int  a = 10, b = 20 ;
    swapv ( a, b ) ;
    printf ( "a = %d b = %d\n", a, b ) ;
    return 0 ;
}
void swapv ( int  x, int  y )
{
    int  t ;
    t = x ;
    x = y ;
    y = t ;
    printf ( "x = %d y = %d\n", x, y ) ;
}
```

The output of the above program would be:

```
x = 20 y = 10
a = 10 b = 20
```

Note that values of **a** and **b** remain unchanged even after exchanging the values of **x** and **y**.

In 'call by reference' the addresses of actual arguments in the call are copied into the formal arguments of the called function. This means that, using these addresses, we can access the actual arguments and hence can manipulate them. The following program illustrates this fact:

```
# include <stdio.h>
```

```
void swapr ( int *, int * ) ;
int main( )
{
    int a = 10, b = 20 ;
    swapr ( &a, &b ) ;
    printf ( "a = %d b = %d\n", a, b ) ;
    return 0 ;
}
void swapr ( int *x, int *y )
{
    int t ;
    t = *x ;
    *x = *y ;
    *y = t ;
}
```

The output of the above program would be:

```
a = 20 b = 10
```

Note that this program manages to exchange the values of **a** and **b** using their addresses stored in **x** and **y**.

Utility of Call by Reference

We know that the **return** statement can return only one value from a function at a time. We can overcome this limitation by using call by reference as shown in the following program.

```
# include <stdio.h>
void areaperi ( int, float *, float * ) ;
int main( )
{
    int radius ;
    float area, perimeter ;
    printf ( "Enter radius of a circle " ) ;
    scanf ( "%d", &radius ) ;
    areaperi ( radius, &area, &perimeter ) ;
    printf ( "Area = %f\n", area ) ;
    printf ( "Perimeter = %f\n", perimeter ) ;
    return 0 ;
}
void areaperi ( int r, float *a, float *p )
```

```
{
    *a = 3.14 * r * r ;
    *p = 2 * 3.14 * r ;
}
```

And here is the output...

```
Enter radius of a circle 5
Area = 78.500000
Perimeter = 31.400000
```

Here, we are making a mixed call, in the sense, we are passing the value of **radius** but, addresses of **area** and **perimeter**. Using the addresses stored in **a** and **p** we can change the values of **area** and **perimeter**. Hence when control returns from the function **areaperi( )**, we are able to output the values of **area** and **perimeter**.

Conclusions

From the programs that we have discussed here, we can draw the following conclusions:

(a) If we want that the value of an actual argument should not get changed in the function being called, pass the actual argument by value.

(b) If we want that the value of an actual argument should get changed in the function being called, pass the actual argument by reference.

(c) If a function is to be made to return more than one value at a time, then return these values indirectly by using a call by reference.

Uses of Pointers

Pointers are popularly used for following purposes:

(a) To return multiple values from a function in an indirect manner, call by reference is used.

(b) To access or manipulate elements of an array or string. This would be discussed in Chapters 13 - 16.

(c) If a large object (like array or structure) is passed to a function by value, a copy of it would be created when the function collects it. This leads to wastage of precious memory space. This can be avoided by passing address of the large object and collecting it in a pointer.

(d) At times, we are required to allocate memory for an object (like array or structure) dynamically when the program is executing. This dynamically allocated memory is later accessed using pointers.

(e) There are different ways in which data can be organized in memory with a view to easily store and access it. To do this, different data structures like, stack, queue, tree, hash table and graph are used. To implement these data structures pointers are used.

(f) Function pointers facilitates implementation of callback mechanism through which a library function can call our function. Function pointers are discussed in Chapter

(g) In embedded systems often parameters like pressure, temperature, etc. are stored at specific pre-determined locations in memory. These values can then be accessed using pointers.

P</> Programs

Problem 9.1

Write a function that receives 5 integers and returns the sum, average and standard deviation of these numbers. Call this function from **main( )** and print the results in **main( )**.

Program

```
/* Function which returns sum, average and standard deviation */
# include <stdio.h>
# include <math.h>
void stats ( int *, int *, double * ) ;
int main( )
{
    int sum, avg ;
    double  stdev ;
    stats ( &sum, &avg, &stdev ) ;
    printf ( "Sum = %d \nAverage = %d \nStandard deviation = %lf\n",
              sum, avg, stdev ) ;
    return 0 ;
}
void stats ( int *sum, int *avg, double *stdev )
{
    int n1, n2, n3, n4, n5 ;
```

```
    printf ( "\nEnter 5 numbers: " ) ;
    scanf ( "%d%d%d%d%d", &n1, &n2, &n3, &n4, &n5 ) ;
    *sum = n1 + n2 + n3 + n4 + n5 ;
    *avg = *sum / 5 ;
    *stdev = sqrt ( ( pow ( ( n1 - *avg ), 2.0 ) + pow ( ( n2 - *avg ), 2.0 ) + \
                    pow ( ( n3 - *avg ), 2.0 ) + pow ( ( n4 - *avg ), 2.0 ) + \
                    pow ( ( n5 - *avg ), 2.0 ) ) / 4 ) ;
}
```

Output

```
Enter 5 numbers: 10 20 30 40 50
Sum = 150
Average = 30
Standard deviation = 15.811388
```

Problem 9.2

Write a program that defines a function that calculates power of one number raised to another and factorial value of a number in one call.

Program

```
# include <stdio.h>
void power_fact ( float, int, int, float *, int * ) ;
int main( )
{
    float a ;
    int b, number, factorial ;
    float pow ;
    printf ( "Enter a and b for calculating a raised to b: " ) ;
    scanf ( "%f %d", &a, &b ) ;
    printf ( "Enter number whose factorial is to be calculated: " ) ;
    scanf ( "%d", &number ) ;
    power_fact ( a, b, number, &pow, &factorial ) ;
    printf ( "Power = %f Factorial = %d", pow, factorial ) ;
    return 0 ;
}
void power_fact ( float x, int y, int num, float *power, int *fact )
{
    float res = 1 ;
```

```
    int i ;
    for ( i = 1 ; i <= y ; i++ )
        res = res * x ;
    *power = res ;
    res = 1 ;
    for ( i = 1 ; i <= num ; i++ )
        res = res * i ;
    *fact = res ;
}
```

Output

```
Enter a and b for calculating a raised to b: 2 5
Enter number whose factorial is to be calculated: 6
Power = 32.000000 Factorial = 720
```

Problem 9.3

Figure 9.4 shows three memory locations and values stored in them. Write a program to declare variables that implement the relationship shown. How will you print the values and addresses shown in the figure? On which machine the program should be executed to get such addresses?

Figure 9.4 Memory-map of 3 variables.

Program

```
#include <stdio.h>
int main( )
{
    float x = 3.14 ;
    float *y ;
    float **z ;
```

```
    = &x ;
    z = &y ;
    printf ( "%p %p %p\n", &x, &y, &z ) ;
    printf ( "%p %p\n", y, z ) ;
    printf ( "%f %f %f", x, *y, **z ) ;
    return 0 ;
}
```

Output

```
0x7ffea600ed9c  0x7ffea600eda0  0x7ffea600eda8
0x7ffea600ed9c  0x7ffea600eda0
3.140000  3.140000  3.140000
```

Exercises

[A] What will be the output of the following programs?

(a)
```
# include <stdio.h>
void fun ( int, int ) ;
int main( )
{
    int  i = 5, j = 2 ;
    fun ( i, j ) ;
    printf ( "%d %d\n", i, j ) ;
    return 0 ;
}
void fun ( int  i, int  j )
{
    i = i * i ;
    j = j * j ;
}
```

(b)
```
# include <stdio.h>
void fun ( int *, int * ) ;
int main( )
{
    int  i = 5, j = 2 ;
    fun ( &i, &j ) ;
    printf ( "%d %d\n", i, j ) ;
```

```
    return 0 ;
}
void fun ( int *i, int *j )
{
    *i = *i * *i ;
    *j = *j * *j ;
}
```

(c)
```
# include <stdio.h>
int main( )
{
    float a = 13.5 ;
    float *b, *c ;
    b = &a ; /* suppose address of a is 1006 */
    c = b ;
    printf ( "%u %u %u\n", &a, b, c ) ;
    printf ( "%f %f %f %f %f\n", a, *(&a), *&a, *b, *c ) ;
    return 0 ;
}
```

[B] Point out the errors, if any, in the following programs:

(a)
```
# include <stdio.h>
int main( )
{
    float p = 23.24 ;
    int *q, **r ;
    q = &p ;
    r = &q ;
    printf ( "%f %f\n", *q, **r ) ;
    return 0 ;
}
```

(b)
```
# include <stdio.h>
int main( )
{
    char ch = 'A' ;
    int k = 35 ;
    float a = 3.14 ;
    printf ( "%p %p %p\n", &ch, &k, &a ) ;
    return 0 ;
}
```

(c)
```
# include <stdio.h>
void function ( int * ) ;
int main( )
{
    int i = 35, *z ;
    z = function ( &i ) ;
    printf ( "%d\n", z ) ;
    return 0 ;
}
void function ( int *m )
{
    return ( *m + 2 ) ;
}
```

[C] Attempt the following questions:

(a) Given three variables **x**, **y**, **z**, write a function to circularly shift their values to right. In other words, if x = 5, y = 8, z = 10, after circular shift y = 5, z = 8, x =10. Call the function with variables **a**, **b**, **c** to circularly shift values.

(b) Define a function that receives weight of a commodity in Kilograms and returns the equivalent weight in Grams, Tons and Pounds. Call this function from **main( )** and print the results in **main( )**.

(c) Define a function to compute the distance between two points and use it to develop another function that will compute the area of the triangle whose vertices are **A(x1, y1)**, **B(x2, y2)**, and **C(x3, y3)**. Use these functions to develop a function which returns a value 1 if the point **(x, y)** lines inside the triangle ABC, otherwise returns a value 0. Would you get any advantage if you develop these functions to work on call by reference principle?

KanNotes

- Pointers are variables which hold addresses of other variables
- Address, Reference, Memory Location, Cell number are same
- & - Address of operator, * - Value at address or Indirection operator
- &, * - Pointer operators

- & can be used only with a variable
- * can be used with variable, constant or expression
- variable is same as *&variable
- Example of pointer usage :

```
int i = 10 ; int *j ; int **k ;
j = &i ; k = &j ;
printf ( "%d %d %d", i, *j, **k ) ;
```

  Here j is an integer pointer. k is a pointer to an integer pointer

- Even if a is a 4-byte variable, &a, gives address of first out of these 4 bytes
- For printing address – use %p.
- Using an integer ptr – Use * to reach integer
- Using a pointer to an integer pointer – Use ** to reach integer
- 3 ways to call a function :
  1) Call by value - when values of variables are passed to the called function
  2) Call by reference - when addresses of variables are passed to the called function
  3) Mixed call - when values of variables and addresses of variables are passed to the called function
- Call by Value - Change in formal arguments does not affect actual arguments
- Call by Reference : Using formal arguments actual arguments can be changed
- Examples of call types :
  1) swapv (a, b) ; - Call by value
  2) swapr (&a, &b) ; - call by reference
  3) sumprod (a, b, c, &s, &p) ; - Mixed call

10 Recursion

"To iterate is human, to recurse devine..."

When it comes to implementing a logic that is expressible in the form of itself, there are two ways to do it. One is the good old way of using loops; another is the smart way of using recursion. This chapter shows you how to adopt the smart way...

Contents

- Recursion
- Programs
- Exercises
- KanNotes

Recursion is an important feature associated with functions in C. Though a bit difficult to understand, it is often the most direct way of programming a complicated logic. This chapter explores recursion in detail.

Recursion

In C, it is possible for a function to call itself. A function is called 'recursive' if a statement within the body of a function calls the same function. Sometimes called 'circular definition', recursion is thus the process of defining something in terms of itself.

Let us now see a simple example of recursion. Suppose we wish to calculate factorial value of an integer. As we know, factorial value of 4 is 4 * 3 * 2 * 1. This can also be expressed as 4! = 4 * 3! where '!' stands for factorial. Thus, factorial of a number can be expressed in the form of itself. Hence this logic can be programmed using recursion as shown in the following program.

```
# include <stdio.h>
int rec ( int  ) ;
int main( )
{
    int a, fact ;
    printf ( "Enter any number: " ) ;
    scanf ( "%d", &a ) ;
    fact = rec ( a ) ;
    printf ( "Factorial value = %d\n", fact ) ;
    return 0 ;
}
int rec ( int  x )
{
    int f ;
    if ( x == 1 )
        return ( 1 ) ;
    else
        f = x * rec ( x - 1 ) ;
    return ( f ) ;
}
```

And here is the output for three runs of the program...

```
Enter any number: 1
```

```
Factorial value = 1
Enter any number: 2
Factorial value = 2
Enter any number: 5
Factorial value = 120
```

Let us understand this recursive factorial function thoroughly. In the first run when the number entered through **scanf( )** is 1, let us see what action does **rec( )** take. The value of **a** (i.e., 1) is copied into **x**. Since **x** turns out to be 1, the condition **if (x == 1)** is satisfied and hence 1 (which is indeed the value of 1 factorial) is returned through the **return** statement.

When the number entered through **scanf( )** is 2, the **(x == 1)** test fails, so we reach the statement,

```
f = x * rec ( x - 1 ) ;
```

And this is where we meet recursion. How do we handle the expression **x * rec (x - 1)**? We multiply **x** by **rec (x - 1)**. Since the current value of **x** is 2, we should calculate the value (2 * rec (1)). We know that the value returned by **rec (1)** is 1, so the expression reduces to (2 * 1), or simply 2. Thus the expression, **x * rec (x - 1)** evaluates to 2, which is stored in the variable **f**, and is returned to **main( )**, where it is duly printed out.

When value of **a** is 3, to visualize how the control flows from one function call to another, look at Figure 10.1.

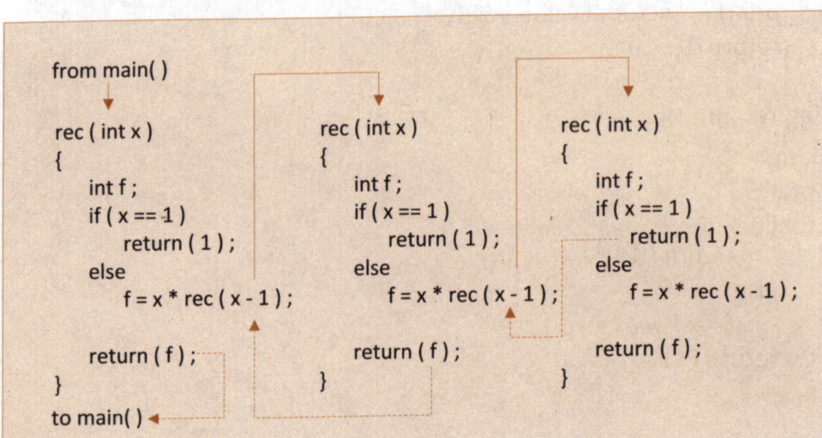

Figure 10.1 Working of recursive **rec( )** function.

First time when **rec( )** is called from **main( )**, **x** collects 3. From here, since **x** is not equal to 1, the **if** block is skipped and **rec( )** is called again with the argument **(x – 1)**, i.e. 2. This is a recursive call. Since **x** is still not equal to 1, **rec( )** is called yet another time, with argument (2 - 1). This time as **x** is 1, control goes back to previous **rec( )** with the value 1, and **f** is evaluated as 2. Similarly, each **rec( )** evaluates its **f** from the returned value, and finally 6 is returned to **main( )**. The flow of execution can be grasped easily by following the arrows shown in Figure 10.1.

Let it be clear that while executing the program, there do not exist so many copies of the function **rec( )**. These have been shown in the figure just to help you keep track of how the control flows during successive recursive calls.

Recursion may seem strange and complicated at first glance, but it is often the most direct way to code an algorithm, and once you are familiar with recursion, the clearest way of doing so.

Whenever we make a function call (recursive or normal), the parameters and the return address get stored at a place in memory known as stack. The stack gets unwound when the control returns from the called function. Thus, during every recursive function call, we are working with a fresh set of parameters.

Also, note that while writing recursive functions, you must have an **if** statement somewhere in the recursive function to force the function to return without recursive call being executed. If you do not do this and you call the function, you will fall in an indefinite loop, and the stack will keep on getting filled with parameters and the return address each time there is a call. The stack would become full soon and you would get a run-time error indicating that the stack has become full. This is a very common error while writing recursive functions. My advice is to use **printf( )** statement liberally during the development of recursive function, so that you can watch what is going on.

P</> Programs

Problem 10.1

A 5-digit positive integer is entered through the keyboard, write a recursive function to calculate sum of digits of the 5-digit number.

Program

```
/* Calculate sum of digits of a five-digit number using recursion */
# include <stdio.h>
int rsum ( int ) ;
int main( )
{
    int num, sum ;
    int n ;
    printf ( "Enter number: " ) ;
    scanf ( "%d", &num ) ;
    sum = rsum ( num ) ;
    printf ( "Sum of digits is %d\n", sum ) ;
    return 0 ;
}
int rsum ( int n )
{
    int s, remainder ;
    if ( n != 0 )
    {
        remainder = n % 10 ;
        s = remainder + rsum ( n / 10 ) ;
    }
    else
        return 0 ;
    return s ;
}
```

Output

```
Enter number: 12345
Sum of digits is 15
```

Problem 10.2

A positive integer is entered through the keyboard, write a program to obtain the prime factors of the number. Modify the function suitably to obtain the prime factors recursively.

Program

```
/* Find Prime Factors of a number recursively */
# include <stdio.h>
void factorize ( int, int ) ;
int main( )
{
    int num ;
    printf ( "Enter a number: " ) ;
    scanf ( "%d", &num ) ;
    printf ( "Prime factors are: " ) ;
    factorize ( num, 2 ) ;
    return 0 ;
}
void factorize ( int n, int i )
{
    if ( i <= n )
    {
        if ( n % i == 0 )
        {
            printf ( "%d ", i ) ;
            n = n / i ;
        }
        else
            i++ ;
        factorize ( n, i ) ;
    }
}
```

Output

```
Enter a number: 60
Prime factors are: 2 2 3 5
```

Problem 10.3

Write a recursive function to obtain the first 25 numbers of a Fibonacci sequence. In a Fibonacci sequence the sum of two successive terms gives the third term. Following are the first few terms of the Fibonacci sequence:

0 1 1 2 3 5 8 13 21 34 55 89....

Program

```
/* Generate first 25 terms of a Fibonacci sequence using recursion */
#include<stdio.h>
int fibo ( int ) ;
int main( )
{
    int terms = 25, i, n = 0 ;
    for ( i = 1 ; i <= terms ; i++ )
    {
        printf ( "%d\t", fibo ( n ) ) ;
        n++ ;
    }
    return 0 ;
}
int fibo ( int n )
{
    if ( n == 0 || n == 1 )
        return n ;
    else
        return ( fibo ( n - 1 ) + fibo ( n - 2 ) ) ;
}
```

Output

```
0     1     1     2     3     5     8     13    21    34    55
89    144   233   377   610   987   1597  2584  4181  6765
10946 17711 28657 46368
```

Exercises

[A] What will be the output of the following programs?

(a)
```
# include <stdio.h>
int main( )
{
    printf ( "I C, you C, we all C\n" ) ;
    main( ) ;
```

```
    return 0 ;
}
```

(b)
```
# include <stdio.h>
# include <stdlib.h>
int main( )
{
    int i = 0 ;
    i++ ;
    if ( i <= 5 )
    {
        printf ( "C adds wings to your thoughts\n" ) ;
        exit ( 0 ) ;
        main( ) ;
    }
    return 0 ;
}
```

[B] Attempt the following questions:

(a) A positive integer is entered through the keyboard, write a function to find the binary equivalent of this number:

(1) Without using recursion
(2) Using recursion

(b) Write a recursive function to obtain the sum of first 25 natural numbers.

(c) There are three pegs labeled A, B and C. Four disks are placed on peg A. The bottom-most disk is largest, and disks go on decreasing in size with the topmost disk being smallest. The objective of the game is to move the disks from peg A to peg C, using peg B as an auxiliary peg. The rules of the game are as follows:

(1) Only one disk may be moved at a time, and it must be the top disk on one of the pegs.
(2) A larger disk should never be placed on the top of a smaller disk.

Write a program to print out the sequence in which the disks should be moved such that all disks on peg A are finally transferred to peg C.

KanNotes

- A function that calls itself is called a recursive function
- Any function, including main() can become a recursive function
- Recursive call always leads to an infinite loop. So, a provision must be made to get outside this infinite loop
- The provision is done by making the recursive call either in the if block or in the else block
- If recursive call is made in the if block, else block should contain the end condition logic
- If recursive call is made in the else block, if block should contain the end condition logic
- Fresh set of variables are born during each function call - normal call or recursive call
- Variables die when control returns from a function
- Recursive function may or may not have a return statement
- Recursion is an alternative for loop in logics which are expressible in the form of themselves
- Recursive calls are slower than an equivalent while / for / do-while loop
- It becomes easy to understand the working of a recursive function if you make several copies of the same function on paper and then perform a dry run of the program

11 Data Types Revisited

"Get to the nitty-gritties..."

Being able to use the data types in a program is one thing, being able to understand how they behave and why they behave that way is quite a different thing. This chapter is about the second thing...

Contents

As seen in Chapter 1, the primary data types could be of three varieties—**char**, **int**, and **float**. Each of them has several variations. For example, a **char** can be an **unsigned char** or a **signed char**. We would take a closer look at these variations of primary data types in this chapter.

To fully define a variable, one needs to mention not only its type but also its storage class. In this chapter, we would also explore the different storage classes and their relevance in C programming.

Integers—*short, long, long long, signed, unsigned*

C offers three variations of the integer data type—**short**, **long** and **long long**. Though their sizes vary across compilers, the following rules apply:

(a) **short** is at least 2 bytes big

(b) **long** is at least 4 bytes big

(c) **long long** is at least 8 bytes big

(d) **short** is never bigger than **int**

(e) **int** is never bigger than **long**

(f) **long** is never bigger than **long long**

Based on the size, the range of each integer type varies. A 2-byte integer can take values from -32768 to +32767, a 4-byte integer can take values from -2147483648 to +2147483647, whereas an 8-byte integer can take values from -9223372036854775808 to 9223372036854775807. The range for a specific compiler is defined in the file "limits.h" that comes with the compiler.

Each of these integers has two further variations—**signed** and **unsigned**. In the signed variety, the highest (leftmost) bit stores the sign of the number—0, if the number is positive, and 1, if the number is negative. On the other hand, in **unsigned** all the bits are used to store the value of the number. These variables can be declared as shown below.

```
short signed int a ;
short unsigned int b ;
signed int i ;
unsigned int j ;
signed long int x ;
```

```
unsigned long int y ;
signed long long int m ;
unsigned long long int n ;
```

In these declarations, **signed** and **int** can be dropped. So, the following declarations would have served the same purpose as the ones made above:

```
short a ;
short unsigned b ;
int i ;
unsigned j ;
long x ;
unsigned long y ;
long long m ;
unsigned long long n ;
```

Depending upon the programming situation, we should use the appropriate type of integer. For example, if a variable is going to only count things, then we can declare it as,

```
unsigned int num_students ;
```

With this, the range of permissible integer values (for a 32-bit compiler) will shift from the range -2147483648 to +2147483647 to the range 0 to 4294967295. This doubles the size of the largest possible value that it can take, since in an **unsigned int**, the left-most bit is not used to store the sign of the number and is free to store the value of the number.

Chars—*signed, unsigned*

Parallel to integers**, char**s also can be **signed** or **unsigned**. Both occupy one byte each, but have different ranges. To begin with, it might appear strange as to how a **char** can have a sign. Consider the statement

```
signed char ch = 'A' ;
```

Here binary equivalent of the ASCII/Unicode value of 'A' (i.e., binary of 65) gets stored in **ch**. And if 65's binary can be stored, then -54's binary can also be stored.

As with integers, **signed** is default. So **signed char** is same as **char** and has a range from -128 to +127. Likewise, an **unsigned char** has a range from 0 to 255.

Note that while assigning a value to an integer or a char, if it exceeds the upper bound, then the appropriate value from negative side of the range gets assigned. Likewise, if the lower bound is exceeded, then the value from the positive side of the range gets assigned. The following program illustrates this:

```
# include <stdio.h>
int main( )
{
    char ch = 128 ;
    char dh = -132 ;
    printf ( "%hhd %hhd\n", ch, ch ) ;
    return 0 ;
}
```

On execution, the program produces the output -128 124. Since **ch** has been defined as a **char**, it cannot take a value bigger than +127. When we attempt to assign it a value 128, it exceeds +127 by 1. So, the first value on the negative side, i.e., -128, gets assigned to **ch**. Similarly, -132 exceeds -128 by 4, so 4th number from positive side, i.e., 124, gets assigned to **dh**. Note that to print the number stored in a **signed char** we should use the format specifier **%hhd**. Similarly, to get numerical output of an **unsigned char** we should use **%hhu**.

Reals—*float, double, long double*

A **float** occupies four bytes in memory and can range from -3.4e38 to +3.4e38. If this is insufficient, then C offers a **double** data type that occupies 8 bytes in memory and has a range from -1.7e308 to +1.7e308. A variable of type **double** can be declared as,

```
double population ;
```

If the situation demands usage of real numbers that lie even beyond the range offered by **double** data type, then there exists a **long double** that can range from -1.7e4932 to +1.7e4932. A **long double** occupies 10 bytes in memory.

The essence of all the data types that we have learnt so far has been captured in Figure 11.1.

Data Type	Range	Bytes	Format
signed char	-128 to +127	1	%c
unsigned char	0 to 255	1	%c
short signed int	-32768 to +32767	2	%hd
short unsigned int	0 to 65535	2	%hu
signed int	-2147483648 to +2147483647	4	%d
unsigned int	0 to 4294967295	4	%u
long signed int	-2147483648 to +2147483647	4	%ld
long unsigned int	0 to 4294967295	4	%lu
long long signed int	-9223372036854775808 to 9223372036854775807	8	%lld
long long unsigned int	0 to 18446744073709551615	8	%llu
float	-3.4e38 to +3.4e38	4	%f
double	-1.7e308 to +1.7e308	8	%lf
long double	-1.7e4932 to +1.7e4932	10	%Lf

Figure 11.1 Data types in C.

A Few More Issues...

Having seen all the variations of the primary types let us look at some more related issues.

(a) In the ranges of **char**s and **int**s, there is an extra number on the negative side. This is because a negative number is stored as 2's compliment of its binary. For example, let us see how -128 is stored. Firstly, binary of 128 is calculated (10000000), then its 1's compliment is obtained (01111111). A 1's compliment is obtained by changing all 0s to 1s and 1s to 0s. Then 2's compliment is obtained by adding 1 to the 1's compliment. Thus, for -128, 10000000 gets stored. This is an 8-bit number and it can be easily accommodated in a **char**. As against this, +128 cannot be stored in a **char** because its binary 010000000 (left-most 0 is for positive sign) is a 9-bit number. However, +127 can be stored as its binary 01111111 turns out to be an 8-bit number.

(b) What happens when we attempt to store +128 in a **char**? The first number on the negative side, i.e., -128 gets stored. This is because from the 9-bit binary of +128, 010000000, only the right-most 8 bits get stored. But when 10000000 is stored, the left-most bit is 1 and it is treated as a sign bit. Thus, the number becomes -128 since it is indeed the binary of -128, as can be understood from (b) above. Similarly, you can verify that an attempt to store +129 in a **char** results in storing -127 in it. In general, if we exceed the range from positive side we end up on the negative side. Vice versa is also true. If we exceed the range from negative side, we end up on positive side.

(c) Sometimes, we come across situations where the constant is small enough to be an **int**, but still we want to give it to be treated as **long**. In such cases, we add the suffix 'L' or 'l' at the end of the number, as in 23L. Likewise, 3.14 is **double** by default. To treat it as a **float** we should use 3.14f, and 3.14l or 3.14L to treat it as a **long double**.

Storage Classes in C

We have already said all that needs to be said about constants, but we are not finished with variables. To fully define a variable, one needs to mention not only its 'type' but also its 'storage class'.

In our programs, we did not mention storage class of the variables used. We were able to get away with this because storage classes have defaults. If we do not specify the storage class of a variable while defining it, the compiler will assume a storage class depending on where the variable is being defined.

A variable's storage class tells us the following things about the variable:

(a) Where would the variable be stored.

(b) What would be the default initial value of the variable.

(c) What would be the scope of the variable; i.e., to which statements the value of the variable would be available.

(d) What would be the life of the variable; i.e., how long would the variable exist.

There are four storage classes in C:

(a) Automatic storage class
(b) Register storage class
(c) Static storage class
(d) External storage class

Let us examine these storage classes one by one.

Automatic Storage Class

The features of an automatic storage class variable are as follows:

Storage:	Memory.
Default value:	An unpredictable value, often called a garbage value.
Scope:	Local to the block in which the variable is defined.
Life:	Till the control remains within the block in which the variable is defined.

Following program indicates how an automatic storage class variable is declared, and the fact that if the variable is not initialized, it contains a garbage value.

```
# include <stdio.h>
int main( )
{
    auto int i, j ;
    printf ( "%d  %d\n", i, j ) ;
    return 0 ;
}
```

The output of the above program could be...

```
1211  221
```

where, 1211 and 221 are garbage values of **i** and **j**. When you run this program, you may get different output depending upon what garbage values lay at addresses allocated to the variables. Note that the keyword for this storage class is **auto**, and not automatic.

Scope and life of an automatic variable can be understood through the following program:

```
# include <stdio.h>
int main( )
{
    auto int i = 1 ;
    {
        auto int i = 2 ;
        {
            auto int i = 3 ;
            printf ( "%d ", i ) ;
        }
        printf ( "%d ", i ) ;
    }
    printf ( "%d\n", i ) ;
    return 0 ;
}
```

The output of the above program would be 3 2 1. Note that the Compiler treats the three **i**'s as different variables, since they are defined in different blocks. All three **i**'s are available to the innermost **printf( )**. This is because the innermost **printf( )** lies in all the three blocks (a block is all statements enclosed { }) in which the three **i**'s are defined. This **printf( )** prints 3 because when all three **i**'s are available, the one which is most local (nearest to **printf( )**) is given a priority.

Once the control comes out of the innermost block, the variable **i** with value 3 dies, and hence the **i** in the second **printf( )** refers to **i** with value 2. Similarly, when the control comes out of the next innermost block, the third **printf( )** refers to the **i** with value 1.

Register Storage Class

The features of a **register** storage class variable are as follows:

Storage:	CPU registers.
Default value:	Garbage value.
Scope:	Local to the block in which the variable is defined.
Life:	Till the control remains within the block in which the variable is defined.

A value stored in a CPU register is accessed faster than the one that is stored in memory. Therefore, if a variable is used at many places in a program, it is better to declare its storage class as **register**. A good example of frequently used variables is loop counters. We can name their storage class as **register** as shown below.

```
register int i ;
for ( i = 1 ; i <= 10 ; i++ )
    printf ( "%d\n", i ) ;
```

Though **i** is of **register** storage class, we cannot say for sure that its value would be stored in a CPU register. That is because the number of CPU registers are limited, and they may be busy doing some other tasks. In such an event, **i** works as if its storage class is **auto**.

A **float** value requires 4 bytes. So, it cannot be stored in a CPU register if the microprocessor has 16-bit CPU registers. If you use **register** storage class for a **float** in such a case, you will not get any error messages. Instead, the compiler would treat it as an **auto** storage class variable.

Also, regardless of whether a variable gets a place in CPU register or not, we can never use **&** on a register storage class variable.

Static Storage Class

The features of a **static** storage class variable are as follows:

Storage:	Memory.
Default value:	Zero.
Scope:	Local to the block in which the variable is defined.
Life:	Value of the variable persists between different function calls.

The following program shows the static storage class in action:

```
#include <stdio.h>
void increment( ) ;
int main( )
{
    increment( ) ;
    increment( ) ;
    increment( ) ;
    return 0 ;
}
void increment( )
```

```
{
    auto int i = 1 ;
    static int j = 1 ;
    i = i + 1 ;
    j = j + 1 ;
    printf ( "%d %d\n", i, j ) ;
}
```

Here is the output of the program...

```
2 2
2 3
2 4
```

No matter how many times we call **increment( ), i** is initialized to 1 every time, whereas **j** is initialized to 1 only during the first call to **increment( )**. When control returns from **increment( )**, the variable **i** dies, whereas **j** being **static**, continues to live with its latest value. **j** dies only when execution of the program comes to an end.

External Storage Class

The features of an external storage class variable are as follows:

Storage:	Memory.
Default value:	Zero.
Scope:	Global.
Life:	As long as the program's execution doesn't come to an end.

External variables differ from those we have already discussed in that their scope is global, not local. External variables are declared outside all functions, and are available to all the statements that care to use them. Here is an example to illustrate this fact.

```
# include <stdio.h>
int i ;
void increment( ) ;
void decrement( ) ;
int main( )
{
    printf ( "\ni = %d", i ) ;
```

```
    increment( ) ;
    increment( ) ;
    decrement( ) ;
    decrement( ) ;
    return 0 ;
}
void increment( )
{
    i = i + 1 ;
    printf ( "on incrementing i = %d\n", i ) ;
}
void decrement( )
{
    i = i - 1 ;
    printf ( "on decrementing i = %d\n", i ) ;
}
```

The output of the program would be as follows:

```
i = 0
on incrementing i = 1
on incrementing i = 2
on decrementing i = 1
on decrementing i = 0
```

From the above output, the variable **i** is available to the functions **increment( )** and **decrement( )** since **i** has been defined outside all functions.

Look at the following program.

```
# include <stdio.h>
int  x = 21 ;
int main( )
{
    extern int  y ;
    printf ( "%d %d\n", x, y ) ;
    return 0 ;
}
int y = 31 ;
```

Here, **x** and **y** both are global variables. Since both have been defined outside all the functions, both enjoy external storage class. Note the difference between the following statements:

```
extern int y ;
int y = 31 ;
```

Here the first statement is a declaration, whereas the second is the definition. When we declare a variable, no space is reserved for it, whereas when we define it, space gets reserved for it in memory. We had to declare **y** since it is being used in **printf( )** before its definition is encountered. There was no need to declare **x** since it was defined before its use. Also remember that a variable can be declared several times but can be defined only once.

Another small issue—what will be the output of the following program?

```
# include <stdio.h>
int x = 10 ;
void display( ) ;
int main( )
{
    int x = 20 ;
    printf ( "%d\n", x ) ;
    display( ) ;
    return 0 ;
}
void display( )
{
    printf ( "%d\n", x ) ;
}
```

Here **x** is defined at two places, once outside **main( )** and once inside it. When the control reaches **printf( )** in **main( )** which **x** gets printed? The local variable **x**, since it gets a preference over the global **x**. Hence the **printf( )** outputs 20. When **display( )** is called and control reaches the **printf( )** there is no such conflict, since local **x** (with value 20) is not available here. Hence, this time, the value of the global **x**, i.e., 10 gets printed.

Which to Use When

We can make a few ground rules for usage of different storage classes in different programming situations with a view to:

(a) economise the memory space consumed by the variables
(b) improve the speed of execution of the program

The rules are as under:

(a) Use **register** storage class for only those variables that are being used very often in a program, like loop counters.

(b) Use **static** storage class only if you want the variable to persist across function calls.

(c) Use **extern** storage class for only those variables that are being used by almost all the functions in the program. This would avoid unnecessary passing of these variables as arguments when making a function call.

(d) If absence of any of the express needs mentioned above, use **auto** storage class.

A Few Subtle Issues

Let us now look at some subtle issues about storage classes.

(a) All **auto** variables defined in a function are created on the stack each time the function is called. These variables die when control goes back from the function. However, if the variables inside the function are defined as **static** then they do not get created on the stack. Instead, they are created in a place in memory called 'Data Segment'. Such variables die only when program execution comes to an end.

(b) A **static** variable can also be defined outside all the functions. The scope of this variable is limited to the same file in which it is declared. This means that the variable would not be available to any function defined in other files.

(c) If a variable is defined outside all functions, then not only is it available to all other functions in the file in which it is defined, but is also available to functions defined in other files. In the other files, the variable should be declared as **extern**. This is shown in the following program:

```
/* PR1.C */
# include <stdio.h>
int i = 35 ;
int fun1( ) ;
int fun2( ) ;
int main( )
{
    printf ( "%d\n", i ) ;
    fun1( ) ;
    fun2( ) ;
    return 0 ;
}
```

```
/* FUNCTIONS.C */
# include <stdio.h>
extern int i ;
int fun1( )
{
    i++ ;
    printf ( "%d\n", i ) ;
    return 0 ;
}
int fun2( )
{
    i-- ;
    printf ( "%d\n", i ) ;
    return 0 ;
}
```

The output of the program would be

```
35
36
35
```

(d) In the following statements the first three are definitions, whereas the last one is a declaration.

```
auto int i ;  static int j ;  register int k ;  extern int l ;
```

When you have imbibed the stuff on storage classes presented in this chapter, do read Chapter 24 for a more detailed explanation.

Exercises

[A] What will be the output of the following programs?

(a)
```
# include <stdio.h>
int i = 0 ;
void val( ) ;
int main( )
{
    printf ( "main's i = %d\n", i ) ;
    i++ ;
    val( ) ;
    printf ( "main's i = %d\n", i ) ;
    val( ) ;
    return 0 ;
}
void val( )
{
    i = 100 ;
    printf ( "val's i = %d\n", i ) ;
    i++ ;
}
```

(b)
```
# include <stdio.h>
int main( )
{
    static int count = 5 ;
    printf ( "count = %d\n", count-- ) ;
    if ( count != 0 )
        main( ) ;
    return 0 ;
}
```

(c)
```
# include <stdio.h>
void fnc( ) ;
int main( )
{
    func( ) ;
    func( ) ;
    return 0 ;
}
void func( )
{
    auto int  i = 0 ;
    register int j = 0 ;
    static int k = 0 ;
    i++ ;  j++ ;  k++ ;
    printf ( "%d % d %d\n", i, j, k ) ;
}
```

(d)
```
# include <stdio.h>
int x = 10 ;
int main( )
{
    int x = 20 ;
    {
        int x  = 30 ;
        printf ( "%d\n", x ) ;
    }
    printf ( "%d\n", x ) ;
    return 0 ;
}
```

[B] Point out the errors, if any, in the following programs:

(a)
```
# include <stdio.h>
int main( )
{
    long  num = 2 ;
    printf ( "%d\n", num ) ;
    return 0 ;
}
```

(b)
```
# include <stdio.h>
```

```
int main( )
{
    char ch = 200 ;
    printf ( "%d\n", ch ) ;
    return 0 ;
}
```

(c)
```
# include <stdio.h>
int main( )
{
    long float a = 25.345e454 ;
    unsigned double b = 25 ;
    printf ( "%lf %d\n", a, b ) ;
    return 0 ;
}
```

(d)
```
# include <stdio.h>
static int y ;
int main( )
{
    static int z ;
    printf ( "%d %d\n", y, z ) ;
    return 0 ;
}
```

[C] State whether the following statements are True or False:

(a) The value of an automatic storage class variable persists between various function invocations.

(b) If the CPU registers are not available, the register storage class variables are treated as static storage class variables.

(c) If we try to use register storage class for a **float** variable the compiler will report an error message.

(d) The default value for automatic variable is zero.

(e) The life of static variable is till the control remains within the block in which it is defined.

(f) If a global variable is to be defined, then the **extern** keyword is necessary in its declaration.

(g) The address of register variable is not accessible.

KanNotes

- Types :

  Integer - short, int, long, long long, signed, unsigned
  Char - signed, unsigned
  Real - float, double, long double

- Sizes of data types may vary from one compiler to another. For example, size of an int is 2 bytes in TC, 4 bytes in VisualStudio

- For all compilers : sizeof (short) <= sizeof (int) <= sizeof (long) <= sizeof (long long)

- In signed, left-most bit is 0/1 (+ve/-ve). In unsigned, all bits contribute to value

- Negative integers are stored as 2s complement

- Number without a decimal point is by default an int. Use suitable suffix to change it :

  365u - unsigned, 365l - long, 365lu, 365ul - long unsigned,
  365ll – long long, 365ull – long long unsigned
  Capital suffix have same effect

- Number with a decimal point is by default a double. Use suitable suffix to change it :

  3.14 - double, 3.14f - float, 3.14L - long double

- Two things are needed to completely define a variable :

  1) Type of variable 2) Storage class of variable

- Type signifies what type of value can be stored in the variable

- Storage classes signifies storage location, default initial value, scope and life

- Automatic storage class :

Default value - garbage, Storage - memory
Scope - local to the block ({ })
Life - till control is in the block in which variable is defined

- Register storage class :
  Default value - garbage, Storage - CPU registers
  Scope - local to the block
  Life - till control is in the block in which variable is defined
- Static storage class :
  Default value - 0, Storage - memory
  Scope - local to the block
  Life - till execution of program does not end
- Extern storage class :
  Default value - 0, Storage - memory
  Scope - Global
  Life - till execution of program does not end
- CPU Registers - Internal memory of Microprocessor
- Definition of a variable reserves space, declaration does not
- Redeclaration of variable is ok, redefinition is not
- int i ; → Definition extern int i ; → declaration
- Local variable gets a priority over global variable of same name
- Out of locals of same name, most local variable gets a priority
- Usage :
  Register - For frequently used variables
  Static - If variable is to live across function calls
  External - If variable is required by all functions
  Automatic - All other cases

12

The C Preprocessor

"Add spick and span..."

Do you think when a game company creates a game for different mobile phones; it maintains different programs for each phone type? It cannot afford to, as making changes in one would necessitate changes in all others. Moreover, with so many phone types around, this would be a difficult proposition. This situation can be smartly handled using preprocessor directives. This chapter shows you how...

Contents

C preprocessor is a program that processes our program before it is passed to the compiler. We can write C programs without knowing anything about the preprocessor or its facilities. But preprocessor is such a great convenience that virtually all C programmers rely on it. This chapter explores the preprocessor directives, and discusses the pros and cons of using them in programs.

Features of C Preprocessor

The C program is known as 'Source Code'. When the source code is passed through 'Preprocessor', it creates 'Expanded Source Code' as per the preprocessor directives used in the source code. Each preprocessor directive begins with a # symbol. Following preprocessor directives may be used in the source code:

(a) Macro expansion
(b) File inclusion
(c) Conditional compilation
(d) Miscellaneous directives

Let us understand these preprocessor directives one-by-one.

Macro Expansion

Look at the following program:

```
# include <stdio.h>
# define PI 3.1428
int main( )
{
    float r = 6.25, area ;
    area = PI * r * r ;
    printf ( "Area of circle = %f\n", area ) ;
    return 0 ;
}
```

In the statement

```
# define PI 3.1428
```

PI is called 'macro template', whereas, 3.1428 is called 'macro expansion'. During preprocessing, every macro template gets replaced with its corresponding macro expansion. Usually, macro templates are written in capital letters. This makes it easy for programmers to identify macro templates while reading the program.

And now an important question—why use **#define** at all? Suppose the constant 3.1428 appears many times in your program. Some day you may wish to change all these values with a more accurate 3.142857. For this you must go through the program and manually change each occurrence of the constant. However, if you have defined PI in a **#define** directive, you only need to change the **#define** directive to:

```
# define PI 3.142857
```

Once done, the change will be made in all occurrences of PI during preprocessing. This convenience may not matter for small programs shown above, but with large programs, macro definitions are almost indispensable.

You may feel that the same purpose could have been served had we used a variable **pi** instead of a macro template **PI**. But for three reasons it would have been a bad idea.

Firstly, it is inefficient, since the compiler can generate faster and more compact code for constants than it can for variables. Secondly, using a variable for what is really a constant encourages sloppy thinking—if something never changes, it is hard to imagine it as a variable. And thirdly, there is always a danger that the variable may inadvertently get altered somewhere in the program. So, it is no longer a constant that you think it is.

Given below are some more sample **#define**s.

```
# define AND &&
# define ARANGE ( a > 25 AND a < 50 )
# define SLOGAN printf ( "In history you can see the future\n" ) ;
```

Macros with Arguments

The macros that we have used so far are called simple macros. Macros can have arguments, just as functions can. Here is a program that illustrates this fact.

```
# include <stdio.h>
# define AREA(x) ( 3.14 * x * x )
int main( )
{
    float r1 = 6.25, r2 = 2.5, a ;
    a = AREA ( r1 ) ;
```

```
    printf ( "Area of circle = %f\n", a ) ;
    a = AREA ( r2 ) ;
    printf ( "Area of circle = %f\n", a ) ;
    return 0 ;
}
```

On execution, the program produces the following output:

```
Area of circle = 122.656250
Area of circle = 19.625000
```

The preprocessor would replace every **AREA(x)** with **(3.14 * x * x)**. As it does this, **x** would be substituted with the argument that we use in the macro. Thus **a = AREA(r1)** would be replaced with **a = (3.14 * r1 * r1)**.

Here are a few more examples of macros with arguments:

```
# define ISDIGIT(n) ( n >= 48 && n <= 57 )
# define ISCAPITAL(ch) ( ch >= 'A' && ch <= 'Z' )
```

Here are some important points to remember while writing macros with arguments:

(a) Do not give a space between macro template and its argument in **#define**. For example, there should be no blank between **AREA** and **(x)** in the definition, #define AREA(x) (3.14 * x * x).

(b) The entire macro expansion should be enclosed within parentheses. Following program shows what would happen if we fail to enclose the macro expansion within parentheses.

```
# include <stdio.h>
# define SQUARE(n) n * n
int main( )
{
    int j ;
    j = 64 / SQUARE ( 4 ) ;
    printf ( "j = %d\n", j ) ;
    return 0 ;
}
```

The above program would output j = 64, whereas, what we expected was j = 4. What went wrong? Well, the macro got expanded to

```
j = 64 / 4 * 4 ;
```

which yielded 64.

(c) Macros can be split into multiple lines, with a '\' (backslash) present at the end of each line, except the last. Given below is one such multiline macro.

```
# define HLINE   for ( i = 0 ; i < 79 ; i++ ) \
                         printf ( "%c", 196 ) ;
```

(d) If you are unable to debug a macro, you should view the expanded code of the program to see how the macro is getting expanded. If your source code is present in the file PR1.C, then the expanded source code would be stored in PR1.I. You need to generate this file at the command prompt by saying:

```
C:\>cpp  PR1.C                    - in Turbo C/C++
$ gcc -E -o PR1.I  PR1.C          - in gcc
```

These commands invoke the C Preprocessor which generates the expanded source code and stores it in a file called PR1.I. You can now open this file and see the expanded source code.

Macros versus Functions

In the above example, a macro **AREA** was used to calculate the area of the circle. We could have defined a function **area( )** for the same. This brings us to a question—which one to use when?

If we use a macro, it would be expanded during preprocessing. As against this, if we use a function, during execution control and value of radius would be passed to **area( )**, area would be calculated and returned.

So, if we use a macro hundred times in a program, the macro expansion (formula) goes into our source code at hundred different places, thus increasing the program size. On the other hand, if a function is used, the formula would occur only once in the function. At hundred places where you need this formula there would be function calls. So, space requirement would now be less. But passing arguments to a function and getting back the returned value does take time and would therefore slow down the program. This gets avoided with macros since they have already been expanded and placed in the source code before compilation. Thus, the trade-off is between memory space and time.

Moral is—if the macro is simple as in our examples, it makes nice shorthand and avoids the overheads associated with function calls. On the other hand, if we have a large macro and it is used often, we ought to replace it with a function.

File Inclusion

The next preprocessor directive that we will explore is file inclusion. It looks like this:

```
# include "filename"
```

It causes the entire contents of **filename** to be inserted into the source code where we have used #include. It is common for the files that are to be included to have a .h extension. This extension stands for 'header file', as its contents when included go to the head of your program.

The prototypes of all the library functions are grouped into different categories and then stored in different header files. For example, prototypes of all Maths-related functions are stored in the file 'math.h', prototypes of input/output functions are stored in the file 'stdio.h', etc.

There exist two ways to write **#include** statement. These are:

```
# include "filename"
# include <filename>
```

The meaning of each of these forms is given below.

# include "mylib.h"	This directive would look for the file **mylib.h** in the current directory as well as the list of directories specified in the include search path.
# include <mylib.h>	This directive would look for the file **mylib.h** in the list of directories specified in the include search path.

The include search path is a list of directories that would be searched for the file being included. Different C compilers let you set the search path in different manner. For Turbo C/C++ compiler the search path can be set up by selecting 'Directories' from the 'Options' menu. On doing this, a dialog box appears. In this dialog box against 'Include Directories', we can specify the search path. We can also specify multiple include paths separated by ';' (semicolon) as shown below.

```
c:\tc\lib ; c:\mylib ; d:\libfiles
```

In Visual Studio the search path for a project can be set by right-clicking the project name in Solution Explorer and selecting "Properties" from the menu that pops up. This brings up a dialog box. You can now set up the search path by going to "Include Directories" in "Configuration Properties" tab.

Suppose we wish to create our own library of functions which we wish to distribute to others. For this the functions should be defined in a ".c" file and their corresponding prototype declarations and macros be declared in a ".h" file. The definitions can then be compiled into a library file (in machine language). While distributing the library, its compiled version and the ".h" file should be given to users. Those who wish to use your library would have to link your compiled library file and include your header file. This way the function definitions in the ".c" file remain with you and are not exposed to users of your library.

Conditional Compilation

We can, if we want, have the compiler skip over part of a source code by inserting the preprocessing commands **#ifdef** and **#endif**, which have the general form given below.

```
# ifdef  macroname
    statement 1 ;
    statement 2 ;
    statement 3 ;
# endif
```

If **macroname** is **#define**d, the block of code will be processed as usual; otherwise not.

Where would **#ifdef** be useful? When would you like to compile only a part of your program? In three cases, discussed below.

(a) We can "comment out" some lines of code that we do not need right now as shown below.

```
int main( )
{
```

```
    # ifdef NOTNOW
        statement 1 ; statement 2 ;
    # endif
    statement 3 ; statement 4 ;
}
```

Here, statements 1 and 2 would get compiled only if the macro NOTNOW is defined, and we have purposefully omitted the definition of this macro. Later, if we want that these statements should also get compiled, we can either delete the **#ifdef** and **#endif** statements or **#define** NOTNOW at the top.

(b) A more sophisticated use of **#ifdef** has to do with making the programs portable, i.e., to make them work on two computers with different configurations. You can do so by isolating the lines of code that must be different for each machine by marking them off with **#ifdef**, as follows:

```
int main( )
{
    # ifdef INTELI7
        code suitable for an Intel I7 machine
    # else
        code suitable for other machines
    # endif
    code common to both the computers
}
```

When we compile this program, it would compile only the code suitable for other machines and the common code, since macro INTELI7 has not been defined. If we want to run the program on an Intel I7 machine, before recompiling the program we need to add a statement at the top saying,

```
# define INTELI7
```

Sometimes, instead of **#ifdef**, the **#ifndef** directive is used. The **#ifndef** (which means 'if not defined') works exactly opposite to **#ifdef**.

(c) Ideally, we should **#include** a file only once. But if by mistake we use multiple **#include**s for the same file, it should get included only once. This can be achieved using **#ifndef** as shown below:

```
/* myfile.h */
# ifndef __myfile_h
    # define __myfile_h
    /* some declarations */
# endif
```

First time the file 'myfile.h' gets included, the preprocessor checks whether a macro called **__myfile_h** is defined or not. Since it is not defined, it gets defined and the rest of the code gets included. Next time we attempt to include the same file, the inclusion is prevented since **__myfile_h** already stands defined. It is a good practice to use this feature in header files. This feature is often called include guard or header guard.

#if and *#elif* Directives

The **#if** directive can be used to test whether an expression evaluates to a non-zero value or not. If the result of the expression is non-zero, then subsequent lines up to a **#else**, **#elif** or **#endif** are compiled, otherwise they are skipped. A simple example of **#if** directive is shown below:

```
int main( )
{
    # if TEST <= 5
        statement 1 ;
    # else
        statement 2 ;
    # endif
}
```

If the expression, **TEST <= 5** evaluates to true, then statement 1 is compiled, otherwise statement 2 is compiled. In place of the expression **TEST <= 5**, other expressions like **(LEVEL == HIGH || LEVEL == LOW)** or **ADAPTER == SVGA** can also be used. If required, we can even use nested conditional compilation directives.

Miscellaneous Directives

There are two more preprocessor directives available, though they are not very commonly used. They are:

(a) #undef
(b) #pragma

#undef Directive

On some occasions, it may be desirable to cause a defined name to become 'undefined'. This can be accomplished by means of the **#undef** directive as shown below:

```
# undef PENTIUM
```

This would cause the definition of PENTIUM to be removed. All subsequent **#ifdef PENTIUM** statements would evaluate to false. In practice, seldom are you required to undefine a macro, but if you are required to, then you know that there is **#undef** to fall back upon.

#pragma Directive

This directive is used to turn certain features on or off. Pragmas vary from one build tool to another. Some pragmas deal with formatting source listings and placing comments in the object file. There are others that allow us to suppress warnings generated by the compiler. Some of these pragmas are discussed below.

(a) **#pragma startup** and **#pragma exit**: These directives allow us to specify functions that are called upon program startup (before **main( )**) or program exit (just before the program terminates). Their usage is as follows:

```
# include <stdio.h>
void fun1( ) ;
void fun2( ) ;
# pragma startup fun1
# pragma exit fun2
int main( )
{
    printf ( "Inside main\n" ) ;
    return 0 ;
}
void fun1( )
{
    printf ( "Inside fun1\n" ) ;
}
void fun2( )
{
    printf ( "Inside fun2\n" ) ;
```

```
}
```

And here is the output of the program.

```
Inside fun1
Inside main
Inside fun2
```

Note that the functions **fun1( )** and **fun2( )** should neither receive nor return any value. If we want two functions to get executed at startup then their pragmas should be defined in the reverse order in which we want to get them called.

(b) **#pragma warn**: On compilation the compiler reports Errors and Warnings in the program, if any. Errors must be corrected. Warnings, on the other hand, offer the programmer a hint or suggestion that something may be *wrong* with a particular piece of code. Two most common situations when warnings are displayed are as under:

- If you have written code that is considered as bad programming practice. For example, if a function does not return a value and you have not declared the return type of this function as **void**.
- If you have written code that might cause run-time errors, such as assigning a value using an uninitialized pointer.

The **#pragma warn** directive tells the compiler whether we want to suppress a specific warning or not. Usage of this pragma is shown below.

```
# include <stdio.h>
# pragma warn –rvl    /* return value */
# pragma warn –par    /* parameter not used */
# pragma warn –rch    /* unreachable code */
int  f1( )
{
    int  a = 5 ;
}
void  f2 ( int  x )
{
    printf ( "Inside f2\n" ) ;
}
int  f3( )
```

```
{
    int x = 6 ;
    return x ;
    x++ ;
}
int main( )
{
    f1( ) ;
    f2 ( 7 ) ;
    f3( ) ;
    return 0 ;
}
```

If you go through the program, you can notice three problems immediately. These are:

(a) Though promised, **f1( )** doesn't return a value.
(b) The parameter **x** passed to **f2( )** is not being used anywhere.
(c) The control can never reach **x++** in **f3( )**.

If we compile the program, we should expect warnings indicating the above problems. However, this does not happen since we have suppressed the warnings using the **#pragma** directives.

If we replace the '–' sign with a '+', then these warnings would be flashed on compilation. Though it is a bad practice to suppress warnings, at times, it becomes useful to suppress them. For example, while compiling a big program you may first want to eliminate all errors and then turn your attention to the warnings. At such times, you may suppress the warnings. Once you have eliminated all errors, then you may turn on the warnings and attend to them.

The Build Process

There are many steps involved in converting a C program into an executable form. Figure 12.1 shows these different steps along with the files created during each stage. Many software development tools hide some of these steps from us. However, if you understand these steps, it will make you a better programmer.

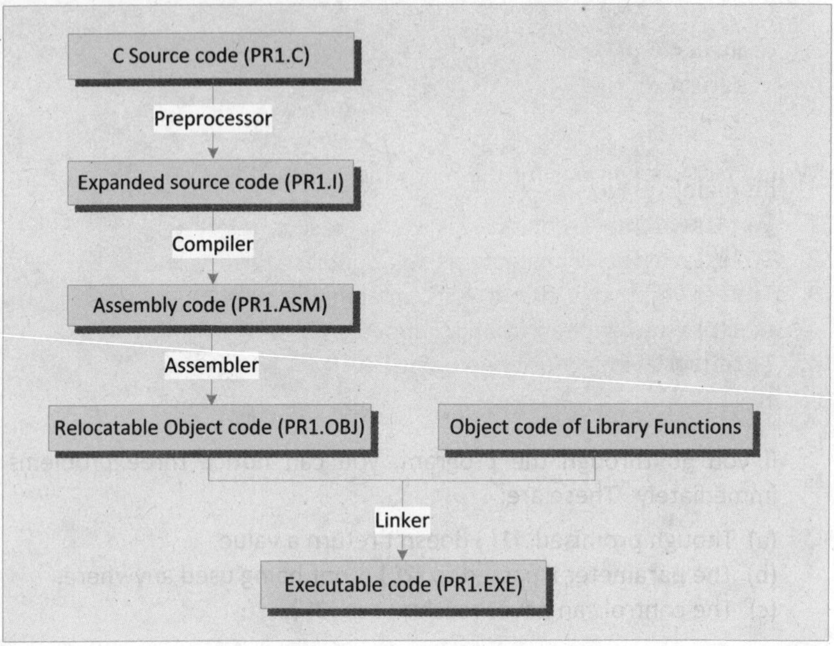

Figure 12.1 Steps involved in the build process.

Figure 12.2 summarizes the role played by each program during the build process.

Program	Input	Output
Editor	Program typed from keyboard	C source code containing program and preprocessor directives
Preprocessor	C source code file	Expanded Source code file created after processing preprocessor directives
Compiler	Expanded Source code file	Assembly language code
Assembler	Assembly language code	Relocatable Object code in machine language
Linker	Object code of our program and object code of library functions	Executable code in machine language

Figure 12.2 Role of programs involved in build process.

Programs

Problem 12.1

Write macro definitions for the following:

1. To test whether a character is a lowercase letter or not.
2. To test whether a character is an uppercase letter or not.
3. To test whether a character is an alphabet or not. Make use of the macros you defined in 1 and 2 above.
4. To obtain the bigger of two numbers.

Program

```
/* Macros ISUPPER, ISLOWER, ISAPLHA, BIG */
# include <stdio.h>
#define ISUPPER(x) ( x >= 65 && x <= 90 ? 1 : 0 )
#define ISLOWER(x) ( x >= 97 && x <= 122 ? 1 : 0 )
#define ISALPHA(x) ( ISUPPER(x) || ISLOWER(x) )
#define BIG(x,y) ( x > y ? x : y )
int main( )
{
    char ch ;
    int d, a, b ;
    printf ( "\nEnter any alphabet/character: " ) ;
    scanf ( "%c", &ch ) ;
    if ( ISUPPER ( ch ) == 1 )
        printf ( "You entered a capital letter\n" ) ;
    if ( ISLOWER ( ch ) == 1 )
        printf ( "You entered a small case letter\n" ) ;
    if ( ISALPHA ( ch ) != 1 )
        printf ( "You entered character other than an alphabet\n" ) ;
    printf ( "Enter any two numbers: " ) ;
    scanf ( "%d%d", &a, &b ) ;
    d = BIG ( a, b ) ;
    printf ( "Bigger number is %d\n", d ) ;
    return 0 ;
}
```

Output

```
Enter any alphabet/character: A
```

```
You entered a capital letter
Enter any two numbers: 10 20
Bigger number is 20
```

Problem 12.2

Write macro definitions with arguments for calculation of area and perimeter of a triangle, a square and a circle. Store these macro definitions in a file "areaperi.h". Include this file in your program, and use the macro definitions for calculating area and perimeter for different squares, triangles and circles.

Program

```
/* areaperi.h */
/* Storing the macro definitions of area and perimeter of circle, triangle
and square in the "areaperi.h" header file */
#define PI 3.1415
#define PERIC( r ) ( 2 * PI * r )
#define AREAC( r ) ( PI * r * r )
#define PERIS( x ) ( 4 * x )
#define AREAS( x ) ( x * x )
#define PERIT( x, y, z ) ( x + y + z )
#define AREAT( b, h ) ( 0.5 * b * h )
```

```
/* Program to use macros in header file "areaperi.h" */
# include <stdio.h>
# include "areaperi.h"
int main( )
{
    int d, a, b ;
    float sid1, sid2, sid3, sid, p_tri, p_cir, p_sqr, a_tri, a_cir,a_sqr ;
    float r, base, height ;
    printf ( "\nEnter radius of circle: " ) ;
    scanf ( "%f", &r ) ;
    p_cir = PERIC ( r ) ;
    printf ( "Circumference of circle = %f\n", p_cir ) ;
    a_cir = AREAC ( r ) ;
    printf ( "Area of circle = %f\n", a_cir ) ;
    printf ( "Enter side of a square: " ) ;
```

```
    scanf ( "%f", &sid ) ;
    p_sqr = PERIS ( sid ) ;
    printf ( "Perimeter of square = %f\n", p_sqr ) ;
    a_sqr = AREAS ( sid ) ;
    printf ( "Area of square = %f\n", a_sqr ) ;
    printf ( "Enter length of 3 sides of triangle: " ) ;
    scanf ( "%f %f %f", &sid1, &sid2, &sid3 ) ;
    p_tri = PERIT ( sid1, sid2, sid3 ) ;
    printf ( "Perimeter of triangle = %f\n", p_tri ) ;
    printf ( "Enter base and height of triangle: " ) ;
    scanf ( "%f %f", &base, &height ) ;
    a_tri = AREAT ( base, height ) ;
    printf ( "Area of triangle = %f\n", a_tri ) ;
    return 0 ;
}
```

Output

```
Enter radius of circle: 5
Circumference of circle = 31.415001
Area of circle = 78.537498
Enter side of a square: 6
Perimeter of square = 24.000000
Area of square = 36.000000
Enter length of 3 sides of triangle: 3 4 5
Perimeter of triangle = 12.000000
Enter base and height of triangle: 4 6
Area of triangle = 12.000000
```

Exercises

[A] Answer the following questions:

(a) A preprocessor directive is:

1. A message from compiler to the programmer
2. A message from compiler to the linker
3. A message from programmer to the preprocessor
4. A message from programmer to the microprocessor

(b) Which of the following are correctly formed **#define** statements?

```
#define  INCH PER FEET  12
#define  SQR (X)  ( X * X )
#define  SQR(X)  X * X
#define  SQR(X)  ( X * X )
```

(c) State True or False:

1. A macro must always be written in capital letters.
2. A macro must always be accommodated in a single line.
3. After preprocessing when the program is sent for compilation the macros are removed from the expanded source code.
4. Macros with arguments are not allowed.
5. In a macro call the control is passed to the macro.

(d) A header file is:

1. A file that contains standard library functions
2. A file that contains function declarations and macros
3. A file that contains user-defined functions
4. A file that is present in current working directory

(e) All macro substitutions in a program are done:

1. Before compilation of the program
2. After compilation of the program
3. During execution of the program
4. During linking of the program

[B] What will be the output of the following programs?

(a)
```
# include <stdio.h>
int main( )
{
    int  i = 2 ;
    # ifdef DEF
        i *= i ;
    # else
        printf ( "%d\n", i ) ;
    # endif
    return 0 ;
}
```

(b)
```
# include <stdio.h>
# define PRODUCT(x) ( x * x )
```

```
int main( )
{
    int i = 3, j, k, l ;
    j = PRODUCT( i + 1 ) ;
    k = PRODUCT( i++ ) ;
    l = PRODUCT ( ++i ) ;
    printf ( "%d %d %d %d\n", i, j, k, l ) ;
    return 0 ;
}
```

(c)
```
# include <stdio.h>
# define PI 3.14
# define AREA( x, y, z ) ( PI * x * x + y * z ) ;
int main( )
{
    float a = AREA ( 1, 5, 8 ) ;
    float b = AREA ( AREA ( 1, 5, 8 ), 4, 5 ) ;
    printf ( " a = %f\n", a ) ;
    printf ( " b = %f\n", b ) ;
    return 0 ;
}
```

[C] Attempt the following questions:

(a) If a macro is not getting expanded as per your expectation, how will you find out how is it being expanded by the preprocessor?

(b) Write macro definitions for the following:

1. To find arithmetic mean of two numbers.
2. To find absolute value of a number.
3. To convert an uppercase alphabet to lowercase.
4. To obtain the biggest of three numbers.

(c) Write macro definitions with arguments for calculation of Simple Interest and Amount. Store these macro definitions in a file "interest.h". Include this file in your program, and use the macro definitions for calculating Simple Interest and Amount.

KanNotes

- Preprocessor expands the source code as per the preprocessor directives used in it.

- 4 types of Preprocessor directives :

  1) Macro Expansion 2) File Inclusion
  3) Conditional Compilation 4) Miscellaneous Directives

- # include "stdio.h" - Searches the file in Include path + Current dir

  # include <stdio.h> - Searches the file in Include path

- Macros - Every template is replaced by its expansion

- Macros have a global effect

- # define PLANK 6.634E-34 - Simple macro

  # define AREA(x) PI * x * x - Macro with argument

- Macros can take multiple arguments - #define CALC(a, b, c) (a + b * c / 3.14)

- Macros can be split over multiple lines. Put a \ at the end of each line, except last line

- Advantage of Macros - Faster than functions

- Advantage of Functions - Occupy less space

- Be aware of side-effects of macros with arguments

  #define SQUARE(y) y * y

  would expand z = SQUARE(3 + 1) into z = 3 + 1 * 3 + 1

- Conditional compilation - Compiles the code only if the condition is true

- Conditional compilation is implemented using #ifdef, #else, #endif, #ifndef, #if

- Miscellaneous directives :

  #undef - undefines a macro that has already been defined
  #pragma inline - used for compilation of program that uses assembly language statements

- There are many other #pragma directives

13 Arrays

"Bringing order to chaos..."

A variable can hold one value at a time. So, if you have 100 values, how many variables will you need? Well, answer is not 100. It is 1, and that variable is a special variable called Array. This chapter shows you how to work with it...

Contents

C language provides a capability that enables the programmer to design a set of similar data types, called array. This chapter describes how arrays can be created and manipulated in C. Pointers and arrays are very closely related. This relationship is also discussed in this chapter.

What are Arrays?

Suppose we wish to arrange the percentage marks obtained by 100 students in ascending order. For this we can either construct 100 variables, each variable containing one student's marks; or construct one variable capable of storing hundred students' marks. Obviously, the second alternative is better as it is easier to handle one variable than handling 100 variables. Such a variable is called an array.

Now a formal definition of an array—an array is a collection of similar elements. These similar elements could be percentage marks of 100 students, or salaries of 300 employees, or ages of 50 employees. What is important is that the elements must be 'similar'. We cannot have an array of 10 numbers, of which 5 are **int**s and 5 are **float**s. Usually, the array of characters is called a 'string', whereas an array of **int**s or **float**s is called simply an array.

A Simple Program using Array

Let us write a program to find average marks obtained by a class of 30 students in a test.

```
# include <stdio.h>
int main( )
{
    int avg, sum = 0 ;
    int i ;
    int marks[ 30 ] ; /* array declaration */
    for ( i = 0 ; i <= 29 ; i++ )
    {
        printf ( "Enter marks " ) ;
        scanf ( "%d", &marks[ i ] ) ; /* store data in array */
    }
    for ( i = 0 ; i <= 29 ; i++ )
        sum = sum + marks[ i ] ; /* read data from an array*/
```

```
    avg = sum / 30 ;
    printf ( "Average marks = %d\n", avg ) ;
    return 0 ;
}
```

There is a lot of new material in this program, so let us understand it part by part.

Array Declaration

Like other variables, an array needs to be declared so that the compiler will know what type of an array and how large an array we want. In our program, we have done this through the statement:

```
int marks[ 30 ] ;
```

Here, [30] tells the compiler how many elements of the type **int** will be in our array. This number is often called the 'dimension' of the array.

Accessing Elements of an Array

Once an array is declared, an individual element in it is referred using marks[0], marks[1], marks[2], etc. The number used in [ ] specifies the element's position in the array. Array elements are counted starting from 0th element. Thus, **marks[2]** is not the second element of the array, but the third. 0, 1, 2 are often called subscripts and the array is called subscripted variable. In our program we have used this form to access array elements in two statements

```
scanf ( "%d", &marks[ i ] ) ;      /* store data in array */
sum = sum + marks[ i ] ;           /* read data from an array*/
```

In the first statement we are passing the address of **marks[i]** to **scanf( )** to receive a value in **marks[i]**. In the second statements we are using **marks[i]** to get a running sum. Since both these statements are used in a loop, each time through the loop, **i** takes a different value. So, each time we are scanning or using a new element from the array. This ability to use variables to represent subscripts is what makes arrays so useful. When all the marks have been added up, the result is divided by 30, the number of students, to get the average.

More on Arrays

Let us now discuss the features which make arrays so convenient to program. We would also learn the possible pitfalls in using them.

Array Initialization

Look at the following array declarations:

```
int num[ 6 ] = { 2, 4, 12, 5, 45, 5 } ;
int n[ ] = { 2, 4, 12, 5, 45, 5 } ;
float press[ ] = { 12.3, 34.2, -23.4, -11.3 } ;
long int gdp[ 10 ] ;
```

This shows that arrays can be initialized while declaring them. When we do so, mentioning the dimension of the array is optional, as in arrays **n[ ]** and **press[ ]** above. Also, note that the array **gdp[ ]** has **auto** storage class and it has not been initialized, so it contains garbage values. If we declare it as a **static** array, all its elements would be set to 0.

Array Elements in Memory

Consider the following array declaration:

```
int arr[ 8 ] ;
```

This would reserve 32 bytes for the array in memory, 4 bytes for each of the 8 integers. The values in it would be garbage values. The array elements would occupy adjacent memory locations as shown in Figure 13.1.

12	34	66	-45	23	346	77	90
65508	65512	65516	65520	65524	65528	65532	65536

Figure 13.1 Layout of an array in memory.

Bounds Checking

Consider the following program:

```
# include <stdio.h>
int main( )
{
    int num[ 40 ], i ;
    for ( i = 0 ; i <= 99 ; i++ )
        num[ i ] = i ;
    return 0 ;
}
```

We have reserved 40 slots for **num[ ]**, whereas we are attempting to fill 100 values into it. When value of **i** goes past 39, the values would simply be placed in locations outside the array. If these locations contain garbage data, then nothing would be lost. But if they contain useful data, it would be overwritten leading to unpredictable results. In some cases, the computer may just hang.

Issue is that there will be no error message to warn us that we are going beyond the array size. Thus, to ensure that we do not reach beyond the array size is entirely the programmer's botheration and not that of compiler.

Passing Array Elements to a Function

Array elements can be passed to a function by value, or by reference. These two calls are illustrated below.

```
/* Demonstration of call by value & call by reference */
# include <stdio.h>
void display1 ( int ) ;
void display2 ( int * ) ;
int main( )
{
    int i ;
    int marks[ ] = { 55, 65, 75, 56, 78, 78, 90 } ;
    for ( i = 0 ; i <= 6 ; i++ )
        display1 ( marks[ i ] ) ;
    for ( i = 0 ; i <= 6 ; i++ )
        display2 ( &marks[ i ] ) ;
    return 0 ;
}
void display1 ( int m )
{
    printf ( "%d ", m ) ;
}
void display2 ( int *n )
{
    printf ( "%d ", *n ) ;
}
```

And here is the output...

```
55 65 75 56 78 78 90
```

```
55 65 75 56 78 78 90
```

Here, to **display1( )** we are passing value of an array element, whereas to **display2( )** we are passing address of an array element. Since at a time only one element or its address is being passed, they are collected in an integer variable **m**, or an integer pointer **n** respectively. Since **n** contains the address of array element, to print out the array element, we are using the 'value at address' operator **(*)**.

Pointers and Arrays

To be able to see what pointers have to do with arrays, let us first learn some pointer arithmetic. Consider the following example:

```
# include <stdio.h>
int main( )
{
    int i = 3, *x ;
    float j = 1.5, *y ;
    char k = 'c', *z ;
    printf ( "Value of i = %d\n", i ) ;
    printf ( "Value of j = %f\n", j ) ;
    printf ( "Value of k = %c\n", k ) ;
    x = &i ; y = &j ; z = &k ;
    printf ( "Original address in x = %u\n", x ) ;
    printf ( "Original address in y = %u\n", y ) ;
    printf ( "Original address in z = %u\n", z ) ;
    x++ ; y++ ; z++ ;
    printf ( "New address in x = %u\n", x ) ;
    printf ( "New address in y = %u\n", y ) ;
    printf ( "New address in z = %u\n", z ) ;
    return 0 ;
}
```

Here is the output of the program.

```
Value of i = 3
Value of j = 1.500000
Value of k = c
Original address in x = 65524
Original address in y = 65520
Original address in z = 65519
New address in x = 65528
```

```
New address in y = 65524
New address in z = 65520
```

Observe the last three lines of the output. 65528 is original address in **x** plus 4, 65524 is original address in **y** plus 4, and 65520 is original address in **z** plus 1. This so happens because every time a pointer is incremented, it points to the immediately next location of its type. So, when an integer pointer **x** is incremented, it points to an address four locations after the current location, since an **int** is always 4 bytes long (under TC/TC++, since **int** is 2 bytes long, new address in **x** would be 65526). Similarly, **y** points to an address 4 locations after the current location and **z** points 1 location after the current location. This is a very important result and can be effectively used while passing the entire array to a function.

The way a pointer can be incremented, it can be decremented as well, to point to earlier locations. Thus, the following operations can be performed on a pointer:

(a) Addition of a number to a pointer.
(b) Subtraction of a number from a pointer.
(c) Subtraction of one pointer from another.
(d) Comparison of two pointer variables.

The program given below illustrates these operations.

```
# include <stdio.h>
int main( )
{
    int arr[ ] = { 10, 20, 30, 45, 67, 56, 74 } ;
    int i = 4, *j, *k, *x, *y ;
    j = &i ;
    j = j + 9 ; /* pointer plus number */
    k = &i ;
    k = k - 3 ; /* pointer minus number */
    x = &arr[ 1 ] ;
    y = &arr[ 5 ] ;
    printf ( "%d\n", y - x ) ;
    j = &arr [ 4 ] ;
    k = ( arr + 4 ) ;
    if ( j == k )
        printf ( "The two pointers point to the same location\n" ) ;
    else
```

```
        printf ( "The two pointers point to different locations\n" ) ;
    return 0 ;
}
```

We are already familiar with the operation of addition/subtraction of a number to/from a pointer. That brings us to the third operation—subtraction of pointers.

x and **y** have been declared as integer pointers and are holding addresses of first and fifth element of the array, respectively. Suppose the array begins at location 65502, then **arr[1]** and **arr[5]** would be present at locations 65506 and 65522 respectively, since each integer in the array occupies 4 bytes in memory. The expression **y - x** would print a value 4, as **y** and **x** are pointing to locations that are 4 integers apart.

Pointer variables can be compared provided both variables point to objects of the same data type. Such comparisons can be useful when both pointer variables point to elements of the same array. The comparison can test for either equality or inequality. Moreover, a pointer variable can be compared with zero (usually expressed as NULL).

Do not attempt the any other operations on pointers, other than the 4 operations mentioned above... they would never work out.

Accessing Array Elements using Pointers

We have learnt these two facts above:

(a) Array elements are always stored in contiguous memory locations.
(b) A pointer when incremented always points to the next location of its type.

Let us now correlate these two facts and access array elements using pointers.

```
# include <stdio.h>
int main( )
{
    int num[ ] = { 24, 34, 12, 44, 56, 17 } ;
    int i, *ptr ;
    ptr = &num[ 0 ] ; /* assign address of zeroth element */
    for ( i = 0 ; i <= 5 ; i++ )
    {
        printf ( "address = %u element = %d\n", ptr, *ptr ) ;
        ptr++ ; /* increment pointer to point to next integer */
```

```
    }
    return 0 ;
}
```

The output of this program would be:

```
address = 65512 element = 24
address = 65516 element = 34
address = 65520 element = 12
address = 65524 element = 44
address = 65528 element = 56
address = 65532 element = 17
```

To understand this output, let us first see how the array elements are arranged in memory. This is shown in Figure 13.2.

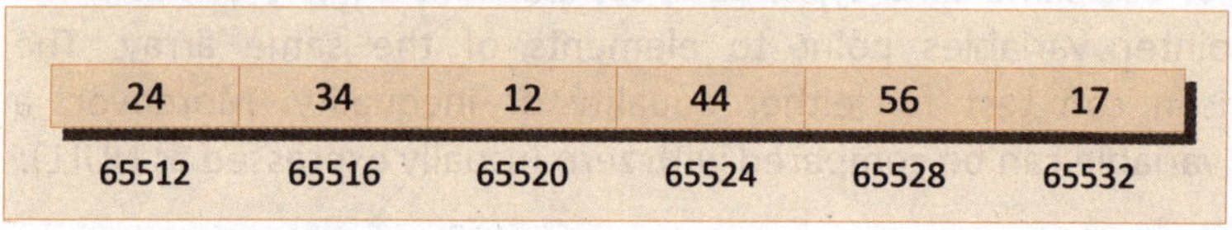

Figure 13.2 Array elements in memory.

In the program, to begin with, we have collected the base address of the array (address of the 0th element) in the variable **ptr** using the statement,

```
ptr = &num[ 0 ] ;  /* assigns address 65512 to j */
```

First time through the loop, **ptr** contains the address 65512, and the value at this address is 24. These are printed using the statement,

```
printf ( "address = %u element = %d\n", ptr, *ptr ) ;
```

On incrementing **ptr**, it points to the next memory location of its type (that is location 65516). But location 65516 contains the second element of the array, therefore when **printf( )** is executed for the second time, it prints out the second element of the array and its address (i.e., 34 and 65516)... and so on till the last element of the array.

So now we know how to access array elements using subscript and using pointer. Obviously, a question arises as to which of the two methods should be used when? Accessing array elements by pointers is faster than accessing them by subscripts. However, from the point of view of convenience in programming, we should observe the following:

Array elements should be accessed using pointers, if the elements are to be accessed in a fixed order, say from beginning to end, or from end to beginning, or every alternate element or any such definite logic.

If there is no fixed logic in accessing the elements, it would be easier to access the elements using a subscript.

Passing an Array to a Function

We already know how to pass individual elements of an array or addresses of individual elements of an array to a function. Let us now see how to pass an entire array to a function. Consider the following program:

```
/* Demonstration of passing an array to a function */
# include <stdio.h>
void display1 ( int  *, int ) ;
void display2 ( int  [ ], int ) ;
int main( )
{
    int num[ ] = { 24, 34, 12, 44, 56, 17 } ;
    display1 ( &num[ 0 ], 6 ) ;
    display2 ( &num[ 0 ], 6 ) ;
    return 0 ;
}
void display1 ( int  *ptr, int  n )
{
    int i ;
    for ( i = 0 ; i <= n - 1 ; i++ )
    {
        printf ( "element = %d\n", *ptr ) ;
        ptr++ ;  /* increment pointer to point to next element */
    }
}
void display2 ( int  ptr[ ], int  n )
{
    int i ;
    for ( i = 0 ; i <= n - 1 ; i++ )
        printf ( "element = %d\n", ptr[ i ] ) ;
}
```

Here, the address of the zeroth element and the number of elements in the array are being passed to the **display1( )** function. The **for** loop accesses the array elements using pointers. Note that it is necessary to pass the total number of elements in the array, otherwise the function would not know when to terminate the **for** loop.

Same parameters are also being passed to **display2( )**. But they are received in a different form

```
void display2 ( int  ptr[ ], int  n )
```

Here, though **ptr** is still an integer pointer, the array notation lets us use the convenient expression **ptr[i]** to access array elements using, without being required to perform any pointer arithmetic on **ptr**.

Note that the address of the zeroth element (often called the base address) can also be passed by just passing the name of the array. Thus, the following two function calls are same:

```
display1 ( &num[ 0 ], 6 ) ;
display1 ( num, 6 ) ;
```

The Real Thing

If you have grasped the concept of storage of array elements in memory and the arithmetic of pointers, here is some real food for thought. Once again consider the following array:

```
int  num[ ] = { 24, 34, 12, 44, 56, 17 } ;
```

We know, that on mentioning the name of the array, we get its base address. Thus, by saying ***num**, we would be able to refer to the zeroth element of the array, that is, 24. One can easily see that ***num** and ***(num + 0)** both refer to 24.

Similarly, by using ***(num + 1)**, we can refer the first element of the array, that is, 34. In fact, this is what the C compiler does internally. When we say, **num[i]**, the C compiler internally converts it to ***(num + i)**. This means that all the following expressions are same:

```
num[ i ]          *( num + i )          *( i + num )          i[ num ]
```

And here is a program to prove my point.

```
/* Accessing array elements in different ways */
# include <stdio.h>
int main( )
{
    int num[ ] = { 24, 34, 12, 44, 56, 17 } ;
    int i ;
    for ( i = 0 ; i <= 5 ; i++ )
    {
        printf ( "address = %u ", &num[ i ] ) ;
        printf ( "element = %d %d ", num[ i ], *( num + i ) ) ;
        printf ( "%d %d\n", *( i + num ), i[ num ] ) ;
    }
    return 0 ;
}
```

The output of this program would be:

```
address = 65512 element = 24 24 24 24
address = 65516 element = 34 34 34 34
address = 65520 element = 12 12 12 12
address = 65524 element = 44 44 44 44
address = 65528 element = 56 56 56 56
address = 65532 element = 17 17 17 17
```

Flexible Arrays

If we do not know the size of an array at the time of writing the program, we can receive it during execution. This is shown below.

```
int max ;
scanf ( "%d", &max ) ;
int arr[ max ] ;
```

This makes the array more flexible, as we do not have to commit to its size at the time of writing the program. This feature has been added in C99 and would be rejected by older compilers, as they expect array dimension to be a positive non-zero integer constant.

The variable-sized arrays can also be created by using a standard library function **malloc( )**. The following program shows how to use it.

```
/* Flexible array size */
# include <stdio.h>
```

```
# include <stdlib.h>
int main( )
{
    int  max, i, *p ;
    printf ( "Enter array size: " ) ;
    scanf ( "%d", &max ) ;
    p = ( int * ) malloc ( max * sizeof ( int ) ) ;
    for ( i = 0 ; i <= 5 ; i++ )
    {
        p[ i ] = i * i ;
        printf ( "%d ", p[ i ] ) ;
    }
    return 0 ;
}
```

To **malloc( )** function we need to pass the number of bytes to allocate in memory. On doing so, it allocates the bytes and returns the base address of the allocated chunk as a **void** pointer. We need to convert the **void** pointer into an **int** pointer. This conversion is necessary since operations cannot be performed on a **void** pointer. The conversion is done using the typecast operation. In the typecast operation the target type should be enclosed within ( ). Once the address is assigned to **p**, it can be used as a normal array through expression **p[i]**.

Returning an Array

The way an array can be passed to a function, it can also be returned from the function. This is shown in the program below.

```
# include <stdio.h>
int * fun ( int *num ) ;
int main( )
{
    int max, *p, i ;
    p = fun ( &max ) ;
    for ( i = 0 ; i < max ; i++ )
        printf ( "%d ", p[ i ] ) ;
    return 0 ;
}
int * fun ( int *num )
{
    static int arr[ ] = { 10, 20, 30, 40, 50 } ;
```

```
    *num = sizeof ( arr ) / sizeof ( arr[ 0 ] ) ;
    return arr ;
}
```

There are a few important points that you should note about the program:

(a) **arr** has been declared as **static** to ensure that it remains alive when control returns from **fun( )** and we can access it in **main( )**.

(b) When we attempt to return the array **arr** from **fun( )** what gets returned is only its base address. Hence return type of **fun( )** is **int ***.

(c) Since a function can return only one value, the address of array is returned explicitly through **return** statement, whereas the array size is returned through **num** using a call by reference.

(d) The number of elements in the array is obtained by dividing the array size by size of its 0th element.

P</> Programs

Problem 13.1

Write a program that interchanges elements at odd position with elements at even position in an array of 10 elements.

Program

```
/* Interachange adjacent elements of an array */
# include <stdio.h>
int main( )
{
    int num[ ] = { 12, 4, 5, 1, 9, 13, 11, 19, 54, 34 } ;
    int i, t ;
    for ( i = 0 ; i <= 9 ; i = i + 2 )
    {
        t = num[ i ] ;
        num [ i ] = num [ i + 1 ] ;
        num [ i + 1 ] = t ;
    }
    for ( i = 0 ; i <= 9 ; i++ )
        printf ( "%d\t", num[ i ] ) ;
    return 0 ;
```

```
}
```

Output

```
4   12   1   5   13   9   19   11   34   54
```

Problem 13.2

Write a program to copy the contents of a 5-element integer array into another array in reverse order.

Program

```
/* Program to copy one array into another in reverse order */
# include <stdio.h>
int main( )
{
    int arr1[ 5 ], arr2[ 5 ], i, j ;
    printf ( "\nEnter 5 elements of array:\n" ) ;
    for ( i = 0 ; i <= 4 ; i++ )
        scanf ( "%d", &arr1[ i ] ) ;
    for ( i = 0, j = 4 ; i <= 4 ; i++, j-- )
        arr2[ j ] = arr1[ i ] ;
    printf ( "Elements in reverse order:\n" ) ;
    for ( i = 0 ; i <= 4 ; i++ )
        printf ( "%d\t", arr2[ i ] ) ;
    return 0 ;
}
```

Output

```
Enter 5 elements of array:
10 20 30 40 50
Elements in reverse order:
50    40    30    20    10
```

Problem 13.3

An array contains 10 integers. Receive the number to be searched in the array as input. Write a program to search this number in the array and display the number of times it occurs in the array.

Program

```
/* Program to find a number and its frequency in array */
# include <stdio.h>
int main( )
{
    int num[ ] = { 7, 3, 5, 4, 6, 7, 2, 4, 6, 7 } ;
    int n, i, count ;
    printf ( "\nEnter an element to search: " ) ;
    scanf ( "%d", &n ) ;
    count = 0 ;
    for ( i = 0 ; i <= 9 ; i++ )
    {
        if ( num[ i ] == n )
            count++ ;
    }
    printf ( "Number %d is found %d time(s) in the array\n", n, count ) ;
    return 0 ;
}
```

Output

```
Enter an element to search: 7
Number 7 is found 3 time(s) in the array
```

Exercises

[A] Answer the following questions:

(a) Are the following array declarations correct?

```
int a (25) ;
int size = 10, b[ size ] ;
```

(b) Which element of the array does this expression reference?

```
num[ 4 ]
```

(c) What is the difference between the 5's in these two expressions?

```
int num[ 5 ] ;
num[ 5 ] = 11 ;
```

(d) What will happen if you try to put so many values into an array when you initialize it that the size of the array is exceeded?

(e) What will happen if you put too few elements in an array when you initialize it?

(f) What will happen if you assign a value to an element of an array whose subscript exceeds the size of the array?

(g) When you pass an array as an argument to a function, what gets passed?

(h) If you don't initialize a static array, what will its elements be set to?

(i) if **int s[5]** is a one-dimensional array of integers, how will you refer to the third element in the array using pointer notation?

[B] Attempt the following questions:

(a) Twenty-five numbers are entered from the keyboard into an array. Write a program to find out how many of them are positive, how many are negative, how many are even and how many odd.

(b) If an array **arr** contains **n** elements, then write a program to check if **arr[0] = arr[n - 1]**, **arr[1] = arr[n - 2]** and so on.

(c) Write a program using pointers to find the smallest number in an array of 25 integers.

(d) Implement the Insertion Sort algorithm shown in Figure 13.3 on a set of 25 numbers.

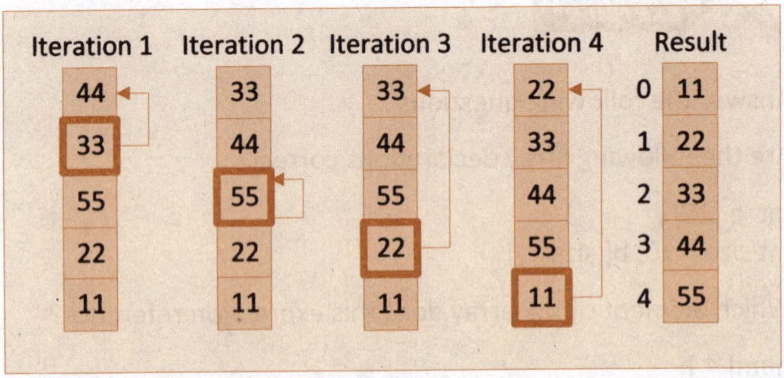

Figure 13.3 Steps involved in Insertion Sort.

(e) Write a program which performs the following tasks:

- Initialize an integer array of 10 elements in **main( )**
- Pass the entire array to a function **modify( )**

- In **modify( )** multiply each element of array by 3
- Return the control to **main( )** and print the new array elements in **main( )**

(f) For the following set of sample data, compute the standard deviation and the mean.

-6, -12, 8, 13, 11, 6, 7, 2, -6, -9, -10, 11, 10, 9, 2

The formula for standard deviation is

$$\frac{\sqrt{(x_i - \bar{x})^2}}{n}$$

where x_i is the data item and $\bar{x}$ is the mean.

(g) The area of a triangle can be computed by the sine law when 2 sides of the triangle and the angle between them are known.

Area = (1 / 2) ab sin (angle)

Given the following 6 triangular pieces of land, write a program to find their area and determine which is largest.

Plot No.	a	b	angle
1	137.4	80.9	0.78
2	155.2	92.62	0.89
3	149.3	97.93	1.35
4	160.0	100.25	9.00
5	155.6	68.95	1.25
6	149.7	120.0	1.75

(h) For the following set of **n** data points (x, y), write a program to compute the correlation coefficient r, given by

$$r = \frac{\sum xy - \sum x \sum y}{\sqrt{[n\sum x^2 - (\sum x)^2][n\sum y^2 - (\sum y)^2]}}$$

x	y
34.22	102.43
39.87	100.93
41.85	97.43
43.23	97.81
40.06	98.32
53.29	98.32
53.29	100.07

54.14	97.08
49.12	91.59
40.71	94.85
55.15	94.65

(i) The **X** and **Y** coordinates of 10 different points are entered through the keyboard. Write a program to find the distance of last point from the first point (sum of distances between consecutive points).

(j) A dequeue is an ordered set of elements in which elements may be inserted or retrieved from either end. Using an array simulate a dequeue of characters and the operations retrieve left, retrieve right, insert left, insert right. Exceptional conditions such as dequeue full or empty should be reported. Use two pointers **left** and **right** for this simulation.

KanNotes

- Array is a variable capable of holding > 1 value at a time
- Two basic properties of an array :
  1) Similarity - All array elements are similar to one another
  2) Adjacency - All array elements are stored in adjacent memory locations
- 2 ways to declare an array :

```
int arr[ 10 ] ;   /* mentioning size is compulsory */
int num[ ] = { 23, 34, 54, 22, 33 } ;   /* size is optional */
```

- Array elements are always counted from 0 onwards. So arr[9] is 10th element
- Arrays have storage classes. Default storage class - auto
- Array elements can be scanned OR calculated :

```
scanf ( "%d %d %d", &arr[ 7 ], &arr[ 8 ], &arr[ 9 ] ) ;
arr[ 5 ] = 3 + 7 % 2 ;
```

- Arithmetic on array elements is allowed :

```
arr[ 6 ] = arr[ 1 ] + arr[ 3 ] / 16 ;
```

- Caution : Bounds checking of an array is programmer's responsibility
- Typical way to process an array element by element :

```
int arr[ 10 ] ;
for ( i = 0 ; i <= 9 ; i++ )
    /* process arr[ i ] */
```

- To obtain address of 0th element of array use :

```
int arr[ 10 ] ; int *p ;
p = arr ;          /* method 1 */
p = &arr[ 0 ] ;  /* method 2 */
```

- Sorting = Arranging array elements in ascending / descending order
- Selection sort - compare 0th element with all others, 1st will others, etc.

  Bubble sort - Compare adjacent elements repeatedly

  Insertion sort – Insert each successive element at appropriate position amongst elements before it
- On incrementing a pointer, it always points to the next location of its type

  On incrementing a float pointer, it points to the next float which is 4 bytes away

  On incrementing an int pointer, it points to the next int which is 4 bytes away

  On incrementing a char pointer, it points to the next char which is 1 byte away
- Only legal pointer operations :

  pointer + number → pointer

  pointer - number → pointer

  pointer - pointer → number

  pointer == pointer
- 5 ways to access array elements using pointers :
  - Set up a pointer holding base address of the array :

    ```
    int arr[ 10 ], *p ;
    ```

p = arr ;

- In a for loop use one of the five expressions :

```
*p ; p++ ;     OR
*(p + i)       OR    *(i + p)     OR
p[i]           OR    i[p]
```

- To pass an array to a function we must always pass two things :

  1) Base address of the array 2) Size of the array

- Array can neither grow nor shrink in size during execution of the program

- We cannot declare an array using int arr[n] and then receive the value of n from keyboard

- We can make the array size flexible by changing the value of MAX suitably :

```
#define MAX 20
Int arr[ MAX ] ;
```

- A variable sized array can be created in two ways"

  Method 1:

```
int max, arr[ max ] ;
scanf ( "%d", &max ) ;
```

  Method 2 :

```
int *p ;
p = ( int * ) malloc ( n * sizeof ( int ) ) ;
```

  Then to access all elements we can use p[i]

14 Multidimensional Arrays

"More the arrays, more the dimensions..."

Multidimensional personalities are always impressive. So are multidimensional arrays. They let you accomplish so much with so few variables. This chapter shows you how to work with a 2-D array and its other cousins...

Contents

In the last chapter we explored arrays with only one dimension. It is also possible for arrays to have two or more dimensions. This chapter describes how multidimensional arrays can be created and manipulated in C.

Two-Dimensional Arrays

The two-dimensional (2-D) array is also called a matrix. Let us see how to create this array and work with it. Here is a sample program that stores roll number and marks obtained by a student side-by-side in a matrix.

```
# include <stdio.h>
int main( )
{
    int stud[ 4 ][ 2 ] ;
    int i, j ;
    for ( i = 0 ; i <= 3 ; i++ )
    {
        printf ( "Enter roll no. and marks" ) ;
        scanf ( "%d %d", &stud[ i ][ 0 ], &stud[ i ][ 1 ] ) ;
    }
    for ( i = 0 ; i <= 3 ; i++ )
        printf ( "%d %d\n", stud[ i ][ 0 ], stud[ i ][ 1 ] ) ;

    return 0 ;
}
```

There are two parts to the program—in the first part, through a **for** loop, we read in the values of roll number and marks, whereas, in the second part through another **for** loop, we print out these values.

Look at the **scanf( )** statement used in the first **for** loop:

```
scanf ( "%d %d", &stud[ i ][ 0 ], &stud[ i ][ 1 ] ) ;
```

In **stud[i][0]** and **stud[i][1]**, the first subscript of the variable **stud**, is row number which changes for every student. The second subscript tells which of the two columns are we talking about—the zeroth column which contains the roll number or the first column which contains the marks. Remember that the counting of rows and columns begin with zero. Thus, 1234 is stored in **stud[0][0]**, 56 is stored in **stud[0][1]** and so on. The complete array arrangement is shown in Figure 14.1.

	column no. 0	column no. 1
row no. 0	1234	56
row no. 1	1212	33
row no. 2	1434	80
row no. 3	1312	78

Figure 14.1 2-D array.

Initializing a 2-D Array

How do we initialize a 2-D array? As simple as this...

```
int stud[ 4 ][ 2 ] = {
                        { 1234, 56 }, { 1212, 33 }, { 1434, 80 }, { 1312, 78 }
                    } ;
```

or even this would work...

```
int stud[ 4 ][ 2 ] = { 1234, 56, 1212, 33, 1434, 80, 1312, 78 } ;
```

of course, with a corresponding loss in readability.

While initializing a 2-D array, it is necessary to mention the second (column) dimension, whereas the first dimension (row) is optional. Thus, the following declarations are perfectly acceptable,

```
int arr[ 2 ][ 3 ] = { 12, 34, 23, 45, 56, 45 } ;
int arr[  ][ 3 ] = { 12, 34, 23, 45, 56, 45 } ;
```

whereas,

```
int arr[ 2 ][  ] = { 12, 34, 23, 45, 56, 45 } ;
int arr[  ][  ] = { 12, 34, 23, 45, 56, 45 } ;
```

would never work.

Memory Map of a 2-D Array

The array arrangement shown in Figure 14.1 is only conceptually true. This is because memory does not contain rows and columns. In memory, whether it is a 1-D or a 2-D array, the array elements are stored in one continuous chain. So, the actual arrangement of array elements of the 2-D array in memory is as shown in Figure 14.2. For want of space I have changed the array name to **s**.

s[0][0]	s[0][1]	s[1][0]	s[1][1]	s[2][0]	s[2][1]	s[3][0]	s[3][1]
1234	56	1212	33	1434	80	1312	78
65508	65512	65516	65520	65524	65528	65532	65536

Figure 14.2 2-D array in memory.

We can easily refer to the marks obtained by the third student using the subscript notation as shown below.

```
printf ( "Marks of third student = %d", s[ 2 ][ 1 ] ) ;
```

Can we not refer to the same element using pointer notation, the way we did in 1-D arrays? Answer is yes. Only the procedure is slightly difficult to understand. So, read on...

Pointers and 2-D Arrays

C language embodies an unusual but powerful capability—it can treat parts of arrays as arrays. More specifically, each row of a 2-D array can be thought of as a 1-D array.

Thus, the declaration,

```
int s[ 5 ][ 2 ] ;
```

can be thought of as setting up an array of 5 elements, each of which is a 1-D array containing 2 integers. We refer to an element of a 1-D array using one subscript. Similarly, if we can imagine **s** to be a 1-D array, then we can refer to its zeroth element as **s[0]**, the next element as **s[1]** and so on. More specifically, **s[0]** gives the address of the zeroth 1-D array, **s[1]** gives the address of the first 1-D array and so on. This fact can be demonstrated by the following program:

```
/* Demo: 2-D array is an array of arrays */
# include <stdio.h>
int main( )
{
```

```
    int s[ 4 ][ 2 ] = {
                        { 1234, 56 }, { 1212, 33 }, { 1434, 80 }, { 1312, 78 }
                    };
    int i ;
    for ( i = 0 ; i <= 3 ; i++ )
        printf ( "Address of %d th 1-D array = %u\n", i, s[ i ] ) ;
    return 0 ;
}
```

And here is the output...

```
Address of 0 th 1-D array = 65508
Address of 1 th 1-D array = 65516
Address of 2 th 1-D array = 65524
Address of 3 th 1-D array = 65532
```

This output is consistent with the addresses shown in Figure 14.2. Each 1-D array starts 8 bytes further along than the last one. Thus **s[0]** and **s[1]** would yield the addresses 65508 and 65516.

Suppose we want to refer to the element **s[2][1]** using pointers. We know that **s[2]** would give the address 65524, the address of the second 1-D array. So **(s[2] + 1)** or (65524 + 1) would give the address 65528. The value at this address can be obtained through ***(s[2] + 1)**. We have already studied while learning 1-D arrays that **num[i]** is same as ***(num + i)**. Similarly, ***(s[2] + 1)** is same as, ***(*(s + 2) + 1)**. Thus, all the following expressions refer to the same element:

```
s[ 2 ][ 1 ]
* ( s[ 2 ] + 1 )
* ( * ( s + 2 ) + 1 )
```

Using these concepts, the following program prints out each element of a 2-D array using pointer notation:

```
/* Pointer notation to access 2-D array elements */
# include <stdio.h>
int main( )
{
    int s[ 4 ][ 2 ] = {
                          { 1234, 56 }, { 1212, 33 }, { 1434, 80 }, { 1312, 78 }
                      };
    int i, j ;
```

```
    for ( i = 0 ; i <= 3 ; i++ )
    {
        for ( j = 0 ; j <= 1 ; j++ )
            printf ( "%d ", *( *( s + i ) + j ) ) ;
        printf ( "\n" ) ;
    }
    return 0 ;
}
```

And here is the output...

```
1234 56
1212 33
1434 80
1312 78
```

Pointer to an Array

If we can have a pointer to an integer, a pointer to a float, a pointer to a char, then can we not have a pointer to an array? We certainly can. The following program shows how to build and use it:

```
/* Usage of pointer to an array */
# include <stdio.h>
int main( )
{
    int s[ 4 ][ 2 ] = {
                        { 1234, 56 }, { 1212, 33 }, { 1434, 80 }, { 1312, 78 }
                    } ;
    int ( *p )[ 2 ] ;
    int i, j, *pint ;
    for ( i = 0 ; i <= 3 ; i++ )
    {
        p = &s[ i ] ;
        pint = ( int * ) p ;
        printf ( "\n" ) ;
        for ( j = 0 ; j <= 1 ; j++ )
            printf ( "%d ", *( pint + j ) ) ;
    }
    return 0 ;
}
```

And here is the output...

```
1234 56
1212 33
1434 80
1312 78
```

Here **p** is a pointer to an array of two integers. Note that the parentheses in the declaration of **p** are necessary. Absence of them would make **p** an array of 2 integer pointers. Array of pointers is covered in a later section in this chapter.

In the outer **for** loop, each time we store the address of a new 1-D array in **p**. Thus, first time through this loop, **p** would contain the address of the zeroth 1-D array. This address is then assigned to an integer pointer **pint**. Lastly, in the inner **for** loop using the pointer **pint**, we have printed the individual elements of the 1-D array to which **p** is pointing.

But why should we use a pointer to an array to print elements of a 2-D array. Is there any situation where we can appreciate its usage better? The entity pointer to an array is immensely useful when we need to pass a 2-D array to a function. This is discussed in the next section.

Passing 2-D Array to a Function

The following program shows how we can pass a 2-D array to a function.

```
/* Passing 2-D array to a function */
# include <stdio.h>
void display ( int  q[  ][ 4 ], int , int ) ;
int main( )
{
    int  a[ 3 ][ 4 ] = {
                        1, 2, 3, 4,
                        5, 6, 7, 8,
                        9, 0, 1, 6
                    } ;
    display ( a, 3, 4 ) ;
    return 0 ;
}
void display ( int  q[  ][ 4 ], int  row, int  col )
{
    int  i, j ;
    for ( i = 0 ; i < row ; i++ )
```

```
    {
        for ( j = 0 ; j < col ; j++ )
            printf ( "%d ", q[ i ][ j ] ) ;
        printf ( "\n" ) ;
    }
    printf ( "\n" ) ;
}
```

And here is the output...

```
1 2 3 4
5 6 7 8
9 0 1 6
```

In the **display( )** function, we have collected the base address of the 2-D array being passed to it in **q**, where **q** is pointer to an array of 4 integers. The declaration of **q** looks like this:

```
int q[  ][ 4 ] ;
```

This is same as saying **int (*q)[4]**. The only advantage in using the form **q[ ][4]** is that, we can now use the more familiar expression **q[i][j]** to access array elements.

Array of Pointers

The way there can be an array of **ints** or an array of **floats**, similarly, there can be an array of pointers. An array of pointers would be a collection of addresses. The addresses present in it can be addresses of isolated variables or addresses of array elements or any other addresses. All rules that apply to an ordinary array apply to the array of pointers as well. I think a program would clarify the concept.

```
# include <stdio.h>
int main( )
{
    int *arr[ 4 ] ;  /* array of integer pointers */
    int i = 31, j = 5, k = 19, l = 71, m ;
    arr[ 0 ] = &i ;
    arr[ 1 ] = &j ;
    arr[ 2 ] = &k ;
    arr[ 3 ] = &l ;
    for ( m = 0 ; m  <= 3 ; m++ )
```

```
        printf ( "%d\n", * ( arr[ m ] ) ) ;
    return 0 ;
}
```

Figure 14.3 shows the contents and the arrangement of the array of pointers in memory. As you can observe, **arr** contains addresses of isolated **int** variables **i, j, k** and **l**. The **for** loop in the program picks up the addresses present in **arr** and prints the values present at these addresses.

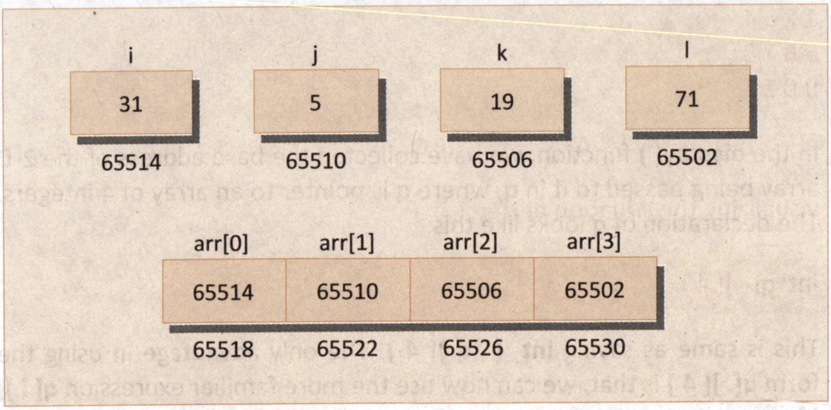

Figure 14.3 Array of pointers.

An array of pointers can even contain the addresses of other arrays' elements. The following program would justify this:

```
# include <stdio.h>
int main( )
{
    static int a[ ] = { 0, 1, 2, 3, 4 } ;
    int *p[ ] = { a, a + 1, a + 2, a + 3, a + 4 } ;
    printf ( "%u %u %d\n", p, *p, * ( *p ) ) ;
    return 0 ;
}
```

I would leave it for you to figure out the output of this program.

3-D Array

I am not going to show a programming example that uses a 3-D array. However, an example of initializing a 3-D array will consolidate your understanding of arrays.

```
int arr[ 3 ][ 4 ][ 2 ] = {
                           {
                               { 2, 4 }, { 7, 8 }, { 3, 4 }, { 5, 6 }
                           },
                           {
                               { 7, 6 }, { 3, 4 }, { 5, 3 }, { 2, 3 }
                           },
                           {
                               { 8, 9 }, { 7, 2 }, { 3, 4 }, { 5, 1 }
                           }
                       };
```

A 3-D array can be thought of as an array of arrays of arrays. The outer array has three elements, each of which is a 2-D array of four 1-D arrays, each of which contains two integers. Figure 14.4 would help you in visualizing the situation better.

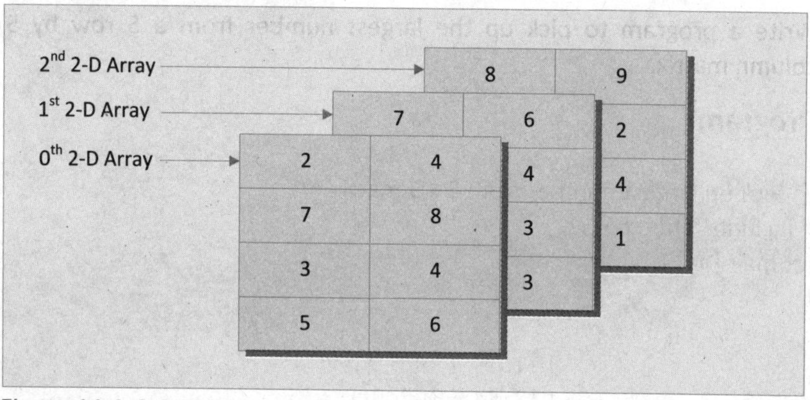

Figure 14.4 3-D array.

Again, remember that the arrangement shown in Figure 14.4 is only conceptually true. In memory, the array elements are stored linearly as shown in Figure 14.5.

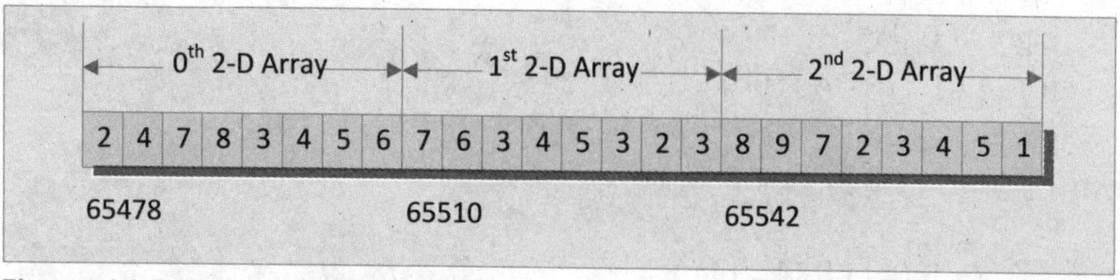

Figure 14.5 3-D array in memory.

How would you refer to the array element 1 in the above array? The first subscript should be [2], since the element is in third 2-D array; the second subscript should be [3] since the element is in fourth row of the 2-D array; and the third subscript should be [1] since the element is in second position in the 1-D array. So element 1 can be referred as **arr[2][3][1]**.

It may be noted here that the counting of array elements even for a 3-D array begins with zero. We can also refer to this element using pointer notation as shown below.

```
*( *( *( arr + 2 ) + 3 ) + 1 )
```

P</> Programs

Problem 14.1

Write a program to pick up the largest number from a 5 row by 5 column matrix.

Program

```
/* Pick up largest number from 5 x 5 matrix */
# include <stdio.h>
int main( )
{
    int a[ 5 ][ 5 ] = {
                        { 11, 1, 7, 9, 7 },
                        { 13, 54, 56, 2, 5 },
                        { 23, 43, 89, 22, 13 },
                        { 14, 15, 17, 16, 19 },
                        { 45, 3, 6, 8, 10 }
                    } ;
    int i, j, big ;
    big = a[ 0 ][ 0 ] ;
    for ( i = 0 ; i <= 4 ; i++ )
    {
        for ( j = 0 ; j <= 4 ; j++ )
        {
            if ( a[ i ][ j ] > big )
                big = a[ i ][ j ] ;
        }
```

```
    }
    printf ( "\nLargest number in the matrix is %d\n", big ) ;
    return 0 ;
}
```

Output

```
Largest number in the matrix is 89
```

Problem 14.2

Write a program to obtain transpose of a 3 x 5 matrix. The transpose of a matrix is obtained by exchanging the elements of each row with the elements of the corresponding column

Program

```
/* Transpose of a matrix */
#include <stdio.h>
int main( )
{
    int mat1[ 3 ][ 5 ] = {
                            1, 2, 3, 4, 5,
                            6, 7, 8, 9, 10,
                            11, 12, 13, 14, 15
                         } ;
    int mat2[ 5 ][ 3 ] ;
    int i, j ;
    for ( i = 0 ; i < 3 ; i++ )
    {
        for ( j = 0 ; j < 5 ; j++ )
            mat2[ j ][ i ] = mat1[ i ][ j ] ;
    }
    for ( i = 0 ; i < 5 ; i++ )
    {
        for ( j = 0 ; j < 3 ; j++ )
            printf ( "%d\t", mat2[ i ][ j ] ) ;
        printf ( "\n" ) ;
    }
    return 0 ;
}
```

Output

```
1   6   11
2   7   12
3   8   13
4   9   14
5   10  15
```

Exercises

[A] What will be the output of the following programs?

(a)
```
# include <stdio.h>
int main( )
{
    int n[ 3 ][ 3 ] = {
                        { 2, 4, 3 }, { 6, 8, 5 }, { 3, 5, 1 }
                      } ;
    printf ( "%d %d %d\n", *n, n[ 1 ][ 1 ], n[ 2 ][ 2 ] ) ;
    return 0 ;
}
```

(b)
```
# include <stdio.h>
int main( )
{
    int n[ 3 ][ 3 ] = {
                        { 2, 4, 3 }, { 6, 8, 5 }, { 3, 5, 1 }
                      } ;
    int i, *ptr ;
    ptr = &n[ 0 ][ 0 ] ;
    for ( i = 0 ; i <= 8 ; i++ )
        printf ( "%d\n", *( ptr + i ) ) ;
    return 0 ;
}
```

(c)
```
# include <stdio.h>
int main( )
{
    int n[ 3 ][ 3 ] = {
                        2, 4, 3, 6, 8, 5, 3, 5, 1
                      } ;
```

```
    int i, j ;
    for ( i = 0 ; i <= 2 ; i++ )
        for ( j = 0 ; j <= 2 ; j++ )
            printf ( "%d %d\n", n[ i ][ j ], *( *( n + i ) + j ) ) ;
    return 0 ;
}
```

[B] Point out the errors, if any, in the following programs:

(a)
```
# include <stdio.h>
int main( )
{
    int twod[ ][ ] = {
                        2, 4, 6, 8
                     } ;
    printf ( "%d\n", twod ) ;
    return 0 ;
}
```

(b)
```
# include <stdio.h>
int main( )
{
    int three[ 3 ][ ] = {
                          { 2, 4, 3 }, { 6, 8, 2 }, { 2, 3, 1 }
                        } ;
    printf ( "%d\n", three[ 1 ][ 1 ] ) ;
    return 0 ;
}
```

[C] Attempt the following questions:

(a) How will you initialize a three-dimensional array **threed[3][2][3]**? How will you refer the first and last element in this array?

(b) Match the following with reference to the program segment given below:

```
int i, j, = 25 ;
int *pi, *pj = & j ;
*pj = j + 5 ;
j = *pj + 5 ;
pj = pj ;
*pi = i + j ;
```

Each integer quantity occupies 2 bytes of memory. The value assigned to **i** begins at (hexadecimal) address F9C and the value assigned to **j** begins at address F9E. Match the value represented by expression in left column with values in the right column.

1.	&i	a.	30
2.	&j	b.	F9E
3.	pj	c.	35
4.	*pj	d.	FA2
5.	i	e.	F9C
6.	pi	f.	67
7.	*pi	g.	unspecified
8.	(pi + 2)	h.	65
9.	(*pi + 2)	i.	F9E
10.	* (pi + 2)	j.	F9E
		k.	FAO
		l.	F9D

(c) Match the following with reference to the following program segment:

```
int x[ 3 ][ 5 ] = {
                    { 1, 2, 3, 4, 5 },
                    { 6, 7, 8, 9, 10 },
                    { 11, 12, 13, 14, 15 }
                  }, *n = &x ;
```

1.	*(*(x + 2) + 1)	a.	9
2.	*(*x + 2) + 5	b.	13
3.	*(*(x + 1))	c.	4
4.	*(*(x) + 2) + 1	d.	3
5.	* (*(x + 1) + 3)	e.	2
6.	*n	f.	12
7.	*(n +2)	g.	14
8.	(*(n + 3) + 1	h.	7
9.	*(n + 5)+1	i.	1
10.	++*n	j.	8
		k.	5
		l.	10
		m.	6

(d) Match the following with reference to the following program segment:

```
unsigned int arr[ 3 ][ 3 ] = {
                               { 2, 4, 6 }, { 9, 1, 10 }, { 16, 64, 5 }
                             } ;
```

1.	**arr	a.	64
2.	**arr < *(*arr + 2)	b.	18
3.	*(arr + 2) / (*(*arr + 1) > **arr)	c.	6
4.	*(arr[1] + 1) | arr[1][2]	d.	3
5.	*(arr[0]) | *(arr[2])	e.	0
6.	arr[1][1] < arr[0][1]	f.	16
7.	arr[2][1] & arr[2][0]	g.	1
8.	arr[2][2] | arr[0][1]	h.	11
9.	arr[0][1] ^ arr[0][2]	i.	20
10.	++**arr + --arr[1][1]	j.	2
		k.	5
		l.	4

(e) Write a program to find if a square matrix is symmetric.

(f) Write a program to add two 6 x 6 matrices.

(g) Write a program to multiply any two 3 x 3 matrices.

(h) Given an array **p[5]**, write a function to shift it circularly left by two positions. Thus, if the original array is { 15, 30, 28, 19, 61 } then after shifting it will be { 28, 19, 61, 15, 30 } Call this function for a 4 x 5 matrix and get its rows left shifted.

KanNotes

- 2-D array is a collection of several 1-D arrays
- If 2-D arrays are initialized at the same place where it is declared, then mentioning the row dimension is optional
- A 2-D array is laid out linearly in memory in row-major fashion i.e., row after row
- Given a 2-D array int a[4][5] ;

  a[2][3] == *a[2] + 3 == *(*(a + 2) + 3)

- int *p[4] ; - p is an array of 4 integer pointers. Size of p = 16 bytes
- int (*p)[4] ; - p is a pointer to an array of 4 integers. Size of p = 4 bytes
- Typical applications of 2-D arrays :

  All matrix and determinant operations

- Applications of 2-D arrays in games :

  Chess, Ludo, Snakes and Ladders, Brainvita, most other board games

- 3-D array is a collection of several 2-D arrays
- Size of a 3-D array is sum of sizes of all its elements
- Following expressions are referring to the element in the 1st row, 3rd column of the 2nd 2-D array :

  a[2][1][3]

  * (a[2][1] + 3)

  * (* (a[2] + 1) + 3)

  * (* (* (a + 2) + 1) + 3)

- For a 3-D array :

  a, *a, **a, will give address

  ***a will give the integer at a[0][0][0]

15 Strings

"Puppetting on strings..."

The way an integer array is a collection of several integers, a character array is a collection of several characters. Well, almost. The 0 that is present at the end of a character array makes it different. What is the importance of this 0, why it matters and what convenience it provides? Well, this chapter has all these answers and more...

Contents

- What are Strings
- More about Strings
- Pointers and Strings
- Standard Library String Functions
    - *strlen( )*
    - *strcpy( )*
    - *strcat( )*
    - *strcmp( )*
- Programs
- Exercises
- KanNotes

In the last chapter, we learnt how to define arrays of various sizes and dimensions, how to initialize them, how to pass them to a function, etc. With this knowledge under our belt, we are ready to handle strings, which are, simply put, a special kind of array.

What are Strings?

The way a group of integers can be stored in an integer array, similarly a group of characters can be stored in a character array. A string is a 1-D array of characters terminated by a '\0'. For example,

```
char name[ ] = { 'H', 'A', 'E', 'S', 'L', 'E', 'R', '\0' } ;
```

'\0' is called null character. Note that '\0' and '0' are not same. ASCII value of '\0' is 0, whereas ASCII value of '0' is 48. Figure 15.1 shows the way a string is stored in memory. Note that the elements of the string are stored in contiguous memory locations.

H	A	E	S	L	E	R	\0
65518	65519	65520	65521	65522	65523	65524	65525

Figure 15.1 String in memory.

The terminating null ('\0') is important, because it is the only way the functions that work with a string can know where the string ends. In fact, a string not terminated by a '\0' is not really a string, but merely a collection of characters.

C concedes the fact that you would use strings very often and hence provides a shortcut for initializing strings. For example, the string used above can also be initialized as,

```
char name[ ] = "HAESLER" ;
```

Note that, in this declaration, '\0' is not necessary. C inserts the null character automatically.

More about Strings

We can use the '\0' present at the end of a string to our advantage while accessing its elements as shown below:

```
/* Program to demonstrate printing of a string */
# include <stdio.h>
int main( )
{
    char name[ ] = "Klinsman" ;
    int i = 0 ;
    while ( name[ i ] != '\0' )
    {
        printf ( "%c", name[ i ] ) ;
        i++ ;
    }
    printf ( "\n" ) ;
    return 0 ;
}
```

And here is the output...

```
Klinsman
```

No big deal. We have initialized a string and then printed its elements in a **while** loop. But instead of changing **i** from 0 to 7 in the **while** loop, we printed characters in the string till we did not encounter '\0'.

Here is another version of the same program; this one uses a pointer to access the array elements.

```
# include <stdio.h>
int main( )
{
    char name[ ] = "Klinsman" ;
    char *ptr ;
    ptr = name ; /* store base address of string */
    while ( *ptr != '\0' )
    {
        printf ( "%c", *ptr ) ;
        ptr++ ;
    }
    printf ( "\n" ) ;
    return 0 ;
}
```

As with an integer array, by mentioning the name of the array, we get the base address (address of the zeroth element) of the array. This base address is stored in the variable **ptr**. Once the base address is obtained in **ptr**, ***ptr** would yield the value at this address, which gets printed promptly through,

```
printf ( "%c", *ptr ) ;
```

Then, **ptr** is incremented to point to the next character in the string. This derives from two facts—array elements are stored in contiguous memory locations and on incrementing a pointer, it points to the immediately next location of its type. This process is carried out until **ptr** points to the last character in the string, that is, '\0'.

In fact, the character array elements can be accessed exactly in the same way as the elements of an integer array. Thus, all the following expressions refer to the same element:

```
name[ i ]
*( name + i )
*( i + name )
i[ name ]
```

Even though there are so many ways (as shown above) to refer to the elements of a character array, rarely is any one of them used. This is because **printf( )** function has got a sweet and simple way of doing it, as shown below. Note that **printf( )** doesn't print the '\0'.

```
char  name[ ] = "Klinsman" ;
printf ( "%s", name ) ;
```

The **%s** used in **printf( )** is a format specifier for printing a string. The same specification can be used to receive a string from the keyboard, as shown below.

```
char  name[ 25 ] ;
printf ( "Enter your name " ) ;
scanf ( "%s", name ) ;
```

While entering the string using **scanf( )**, we must be cautious about two things:

(a) The length of the string should not exceed the dimension of the character array. This is because the C compiler does not perform bounds checking on arrays. Hence, if you carelessly exceed the bounds, there is a danger of overwriting something important.

(b) **scanf( )** is not capable of receiving multi-word strings. Therefore, if we receive names such as 'Debashish Roy' in a string only 'Debashish' would get stored in it.

If we are prepared to take the trouble, we can make **scanf( )** accept multi-word strings by writing it in this manner:

```
char name[ 25 ] ;
printf ( "Enter your full name " ) ;
scanf ( "%[ ^\n ]s", name ) ;
```

Here, **[^\n]** indicates that **scanf( )** will keep receiving characters into **name[ ]** until \n is encountered. Though workable, this is not the best of the ways to call a function, you would agree.

The way to get around this limitation is by using the function **gets( )**. The usage of functions **gets( )** and its counterpart **puts( )** is shown below.

```
# include <stdio.h>
int main( )
{
   char name[ 25 ] ;
   printf ( "Enter your full name: " ) ;
   gets ( name ) ;
   puts ( "Hello!" ) ;
   puts ( name ) ;
   return 0 ;
}
```

And here is the output...

```
Enter your full name: Debashish Roy
Hello!
Debashish Roy
```

The program and the output are self-explanatory except for the fact that, **puts( )** can display only one string at a time (hence the use of two **puts( )** in the program above). Also, on displaying a string, unlike **printf( )**, **puts( )** places the cursor on the next line. Though **gets( )** is capable of receiving only one string at a time, the plus point with **gets( )** is that it can receive a multi-word string. However, there is a pitfall in using **gets( )**. This is discussed in Chapter 18, along with a solution to overcome it.

Pointers and Strings

Suppose we wish to store "Hello". We may either store it in a string or we may ask the C compiler to store it at some location in memory and assign the address of the string to a **char** pointer. This is shown below.

```
char str1[ ] = "Hello", str2[ 20 ] = "Hi" ;
char *p = "Hello", *s = "Hi" ;
```

There is a subtle difference in usage of these two forms.

Here **str1** acts as a constant pointer to a string, whereas, **p** acts as a pointer to a constant string. As a result, observe which operations are permitted on them, and which are not:

```
str1 = "Adieu" ;      /* error, constant pointer cannot change */
str1 = str2 ;         /* error, constant pointer cannot change */
str1++ ;              /* error, constant pointer cannot change */
*str1 = 'Z' ;         /* works, because string is not constant */
p = "Adieu" ;         /* works, because pointer is not constant */
p = s ;               /* works, because pointer is not constant */
p++ ;                 /* works, because pointer is not constant */
*p = 'M' ;            /* error, because string is constant */
```

The keyword **const** can also be used in context of variables of type **int**, **float**, etc. as shown below:

```
const float pi = 3.14 ;
```

Standard Library String Functions

With every C compiler, a large set of useful string handling library functions are provided. Figure 15.2 lists the more commonly used string functions along with their purpose.

Function	Use
strlen	Finds length of a string
strlwr	Converts a string to lowercase
strupr	Converts a string to uppercase
strcat	Appends a string at the end of another
strncat	Appends first n characters of a string at the end of another
strcpy	Copies a string into another
strncpy	Copies first n characters of a string into another
strcmp	Compares two strings
strncmp	Compares first n characters of two strings
strcmpi	Compares two strings by ignoring the case
stricmp	Compares two strings without regard to case (identical to strcmpi)
strnicmp	Compares first n characters of two strings without regard to case
strdup	Duplicates a string
strchr	Finds first occurrence of a given character in a string
strrchr	Finds last occurrence of a given character in a string
strstr	Finds first occurrence of a given string in another string
strset	Sets all characters of string to a given character
strnset	Sets first n characters of a string to a given character
strrev	Reverses string

Figure 15.2 Standard library string functions.

From the list given in Figure 15.2, we shall discuss functions **strlen( )**, **strcpy( )**, **strcat( )** and **strcmp( )**, since these are very commonly used. This will also illustrate how the library functions in general handle strings. Let us study these functions one by one.

strlen( )

This function counts the number of characters present in a string. Its usage is illustrated in the following program:

```
# include <stdio.h>
# include <string.h>
int main( )
{
    char arr[ ] = "Bamboozled" ;
    int len1, len2 ;
```

```
    len1 = strlen ( arr ) ;
    len2 = strlen ( "Humpty Dumpty" ) ;
    printf ( "string = %s length = %d\n", arr, len1 ) ;
    printf ( "string = %s length = %d\n", "Humpty Dumpty", len2 ) ;
    return 0 ;
}
```

The output would be...

```
string = Bamboozled length = 10
string = Humpty Dumpty length = 13
```

Note that, while calling the function **strlen( )**, we are passing the base address of the string. This function returns the length of the string. While calculating the length, it doesn't count '\0'.

Can we not write a function **xstrlen( )**, which imitates the standard library function **strlen( )**? Let us give it a try...

```
/* A look-alike of the function strlen( ) */
# include <stdio.h>
int xstrlen ( char * ) ;
int main( )
{
    char arr[ ] = "Bamboozled" ;
    int len1, len2 ;
    len1 = xstrlen ( arr ) ;
    len2 = xstrlen ( "Humpty Dumpty" ) ;
    printf ( "string = %s length = %d\n", arr, len1 ) ;
    printf ( "string = %s length = %d\n", "Humpty Dumpty", len2 ) ;
    return 0 ;
}
int xstrlen ( char *s )
{
    int length = 0 ;
    while ( *s != '\0' )
    {
        length++ ;
        s++ ;
    }
    return ( length ) ;
}
```

The output would be...

```
string = Bamboozled length = 10
string = Humpty Dumpty length = 13
```

The function **xstrlen( )** is fairly simple. All that it does is, it keeps counting the characters till it reaches the end of the string, i.e. up to '\0'.

strcpy( )

This function copies the contents of one string into another. The base addresses of the target and source strings should be supplied to this function. Here is an example of **strcpy( )** in action...

```
# include <stdio.h>
# include <string.h>
int main( )
{
    char  source[ ] = "Sayonara", target[ 20 ] ;
    strcpy ( target, source ) ;
    printf ( "source string = %s\n", source ) ;
    printf ( "target string = %s\n", target ) ;
    return 0 ;
}
```

And here is the output...

```
source string = Sayonara
target string = Sayonara
```

On supplying the base addresses, **strcpy( )** goes on copying the characters in source string into the target string till it encounters the end of source string ('\0'). It is our responsibility to see to it that the target string's dimension is big enough to hold the string being copied into it. Thus, a string gets copied into another, piece-meal, character-by-character. There is no short-cut for this. Let us now attempt to mimic **strcpy( )**, via our own string copy function, which we will call **xstrcpy( )**.

```
# include <stdio.h>
void xstrcpy ( char  *, char  * ) ;
int main( )
{
    char  source[ ] = "Sayonara", target[ 20 ] ;
    xstrcpy ( target, source ) ;
```

```
    printf ( "source string = %s\n", source ) ;
    printf ( "target string = %s\n", target ) ;
    return 0 ;
}
void xstrcpy ( char *t, char *s )
{
    while ( *s != '\0' )
    {
        *t = *s ; s++ ; t++ ;
    }
    *t = '\0' ;
}
```

The output of the program would be...

```
source string = Sayonara
target string = Sayonara
```

Note that having copied all the elements of source string into the target string, it is necessary to place a '\0' into the target string, to mark its end.

If you look at the prototype of **strcpy( )** standard library function, it looks like this...

```
strcpy ( char *t, const char *s ) ;
```

We didn't use the keyword const in our version of **xstrcpy( )** and still our function worked correctly. So, what is the need of the **const** qualifier?

What would happen if we add the following line before the **while** loop in **xstrcpy( )**?

```
*s = 'K' ;
```

This would change the source string to "Kayonara". We can ensure that the source string doesn't change even accidentally in **xstrcpy( )** by changing the definition as follows:

```
void xstrcpy ( char *t, const char *s )
{
    /* copying code */
}
```

By declaring **char *s** as **const**, we are declaring that the source string should remain constant (should not change). It also reminds anybody reading the program listing that the variable is not intended to change.

strcat( )

This function concatenates the source string at the end of the target string. For example, "Bombay" and "Nagpur" on concatenation would result in a string "BombayNagpur". Here is an example of **strcat( )** at work.

```
# include <stdio.h>
# include <string.h>
int main( )
{
    char  source[ ] = "Folks!", target[ 30 ] = "Hello" ;
    strcat ( target, source ) ;
    printf ( "source string = %s\n", source ) ;
    printf ( "target string = %s\n", target ) ;
    return 0 ;
}
```

And here is the output...

```
source string = Folks!
target string = HelloFolks!
```

Note that the target string has been made big enough to hold the final string. I leave it to you to develop your own **xstrcat( )** on lines of **xstrlen( )** and **xstrcpy( )**.

strcmp( )

This function compares two strings to find out whether they are same or different. The two strings are compared character-by-character until there is a mismatch or we reach end of any string, whichever occurs first. If the two strings are identical, **strcmp( )** returns a value zero. If they are not, it returns the numeric difference between the ASCII values of the first non-matching pair of characters. Here is a program which puts **strcmp( )** in action.

```
# include <stdio.h>
# include <string.h>
```

```
int main( )
{
    char string1[ ] = "Jerry", string2[ ] = "Ferry" ;
    int i, j, k ;
    i = strcmp ( string1, "Jerry" ) ;
    j = strcmp ( string1, string2 ) ;
    k = strcmp ( string1, "Jerry boy" ) ;
    printf ( "%d %d %d\n", i, j, k ) ;
    return 0 ;
}
```

And here is the output...

```
0 4 -32
```

In the first call to **strcmp( )**, the two strings are identical—"Jerry" and "Jerry"—hence the value returned by **strcmp( )** is zero. In the second call, the first character of "Jerry" does not match with the first character of "Ferry" and the result is 4, which is the numeric difference between ASCII value of 'J' and ASCII value of 'F'. In the third call to **strcmp( )**, "Jerry" doesn't match with "Jerry boy", because the null character at the end of "Jerry" doesn't match the blank in "Jerry boy". The value returned is -32, which is ASCII value of null character minus ASCII value of space, i.e., '\0' minus ' ', which is equal to -32.

The exact value of mismatch rarely concerns us. All that we usually want to know is whether the first string is alphabetically before the second string. If it is, a negative value is returned; if it is not, then a positive value is returned. Try to implement this logic in a user-defined function **xstrcmp( )**.

P</> Programs

Problem 15.1

Write a program that extracts part of the given string from the specified position. For example, if from the sting "Working with strings is fun", starting from position 3, 4 characters are extracted then it should return "king".

Program

```
/* To extract a substring from a string */
# include <stdio.h>
# include <stdlib.h>
# include <string.h>
int main( )
{
    char str[ 20 ], news[ 20 ] ;
    char *s, *t ;
    int pos, n, i ;
    printf ( "\nEnter a string: " ) ;
    scanf ( "%s", str ) ;
    printf ( "Enter position and no. of characters to extract: " ) ;
    scanf ( "%d %d", &pos, &n ) ;
    s = str ;
    t = news ;
    if ( pos < 0 || pos > strlen ( str ) )
    {
        printf ( "Improper position value" ) ;
        exit ( 1 ) ;
    }
    if ( n < 0 )
        n = 0 ;
    if ( n > strlen ( str ) )
        n = n - strlen ( str ) - 1 ;
    s = s + pos ;
    for ( i = 0 ; i < n ; i++ )
    {
        *t = *s ;
        s++ ;
        t++ ;
    }
    *t = '\0' ;
    printf ( "The substring is: %s\n", news ) ;
    return 0 ;
}
```

Output

```
Enter a string: Nagpur
```

```
Enter position and no. of characters to extract: 3 10
The substring is: pur
```

Problem 15.2

Write a program that converts a string like "124" to an integer 124.

Program

```
/* To convert a string to an integer */
# include <stdio.h>
int main( )
{
    char str[ 6 ] ;
    int num = 0, i ;
    printf ( "Enter a string containing a number: " ) ;
    scanf ( "%s", str ) ;
    for ( i = 0 ; str [ i ] != '\0' ; i++ )
    {
        if ( str[ i ] >= 48 && str[ i ] <= 57 )
            num = num * 10 + ( str[ i ] - 48 ) ;
        else
        {
            printf ( "Not a valid string\n" ) ;
            return 1 ;
        }
    }
    printf ( "The number is: %d\n", num ) ;
    return 0 ;
}
```

Output

```
Enter a string containing a number: 237
The number is: 237
```

Problem 15.3

Write a program that generates and prints the Fibonacci words of order 0 through 5. For example, f(0) = "A", f(1) = "B", f(2) = "BA", f(3) = "BAB", f(4) = "BABBA", etc.

Program

```
/* Generate Fibonacci words of order 0 through 5 */
#include <stdio.h>
#include <string.h>
int main( )
{
    char str[ 50 ] ;
    char lastbutoneterm[ 50 ] = "A" ;
    char lastterm[ 50 ] = "B" ;
    int i ;
    for ( i = 1 ; i <= 5 ; i++ )
    {
        strcpy ( str, lastterm ) ;
        strcat ( str, lastbutoneterm ) ;
        printf ( "%s\n", str ) ;
        strcpy ( lastbutoneterm, lastterm );
        strcpy ( lastterm, str ) ;
    }
    return 0 ;
}
```

Output

```
BA
BAB
BABBA
BABBABAB
BABBABABBABBA
```

Exercises

[A] What will be the output of the following programs?

(a)
```
# include <stdio.h>
int main( )
{
    char  c[ 2 ] = "A" ;
    printf ( "%c\n", c[ 0 ] ) ;
    printf ( "%s\n", c ) ;
```

```
        return 0 ;
    }
```

(b)
```
    # include <stdio.h>
    int main( )
    {
        char s[ ] = "Get organized! Learn C!!" ;
        printf ( "%s\n", &s[ 2 ] ) ;
        printf ( "%s\n", s ) ;
        printf ( "%s\n", &s ) ;
        printf ( "%c\n", s[ 2 ] ) ;
        return 0 ;
    }
```

(c)
```
    # include <stdio.h>
    int main( )
    {
        char s[ ] = "Borrowers of books spoil the symmetry of shelves" ;
        int i = 0 ;
        while ( s[ i ] != 0 )
        {
            printf ( "%c %c\n", s[ i ], *( s + i ) ) ;
            printf ( "%c %c\n", i[ s ], *( i + s ) ) ;
            i++ ;
        }
        return 0 ;
    }
```

(d)
```
    # include <stdio.h>
    int main( )
    {
        char str1[ ] = { 'H', 'e', 'l', 'l', 'o', 0 } ;
        char str2[ ] = "Hello" ;
        printf ( "%s\n", str1 ) ;
        printf ( "%s\n", str2 ) ;
        return 0 ;
    }
```

(e)
```
    # include <stdio.h>
    int main( )
    {
        printf ( 5 + "Good Morning " ) ;
        printf ( "%c\n", "abcdefgh"[ 4 ] ) ;
```

```
    return 0 ;
}
```

(f)
```
# include <stdio.h>
int main( )
{
    printf ( "%d %d  %d\n", sizeof ( '3' ), sizeof ( "3" ), sizeof ( 3 ) ) ;
    return 0 ;
}
```

[B] Fill in the blanks:

(a) "A" is a ____________ whereas 'A' is a _____________.

(b) A string is terminated by a ______ character.

(c) The array **char name[10]** can consist of a maximum of _____ characters.

(d) The array elements are always stored in _________ memory locations.

[C] Attempt the following questions:

(a) If the string "Alice in wonder land" is fed to the following **scanf( )** statement, what will be the contents of arrays **str1**, **str2**, **str3** and **str4**?

```
scanf ( "%s%s%s%s", str1, str2, str3, str4 ) ;
```

(b) To uniquely identify a book a 10-digit ISBN (International Standard Book Number) is used. The rightmost digit in ISBN is a checksum digit. This digit is determined from the other 9 digits using the condition that $d_1 + 2d_2 + 3d_3 + ... + 10d_{10}$ must be a multiple of 11 (where d_i denotes the ith digit from the right). The checksum digit d_1 can be any value from 0 to 10: the ISBN convention is to use the value X to denote 10. Write a program that receives a 10-digit integer, computes the checksum, and reports whether the ISBN number is correct or not.

(c) A Credit Card number is usually a 16-digit number. A valid Credit Card number would satisfy a rule explained below with the help of a dummy Credit Card number—4567 1234 5678 9129. Start with the rightmost - 1 digit and multiply every other digit by 2.

```
4 5 6 7   1 2 3 4   5 6 7 8   9 1 2 9

8  12     2   6     10  14    18   4
```

Then subtract 9 from numbers that are larger than 10. Thus, we get:

8 3 2 6 1 5 9 4

Add them all up to get 38.

Add all the other digits (5, 7, 2, 4, 6, 8, 1, 9) to get 42.

Sum of 38 and 42 is 80. Since 80 is divisible by 10, the Credit Card number is valid.

Write a program that receives a Credit Card number and checks using the above rule whether the Credit Card number is valid.

KanNotes

- Strings are character arrays ending with '\0'. '\0' is called String Terminator
- Other arrays do not end with '\0'
- ASCII values : '0' = 48 '\0' = 0
- Ways to output strings :
```
char name[ ] = "Sanjay" ;
printf ( "%s\n", name ) ;
puts ( name ) ;
```
- Ways to input strings :
```
char name[ 30 ] ;
scanf ( "%s", name ) ;
gets ( name ) ;
```
- To receive multiword strings :
```
scanf ( "%[^\n]s", name ) ;   /* means accept everything except \n */
gets ( name ) ;
```
- Prefer scanf( ) for receiving name of city, gets( ) for receiving name and surname
- 3 = integer 3.0 = double
  '3' = character "3" = string ending with '\0'

- Standard way of processing a string :

```
char str[] = "Blah blah blah" ; char *p ;
p = str ;
while ( *p != '\0' )
{
    /* process current character given by *p */
    p++ ;
}
```

- printf ("Hello") ; - passes base address of string to printf( )

- Useful string functions :

```
int l = strlen ( str ) ;  /* returns length of string str */
strcpy ( target, source ) ;  /* copies source string to target string */
strcat ( target, source ) ;  /* appends source at the end of target */
int l = strcmp ( str1, str2 ) ; /* returns 0 if strings are equal,
                                   nonzero if they are unequal */
strupr ( str ) ;   /* converts string str to uppercase */
strlwr ( str ) ;   /* converts string str to lowercase */
toupper ( ch ) ;   /* converts character ch to uppercase */
tolower ( ch ) ;   /* converts character ch to lowercase */
```

- #include <string.h> for prototypes of library string functions

- char p[] = "Nagpur" ;

  p is a constant pointer to string
  p cannot be changed
  Nagpur can be changed

- char *p = "Nagpur" ;

  p is a pointer to a constant string
  p can be changed
  Nagpur cannot be changed

16 Handling Multiple Strings

"More Puppets, More Strings..."

Instead of creating several arrays of integers, create a 2D array of integers. Instead of creating several arrays of characters, create a 2-D array of characters. Well, do not. Why? Read on, this chapter provides the answer...

Contents

- 2-D Array of Characters
- Array of Pointers to Strings
- Limitation of Array of Pointers to Strings
- Programs
- Exercises
- KanNotes

In the last chapter, we learnt how to deal with individual strings. But often we are required to deal with a set of strings rather an isolated string. This chapter discusses how such situations can be handled effectively.

2-D Array of Characters

In Chapter 14 we saw several examples of 2-D integer arrays. Let us now look at a similar entity, but one dealing with characters. Our example program asks you to type your name. When you do so, it checks your name against a list of names to see if you are worthy of entry to the palace. Here is the program...

```
# include <stdio.h>
# include <string.h>
int main( )
{
    char list[ 6 ][ 20 ] = {
                              "akshay", "parag", "raman",
                              "srinivas", "gopal", "rajesh"
                          } ;
    int i ;
    char yourname[ 20 ] ;
    printf ( "Enter your name " ) ;
    scanf ( "%s", yourname ) ;
    for ( i = 0 ; i <= 5 ; i++ )
    {
        if ( strcmp ( &list[ i ][ 0 ], yourname ) == 0 )
        {
            printf ( "Welcome, you can enter the palace\n" ) ;
            return 0 ;
        }
    }
    printf ( "Sorry, you are a trespasser" ) ;
    return 0 ;
}
```

And here is the output for two sample runs of this program...

```
Enter your name dinesh
Sorry, you are a trespasser
Enter your name raman
Welcome, you can enter the palace
```

Notice how the two-dimensional character array has been initialized. The first dimension gives the number of names in the array, whereas the second dimension gives the length of each item in the array.

Instead of initializing names, had these names been supplied from the keyboard, the program segment would have looked like this...

```
for ( i = 0 ; i <= 5 ; i++ )
    scanf ( "%s", &list[ i ][ 0 ] ) ;
```

While comparing the strings using the function **strcmp( )**, the addresses of the strings being compared are passed to it. If the two strings match, **strcmp( )** would return a value 0, otherwise it would return a non-zero value.

The names would be stored in the memory as shown in Figure 16.1. Note that each string ends with a '\0'. The arrangement, as you can appreciate, is similar to that of a 2-D numeric array.

65454	a	k	s	h	a	y	\0			
65474	p	a	r	a	g	\0				
65494	r	a	m	a	n	\0				
65514	s	r	i	n	i	v	a	s	\0	
65534	g	o	p	a	l	\0				
65554	r	a	j	e	s	h	\0			

65573 (last location)

Figure 16.1 2-D array of characters in memory.

Here, 65454, 65474, etc., are the base addresses of successive names. As seen in Figure 16.1 some of the names do not occupy all the bytes reserved for them. For example, even though 20 bytes are reserved for storing the name "akshay", it occupies only 7 bytes. Thus, 13 bytes go waste. Similarly, for each name, there is some amount of wastage. This wastage can be avoided using an 'array of pointers to strings'.

Array of Pointers to Strings

As we know, a pointer variable always contains an address. Therefore, if we construct an array of pointers, it would contain several addresses.

Following code snippet shows how names can be stored using an array of pointers.

```
char *names[ ] = {
                    "akshay", "parag", "raman",
                    "srinivas", "gopal", "rajesh"
               };
```

In this declaration, **names[ ]** is an array of pointers. It contains base addresses of different names. This is depicted in Figure 16.2.

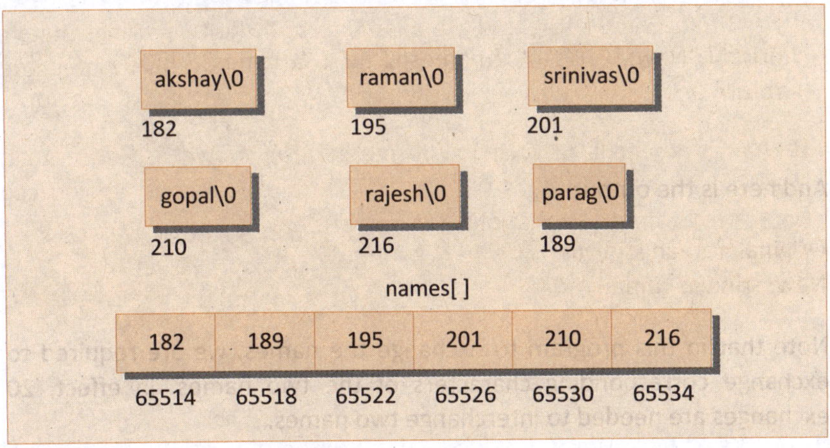

Figure 16.2 Array of pointers to strings.

In 2-D array of characters, the strings occupied 120 bytes. As against this, in array of pointers, the strings occupy only 41 bytes and the array occupies 24 bytes—a total of 65 bytes. Thus, there is a net saving of 55 bytes. A substantial saving, you would agree.

Another advantage of use of array of pointers to store strings is it permits easy manipulation of the strings. This is shown by the following programs. The first one uses a 2-D array of characters to store the names, whereas the second uses an array of pointers to strings. The purpose of both the programs is very simple. We want to exchange the position of the names “raman” and “srinivas”.

```
/* Exchange names using 2-D array of characters */
# include <stdio.h>
int main( )
{
    char names[ ][ 20 ] = {
                            "akshay", "parag", "raman",
```

```
                          "srinivas", "gopal", "rajesh"
                       } ;
    int i ;
    char t ;
    printf ( "Original: %s %s\n", &names[ 2 ][ 0 ], &names[ 3 ][ 0 ] ) ;
    for ( i = 0 ; i <= 19 ; i++ )
    {
        t = names[ 2 ][ i ] ;
        names[ 2 ][ i ] = names[ 3 ][ i ] ;
        names[ 3 ][ i ] = t ;
    }
    printf ( "New: %s %s\n", &names[ 2 ][ 0 ], &names[ 3 ][ 0 ] ) ;
    return 0 ;
}
```

And here is the output...

```
Original: raman srinivas
New: srinivas raman
```

Note that in this program to exchange the names, we are required to exchange corresponding characters of the two names. In effect, 20 exchanges are needed to interchange two names.

Let us see, if the number of exchanges can be reduced by using an array of pointers to strings. Here is the program...

```
# include <stdio.h>
int main( )
{
    char *names[ ] = {
                          "akshay", "parag", "raman",
                          "srinivas", "gopal", "rajesh"
                     } ;
    char *temp ;
    printf ( "Original: %s %s\n", names[ 2 ], names[ 3 ] ) ;
    temp = names[ 2 ] ;
    names[ 2 ] = names[ 3 ] ;
    names[ 3 ] = temp ;
    printf ( "New: %s %s\n", names[ 2 ], names[ 3 ] ) ;
    return 0 ;
}
```

And here is the output...

```
Original: raman srinivas
New: srinivas raman
```

The output is same as the earlier program. In this program to exchange the names we have just exchanged their addresses stored in the array of pointers. Thus, by effecting just one exchange, we can interchange names. This makes handling strings very convenient.

Thus, from the point of view of efficient memory usage and ease of programming, an array of pointers to strings scores over a 2-D character array.

Limitation of Array of Pointers to Strings

To set up strings in a 2-D array of characters, we can either initialize it while declaring it, or receive the strings using **scanf( )** function. Unlike this, while using an array of pointers to strings we can only initialize it during declaration. Thus, the following code would never work:

```
char *names[ 6 ] ;
scanf ( "%s", names[ 0 ] ) ;
```

Here while declaring the array, it contains garbage addresses. And it would be incorrect to send one of these garbage address to **scanf( ).**

To overcome this difficulty we should first use **scanf( )** to receive a name in string **n[ ]**. Then using **malloc( )** allocate the space needed to accommodate the name and then copy the name into this space. This is shown below.

```
# include <stdio.h>
# include <string.h>
# include <stdlib.h>
int main( )
{
    char *names[ 6 ], n[ 50 ] ;
    int len, i ;
    char *p ;
    for ( i = 0 ; i <= 5 ; i++ )
    {
        printf ( "Enter name: " ) ;
```

```
        scanf ( "%s", n ) ;
        len = strlen ( n ) ;
        p = ( char * ) malloc ( len + 1 ) ;  /* +1 for accommodating \0 */
        strcpy ( p, n ) ;
        names[ i ] = p ;
    }
    for ( i = 0 ; i <= 5 ; i++ )
        printf ( "%s\n", names[ i ] ) ;
    return 0 ;
}
```

malloc( ) receives number of bytes to be allocated and returns the base address of the chunk of memory that it allocates. The returned address is of the type **void ***. A **void *** means a pointer which is a legal address but it is not address of a **char**, or address of an **int**, or address of any other data type. Hence it has been converted into **char *** using a C language feature called typecasting. Typecasting will be discussed in detail in Chapter 22. The prototype of **malloc( )** has been declared in the header file 'stdlib.h'.

P</> Programs

Problem 16.1

Write a program to store a few strings using an array of pointers to strings. Receive a string and check if it is present in the array.

Program

```
/* Search a string in an array */
# include <stdio.h>
# include <string.h>
int main( )
{
    char *str[ ] = {
                        "We will teach you how to...",
                        "Move a mountain", "Level a building",
                        "Erase the past", "Make a million",
                        "...all through C!"
                    } ;
    char str1[ 20 ], *p ;
    int i ;
```

```
    printf ( "\nEnter string to be searched: " ) ;
    scanf ( "%s", str1 ) ;
    p = NULL ;
    for ( i = 0 ; i < 6 ; i++ )
    {
        p = strstr ( str[ i ], str1 ) ;
        if ( p != NULL )
        {
            printf ( "%s found in the array", str1 ) ;
            return 0 ;
        }
    }
    printf ( "%s not found in the array", str1 ) ;
    return 0 ;
}
```

Output

```
Enter string to be searched: Million
Million not found in the array
```

Problem 16.2

Write a program to alphabetically sort a set of names stored using an array of pointers to strings.

Program

```
/* Sort strings alphabetically */
# include <stdio.h>
# include <string.h>
int main( )
{
    char *str[ ] =  {
                        "Rajesh", "Ashish", "Milind",
                        "Pushkar", "Akash"
                    } ;
    char *t ;
    int i, j ;
    for ( i = 0 ; i < 5 ; i++ )
    {
```

```
        for ( j = i + 1 ; j < 5 ; j++ )
        {
            if ( ( strcmp ( str[ i ], str[ j ] ) ) > 0 )
            {
                t = str[ i ] ;  str[ i ] = str[ j ] ;  str[ j ] = t ;
            }
        }
    }
    for ( i = 0 ; i < 5 ; i++ )
        printf ( "%s\t", str[ i ] ) ;
    return 0 ;
}
```

Output

```
Akash   Ashish   Milind   Pushkar   Rajesh
```

Problem 16.3

Write a program to reverse the strings stored in an array of pointers to strings:

Program

```
/* Reverse strings stored in an array of pointers */
# include <stdio.h>
# include <string.h>
void xstrrev ( char *ss ) ;
int main( )
{
    char  str[ ][ 35 ] = {
                            "To ere is human...",
                            "But to really mess things up...",
                            "One needs to know C !!"
                        } ;
    int  i ;
    for ( i = 0 ; i <= 2 ; i++ )
    {
        xstrrev ( str[ i ] ) ;
        printf ( "%s\n", str[ i ] ) ;
    }
```

```
    return 0 ;
}
void xstrrev ( char *s )
{
    int l, i ;
    char *t, temp ;
    l = strlen ( s ) ;
    t = s + l - 1 ;
    for ( i = 1 ; i <= l / 2 ; i++ )
    {
        temp = *s ; *s = *t ; *t = temp ;
        s++ ; t-- ;
    }
}
```

Output

```
...namuh si ere oT
...pu sgniht ssem yllaer ot tuB
!! C wonk ot sdeen enO
```

Exercises

[A] Answer the following questions:

(a) How many bytes in memory would be occupied by the following array of pointers to strings? How many bytes would be required to store the same strings in a two-dimensional character array?

```
char *mess[ ] = {
                    "Hammer and tongs", "Tooth and nail",
                    "Spit and polish", "You and C"
                } ;
```

(b) Write a program to delete all vowels from a sentence. Assume that the sentence is not more than 80 characters long.

(c) Write a program that will read a line and delete from it all occurrences of the word 'the'.

(d) Write a program that stores a set of names of individuals and abbreviates the first and middle name to their first letter.

(e) Write a program to count the number of occurrences of any two vowels in succession in a line of text. For example, in the following sentence:

"Please read this application and give me gratuity"

such occurrences are ea, ea, ui.

(f) Write a program that receives an integer (less than or equal to nine digits in length) and prints out the number in words. For example, if the number input is 12342, then the output should be Twelve Thousand Three Hundred Forty Two.

KanNotes

- 2 ways to handle multiple related strings :

  1) Using 2-D array of strings
  2) Using array of pointers to strings

- Pros and cons of using 2-D array of strings :

  Pros :
  Easy to process using 2 for loops and expression str[i][j]

  Cons :
  Leads to wastage of precious memory space
  Leads to tedious processing of array elements

- Pros and cons of using array of pointers to strings :
  Pros :
  Easy to process
  Saves space

  Cons :
  Cannot change strings. Their relative positions in the array can be changed
  Cannot receive strings from keyboard easily. Can be done by allocating space for each string using malloc() and then assigning the addresses returned by malloc() to the array elements

17 Structures

"Address the heterogeneous world ..."

Imagine a railway reservation system. The data in it like name, age, gender, address, distance of travel, source and destination stations, is dissimilar. How can this dissimilar data be kept together? Well, this chapter has the answer...

Contents

C language provides arrays and strings to let us handle similar data. But real-world data is usually dissimilar. For example, a 'book' is a collection of items like title, author, publisher, number of pages, date of publication, etc. For dealing with such data C provides a data type called 'structure', which is the topic of this chapter.

Why use Structures?

Suppose we wish to store in memory name (a string), price (a float) and number of pages (an int) of 3 books. To do this we can take following approaches:

(a) Construct 3 arrays for storing names, prices and number of pages.
(b) Use a structure variable.

Let us examine these two approaches one-by-one. For the sake of programming convenience, let us assume that the names of books are single character long. Here is a program that uses 3 arrays.

```
# include <stdio.h>
int main( )
{
    char  name[ 3 ] ;
    float  price[ 3 ] ;
    int  pages[ 3 ], i ;
    printf ( "Enter names, prices and no. of pages of 3 books\n" ) ;
    for ( i = 0 ; i <= 2 ; i++ )
        scanf ( "%c %f %d", &name[ i ], &price[ i ], &pages[ i ] ) ;
    printf ( "And this is what you entered\n" ) ;
    for ( i = 0 ; i <= 2 ; i++ )
        printf ( "%c %f %d\n", name[ i ], price[ i ], pages[ i ] ) ;
    return 0 ;
}
```

And here is the sample run...

```
Enter names, prices and no. of pages of 3 books
A 100.00 354
C 256.50 682
F 233.70 512
And this is what you entered
A 100.000000 354
C 256.500000 682
```

```
F 233.700000 512
```

Though this approach works, it has following limitations:

(a) It obscures the fact that we are dealing with characteristics related to a single entity—the book.

(b) If we wish to store more items related to a book (publisher, date of publication, etc.), we would be required to create more arrays.

These limitations can be overcome by following the second approach—using a special data type called structure. It lets us group several similar/dissimilar data types together. The following example illustrates the use of this data type:

```
# include <stdio.h>
int main( )
{
    struct book
    {
        char name ; float price ; int pages ;
    } ;
    struct book b1, b2, b3 ;
    printf ( "Enter names, prices & no. of pages of 3 books\n" ) ;
    scanf ( "%c %f %d", &b1.name, &b1.price, &b1.pages ) ;
    scanf ( "%c %f %d", &b2.name, &b2.price, &b2.pages ) ;
    scanf ( "%c %f %d", &b3.name, &b3.price, &b3.pages ) ;
    printf ( "And this is what you entered\n" ) ;
    printf ( "%c %f %d\n", b1.name, b1.price, b1.pages ) ;
    printf ( "%c %f %d\n", b2.name, b2.price, b2.pages ) ;
    printf ( "%c %f %d\n", b3.name, b3.price, b3.pages ) ;
    return 0 ;
}
```

And here is the output...

```
Enter names, prices and no. of pages of 3 books
A 100.00 354
C 256.50 682
F 233.70 512
And this is what you entered
A 100.000000 354
C 256.500000 682
F 233.700000 512
```

The program begins with declaration of a user-defined data type called **struct book**, containing 3 structure elements—**name**, **price** and **pages**. Then we have defined 3 structure variables **b1**, **b2**, **b3** of the type **struct book**. Each of these variables consists of a character variable called **name**, a float variable called **price** and an integer variable called **pages**.

Then we have received values into these variables using **scanf( )** and printed them out using **printf( )**. Note that to access each element of a structure variable we have used the dot (.) operator, as in, **b1.name**, **b1.price** and **b1.pages**.

You would agree that this second approach is better than the previous approach using arrays as it keeps dissimilar but related characteristics of a book (name, price, pages) together.

Array of Structures

In the second approach used above, if the number of books increase, instead of creating more variables like **b4**, **b5**, **b6**, etc. we should create an array of structures as illustrated in the following program:

```
/* Usage of an array of structures */
# include <stdio.h>
void linkfloat( ) ;
int main( )
{
    struct book
    {
        char name ; float price ; int pages ;
    } ;
    struct book b[ 10 ] ;
    int i ; int dh;
    for ( i = 0 ; i <= 9 ; i++ )
    {
        printf ( "Enter name, price and pages\n" ) ;
        scanf ( "%c %f %d", &b[ i ].name, &b[ i ].price, &b[ i ].pages ) ;
        while ((dh = getchar( )) != '\n' )
            ;
    }
    for ( i = 0 ; i <= 9 ; i++ )
        printf ( "%c %f %d\n", b[ i ].name, b[ i ].price, b[ i ].pages ) ;
    return 0 ;
}
```

```
void linkfloat( )
{
    float a = 0, *b ;
    b = &a ;    /* cause emulator to be linked */
    a = *b ;    /* suppress the warning - variable not used */
}
```

Notice how the array of structures is declared...

```
struct book  b[ 10 ] ;
```

This array provides space in memory for 10 structures of the type **struct book**. Thus, by using one array we can take care of many books, each having many data items.

To refer to zeroth book's price we use **b[0].price**, to refer to first book's price we use **b[1].price**, etc.

When we supply first record to **scanf( )** the values entered are assigned to different structure elements, but the enter that we hit remains in the keyboard buffer. If we leave it there, the next call to **scanf( )** would take this enter and move ahead. To prevent this from happening we must flush out the keyboard buffer. This is what is being achieved through the **while** loop following the **scanf( )**. Some texts may use **fflush (stdin)** instead of the **while** loop to get the same effect. But this is not a portable way of clearing the input buffer, and may not work with all compilers.

If we don't define the **linkfloat( )** function, we may get an error "Floating-Point Formats Not Linked" with some C Compilers. How can we force the formats to be linked? That's where the **linkfloat( )** function comes in. It forces linking of the floating-point emulator into an application. There is no need to call this function; we just need to define it in our program.

Intricacies of Structures

We now know how to declare a structure, how to create structure variables, how to create an array of structures and how to access structure elements. It is time to explore the intricacies of structures.

Structure Declaration

Declaration of a structure does not reserve any space in memory. All that it does is, it defines the 'form' of the structure.

We can combine the declaration of the structure type and definition of structure variables in one statement as shown below. When we do so, mentioning the structure name is optional.

```
struct
{
    char name ; float price ; int pages ;
} b1, b2, b3 ;
```

Like primary variables, pointers, arrays and strings, structure variables too can be initialized where they are declared. The syntax to do so is quite similar to the one that is used to initialize arrays.

```
struct book
{
    char name[ 10 ] ; float price ; int pages ;
} ;
struct book b1 = { "Basic", 130.00, 550 } ;
struct book b2 = { "Physics", 150.80, 800 } ;
struct book b3 = { 0 } ;
```

If a structure variable is initiated to a value { 0 }, then all its elements are set to value 0, as in **b3** above. This is a handy way of initializing structure variables. In absence of this, we would have been required to initialize each individual element to a value 0.

Usually, structure type declaration appears at the top of the source code file, before any variables or functions are defined. In very large programs they are put in a separate header file, and the file is #included in the program we wish to use this structure type.

Storage of Structure Elements

Structure elements are always stored in contiguous memory locations. The following program illustrates this fact:

```
/* Memory map of structure elements */
# include <stdio.h>
int main( )
{
    struct book
    {
        char name ; float price ; int pages ;
    } ;
```

```
    struct book b1 = { 'B', 130.00, 550 } ;
    printf ( "Address of name = %u\n", &b1.name ) ;
    printf ( "Address of price = %u\n", &b1.price ) ;
    printf ( "Address of pages = %u\n", &b1.pages ) ;
    return 0 ;
}
```

Here is the output of the program...

```
Address of name = 65518
Address of price = 65519
Address of pages = 65523
```

The structure elements are stored in memory as shown in Figure 17.1.

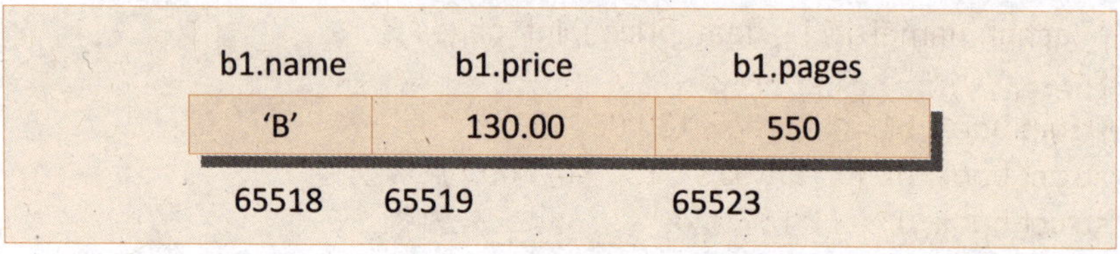

Figure 17.1 Layout of structure variable in memory.

In an array of structures, all elements of the array are stored in adjacent memory locations.

Copying of Structure Elements

Structure elements can be copied either piece-meal or all at one shot. Both these approaches are shown in the following example:

```
# include <stdio.h>
# include <string.h>
int main( )
{
    struct employee
    {
        char name[ 10 ] ; int age ; float salary ;
    } ;
    struct employee e1 = { "Sanjay", 30, 5500.50 } ;
    struct employee e2, e3 ;
    /* piece-meal copying */
    strcpy ( e2.name, e1.name ) ; /* e2.name = e1. name is wrong */
    e2.age = e1.age ;
```

```
    e2.salary = e1.salary ;
    /* copying all elements at one go */
    e3 = e2 ;
    printf ( "%s %d %f\n", e1.name, e1.age, e1.salary ) ;
    printf ( "%s %d %f\n", e2.name, e2.age, e2.salary ) ;
    printf ( "%s %d %f\n", e3.name, e3.age, e3.salary ) ;
    return 0 ;
}
```

The output of the program would be...

```
Sanjay 30 5500.500000
Sanjay 30 5500.500000
Sanjay 30 5500.500000
```

If all elements are to be copied, copying at one shot is preferred, whereas, if we wish to copy only some of the elements, we need to take the piece-meal approach.

Nested Structures

One structure can be nested within another structure. Using this facility, complex data types can be created. The following program shows nested structures at work:

```
# include <stdio.h>
int main( )
{
    struct address
    {
        char phone[ 15 ] ; char city[ 25 ] ; int pin ;
    } ;
    struct emp
    {
        char name[ 25 ] ; struct address a ;
    } ;
    struct emp e = { "jeru", "2531046", "nagpur", 10 };
    printf ( "name = %s phone = %s\n", e.name, e.a.phone ) ;
    printf ( "city = %s pin = %d\n", e.a.city, e.a.pin ) ;
    return 0 ;
}
```

And here is the output...

```
name = jeru phone = 2531046
city = nagpur pin = 10
```

Notice the method used to access the element of a structure that is part of another structure. For this, the dot operator is used twice, as in the expressions, **e.a.pin** or **e.a.city**.

Nested structures can be surprisingly self-descriptive, for example:

```
maruti.engine.bolt.large.qty
```

This clearly signifies that we are referring to the quantity of large sized bolts that fit on an engine of a maruti car.

Passing Structure Elements / Structure Variables

We may either pass individual structure elements or the entire structure variable to a function as shown in the following program:

```
/* Passing individual structure elements */
# include <stdio.h>
struct book
{
    char  name[ 25 ] ;  char  author[ 25 ] ;  int  pages ;
} ;
void display1 ( char  *, char  *, int ) ;
void display2 ( struct book ) ;
void display3 ( struct book * ) ;
int main( )
{
    struct book b1 = { "Let Us C", "YPK", 464 } ;
    display1 ( b1.name, b1.author, b1.pages ) ;
    display2 ( b1 ) ;
    display3 ( &b1 ) ;
    return 0 ;
}
void display1 ( char  *n, char  *a, int  pg )
{
    printf ( "%s %s %d\n", n, a, pg ) ;
}
void display2 ( struct book  b )
{
```

```
    printf ( "%s %s %d\n", b.name, b.author, b.pages ) ;
}
void display3 ( struct book *pb )
{
    printf ( "%s %s %d\n", pb->name, pb->author, pb->pages ) ;
}
```

And here is the output...

```
Let Us C YPK 464
Let Us C YPK 464
Let Us C YPK 464
```

Observe that in the declaration of the structure, **name** and **author** are arrays. Therefore, when we called the **display1( )** using,

```
display1 ( b1.name, b1.author, b1.pages ) ;
```

we passed base addresses of the arrays **name** and **author**, but the value stored in **pages**. Thus, this is a mixed call—a call by reference as well as a call by value. **display1( )** proceeds to print the two strings and integer.

The structure variable **b1** has been passed by value to **display2( )** and by reference to **display3( )**. **b1** passed to **display2( )** is collected in variable **b** of the type **struct book**. Likewise, address of **b1** passed to **display3( )** is collected in 'structure pointer' or 'pointer to a structure' **pb**. (Refer Figure 17.2.)

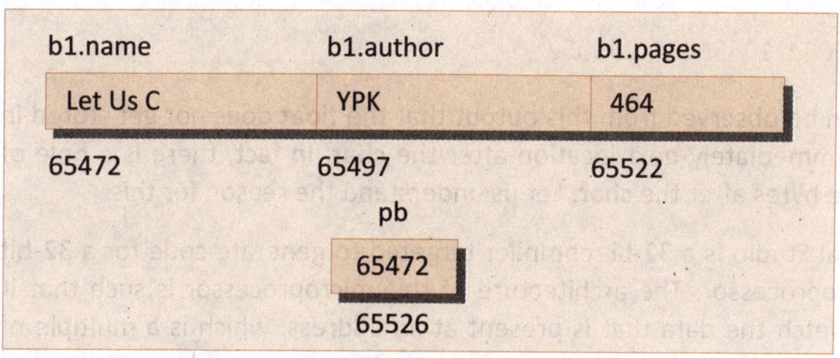

Figure 17.2 Pointer to a structure.

Since we need **struct book** in both **display2( )** and **display3( )** it has been declared globally. **display2( )** accesses and prints the elements of **b** using the '.' operator.

Observe carefully, how **printf( )** is used in **display3( )** to print structure elements. We cannot use **pb.name** or **pb.pages** because **pb** is not a structure variable but a pointer to a structure. In such cases C provides an operator **->** to refer to the structure elements. Remember that on the left-hand side of the **'->'** operator, there must always be a pointer to a structure.

Packing Structure Elements

Consider the following code snippet:

```
struct emp
{
    int a ;  char ch ;  float s ;
} ;
struct emp e ;
printf ( "%u %u %u\n", &e.a, &e.ch, &e.s ) ;
```

If we execute this program using TC/TC++ Compiler we get the addresses as:

```
65518  65520  65521
```

As expected, in memory the **char** begins immediately after the **int** and **float** begins immediately after the **char**.

However, if we run the same program using Visual Studio compiler then the output turns out to be:

```
1245044  1245048  1245052
```

It can be observed from this output that the **float** does not get stored in the immediately next location after the **char**. In fact, there is a hole of three bytes after the **char**. Let us understand the reason for this.

Visual Studio is a 32-bit compiler targeted to generate code for a 32-bit microprocessor. The architecture of this microprocessor is such that it can fetch the data that is present at an address, which is a multiple of four much faster than the data present at any other address. Hence the compiler aligns every element of a structure at an address that is multiple of four. Hence the three holes between the **char** and the **float**.

However, some programs need to exercise precise control over the memory areas where data is placed. For example, suppose we wish to read the contents of the boot sector (first sector on the hard disk) into a structure. For this the byte arrangement of the structure elements must match the arrangement of various fields in the boot sector of the disk. The **#pragma pack** directive offers a way to fulfil this requirement. This directive specifies packing alignment for structure members. The pragma takes effect at the first structure declaration after the pragma is seen.

Visual Studio compiler supports this feature, whereas Turbo C/C++ does not. The following code shows how to use this directive:

```
# pragma pack(1)
struct emp
{
    int a ;  char ch ;  float s ;
} ;
# pragma pack( )
struct emp e ;
printf ( "%u %u %u\n", &e.a, &e.ch, &e.s ) ;
```

Here, **#pragma pack (1)** lets each structure element to begin on a 1-byte boundary as justified by the output of the program given below.

```
1245044 1245048 1245049
```

Uses of Structures

Structures are very useful in Database Management to maintain data about employees in an organization, books in a library, items in a store, financial accounting transactions in a company, etc. They are also used for many other purposes like:

(a) Changing the size of the cursor
(b) Clearing the contents of the screen
(c) Placing the cursor at an appropriate position on screen
(d) Drawing any graphics shape on the screen
(e) Receiving a key from the keyboard
(f) Checking the memory size of the computer
(g) Finding out the list of equipment attached to the computer
(h) Formatting a disk
(i) Hiding a file from the directory
(j) Displaying the directory of a disk
(k) Sending the output to printer
(l) Interacting with the mouse

And that is certainly a very impressive list! At least impressive enough to make you realize how important a data type a structure is and to be thorough with it if you intend to program any of the above applications.

P</> Programs

Problem 17.1

A stack is a data structure in which addition of new element or deletion of existing element always takes place at the same end known as 'top' of stack. Write a program to implement a stack using a linked list.

Program

```
/* Implementation of stack using a linked list */
# include <stdlib.h>
# include <stdio.h>
struct node
{
    int data ; struct node *link ;
} ;
void push ( struct node **s, int item ) ;
int pop ( struct node **s ) ;
int main( )
{
    struct node *top ;
    int t, i, item ;
    top = NULL ;
    push ( &top, 45 ) ; push ( &top, 28 ) ;
    push ( &top, 63 ) ; push ( &top, 55 ) ;
    item = pop ( &top ) ;
    printf ( "Popped : %d\n", item ) ;
    item = pop ( &top ) ;
    printf ( "Popped : %d\n", item ) ;
    return 0 ;
}
void push ( struct node **s, int item )
{
    struct node *q ;
    q = ( struct node * ) malloc ( sizeof ( struct node ) ) ;
    q -> data = item ;
```

```
    q -> link = *s ;
    *s = q ;
}
int pop ( struct node **s )
{
    int item ;
    struct node *q ;
    if ( *s == NULL )
        printf ( "Stack is empty\n" ) ;
    else
    {
        q = *s ;
        item = q -> data ;
        *s = q -> link ;
        free ( q ) ;
        return ( item ) ;
    }
}
```

Output

```
Popped : 55
Popped : 63
```

Problem 17.2

In a data structure called queue the addition of new element takes place at the end (called 'rear' of queue), whereas deletion takes place at the other end (called 'front' of queue). Write a program to implement a queue using a linked list.

Program

```
/* Implementation of a queue using linked list */
# include <stdio.h>
# include <stdlib.h>
struct queue
{
    int item ; struct queue *link ;
} ;
struct queue *rear, *front ;
```

```
void add ( int  item ) ;
int del_queue( ) ;
int main( )
{
    int  item ;
    rear = front = NULL ;
    add ( 10 ) ;  add ( 20 ) ;  add ( 30 ) ;
    add ( 40 ) ;  add ( 50 ) ;  add ( 60 ) ;
    item = del_queue( ) ;
    printf ( "Deleted Item = %d\n", item ) ;
    item = del_queue( ) ;
    printf ( "Deleted Item = %d\n", item ) ;
    return 0 ;
}
void add ( int  item )
{
    struct queue *q = ( struct queue * ) malloc ( sizeof ( struct queue ) ) ;
    q -> item = item ;
    q -> link = NULL ;
    if ( rear == NULL )
    {
        rear = q ;  front = q ;
    }
    else
    {
        q -> link = rear ;  rear = q ;
    }
}
int del_queue( )
{
    int  item ;
    struct queue *q = rear ;
    if ( front == NULL )
    {
        printf ( "Queue is empty\n" ) ;
        return -1;
    }
    else
    {
        if ( front == rear )
        {
```

```
            item = q -> item ;  front = rear = NULL ;
            free( q ) ;
        }
        else
        {
            while( q -> link -> link != NULL )
                q = q -> link ;
            item = q -> link -> item ;
            free( q -> link ) ;
            front = q ;
            q -> link = NULL ;
        }
    }
    return item ;
}
```

Output

```
Deleted Item = 10
Deleted Item = 20
```

Exercises

[A] Answer the following questions:

(a) Given the statement,

maruti.engine.bolts = 25 ;

which of the following is True?

1. bolts is a structure variable
2. engine is a structure variable
3. maruti is a structure variable
4. Option 2. and 3.

(b)

```
struct time
{
    int hours ; int minutes ; int seconds ;
} t ;
struct time *pt ;
pt = &t ;
```

With reference to the above declarations which of the following refers to **seconds** correctly:

1. pt.seconds
2. pt -> seconds
3. time.seconds
4. time->seconds

[B] Attempt the following questions:

(a) Create a structure called **student** that can contain data given below:

Roll number, Name, Department, Course, Year of joining

Assume that there are not more than 450 students in the college.

(1) Write a function to print names of all students who joined in a particular year.

(2) Write a function to print the data of a student whose roll number is received by the function.

(b) Create a structure that can contain data of customers in a bank. The data to be stored is Account number, Name and Balance in account. Assume maximum of 200 customers in the bank.

(1) Define a function to print the Account number and name of each customer with balance below Rs. 1000.

(2) If a customer requests for withdrawal or deposit, it should receive as input Account number, amount and code (1 for deposit, 0 for withdrawal).

Define a function that prints a message, "The balance is insufficient for the specified withdrawal", if on withdrawal the balance falls below Rs. 1000.

(c) An automobile company has serial number for engine parts starting from AA0 to FF9. The other characteristics of parts are year of manufacture, material and quantity manufactured.

(1) Create a structure to store information corresponding to a part.

(2) Write a program to retrieve information on parts with serial numbers between BB1 and CC6.

(d) A record contains name of cricketer, his age, number of test matches that he has played and the average runs that he has scored. Create an array of structures to hold records of 20 such cricketers and then write a program to read these records and arrange them in ascending order by average runs. Use the **qsort( )** standard library function.

(e) Suppose there is a structure called **employee** that holds information like employee code, name and date of joining. Write a program to create an array of structures and enter some data into it. Then ask the user to enter current date. Display the names of those employees whose tenure is greater than equal to 3 years.

(f) Create a structure called **library** to hold accession number, title of the book, author name, price of the book, and flag indicating whether book is issued or not. Write a menu-driven program that implements the working of a library. The menu options should be:

1. Add book information
2. Display book information
3. List all books of given author
4. List the title of book specified by accession number
5. List the count of books in the library
6. List the books in the order of accession number
7. Exit

(g) Define a function that compares two given dates. To store a date, use a structure that contains three members namely day, month and year. If the dates are equal the function should return 0, otherwise it should return 1.

kn KanNotes

- Structure is a collection of dissimilar (usually) elements stored in adjacent locations

  Structure is also known as - User-defined data type / Secondary data type / Aggregate data type / Derived data type

- Terminology :

  struct employee { char name ; int age ; float salary ; } ;
  struct employee e1, e2, e[10] ;

  struct - Keyword employee - Structure name / tag

name, age, salary - Structure elements / Structure members
e1, e2 - Structure variables e[ ] - Array of structures

- Structure elements are stored in adjacent memory locations

- Size of structure variable = sum of sizes of structure elements

- 2 ways to copy structure elements :

```
struct emp e1 = { "Rahul", 23, 4000.50 } ;
struct emp e2, e3 ;
e2.n = e1.n ; e2.a = e1.a ; e2.s = e1.s ;  → Piecemeal copying
e3 = e1 ;  → Copying at one shot
```

- Structures can be nested :

```
struct address { char city[ 20 ] ; long int pin ; } ;
struct emp { char n[ 20 ] ; int age ; struct address a ; float s ; } ;
struct emp e ;
```

  To access city and pin we should use e.a.city and e.a.pin

- To access structure elements using structure variable, use . operator as in

```
struct emp e ; printf ( "%s %d %f", e.name, e.age, e.sal ) ;
```

- To access structure elements using structure pointer, use -> operator as in

```
struct emp e ; struct emp *p ;
p = &e ;
printf ( "%s %d %f", p->name, p->age, p->sal ) ;
```

- If a structure contains a pointer to itself, it is called a self-referential structure :

```
struct node { int data ; struct node *link ; } ;
```

- Uses of structures :

  Database Management   Displaying characters
  Printing on printer   Mouse Programming
  Graphics Programming   All Disk Operations

18 Console Input / Output

"Input from keyboard, Output to screen"

I want to print names, ages and salaries of 5 persons on the screen. The names and ages should be left-justified and properly aligned one below the other. The salaries should be aligned with the decimal point and only two digits should be printed after decimal point. To achieve all this, you need formatted console printing functions. This chapter shows you which one of them to use and how…

Contents

C language has no provision for receiving data from any of the input devices (like say keyboard, disk, etc.), or for sending data to the output devices (like say monitor, disk, etc.). Then how do we manage Input/Output (I/O)? Well, that is what we intend to explore in this chapter.

Types of I/O

Though C has no keywords to perform I/O, it must be dealt with at some point or the other. There is not much use of writing a program that spends all its time telling itself a secret.

Each Operating System (OS) has its own way of inputting and outputting data from and to the files and devices. So, functions are defined that can carry out I/O keeping in mind the particular operating system's I/O facilities. These functions are then compiled and made available to users in the form of libraries.

Since I/O facilities are OS dependent, definition of an I/O function for one OS would be different than the one for another OS, even though the behavior of both functions would be same.

There are numerous library functions available for I/O. These can be classified into two broad categories:

(a) Console I/O functions - Functions to receive input from keyboard and display output to screen.

(b) File I/O functions - Functions to perform I/O operations on files on a disk.

In this chapter we would be discussing only Console I/O functions. File I/O functions would be discussed in Chapter 19.

Console I/O Functions

The screen and keyboard together are called a console. Console I/O functions can be further classified into two categories—formatted and unformatted console I/O functions.

Formatted functions allow the input read from keyboard or output to screen to be formatted as per our requirements. For example, while displaying values of average marks and percentage marks on the screen, details like where this output would appear on the screen, how many spaces would be present between the two values, the number of places after the decimal points, etc., can be controlled using formatted functions. The functions available under each of these two categories are shown in Figure 18.1.

Console Input/Output functions

Formatted functions

Type	**Input**	**Output**
char	scanf( )	printf( )
int	scanf( )	printf( )
float	scanf( )	printf( )
string	scanf( )	printf( )

Unformatted functions

Type	**Input**	**Output**
char	getchar( )	putchar( )
int	-	-
float	-	-
string	gets( )	puts( )

Figure 18.1 Console I/O functions.

Let us now discuss these console I/O functions in detail.

Formatted Console I/O Functions

As can be seen from Figure 18.1, the functions **printf( ),** and **scanf( )** fall under the category of formatted console I/O functions. These functions allow us to supply input in a fixed format and obtain output in specified form. Let us discuss these functions one-by-one.

General form of **printf( )** looks like this...

```
printf ( "format string", list of variables ) ;
```

The format string can contain:

(a) Characters that are simply printed as they are
(b) Format specifications that begin with a % sign
(c) Escape sequences that begin with a \ sign

For example, look at the following code snippet:

```
int avg = 346 ;
float per = 69.2 ;
printf ( "Average = %d\nPercentage = %f\n", avg, per ) ;
```

The output of this code snippet would be...

```
Average = 346
Percentage = 69.200000
```

During execution **printf( )** function examines the format string from left to right. Till it does not come across either a **%** or a \, it continues to display the characters that it encounters, on to the screen. In this example, **Average =** is displayed on the screen. When it comes across a format specifier, it picks up the first variable in the list of variables and prints its value in the specified format. In this example, when **%d** is met, the variable **avg** is picked up and its value is printed. Similarly, when an escape sequence is met, it takes suitable action. In this example, when **\n** is met, it places the cursor at the beginning of the next line. This process continues till the end of format string is reached.

Format Specifications

The **%d** and **%f** used in the **printf( )** are called format specifiers. Figure 18.2 gives a list of format specifiers that can be used with the **printf( )** function.

Data type		Format specifier
Integer	signed short	%hd
	unsigned short	%hu
	int	%d or %i
	unsigned int	%u
	singed long	%ld
	unsigned long	%lu
	signed long long	%lld
	unsigned long long	%llu
	unsigned hexadecimal	%x
	unsigned octal	%o
Real	float	%f
	double	%lf
	long double	%Lf
Character	signed character	%c
	unsigned character	%c
String		%s

Figure 18.2 Different format specifiers.

We can provide optional specifiers shown in Figure 18.3 in the format specifications.

Specifier	Description
w	Digits specifying field width
.	Decimal point separating field width from precision (precision means number of places after the decimal point)
d	Digits specifying precision
-	Minus sign for left justifying output in specified field width

Figure 18.3 Optional format specifiers.

The field-width specifier tells **printf( )** how many columns on screen should be used while printing a value. For example, **%10d** says, "print the variable as a decimal integer in a field of 10 columns". If the value to be printed happens not to fill up the entire field, the value is right justified and is padded with blanks on the left.

If we include the minus sign in format specifier (as in **%-10d**), this means left-justification is desired and the value will be padded with blanks on the right.

If the field-width used turns out to be less than what is required to print the number, the field-width is ignored and the complete number is printed. Here is an example that illustrates all these features.

```
# include <stdio.h>
int main( )
{
    int  weight = 63 ;
    printf ( "weight is %d kg\n", weight ) ;
    printf ( "weight is %2d kg\n", weight ) ;
    printf ( "weight is %4d kg\n", weight ) ;
    printf ( "weight is %6d kg\n", weight ) ;
    printf ( "weight is %-6d kg\n", weight ) ;
    printf ( "weight is %1d kg\n", weight ) ;
    return 0 ;
}
```

The output of the program would look like this ...

```
Columns   0123456789012345678901234567890
          weight  is  63  kg
          weight  is  63  kg
          weight  is     63  kg
          weight  is        63 kg
          weight  is  63       kg
          weight  is  63  kg
```

Specifying the field width can be useful in creating tables of numeric values with the numbers lined up properly, as the following program demonstrates:

```
# include <stdio.h>
int main( )
{
    printf ( "%10.1f %10.1f %10.1f\n", 5.0, 13.5, 133.9 ) ;
    printf ( "%10.1f %10.1f %10.1f\n", 305.0, 1200.9, 3005.3 );
    return 0 ;
}
```

This results into a much better output...

```
01234567890123456789012345678901
       5.0       13.5      133.9
     305.0     1200.9     3005.3
```

Note that the specifier **%10.1f** specifies that a float be printed right-aligned within 10 columns, with one place beyond the decimal point.

The format specifiers can be used even while displaying a string of characters. The following program would clarify this point:

```
# include <stdio.h>
int main( )
{
    char  firstname1[  ] = "Sandy" ;
    char  surname1[  ] = "Malya" ;
    char  firstname2[  ] = "AjayKumar" ;
    char  surname2[  ] = "Gurubaxani" ;
    printf ( "%20s%20s\n", firstname1, surname1 ) ;
    printf ( "%20s%20s\n", firstname2, surname2 ) ;
    return 0 ;
}
```

And here's the output...

```
01234567890123456789012345678901234567890
               Sandy               Malya
           AjayKumar          Gurubaxani
```

The format specifier **%20s** prints the string in these 20 columns with right justification. This helps lining up names of different lengths properly. Obviously, the format **%-20s** would have left-justified the string. Had we used **%-20.10s** it would have meant left-justify the string in 20 columns and print only first 10 characters of the string.

Escape Sequences

All escape sequences begin with a \. They are called because the backslash symbol (\) is considered as an 'escape' character—it causes an escape from the normal interpretation of a string, so that the next character is recognized as one having a special meaning. Figure 18.4 shows a complete list of these escape sequences.

Escape Seq.	Purpose	Escape Seq.	Purpose
\n	New line	\t	Tab
\v	Vertical tab	\b	Backspace
\r	Carriage return	\f	Form feed
\a	Alert	\'	Single quote
\"	Double quote	\\	Backslash
\?	Question mark	\xhh	Char in hex value

Figure 18.4 Escape sequences.

The following program shows usage of escape sequences **\n**, **\t** and **\v**.

```
# include <stdio.h>
int main( )
{
    printf ( "Maths teaches reasoning,\nnot Algebra & geometry\n" ) ;
    printf ( "Future of learning \r is remote\n" ) ;
    printf ( "You\tmust\tbe\tcrazy\vto\thate\tthis\tbook\n" ) ;
    return 0 ;
}
```

And here is the output...

```
01234567890123456789012345678901234567890123456789012345...
Maths teaches reasoning,
not Algebra & geometry
is remotelearning
You     must    be      crazy
                        to      hate    this    book
```

The **\n** takes the cursor to beginning of next line. Hence in the first **printf( )** message after the word 'reasoning,' is printed on the next line. In the second **printf( )**, **\r** positioned the cursor to the beginning of the line in which it is currently placed. Hence, the message got overwritten.

While using **\t** an 80-column screen is divided into 10 print zones of 8 columns each. Using a **\t** moves the cursor to the beginning of next print zone. For example, if cursor is positioned in column 5, then printing a **\t** takes the cursor to column 8. **\v** moves the cursor in the next line below its current position.

\b moves the cursor one position to the left of its current position. **\a** alerts the user by sounding the speaker inside the computer. Form feed advances the computer stationery attached to the printer to the top of the next page. Characters single quote, double quote, backslash and question mark can be printed by preceding them with the backslash. Thus, the statement,

```
printf ( "He said, \"How\'s life\?\"" ) ;
```

will print...

```
He said, "How's life?"
```

Finally, the character 'A' can be printed using decimal or its octal and hexadecimal representation using the following statement:

```
printf ( "%c %c %c", 65, '\101', '\x41' ) ;
```

Ignoring Characters

Sometimes we may wish to ignore some of the characters supplied as input. For example, while receiving a date we may wish to ignore the separator like '.', '/' or '-'. This can be done using **%*c**. This means if a '.' or '/' or '-' is entered it would be matched and ignored. The * ensures that the character entered does not get assigned to any variable in the variable list.

```
printf ( "Enter date in dd/mm/yy or dd.mm.yy or dd-mm-yy format\n") ;
scanf ( "%d%*c%d%*c%d", &dd, &mm, &yy ) ;
printf ( "%d/%d%/%d\n", dd, mm, yy ) ;
```

Mismatch

If there is a mismatch in the specifier and the type of value being printed, **printf( )** attempts to perform the specified conversion, and does its best to produce a proper result. Sometimes the result is nonsensical, as in case when we ask it to print a string using **%d**. Sometimes the result is useful, as in the case we ask **printf( )** to print ASCII value of a character using **%d**. Sometimes the result is disastrous and the entire program blows up.

The following program shows a few of these conversions, some sensible, some weird:

```
# include <stdio.h>
int main( )
{
    char ch = 'z' ;
    int i = 125 ;
    float a = 12.55 ;
    char s[ ] = "hello there !" ;
    printf ( "%c %d %f\n", ch, ch, ch ) ;
    printf ( "%s %d %f\n", s, s, s ) ;
    printf ( "%c %d %f\n",i ,i, i ) ;
    printf ( "%f %d\n", a, a ) ;
    return 0 ;
}
```

And here is the output...

```
z 122 -9362831782501783000000000000000000000000000.000000
hello there ! 3280 -
9362831782501783000000000000000000000000000.000000
} 125 -9362831782501783000000000000000000000000000.000000
12.550000 0
```

I would leave it to you to analyze the results by yourselves. You would find that some of the conversions are quite sensible.

Let us now turn our attention to **scanf( )**. The **scanf( )** function allows us to enter data from keyboard that will be formatted in a certain way.

The general form of **scanf( )** statement is as follows:

```
scanf ( "format string", list of addresses of variables ) ;
```

For example:

```
scanf ( "%d %f %c", &c, &a, &ch ) ;
```

Note that we are sending addresses of variables to **scanf( )** function. This is necessary because the values received from keyboard must be dropped into variables corresponding to these addresses. The values that are supplied through the keyboard must be separated by either blank(s), Tab(s), or newline(s). Do not include these escape sequences in the format string. All the format specifications that we learnt in **printf( )** function are applicable to **scanf( )** function as well.

sprintf( ) and *sscanf( )* Functions

The **sprintf( )** function works similar to the **printf( )** function except for one small difference. Instead of sending the output to the screen as **printf( )** does, this function writes the output to a string. The following program illustrates this:

```
# include <stdio.h>
int main( )
{
    int i = 10 ;
    char ch = 'A' ;
    float a = 3.14 ;
    char str[ 20 ] ;
    printf ( "%d %c %f\n", i, ch, a ) ;
    sprintf ( str, "%d %c %f", i, ch, a ) ;
    printf ( "%s\n", str ) ;
    return 0 ;
}
```

In this program, the **printf( )** prints out the values of **i**, **ch** and **a** on the screen, whereas **sprintf( )** stores these values in the string **str**. Since the string **str** is present in memory, what is written into **str** using **sprintf( )** doesn't get displayed on the screen. Once **str** has been built, its contents can be displayed on the screen. In our program this is achieved by the second **printf( )** statement.

The counterpart of **sprintf( )** is the **sscanf( )** function. It allows us to read characters from a string and to convert and store them in C variables according to specified formats. The **sscanf( )** function comes in handy for in-memory conversion of characters to values. You may find it convenient to read in strings from a file and then extract values from a string by using **sscanf( )**. The usage of **sscanf( )** is same as **scanf( )**, except that the first argument is the string from which reading is to take place.

Unformatted Console I/O Functions

There are several standard library functions available under this category—those that can deal with a single character and those that can deal with a string of characters. For openers, let us look at those which handle one character at a time.

fgetchar( ) and *fputchar( )*

The **fgetchar( )** function (or its equivalent **getchar( )** macro) lets you read a single character entered from keyboard. The character that is typed has to be followed by Enter key. Its counterpart is **fputchar( )** (or its equivalent **putchar( )** macro) which displays a character on the screen. Their usage is shown in the following program:

```
# include <stdio.h>
int main( )
{
    char ch ;
    printf ( "\nType any alphabet" ) ;
    ch = getchar( ) ; /* must be followed by enter key */
    printf ( "You typed " ) ;
    putchar ( ch ) ;
    return 0 ;
}
```

With **fgetchar( )** you need to hit the Enter key before the function can digest what you have typed. However, we may want a function that will read a single character the instant it is typed without waiting for the Enter key to be hit. There is no standard function to achieve this and there are different solutions for different OS.

Compilers like Turbo C and Visual Studio provide function called **getch( )** to achieve this. Its prototype is present in the file **conio.h**. This function reads a single character from keyboard. But it does not use any buffer, so the entered character is immediately returned without waiting for the enter key. In Linux-based systems the same effect can be obtained by doing some terminal settings using **stty** command.

gets( ) and *puts( )*

gets( ) receives a string from the keyboard. It is terminated when an Enter key is hit. Thus, spaces and tabs are perfectly acceptable as part of the input string. More exactly, **gets( )** function gets a newline (**\n**) terminated string of characters from the keyboard and replaces the **\n** with a **\0**. The **puts( )** function works exactly opposite to **gets( )** function. It outputs a string to the screen.

Here is a program which illustrates the usage of these functions.

```
# include <stdio.h>
int main( )
{
    char  footballer[ 40 ] ;
    puts ( "Enter name" ) ;
    gets ( footballer ) ;  /* sends base address of array */
    puts ( "Happy footballing!" ) ;
    puts ( footballer ) ;
    return 0 ;
}
```

Following is the sample output:

```
Enter name
Lionel Messi
Happy footballing!
Lionel Messi
```

Why did we use two **puts( )** functions to print "Happy footballing!" and "Lionel Messi"? Because, unlike **printf( ), puts( )** can output only one string at a time. If we attempt to print two strings using **puts( ),** only the first one gets printed. Similarly, unlike **scanf( ), gets( )** can be used to read only one string at a time.

A word of caution! While using **gets( )** if the length of the input string is bigger than the size of the string passed to **gets( )** then we may end up exceeding the bounds of the string, which is dangerous. This can be avoided using **fgets( )** function as shown below:

```
char str[ 20 ] ;
puts ( "Enter a string: " ) ;
fgets ( str, 20, stdin ) ;
puts ( str ) ;
```

Here is the sample interaction with this code snippet...

```
Enter a string:
It is safe to use fgets than gets
It is safe to use f
```

Note that only 19 characters were stored in **str[ ]** followed by a '\0'. So, bounds of the string were not exceeded. Here **stdin** represents standard input device, i.e., keyboard.

Exercises

[A] What will be the output of the following programs?

(a)
```
# include <stdio.h>
# include <ctype.h>
int main( )
{
    char ch ;
    ch = getchar( ) ;
    if ( islower ( ch ) )
        putchar ( toupper ( ch ) ) ;
    else
        putchar ( tolower ( ch ) ) ;
    return 0 ;
}
```

(b)
```
# include <stdio.h>
int main( )
{
    int i = 2 ;
    float f = 2.5367 ;
    char str[ ] = "Life is like that" ;
    printf ( "%4d\t%3.3f\t%4s\n", i, f, str ) ;
```

```
    return 0 ;
}
```

(c)
```
# include <stdio.h>
int main( )
{
    printf ( "More often than \b\b not \rthe person who \
              wins is the one who thinks he can!\n" ) ;
    return 0 ;
}
```

(d)
```
# include <conio.h>
char p[ ] = "The sixth sick sheikh's sixth ship is sick" ;
int main( )
{
    int i = 0 ;
    while ( p[ i ] != '\0' )
    {
        putchar ( p[ i ] ) ;
        i++ ;
    }
    return 0 ;
}
```

[B] Point out the errors, if any, in the following programs:

(a)
```
# include <stdio.h>
int main( )
{
    int i ;
    char a[ ] = "Hello" ;
    while ( a != '\0' )
    {
        printf ( "%c", *a ) ;
        a++ ;
    }
    return 0 ;
}
```

(b)
```
# include <stdio.h>
int main( )
{
    double dval ;
```

```
    scanf ( "%f", &dval ) ;
    printf ( "Double Value = %lf\n", dval ) ;
    return 0 ;
}
```

(c)
```
# include <stdio.h>
int main( )
{
    int ival ;
    scanf ( "%d\n", &n ) ;
    printf ( "Integer Value = %d\n", ival ) ;
    return 0 ;
}
```

(d)
```
# include <stdio.h>
int main( )
{
    int dd, mm, yy ;
    printf ( "Enter date in dd/mm/yy or dd-mm-yy format\n" ) ;
    scanf ( "%d%*c%d%*c%d", &dd, &mm, &yy ) ;
    printf ( "The date is: %d - %d - %d\n", dd, mm, yy ) ;
    return 0 ;
}
```

(e)
```
# include <stdio.h>
int main( )
{
    char text ;
    sprintf ( text, "%4d\t%2.2f\n%s", 12, 3.452, "Merry Go Round" ) ;
    printf ( "%s\n", text ) ;
    return 0 ;
}
```

(f)
```
# include <stdio.h>
int main( )
{
    char buffer[ 50 ] ;
    int no = 97;
    double val = 2.34174 ;
    char name[ 10 ] = "Shweta" ;
    sprintf ( buffer, "%d %lf %s", no, val, name ) ;
    printf ( "%s\n", buffer ) ;
    sscanf ( buffer, "%4d %2.2lf %s", &no, &val, name ) ;
```

```
    printf ( "%s\n", buffer ) ;
    printf ( "%d %lf %s\n", no, val, name ) ;
    return 0 ;
}
```

[C] Answer the following questions:

(a) To receive the string "We have got the guts, you get the glory!!" in an array **char str[100]** which of the following functions would you use?

1. scanf ("%s", str) ;
2. gets (str) ;
3. getchar (str) ;
4. fgetchar (str) ;

(b) If an integer is to be entered through the keyboard, which function would you use?

1. scanf( )
2. gets( )
3. getche( )
4. getchar( )

(c) Which of the following can a format string of a **printf( )** function contain:

1. Characters, format specifications and escape sequences
2. Character, integers and floats
3. Strings, integers and escape sequences
4. Inverted commas, percentage sign and backslash character

(d) The purpose of the field-width specifier in a **printf( )** function is to:

1. Control the margins of the program listing
2. Specify the maximum value of a number
3. Control the size of font used to print numbers
4. Specify how many columns should be used to print the number

(e) If we are to display the following output properly aligned which format specifiers would you use?

```
Discovery of India            Jawaharlal Nehru       425.50
My Experiments with Truth     Mahatma Gandhi         375.50
Sunny Days                    Sunil Gavaskar          95.50
One More Over                 Erapalli Prasanna       85.00
```

KanNotes

- I/O in C is always done using functions, not using keywords
- All I/O functions can be divided into 2 broad categories :

  1) Console I/O functions : a) Formatted b) Unformatted
  2) Disk I/O functions
- The formatted console I/O functions can force the user to receive the input in a fixed format and display the output in a fixed format.
- All formatted Console I/O is done using printf() and scanf()
- Examples of formatting :

  %20s – right-align a string in 20 columns
  %-10d – left-align an integer in 10 columns
  %12.4f – right-align a float in 12 columns with 4 places beyond decimal point
- Escape sequences :

  \n - positions cursor on next line
  \r - positions cursor at beginning of same line
  When we hit enter \r is generated and is converted into \r\n
  \t - positions cursor at beginning of next print zone. 1 print zone = 8 columns
  \v – positions cursor in the next line below current cursor position
  \', \", \?, \\ - produces ' " ? \ in the output
  \xhh – represents ASCII character in hexadecimal notation
- scanf( ) can contain format specifier like %10.2f, but it is too restrictive, hence rarely used
- Unformatted console I/O functions :

  char - fgetchar(), fputchar(). fgetchar() - Waits for enter
  int / float - no functions
  string - gets(), puts(), fgets(), fputs()

19 File Input / Output

"Save in file, what you will need in future"

Once you know how to read / write data from / to file, you have crossed a major hurdle. With this knowledge under your belt, you will be able to write many useful programs. This chapter shows you how...

Contents

Often data is so large that all of it cannot be stored in memory and only a limited amount of it can be displayed on the screen. Also, memory is volatile and its contents would be lost once the program is terminated. At such times, it becomes necessary to store the data in a 'file' on disk so that it can be later retrieved, used and displayed either in part or in whole. This chapter discusses how file I/O operations can be performed.

File Operations

There are different operations that can be carried out on a file. These are:

(a) Creation of a new file
(b) Opening an existing file
(c) Reading from a file
(d) Writing to a file
(e) Moving to a specific location in a file (seeking)
(f) Closing a file

Let us write a program to read a file and display its contents on the screen. We will first list the program and show what it does, and then dissect it line-by-line. Here is the listing...

```
/* Display contents of a file on screen. */
# include <stdio.h>
int main( )
{
    FILE *fp ;
    char ch ;
    fp = fopen ( "PR1.C", "r" ) ;
    while ( 1 )
    {
        ch = fgetc ( fp ) ;
        if ( ch == EOF )
            break ;
        printf ( "%c", ch ) ;
    }
    printf ( "\n" ) ;
    fclose ( fp ) ;
    return 0 ;
}
```

On execution of this program, it displays the contents of the file 'PR1.C' on the screen. Let us now understand how it does the same.

Opening a File

The basic logic of the program is as follows:

(a) Read a character from file.

(b) Display the character read on the screen.

(c) Repeat steps (a) and (b) for all characters in the file.

It would be quite inefficient to access the disk every time we want to read a character from it. It would be more sensible to read the contents of the file into a buffer (a chunk in memory) while opening the file and then read the file character by character from the buffer rather than from the disk. This is shown in Figure 19.1.

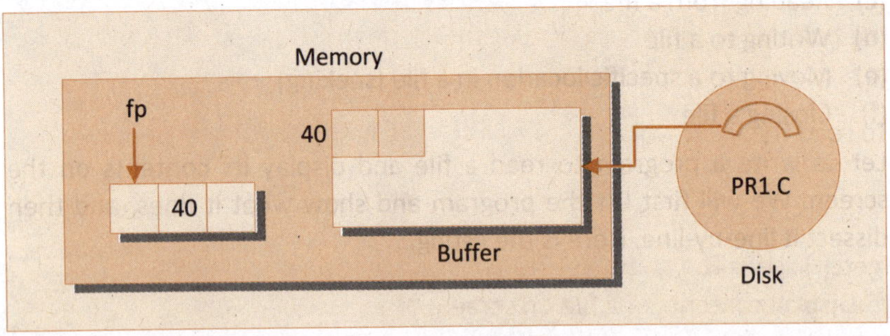

Figure 19.1 File read operation.

Same argument also applies to writing information in a file. Instead of writing characters in the file on the disk one character at a time, it would be more efficient to write characters in a buffer and then finally transfer the contents from the buffer to the disk.

Before we can read (or write) information from (to) a file on a disk we must open the file. To open the file we have called the function **fopen( )**. It would open a file **"PR1.C"** in **'read'** mode since we intend to read the file contents. In fact **fopen( )** performs three important tasks when you open the file in **"r"** mode:

(a) It locates the file to be opened, on the disk.

(b) It loads the file from the disk into a buffer.

(c) It sets up a character pointer which points to the first character of the buffer.

(d) It sets up a **FILE** structure and returns its address.

Let us understand the purpose of the **FILE** structure. To be able to successfully read from a file, information like mode of opening, size of file, place in the file from where the next read operation would be performed, etc., must be maintained. Since all this information is inter-related, all of it is set by **fopen( )** in a structure called **FILE**. **fopen( )** returns the address of this structure, which we have collected in the structure pointer **fp**. We have declared **fp** as follows:

```
FILE *fp ;
```

The **FILE** structure has been declared in the header file "stdio.h" (standing for standard input/output header file).

Reading from a File

A call to **fopen( )** sets up a pointer that points to the first character in the buffer. This pointer is one of the elements of the structure to which **fp** is pointing (refer Figure 19.1).

To read the file's contents from buffer we have called **fgetc( )** as under.

```
ch = fgetc ( fp ) ;
```

fgetc( ) reads the character from the current pointer position, advances the pointer position so that it now points to the next character, and returns the character that is read, which we have collected in the variable **ch**. Note that once the file has been opened, we no longer refer to the file by its name, but through the file pointer **fp**.

We have used the function **fgetc( )** in an infinite **while** loop. We should break out of this loop when all the characters from the file have been read. But how would we know this? Well, **fgetc( )** returns a macro EOF (End of File), once all the characters have been read and we attempt to read one more character. The EOF macro is defined in the file "stdio.h".

Closing the File

When we have finished reading from the file, we need to close it. This is done using the function **fclose( )** through the statement,

```
fclose ( fp ) ;
```

Once we close the file, we can no longer read from it using **fgetc( )**. Note that to close the file, we don't use the filename but the file pointer **fp**.

On closing the file, the buffer associated with the file is removed from memory.

In this program we have opened the file for reading. Suppose we open a file with an intention to write characters into it. This time too, a buffer would get associated with it. When we attempt to write characters into this file using **fputc( )** the characters would get written to the buffer. When we close this file using **fclose( )** two operations would be performed:

(a) The characters in the buffer would be written to the file on the disk.
(b) The buffer would be eliminated from memory.

You can imagine a possibility when the buffer may become full before we close the file. In such a case the buffer's contents would be written to the disk the moment it becomes full. This buffer management is done for us by the library functions.

Counting Characters, Tabs, Spaces, ...

Having understood the first file I/O program, let us write a program that will read a file and count how many characters, spaces, tabs and newlines are present in it. Here is the program...

```
/* Count chars, spaces, tabs and newlines in a file */
# include <stdio.h>
int main( )
{
    FILE *fp ;
    char ch ;
    int nol = 0, not = 0, nob = 0, noc = 0 ;
    fp = fopen ( "PR1.C", "r" ) ;
    while ( 1 )
    {
        ch = fgetc ( fp ) ;
        if ( ch == EOF )
            break ;
        noc++ ;
        if ( ch == ' ' )
            nob++ ;
        if ( ch == '\n' )
            nol++ ;
        if ( ch == '\t' )
            not++ ;
```

```
    }
    fclose ( fp ) ;
    printf ( "Number of characters = %d\n", noc ) ;
    printf ( "Number of blanks = %d\n", nob ) ;
    printf ( "Number of tabs = %d\n", not ) ;
    printf ( "Number of lines = %d\n", nol ) ;
    return 0 ;
}
```

Here is a sample run...

```
Number of characters = 125
Number of blanks = 25
Number of tabs = 13
Number of lines = 22
```

The above statistics are true for a file "PR1.C", which I had on my disk. You may give any other filename and obtain different results. I believe the program is self-explanatory. In this program too, we have opened the file for reading and then read it character-by-character. Let us now try a program that needs to open a file for writing.

A File-Copy Program

We have already used the function **fgetc( )** which reads characters from a file. Its counterpart is a function called **fputc( )** which writes characters to a file. As a practical use of these character I/O functions, we can copy the contents of one file into another, as demonstrated in the following program. This program reads the contents of a file and copies them into another file, character-by-character.

```
# include <stdio.h>
# include <stdlib.h>
int main( )
{
    FILE *fs, *ft ;
    char ch ;
    fs = fopen ( "PR1.C", "r" ) ;
    if ( fs == NULL )
    {
        puts ( "Cannot open source file" ) ; exit ( 1 ) ;
    }
    ft = fopen ( "PR2.C", "w" ) ;
```

```
    if ( ft == NULL )
    {
        puts ( "Cannot open target file" ) ;
        fclose ( fs ) ; exit ( 2 ) ;
    }
    while ( 1 )
    {
        ch = fgetc ( fs ) ;
        if ( ch == EOF )
            break ;
        else
            fputc ( ch, ft ) ;
    }
    fclose ( fs ) ; fclose ( ft ) ;
    return 0 ;
}
```

There is a possibility that when we try to open a file using the function **fopen( )**, the file may not be opened. While opening the file in "**r**" mode, this may happen because the file being opened may not be present on the disk at all. And you obviously cannot read a file that does not exist.

Similarly, while opening the file for writing, **fopen( )** may fail due to a number of reasons, like, disk space may be insufficient to create a new file, or you may not have write permission to the disk or the disk is damaged and so on.

If **fopen( )** fails to open a file it returns a value NULL (defined in "stdio.h" as **#define NULL 0**). In this program we have handled this possibility by checking whether **fs** and **ft** are set to NULL. If any of them has been set to NULL we have called the **exit( )** function to terminate the execution of the program.

Usually, a value 0 is passed to **exit( )** if the program termination is normal. A non-zero value indicates an abnormal termination of the program. If there are multiple exit points in the program, then the value passed to **exit( )** can be used to find out from where the execution of the program got terminated.

The **fputc( )** function writes a character to a file pointed to by **ft**. The writing process continues till all characters from the source file have been written to the target file, following which the **while** loop terminates.

Note that this file-copy program can copy only text files. To copy binary files with extension .EXE or .JPG, we need to open the files in binary mode, which is dealt with in detail in a later section.

File Opening Modes

Following is a list of modes in which a file can be opened along with the tasks performed by **fopen( )** when the file is opened.

"r" Searches file. If file is opened successfully **fopen( )** loads it into memory and sets up a pointer which points to the first character in it. If the file cannot be opened, **fopen( )** returns NULL.

Operations possible – reading from the file.

"w" Searches file. If the file exists, its contents are overwritten. If the file does not exist, a new file is created. Returns NULL, if unable to open file.

Operations possible – writing to the file.

"a" Searches file. If file is opened successfully **fopen( )** loads it into memory and sets up a pointer that points to the last character in it. If the file does not exist, a new file is created. Returns NULL, if unable to open file.

Operations possible - adding new contents at the end of file.

"r+" Searches file. If file is opened successfully **fopen( )** loads it into memory and sets up a pointer that points to the first character in it. Returns NULL, if unable to open the file.

Operations possible - reading existing contents, writing new contents, modifying existing contents of the file.

"w+" Searches file. If the file exists, its contents are overwritten. If the file does not exist, a new file is created. Returns NULL, if unable to open file.

Operations possible - writing new contents, reading them back and modifying existing contents of the file.

"a+" Searches file. If file is opened successfully **fopen( )** loads it into memory and sets up a pointer that points to the first character in it. If the file does not exist, a new file is created. Returns NULL, if unable to open file.

Operations possible - reading existing contents, appending new contents to end of file. Cannot modify existing contents.

String (Line) I/O in Files

For many purposes, character I/O is just what is needed. However, in some situations, the usage of functions that read or write entire strings might turn out to be more efficient. Here is a program that writes strings to a file using **fputs( )** and then reads them back using **fgets( )**.

```
/* Receives strings from keyboard and writes them to file */
# include <stdio.h>
# include <stdlib.h>
# include <string.h>
int main( )
{
    FILE *fp ;
    char str[ 80 ] ;
    fp = fopen ( "POEM.TXT", "w" ) ;
    if ( fp == NULL )
    {
        puts ( "Cannot open file" ) ; exit ( 1 ) ;
    }
    printf ( "\nEnter a few lines of text:\n" ) ;
    while ( strlen ( gets ( str ) ) > 0 )
    {
        fputs ( str, fp ) ; fputs ( "\n", fp ) ;
    }
    fclose ( fp ) ;

    /* read the file back */
    printf ( "\nFile contents are being read now...\n" , s ) ;
    fp = fopen ( "POEM.TXT", "r" ) ;
    if ( fp == NULL )
    {
        puts ( "Cannot open file" ) ; exit ( 2 ) ;
    }
    while ( fgets ( str, 79, fp ) != NULL )
        printf ( "%s" , str ) ;
    fclose ( fp ) ;
```

```
return 0 ;
}
```

And here is a sample run of the program...

```
Enter a few lines of text:
Shining and bright, they are forever,
so true about diamonds,
more so of memories,
especially yours!

File contents are being read now...
Shining and bright, they are forever,
so true about diamonds,
more so of memories,
especially yours!
```

During execution, after entering each string hit Enter. To terminate the execution of the loop, hit Enter at the beginning of a line. This creates a string of zero length, which the program recognizes as the signal to end the loop.

We have set up a character array **str** to receive a string; **fputs( )** function writes the contents of this array to the file. Since **fputs( )** does not automatically add a newline character to the end of the string, we must do this explicitly to make it easier to read the string back from the file.

While reading the file, the function **fgets( )** takes three arguments. The first argument is the address where the string is stored. The second argument is the maximum length of the string. This argument prevents **fgets( )** from reading in too long a string and overflowing the array. The third argument is the pointer to the structure **FILE**. On reading a line from the file, the string **str** would contain the line contents a '\n' followed by a '\0'. Thus the string is terminated by **fgets( )** and we do not have to terminate it specifically. When all the lines from the file have been read, we attempt to read one more line, in which case **fgets( )** returns a **NULL**.

Text Files and Binary Files

All the programs that we wrote in this chapter so far worked on text files. A text file contains only textual information like alphabets, digits and special symbols. A good example of a text file is any C program, say PR1.C.

As against this, a binary file is merely a collection of bytes. This collection might be a compiled version of a C program (say PR1.EXE), or music data stored in a MP4 file or a picture stored in a JPG file.

A very easy way to find out whether a file is a text file or a binary file is to open that file in Notepad. If on opening the file you can make out what is displayed then it is a text file, otherwise it is a binary file.

From the programming angle there are two main areas where text and binary mode files are different. These are discussed below.

Text versus Binary Mode: Newlines

In text mode, a newline character is converted into the carriage return-linefeed combination before being written to the file. Likewise, the carriage return-linefeed combination in the file is converted back into a newline when the file is read back. If a file is opened in binary mode, these conversions do not take place.

Text versus Binary Mode: Storage of Numbers

While using text mode, numbers are stored as character strings. Thus, an integer 12579 occupies 4 bytes in memory, but when written to the file it would occupy 5 bytes, 1 byte per character. Similarly, the floating-point number 1234.56 would occupy 7 bytes in file. Thus, numbers with more digits would require more storage space.

Hence if large amount of numerical data is to be stored in a disk file, using text mode may turn out to be inefficient. The solution is to open the file in binary mode and use functions **fread( )** and **fwrite( )** which work with numbers in binary format. As a result, each number would occupy same number of bytes on disk as it occupies in memory.

Record I/O in Files

Suppose we wish to perform I/O of data about employees from/to file. For this we would have to create a **struct employee** and then use the following functions to read/write employee data from/to file.

File opened in text mode - **fscanf( ) / fprintf( )**
File opened in binary mode - **fread( ) / fwrite( )**

Given below is the code snippet that shows how to use these functions. You may replace the comments with actual code to make it a fully workable program.

```
/* Writes / Reads records to / from a file in text / binary mode */
# include <stdio.h>
int main( )
{
    FILE *fp ;
    struct emp
    {
        char name[ 40 ] ; int age ; float bs ;
    } ;
    struct emp e ;
    char ch = 'Y' ;
    fp = fopen ( "EMPLOYEE.DAT", "w" ) ;
    while ( ch == 'Y' )
    {
        printf ( "Enter name, age, salary: " ) ;
        scanf ( "%s %d %f", e.name, &e.age, &e.bs ) ;
        fprintf ( fp, "%s %d %f\n", e.name, e.age, e.bs ) ;
        printf ( "Another record: " ) ;
        ch = fgetchar( ) ;
    }
    fclose ( fp ) ;
    fp = fopen ( "EMPLOYEE.DAT", "r" ) ;
    while ( fscanf ( fp, "%s %d %f", e.name, &e.age, &e.bs ) != EOF )
        printf ( "%s %d %f\n", e.name, e.age, e.bs ) ;
    fclose ( fp ) ;

    ch = 'Y' ;
    fp = fopen ( "EMP.DAT", "wb" ) ;
    while ( ch == 'Y' )
    {
        printf ( "Enter name, age, salary: " ) ;
        scanf ( "%s %d %f", e.name, &e.age, &e.bs ) ;
        fwrite ( &e, sizeof ( e ), 1, fp ) ;
        printf ( "Another record: " ) ;
        ch = fgetchar( ) ;
    }
    fclose ( fp ) ;
```

```
    fp = fopen ( "EMP.DAT", "rb" ) ;
    while ( fread ( &e, sizeof ( e ), 1, fp ) == 1 )
        printf ( "%s %d %f\n", e.name, e.age, e.bs ) ;
    fclose ( fp ) ;
    return 0 ;
}
```

Note that we have opened the binary file 'EMP.DAT' in "**rb**" and "**wb**" modes. While opening the file in text mode we can use either "**r**" or "**rt**", but since text mode is the default mode, we usually drop the '**t**'.

To read / write a record in a text mode file we have used **fscanf( )** and **fprintf( )** respectively. They work same as **scanf( )** and **printf( )** except that they have an additional first argument **fp**. This argument indicates the file on which they are supposed to work.

To read / write a record in a binary mode file we have used **fread( )** and **fwrite( )** respectively. Let us understand the following call:

```
fwrite ( &e, sizeof ( e ), 1, fp ) ;
```

Suppose the address of **e** is 400 and size of **e** is 48 bytes. So the above call means—starting with address 400, write next 48 bytes, once, into a file pointed to by **fp**.

Likewise, the call,

```
fwrite ( &e, sizeof ( e ), 1, fp ) ;
```

would mean—from a file pointed to by **fp**, read once, 48 bytes and store them at an address starting from 400.

The text file-based record I/O has two disadvantages:

(a) The numbers would occupy a greater number of bytes, as each number is stored as a character string.

(b) If the number of fields in the structure increase (say, by adding address, house rent allowance, etc.), writing structures using **fprintf( )**, or reading them using **fscanf( )**, would become tedious.

Modifying Records

We know how to read or write records from / to a binary mode fle. But what if we are to modify an existing record? Well, when we open a file **fopen( )** returns a pointer to a structure. This structure contains a pointer which points to the first record in the file. **fread( )** always reads a record from where the pointer is currently placed. Similarly, **fwrite( )** always writes a record where the pointer is currently placed. On using the function **fread( )** or **fwrite( )**, the pointer moves to the beginning of the next record. On closing a file, the pointer is deactivated.

The **rewind( )** function places the pointer to the beginning of the file, irrespective of where it is present right now. The **fseek( )** function lets us move the pointer from one record to another. These functions have been used in the following code to modify an existing record in a file.

```
int recsize ;
recsize = sizeof ( struct emp ) ;
printf ( "\nEnter name of employee to modify: " ) ;
scanf ( "%s", empname ) ;
rewind ( fp ) ;
while ( fread ( &e, recsize, 1, fp ) == 1 )
{
    if ( strcmp ( e.name, empname ) == 0 )
    {
        printf ( "\nEnter new name, age & bs " ) ;
        scanf ( "%s %d %f", e.name, &e.age, &e.bs ) ;
        fseek ( fp, -recsize, SEEK_CUR ) ;
        fwrite ( &e, recsize, 1, fp ) ;
        break ;
    }
}
```

To move the pointer to the previous record from its current position, we have used the function,

```
fseek ( fp, -recsize, SEEK_CUR ) ;
```

-recsize moves the pointer back by **recsize** bytes from the current position. **SEEK_CUR** is a macro defined in "stdio.h".

Similarly, if we wish to place the pointer beyond the last record in the file, we can use

```
fseek ( fp, 0, SEEK_END ) ;
```

In fact, -**recsize** or **0** are just the offsets that tell the compiler by how many bytes should the pointer be moved from a reference position. The reference position could be **SEEK_END**, **SEEK_CUR** or **SEEK_SET**. **SEEK_END** means move the pointer from the end of the file, **SEEK_CUR** means move the pointer with reference to its current position and **SEEK_SET** means move the pointer with reference to the beginning of the file.

Once the pointer has been properly positioned, we have written a new record that overwrites an existing record.

If we wish to know where the pointer is positioned right now, we can use the function **ftell( )**. It returns this position as a **long int** which is an offset from the beginning of the file. A sample call to **ftell( )** is shown below.

```
long int  position ;
position = ftell ( fp ) ;
```

Low-Level File I/O

In low-level File I/O, data cannot be written as individual characters, or as strings or as formatted data. There is only one way to read/write data in low-level file I/O functions—as a buffer full of bytes.

Writing a buffer full of data resembles the **fwrite( )** function. However, unlike **fwrite( )**, the programmer must set up the buffer for the data, place the appropriate values in it before writing, and take them out after writing. Thus, the buffer in the low-level I/O functions is part of the program, rather than being invisible as in high-level file I/O functions.

Low-level file I/O functions offer following advantages:

(a) Since these functions parallel the methods that the OS uses to write to the disk, they are more efficient than high-level file I/O functions.

(b) Since there are fewer layers of routines to go through, low-level I/O functions operate faster than their high-level counterparts.

Let us now write a program that uses low-level file input/output functions.

A Low-level File-copy Program

Earlier we had written a program to copy the contents of one file to another on a character-by-character basis. We can rewrite the same program to read a chunk of bytes from the source file and then write this chunk into the target file. While doing so, the chunk would be read into the buffer and would be written to the file from the buffer. We would manage the buffer ourselves, rather than relying on the library functions to do so. This is what is low-level about this program. Here is a program which shows how this can be done.

```
/* File-copy program which copies text, .com and .exe files */
# include <fcntl.h>
# include <sys\types.h>   /* use sys/types.h for Linux */
# include <sys\stat.h>    /* use sys/stat.h for Linux */
# include <stdlib.h>
# include <stdio.h>
int main( )
{
    char  buffer[ 512 ], source[ 128  ], target[ 128  ] ;
    int  in, out, bytes ;
    printf ( "\nEnter source file name: " ) ;
    gets ( source ) ;
    in = open ( source, O_RDONLY | O_BINARY ) ;
    if ( in == -1 )
    {
        puts ( "Cannot open file" ) ;  exit ( 1 ) ;
    }
    printf ( "\nEnter target file name: " ) ;
    gets ( target ) ;
    out = open ( target, O_CREAT | O_BINARY | O_WRONLY, S_IWRITE) ;
    if ( out == -1 )
    {
        puts ( "Cannot open file" ) ;
        close ( in ) ;  exit ( 2 ) ;
    }
    while ( ( bytes = read ( in, buffer, 512 ) ) > 0 )
        write ( out, buffer, bytes ) ;
    close ( in ) ;  close ( out ) ;
    return 0 ;
}
```

Declaring the Buffer

The first difference that you will notice in this program is that we declare a character buffer,

```
char  buffer[ 512 ] ;
```

This is the buffer in which the data read from the file will be placed. The size of this buffer is important for efficient operation. Depending on the operating system, buffers of certain sizes are handled more efficiently than others.

Opening a File

We have opened two files in our program, one is the source file from which we read the information, and the other is the target file into which we write the information read from the source file.

As in high-level file I/O, the file must be opened before we can access it. This is done using the statement,

```
in = open ( source, O_RDONLY | O_BINARY ) ;
```

As usual, we have to supply to **open( )**, the filename and the mode in which we want to open the file. The possible file opening modes are given below.

O_APPEND - Opens a file for appending

O_CREAT - Creates a new file for writing (no effect if file exists)

O_RDONLY - Opens a new file for reading only

O_RDWR - Creates a file for both reading and writing

O_WRONLY - Creates a file for writing only

O_BINARY - Opens a file in binary mode

O_TEXT - Opens a file in text mode

These 'O-flags' are defined in the file "fcntl.h". So, this file must be included in the program while using low-level file I/O. When two or more O-flags are used together, they are combined using the bitwise OR operator (|). Chapter 21 discusses bitwise operators in detail.

The other statement used in our program to open the file is,

```
out = open ( target, O_CREAT | O_BINARY | O_WRONLY, S_IWRITE ) ;
```

Note that since the target file does not exist when it is being opened, we have used the O_CREAT flag, and since we want to write to the file, we have used O_WRONLY. And finally, since we want to open the file in binary mode, we have used O_BINARY.

Whenever O_CREAT flag is used, another argument must be added to **open( )** function to indicate the read/write status of the file to be created. This argument is called 'permission argument'. Permission arguments could be any of the following:

S_IWRITE - Writing to the file permitted
S_IREAD - Reading from the file permitted

To use these permissions, both the files "types.h" and "stat.h" present in "sys" folder must be **#include**d in the program along with "fcntl.h".

File Handles

Instead of returning a FILE pointer as **fopen( )** did, in low-level file I/O, **open( )** returns an integer value called 'file handle'. This is a number assigned to a particular file, which is used thereafter to refer to the file. If **open( )** returns a value of -1, it means that the file couldn't be successfully opened.

Interaction between Buffer and File

The following statement reads the file or as much of it as will fit into the buffer:

```
bytes = read ( in, buffer, 512 )
```

Here the first argument is file handle, the second is the address of the buffer and the third is the maximum number of bytes we want to read.

For copying the file, we must use both the **read( )** and the **write( )** functions in a **while** loop. The **read( )** function returns the number of bytes actually read. This is assigned to the variable **bytes**. This variable is used to tell **write( )** how many bytes to write from the buffer to the target file.

P</> Programs

Problem 19.1

Write a program to read a file and display its contents along with line numbers before each line.

Program

```
/* Program to display a file with line numbers */
```

```
# include <stdio.h>
# include <stdlib.h>
int main( )
{
    FILE *fp ;
    char ch, source[ 67 ] ; /* max path length for some OS is 66 chars */
    int count = 1 ;
    printf ( "\nEnter file name: " ) ;
    scanf ( "%s", source ) ;
    fp = fopen ( source, "r" ) ;
    if ( fp == NULL )
    {
        puts ( "Unable to open the file." ) ; exit ( 0 ) ;
    }
    printf ( "\n%3d: ", count ) ;
    while ( ( ch = getc( fp ) ) != EOF )
    {
        if ( ch == '\n' )
        {
            count++ ;
            printf ( "\n%3d: ", count ) ;
        }
        else
            printf ( "%c", ch ) ;
    }
    fclose ( fp ) ;
    return 0 ;
}
```

Output

```
Enter the file name: Sample.txt
  1: What is this life
  2: if full of care
  3: We have no time
  4: to stand and stare!
```

Problem 19.2

Write a program to append the contents of one file at the end of another.

Program

```
/* Append contents of one file at the end of another */
# include <stdio.h>
# include <stdlib.h>
# include <string.h>
int main( )
{
    FILE *fs, *ft ;
    char  source[ 67 ], target[ 67 ], str[ 80 ] ;
    puts ( "Enter source file name: " ) ;
    gets ( source ) ;
    puts ( "Enter target file name: " ) ;
    gets ( target ) ;
    fs = fopen ( source, "r" ) ;
    if ( fs == NULL )
    {
        puts ( "Unable to open source file" ) ; exit ( 0 ) ;
    }
    ft = fopen ( target, "a" ) ;
    if ( ft == NULL )
    {
        fclose ( fs ) ;
        puts ( "Unable to open target file" ) ; exit ( 0 ) ;
    }
    while ( fgets ( str, 79, fs ) != NULL )
        fputs ( str, ft ) ;
    printf ( "Appending file completed!!" ) ;
    fclose ( fs ) ;
    fclose ( ft ) ;
    return 0 ;
}
```

Output

```
Enter source file name:
Sample.txt
Enter target file name:
NewSample.txt
Appending file completed!!
```

Exercises

[A] Answer the following questions:

(a) In which file FILE structure is defined?

(b) If a file contains the line "I am a boy\r\n" then on reading this line into the array **str[ ]** using **fgets( )** what would **str[ ]** contain?

(c) State True or False:

1. The disadvantage of high-level file I/O functions is that the programmer has to manage the file buffers.
2. If a file is opened for reading, it is necessary that the file must exist.
3. If a file opened for writing already exists, its contents would be overwritten.
4. For opening a file in append mode it is necessary that the file should exist.

(d) On opening a file for reading which of the following activities are performed:

1. The disk is searched for existence of the file.
2. The file contents are brought into memory.
3. A pointer is set up which points to the first character in the file.
4. All the above.

(e) Is it necessary that a file created in text mode must always be opened in text mode for subsequent operations?

[B] Attempt the following questions:

(a) Suppose a file contains student records with each record containing name and age of a student. Write a program to read these records and display them in sorted order by name.

(b) Write a program to copy contents of one file to another. While doing so replace all lowercase characters to their equivalent uppercase characters.

(c) Write a program that merges lines alternately from two files and writes the results to a new file. If one file has a smaller number of lines than the other, the remaining lines from the larger file should be simply copied into the target file.

(d) Write a program to encrypt/decrypt a file using:

(1) Offset cipher: In this cipher each character from the source file is offset with a fixed value and then written to the target file.

For example, if character read from the source file is 'A', then write a character represented by 'A' + 128 to the target file.

(2) Substitution cipher: In this cipher for each character read from the source file a corresponding predetermined character is written to the target file.

For example, if character 'A' is read from the source file, then a '!' would be written to the target file. Similarly, every 'B' would be substituted by '5' and so on.

(e) In the file 'CUSTOMER.DAT' there are 10 records with the following structure:

```
struct customer
{
   int accno ; char name[ 30 ] ; float balance ;
} ;
```

In another file 'TRANSACTIONS.DAT' there are several records with the following structure:

```
struct trans
{
   int accno ; char trans_type ; float amount ;
} ;
```

The element **trans_type** contains D/W indicating deposit or withdrawal of amount. Write a program to update 'CUSTOMER.DAT' file, i.e., if the **trans_type** is 'D' then update the **balance** of 'CUSTOMER.DAT' by adding **amount** to balance for the corresponding **accno**. Similarly, if **trans_type** is 'W' then subtract the **amount** from **balance**. However, while subtracting the amount ensure that the amount should not get overdrawn, i.e., at least 100 Rs. should remain in the account.

(f) There are 10 records present in a file with the following structure:

```
struct date { int d, m, y ; } ;
struct employee
{
   int empcode[ 6 ] ; char empname[ 20 ] ;
```

```
    struct date join_date ; float salary ;
} ;
```

Write a program to read these records, arrange them in ascending order by **join_date** and write them to a target file.

(g) A hospital keeps a file of blood donors in which each record has the format:

Name: 20 columns Address: 40 columns
Age: 2 columns Blood Type: 1 column (Type 1, 2, 3 or 4)

Write a program to read the file and print a list of all blood donors whose age is below 25 and whose blood type is 2.

(h) Given a list of names of students in a class, write a program to store the names in a file on disk. Make a provision to display the **n**th name in the list, where **n** is read from the keyboard.

(i) Assume that a Master file contains two fields—roll number and name of the student. At the end of the year, a set of students join the class and another set leaves. A Transaction file contains the roll numbers and an appropriate code to add or delete a student.

Write a program to create another file that contains the updated list of names and roll numbers. Assume that the Master file and the Transaction file are arranged in ascending order by roll numbers. The updated file should also be in ascending order by roll numbers.

(j) Given a text file, write a program to create another text file deleting the words "a", "the", "an" and replacing each one of them with a blank space.

KanNotes

- File I/O functions :
  a) High level :
     1) Text mode - (i) Formatted (ii) Unformatted
     2) Binary mode
  b) Low Level
- High level text mode formatted file I/O functions: fprintf(), fscanf()
- High level text mode, unformatted file I/O functions :

  char - fgetc(), fputc()

int, float - no functions
string - fgets(), fputs()

- I/O is always done using a buffer of suitable size

  High level file I/O functions manage the buffer themselves
  While using Low level file I/O functions we have to manage the buffer

- Functions to open and close a file :

  High level - fopen(), fclose()
  Low level - open(), close()

- FILE *fp = fopen ("temp.dat", "r") ;

  FILE is a structure declared in stdio.h
  fopen() - Creates buffer, Creates structure
  - Returns address of structure which is assigned to fp

- ch = fgetc (fp) ; - Reads char, Shifts pointer to next char
  Returns ASCII value of character read
  Returns EOF if no character is left for reading

- To read a file character by character till we do not reach the end :

  while ((ch = fgetc (fp)) != EOF)

- To read a file line by line till we do not reach the end :

  char str[80] ;
  while (fgets (fp, str, 79) != NULL)

- EOF and NULL are macros defined in stdio.h

  #define EOF -1
  #define NULL 0

- fopen() :

  To open file for reading in text mode - "rt" or "r"
  To open file for writing in text mode - "wt" or "w"
  To open file for reading in binary mode - "rb"
  To open file for writing in binary mode - "wb"

- Difference :

  fs = fopen (s,"r") ; - Returns NULL if file is absent

```
                              Returns address of FILE structure, if present
ft = fopen ( t, "w" ) ; - Creates new file if file is absent
                              Overwrites file, if present
fclose ( fs ) ; - Vacates the buffer
fclose ( ft ) ; - Writes buffer to disk, vacates the buffer
```

- To read / write record to a file in text mode :

```
struct emp e = { "Ajay", 24, 4500.50 } ;
fprintf ( fp, "%s %d %f\n", e.name, e.age, e.sal ) ;
 while ( fscanf ( fp, "%s %d %f\n", e.name, &e.age, &e.sal ) != EOF)
```

- To read / write record to a file in binary mode :

```
struct emp e = { "Ajay", 24, 4500.50 } ;
fwrite ( &e, sizeof ( e ), 1, fp ) ;
while ( fread ( &e, sizeof ( e ), 1, fp ) != EOF )
```

- To move the pointer in a file ;

```
fseek ( fp, 512L, SEEK_SET ) ;
```

Moves the pointer 512 bytes from the beginning of file

- Other macros :

SEEK_END - from end of file

SEEK_CUR - from the current position of the pointer

- To read / write a buffer of 512 characters using low level file I/O functions :

```
int in, out ; char buffer[ 512 ] ;
out = open ( "trial.dat", O_WRONLY | O_BINARY | O_CREAT ) ;
in = open ( "sample.dat", O_RDONLY | O_BINARY ) ;
write ( out, buffer, 512 ) ;
n = read ( in, buffer, 512 ) ; /* n - no. of bytes read successfully */
```

- Include three files while doing low level file I/O :

```
#include <fcntl.h>
#include <sys\stat.h>
#include <sys\types.h>
```

20 More Issues In Input/Output

"More the merrier..."

Ever wondered how some programs can receive input at command-line itself? And how they can redirect their input and output with ease? Well, nothing great, that is, once you have gone through this chapter...

Contents

In Chapters 18 and 19 we saw how Console I/O and File I/O operations are done in C. There are still some more issues related with input/output that remain to be understood. These issues help in making the I/O operations more elegant.

Using *argc* and *argv*

While executing the file-copy program in Chapter 19, we are prompted to enter the source and target filenames. Instead of the program prompting us to enter these filenames, we should be able to supply them at command prompt, in the form:

```
filecopy PR1.C PR2.C
```

where, 'filecopy' is the executable form of our C program, 'PR1.C' is the source filename and 'PR2.C' is the target filename. The command prompt is C:\> if you are using command window, Search box if you are using Windows 10 and $ prompt if you are using Linux.

This improvement is possible by passing the source filename and target filename to the function **main( )**. This is illustrated in the program given below.

```
# include <stdio.h>
# include <stdlib.h>
int main ( int argc, char *argv[ ] )
{
    FILE *fs, *ft ;
    char ch ;
    if ( argc != 3 )
    {
        puts ( "Improper number of arguments\n" ) ;
        exit ( 1 ) ;
    }
    fs = fopen ( argv[ 1 ], "r" ) ;
    if ( fs == NULL )
    {
        puts ( "Cannot open source file\n" ) ;
        exit ( 2 ) ;
    }
    ft = fopen ( argv[ 2 ], "w" ) ;
    if ( ft == NULL )
    {
```

```
        puts ( "Cannot open target file\n" ) ;
        fclose ( fs ) ;
        exit ( 3 ) ;
    }
    while ( 1 )
    {
        ch = fgetc ( fs ) ;
        if ( ch == EOF )
            break ;
        else
            fputc ( ch, ft ) ;
    }
    fclose ( fs ) ;
    fclose ( ft ) ;
    return 0 ;
}
```

The arguments that we pass to **main( )** at the command prompt are called command-line arguments. The function **main( )** can have two arguments, traditionally named as **argc** and **argv**. Out of these, **argv** is an array of pointers to strings and **argc** is an **int** whose value is equal to the number of strings to which **argv** points.

When the program is executed, the strings on the command-line are passed to **main( )**. More precisely, the strings at the command-line are stored in memory and address of the first string is stored in **argv[0]**, address of the second string is stored in **argv[1]** and so on. The argument **argc** is set to the number of strings given at the command-line. For example, in our sample program, if at the command prompt we give,

```
filecopy  PR1.C  PR2.C
```

then,

```
argc would contain 3
argv[ 0 ] would contain base address of the string 'filecopy'
argv[ 1 ] would contain base address of the string 'PR1.C'
argv[ 2 ] would contain base address of the string 'PR2.C'
```

Whenever we pass arguments to **main( )**, it is a good habit to check whether the correct number of arguments have been passed to **main( )** or not. In our program this has been done through,

```
if ( argc != 3 )
{
    puts ( "Improper number of arguments\n" ) ;
    exit ( 1 ) ;
}
```

Rest of the program is same as the earlier file-copy program.

One final comment... the **while** loop that we have used in our program can be written in a more compact form, as shown below.

```
while ( ( ch = fgetc ( fs ) ) != EOF )
    fputc ( ch, ft ) ;
```

This avoids the usage of an indefinite loop and a **break** statement to terminate the loop. Here, first **fgetc (fs)** gets the character from the file, assigns it to the variable **ch**, and then **ch** is compared against **EOF**. Remember that it is necessary to put the expression

```
ch = fgetc ( fs )
```

within a pair of parentheses, so that first the character read is assigned to variable **ch** and then it is compared with **EOF**.

There is one more way of writing the **while** loop. It is shown below.

```
while ( !feof ( fs ) )
{
    ch = fgetc ( fs ) ;
    fputc ( ch, ft ) ;
}
```

Here, **feof( )** is a function that returns a 0 if end of file is not reached. Hence we use the **!** operator to negate this 0 to a truth value. When the end of file is reached, **feof( )** returns a non-zero value, **!** makes it 0 and since now the condition evaluates to false, the **while** loop gets terminated.

Note that the following three methods for opening a file are same, since in each one of them, essentially a base address of the string (pointer to a string) is being passed to **fopen( )**.

```
fs = fopen ( "PR1.C" , "r" ) ;
```

```
fs = fopen ( filename, "r" ) ;
fs = fopen ( argv[ 1 ] , "r" ) ;
```

Detecting Errors in Reading/Writing

Not at all times when we perform a read or write operation on a file, are we successful in doing so. So, there must be a provision to test whether our attempt to read/write was successful or not.

The standard library function **ferror( )** reports any error that might have occurred during a read/write operation on a file. It returns a zero if the read/write is successful and a non-zero value in case of a failure. The following program illustrates the usage of **ferror( )**:

```
# include <stdio.h>
int main( )
{
    FILE *fp ;
    char ch ;
    fp = fopen ( "TRIAL", "w" ) ;
    while ( !feof ( fp ) )
    {
        ch = fgetc ( fp ) ;
        if ( ferror( ) )
        {
            perror ( "TRIAL" ) ;
            break ;
        }
        else
            printf ( "%c", ch ) ;
    }
    fclose ( fp ) ;
    return 0 ;
}
```

In this program, the **fgetc( )** function would obviously fail first time around since the file has been opened for writing, whereas **fgetc( )** is attempting to read from the file. The moment the error occurs, **ferror( )** returns a non-zero value and the **if** block gets executed. Instead of printing the error message using **printf( )**, we have used the standard library function **perror( )** to print the error message.

When the error occurs, the error message that is displayed is:

```
TRIAL: Permission denied
```

This means we can precede the system error message with any message of our choice. In our program, we have just displayed the filename in place of the error message.

Standard File Pointers

To perform reading or writing operations on a file, we need to use **fopen( )** to set up a file pointer to refer to this file. Most OSs also predefine pointers for three standard files. To access these pointers, we need not use **fopen( )**. These standard file pointers are shown in Figure 20.1.

Standard File pointer	Description
stdin	Standard input device (Keyboard)
stdout	Standard output device (Monitor)
stderr	Standard error device (Monitor)

Figure 20.1 Standard file pointers.

So if we use the statement **ch = fgetc (stdin)**, it would read a character from the keyboard rather than from a file. We can use this statement without any need to use **fopen( )** or **fclose( )** function calls.

I/O Redirection

Most operating systems incorporate a powerful feature called I/O redirection that allows a program to read from and write to files, even when such a capability has not been incorporated in the program.

Normally a C program receives its input from the standard input device, which is assumed to be the keyboard, and sends its output to the standard output device, which is assumed to be the monitor. In other words, the OS makes certain assumptions about where input should come from and where output should go. Redirection permits us to change these assumptions.

For example, using redirection the output of the program that normally goes to the monitor can be sent to the disk or the printer without really making a provision for it in the program. This is often a more convenient and flexible approach than providing a separate function in the program to write to the disk or printer. Similarly, redirection can be used to read information from disk file directly into a program, instead of receiving the input from keyboard.

To use redirection facility, we need is to execute the program from the command prompt, inserting the redirection symbols at appropriate places. Let us understand this process with the help of a program.

Redirecting the Output

Let's see how we can redirect the output of a program, from the screen to a file. We'll start by considering the simple program shown below.

```
/* File name: util.c */
# include <stdio.h>
int main( )
{
    char ch ;
    while ( ( ch = fgetc ( stdin ) ) != EOF )
        fputc ( ch, stdout ) ;
    return 0 ;
}
```

On compiling this program, we would get an executable file UTIL.EXE. Normally, when we execute this file, the **fputc( )** function will cause whatever we type to be printed on screen, until we type Ctrl-Z, at which point the program will terminate, as shown in the following sample run. The Ctrl-Z character is often called end of file character.

```
C>UTIL.EXE
perhaps I had a wicked childhood,
perhaps I had a miserable youth,
but somewhere in my wicked miserable past,
there must have been a moment of truth ^Z
C>
```

Now let us see what happens when we invoke this program in a different way, using redirection:

```
C>UTIL.EXE  > POEM.TXT
C>
```

The redirection operator, '>', causes any output intended for the screen to be redirected to the file POEM.TXT. Can we prove that the output has indeed gone to the file POEM.TXT? Yes, by opening the file POEM.TXT in any editor. You would see the result of our typing sitting in this file.

Note that the data to be redirected to a file does not need to be typed by a user at the keyboard; the program itself can generate it. Any output normally sent to the screen can be redirected to a disk file. As an example, consider the following program for generating the ASCII table on screen:

```
/* File name: ascii.c*/
# include <stdio.h>
int main( )
{
    int ch ;
    for ( ch = 0 ; ch <= 255 ; ch++ )
        printf ( "%d %c\n", ch, ch ) ;
    return 0 ;
}
```

When this program is compiled and then executed at command prompt using the redirection operator,

```
C>ASCII.EXE > TABLE.TXT
```

the output is written to the file. This can be a useful capability any time you want to capture the output in a file, rather than displaying it on the screen.

Redirecting the Input

We can also redirect input to a program so that, instead of reading a character from the keyboard, a program reads it from a file. To redirect the input, we need to have a file containing some text. Suppose we use a file called NEWPOEM.TXT containing the following lines:

```
Let's start at the very beginning,
A very good place to start!
```

We will assume that using some text editor these lines have been placed in the file NEWPOEM.TXT. Now, we use the input redirection operator '<' before the file, as shown below.

```
C>UTIL.EXE < NEWPOEM.TXT
Let's start at the very beginning,
A very good place to start!
C>
```

The lines are printed on the screen with no further effort on our part.

Both Ways at Once

Redirection of input and output can be done together; the input for a program can come from a file via redirection, at the same time its output can be redirected to a file. Such a program is called a filter. The following command demonstrates this process:

```
C>UTIL.EXE < NEWPOEM.TXT > POETRY.TXT
```

In this case, our program receives the redirected input from the file NEWPOEM.TXT and instead of sending the output to the screen; it redirects it to the file POETRY.TXT.

While using such multiple redirections, do not try to send output to the same file from which you are receiving input. This is because the output file is erased before it is written to. So, by the time we manage to receive the input from a file, it is already erased.

Redirection can be a powerful tool for developing utility programs to examine or alter data in files. Another OS operator can be used to relate two programs directly, so that the output of one is fed directly into another, with no files involved. This is called 'piping', and is done using the operator '|', called pipe. We will not pursue this topic, but you can read about it in the OS Help.

Exercises

[A] Answer the following questions:

(a) How will you use the program given below to perform the following operations?

- Copy the contents of one file into another.
- Create a new file and add some text to it.
- Display the contents of an existing file.

```
# include <stdio.h>
```

```
int main( )
{
    char ch, str[ 10 ] ;
    while ( ( ch = fgetc ( stdin ) ) != -1 )
        fputc ( ch, stdout ) ;
    return 0 ;
}
```

(b) State True or False:

1. We can send arguments at command-line even if we define **main( )** function without parameters.
2. To use standard file pointers we don't need to open the file using **fopen( )**.
3. The zeroth element of **argv** array points to the name of the executable file.

(c) Write a program using command-line arguments to search for a word in a file and replace it with the specified word. The usage of the program is shown below.

C> change <old word> <new word> <filename>

(d) Write a program that can be used at command prompt as a calculating utility. The usage of the program is shown below.

C> calc <switch> <n> <m>

where, **n** and **m** are two integer operands and **switch** is either an arithmetic operator or a comparison operator. If arithmetic operator is supplied, the output should be the result of the operation. If comparison operator is supplied then the output should be **True** or **False**.

KanNotes

- C>, $ are called command prompts in Windows and Linux respectively
- Command-line arguments are arguments provided to main( ) from command-line
- Command-line args are collected in main() in variables argc and argv

  argc - Count of arguments
  argv - Vector (array) of arguments

Any variable names other than argc, argv are ok

- char *argv[ ] is an array of pointers to strings. So all arguments are received as strings and their addresses are stored in argv[ ]

- Errors in reading / writing from / to a file can be detected using ferror() and reported using perror() :

```
ch = fgetc ( fp ) ;
if ( ferror() )
    perror ( "Error while reading" ) ;
```

- Most OSs predefine pointers for three standard files :

  stdin - standard input device - keyboard
  stdout - standard output device - monitor
  stderr - standard error device - monitor

- To use and give up these pointers, we need not use fopen() and fclose()

- The statement ch = fgetc (stdin) would read a character from the keyboard

- If a program uses stdin then using < at command prompt input can be redirected to be received from a file

- If a program uses stdout and stderr then using > at command prompt output and error messages can be redirected to a file

- The operators < and > are called redirection operators

21 Operations On Bits

"Bit by bit, I take a byte..."

Char is one byte long, and char is the smallest entity that we can handle in a C program. But, at times, we may want to access or manipulate individual bits of a byte. How can this be done? Well, this chapter has the answer...

Contents

So far the smallest element in memory on which we were able to operate was a byte, i.e. a **char**. However, we have not attempted to look within a byte to see how it is constructed out of individual bits, and how these bits can be manipulated. Being able to operate on a bit-level, can be very important in programming, especially when a program must interact with the hardware. Let us now delve inside the byte and see how it is constructed and how it can be manipulated effectively.

Bit Numbering and Conversion

A bit (short for Binary Digit) is the most basic unit of information. It can take a value 0 or 1. 4 bits together form a nibble, 8 bits form a byte, 16 bits form a word and 32 bits form a double-word. Bits are numbered from zero onwards, increasing from right to left as shown in Figure 21.1.

C language understands decimal, octal and hexadecimal numbering systems. It does not understand binary numbering system. As against this, hardware understands only binary. Hence while programming a hardware, we are often required to convert the binary numbers into decimal or hexadecimal numbers. Let us see how this conversion can be done. Figure 21.1 shows how binary values 10110110 and 00111100 are converted to decimal numbers.

7	6	5	4	3	2	1	0
1	0	1	1	0	1	1	0

$0 * 2^0 + 1 * 2^1 + 1 * 2^2 + 0 * 2^3 + 1 * 2^4 + 1 * 2^5 + 0 * 2^6 + 1 * 2^7$

$= 2 + 4 + 16 + 32 + 128$

$= 182$

7	6	5	4	3	2	1	0
0	0	1	1	1	1	0	0

$0 * 2^0 + 0 * 2^1 + 1 * 2^2 + 1 * 2^3 + 1 * 2^4 + 1 * 2^5 + 0 * 2^6 + 0 * 2^7$

$= 4 + 8 + 16 + 32$

$= 60$

Figure 21.1 Conversion from Binary to Decimal.

As you can see from Figure 21.1, the binary to decimal conversion process involves remembering powers of 2. This is alright if the binary number is a 8-bit number, but if it is a 16-bit number then remembering powers like 2^{15}, 2^{14}, 2^{13}, etc., is difficult. A much easier method is to convert binary numbers to hexadecimal numbers. In hexadecimal numbering system each number is built using a combination of digits 0 to 9 and A to F. Digits A to F are symbols that are used to represent values 10 to 15. Each hexadecimal digit can be represented using a 4-bit nibble as shown in Figure 21.2.

Hex	Binary	Hex	Binary	Hex	Binary	Hex	Binary
0	0000	4	0100	8	1000	C	1100
1	0001	5	0101	9	1001	D	1101
2	0010	6	0110	A	1010	E	1110
3	0011	7	0111	B	1011	F	1111

Figure 21.2 Binary nibbles and their Hexadecimal equivalents.

Using Figure 21.2, it is very easy to convert binary values into their equivalent hexadecimal values. This is shown in Figure 21.3.

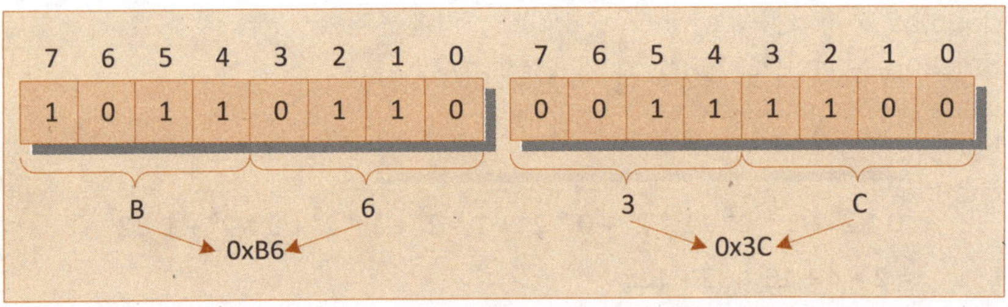

Figure 21.3 Binary to Hexadecimal conversion.

You would agree it is easier to represent the binary number in hex rather than in decimal as it involves neither multiplication nor addition. Quick now, what is binary 1100 in hex? That is right—C. You are already getting the feel of it. With a little practice, it is easy to translate even long numbers into hex. For example, 1100 0101 0011 1010 binary is C53A hex.

Bit Operations

Now that we have understood the bit numbering and the binary to hex conversion process, it is time to access and manipulate bits. Here are some examples of operations that we may wish to perform on bits:

(a) Set bit 3 to 0
(b) Set bit 5 to 1
(c) Check whether bit 6 is 1 (on) or 0 (off)

In (a) and (b) bits are being manipulated (a write operation), whereas, in (c) a bit is being accessed (a read operation). To be able to access or manipulate individual bits, C language provides a powerful set of operators. These are shown in Figure 21.4.

Operator	Meaning
~	One's complement
>>	Right shift
<<	Left shift
&	Bitwise AND
|	Bitwise OR
^	Bitwise XOR(Exclusive OR)

Figure 21.4 Bitwise operators.

These operators can operate on **int**s and **char**s but not on **float**s and **double**s. Before we examine these operators, let me introduce you to a function called **showbits( )**. Its job is to display binary equivalent of the value that it receives. We are going to use this function at several places, but we are going to discuss its details only towards the end of this chapter. Let us now explore the various bitwise operators one-by-one.

One's Complement Operator

On taking one's complement of a number, all 1's present in it are changed to 0's and all 0's are changed to 1's. For example, one's complement of 65, i.e., one's complement of 01000001 (binary equivalent of 65) is 10111110. One's complement operator is represented by the symbol ~ (tilde). Following program shows one's complement operator in action:

```
#include <stdio.h>
int main( )
{
    unsigned char ch = 32, dh ;
    dh = ~ch ;
```

```
    printf ( "~ch = %d\n", dh ) ;
    printf ( "~ch = %x\n", dh ) ;
    printf ( "~ch = %X\n", dh ) ;
    printf ( "~ch = %#X\n", dh ) ;
    return 0 ;
}
```

On execution the program produces the following output:

```
~ch = 223
~ch = df
~ch = DF
~ch = 0xDF
```

Here **ch** contains a value 32, whose binary equivalent is 00100000. On taking one's complement of it, we get 11011111, which in decimal is 223. As we learnt earlier, hexadecimal equivalent of 11011111 is DF. The hexadecimal equivalent gets printed in small case if we use **%x** and in capital if we use **%X**. **#X** prints 0x before the hexadecimal number.

Right Shift and Left Shift Operators

The right shift operator is represented by >>. It needs two operands. Thus, **ch >> 3** would shift all bits in **ch** three places to the right. Similarly, **ch >> 5** would shift all bits 5 places to the right. If **ch** contains the bit pattern 11010111, then, **ch >> 1** would give 01101011 and **ch >> 2** would give 00110101.

Note that as the bits are shifted to the right, blanks are created on the left. These blanks get filled with zeros.

The left shift operator (<<) is similar to the right shift operator (>>), the only difference being that the bits are shifted to the left, and for each bit shifted, a 0 is added to the right of the number.

The following program demonstrates the use of >> and << operators:

```
# include <stdio.h>
void showbits ( unsigned char ) ;
int main( )
{
    unsigned char num = 225, k ;
    printf ( "\nDecimal %d is same as binary ", num ) ;
    showbits ( num ) ;
```

```
    k = num >> 1 ;
    printf ( "\n%d right shift 1 gives ", num ) ;  showbits ( k ) ;
    k = num >> 2 ;
    printf ( "\n%d right shift 2 gives ", num ) ;  showbits ( k ) ;
    k = num << 1 ;
    printf ( "\n%d left shift 1 gives ", num ) ;  showbits ( k ) ;
    k = num << 2 ;
    printf ( "\n%d left shift 2 gives ", num ) ;  showbits ( k ) ;
    return 0 ;
}
void showbits ( unsigned char  n )
{
    int i ;
    unsigned char  j, k, andmask ;
    for ( i = 7 ; i >= 0 ; i-- )
    {
        j = i ;
        andmask = 1 << j ;
        k = n & andmask ;
        k == 0 ? printf ( "0" ) : printf ( "1" ) ;
    }
}
```

The output of the above program would be...

```
Decimal 225 is same as binary 11100001
225 right shift 1 gives 01110000
225 right shift 2 gives 00111000
225 left shift 1 gives 11000010
225 left shift 2 gives 10000100
```

Note that shifting the operand 1 bit to right is same as dividing it by 2 and ignoring the remainder. Thus,

```
64 >> 1 gives 32
64 >> 2 gives 16
128 >> 2 gives 32
```

but,

```
27 >> 1 is 13
49 >> 1 is 24
```

Likewise, left-shifting by 1 would mean multiplying by 2.

A Word of Caution

In the expression **a >> b** if **b** is negative the result is unpredictable. If **a** is negative then its left most bit (sign bit) would be 1. On right shifting **a** it would result in extending the sign bit. For example, if **a** contains -5, then its binary equivalent would be 11111011. On right shifting it by 1, right-most bit, i.e., 1 is lost; other bits are shifted one position to the right and the sign is extended, i.e., it is preserved as 1. This yields 11111101, which is equal to -3. The following program would help you get a clear picture of this:

```
# include <stdio.h>
void showbits ( unsigned char ) ;
int main( )
{
    char num = -5, j, k ;
    printf ( "\nDecimal %d is same as binary ", num ) ;
    showbits ( num ) ;
    for ( j = 1 ; j <= 3 ; j++ )
    {
        k = num >> j ;
        printf ( "\n%d right shift %d gives ", num, j ) ;
        showbits ( k ) ;
    }
    return 0 ;
}
void showbits ( unsigned char  n )
{
    int i ;
    unsigned char  j, k, andmask ;
    for ( i = 7 ; i >= 0 ; i-- )
    {
        j = i ;
        andmask = 1 << j ;
        k = n & andmask ;
        k == 0 ? printf ( "0" ) : printf ( "1" ) ;
    }
}
```

The output of the above program would be...

```
Decimal -5 is same as binary 11111011
-5 right shift 1 gives 11111101
-5 right shift 2 gives 11111110
-5 right shift 3 gives 11111111
```

Utility of << Operator

The left shift operator is often used to create a number with a particular bit in it set to 1. For example, we can create a number with its 3rd bit set to 1 by using the expression 1 << 3. Binary value of 1 is 00000001. On left-shifting this by 3 we get 00001000. Thus, we are able to create a number with its 3rd bit set to 1. Such operations are frequently required while writing programs that interact with hardware or while building embedded systems or IoT systems. Hence it is often done using a macro as shown below.

```
# define _BV(x) ( 1 << x )
```

The _**BV** macro stands for **Bit Value**. Its argument indicates which bit in the number would be set when this macro is used. As you must have guessed, during processing the macro **_BV(3)** would get expanded to **1 << 3**, yielding 00001000.

Bitwise AND, OR and XOR Operators

These operators are represented using **&, |** and **^** respectively. All of them operate on two operands of same type (either **char** or **int**). The second operand is often called a mask. These operators operate on pairs of bits to yield resultant bits. The rules that decide the values of resultant bits are given by Truth Tables shown in Figure 21.5.

&	0	1
0	0	1
1	0	1

|	0	1
0	0	1
1	1	1

^	0	1
0	0	1
1	1	0

Figure 21.5 Truth tables of &, | and ^ operators.

The examples given below show what happens when these operators are used on the same operands. The rules given in the Figure 21.5 are applied to each pair of bits one-by-one to obtain the result. Work through the Truth Tables and confirm that the results obtained are correct.

```
  10101101  Original value       10101101         10101101
& 00100000  AND mask           | 00100000       ^ 00100000
  --------------               --------------   --------------
  00100000  Result               00100000         00100000
```

Thus, it must be clear that the operation is being performed on individual bits, and the operation performed on one pair of bits is completely independent of the operation performed on the other pairs.

Utility of & Operator

& operator is used for two purposes:

(a) To check whether a particular bit of an operand is ON or OFF.

(b) To turn OFF a particular bit.

Both these uses are discussed in the following example.

Suppose, from the bit pattern 10101101 (0xAD), we want to check whether bit number 5 is ON (1) or OFF (0). Since we want to check the bit number 5, the second operand for the AND operation should be 00100000. This second operand if often known as AND mask. The ANDing operation is shown below.

```
10101101      Original bit pattern
00100000      AND mask
--------------
00100000      Resulting bit pattern
```

The resulting value that we get is 32 (or 0x20), which is same as the value of the second operand. The result turned out to be 32 (or 0x20) since the fifth bit of the first operand is ON. Had it been OFF, the bit number 5 in the resulting bit pattern would have evaluated to 0 and the complete bit pattern would have been 00000000.

Thus, depending upon the bit number to be checked in the first operand, we decide the second operand, and on ANDing these two operands the result decides whether the bit was ON or OFF. If the bit is ON (1), the resulting value turns out to be a non-zero value, which is equal to the value of second operand. If the bit is OFF (0), the result is zero, as seen above.

Let us now turn our attention to the second use of the AND operator. As you can see, in the bit pattern 10101101 (0xAD), 3rd bit is ON. To put it off, we need to AND the 3rd bit with 0. While doing so the values of other bits in the pattern should not get disturbed. For this we need to AND the other bits with 1. This operation is shown below.

```
10101101        Original bit pattern
11110111        AND mask
--------------
10100101        Resulting bit pattern
```

The following program puts into action both the uses of & operator:

```
# include <stdio.h>
void showbits ( unsigned  char ) ;
int main( )
{
    unsigned  char  num = 0xAD, j ;
    printf ( "\nValue of num = " ) ;
    showbits ( num ) ;
    j = num & 0x20 ;
    if ( j == 0 )
        printf ( "\nIts fifth bit is off" ) ;
    else
        printf ( "\nIts fifth bit is on" ) ;

    j = num & 0x08 ;
    if ( j == 0 )
        printf ( "\nIts third bit is off" ) ;
    else
    {
        printf ( "\nIts third bit is on" ) ;
        num = num & 0xF7 ;
        printf ( "\nNew value of num = " ) ;
        showbits ( num ) ;
        j = num & 0x08 ;
        if ( j == 0 )
            printf ( "\nNow its third bit is turned off" ) ;
    }
```

```
    return 0 ;
}
void showbits ( unsigned  char  n )
{
    int  i ;
    unsigned  char  j, k, andmask ;
    for ( i = 7 ; i >= 0 ; i-- )
    {
        j = i ;
        andmask = 1 << j ;
        k = n & andmask ;
        k == 0 ? printf ( "0" ) : printf ( "1" ) ;
    }
}
```

And here is the output...

```
Value of num = 10101101
Its fifth bit is on
Its third bit is on
New value of num = 10100101
Now its third bit is turned off
```

Note the use of **&** operator in the statements:

```
j = num & 0x20 ;
j = num & 0x08 ;
num = num & 0xF7 ;
```

A quick glance at these statements does not indicate what operation is being carried out through them. Hence a better idea is to use the macro **_BV** as shown below.

```
# define _BV(x)  ( 1 << x )
j = num & _BV( 5 ) ;
j = num & _BV( 3 ) ;
num = num & ~_BV( 3 ) ;
```

In the last statement **_BV(3)** would yield 00001000 and one's complement of this number would fetch 11110111.

Utility of | Operator

Bitwise OR operator is used to put ON a particular bit in a number. Let us consider the bit pattern 11000011. If we want to put ON bit number 3, then the OR mask to be used would be 00001000. Note that all the other bits in the mask are set to 0 and only the bit, which we want to set ON in the resulting value is set to 1. The code snippet which will achieve this is given below.

```
# define _BV(x)  ( 1 << x )
unsigned char  num = 0xC3 ;
num = num | _BV( 3 ) ;
```

Utility of ^ Operator

XOR operator is used to toggle (change) a bit ON or OFF. A number XORed with another number twice gives the original number. The following program shows how to toggle bit number 2 and 3 in a number 0x32:

```
# include <stdio.h>
int main( )
{
    unsigned char  b = 0x32 ;   /* Binary 00110010 */
    b = b ^ 0x0C ;
    printf ( "%#02x\n", b ) ;    /* prints 0x3E which is 00111110*/
    b = b ^ 0x0C ;
    printf ( "%#02x\n", b ) ;    /* prints 0x32 which is 00110010 */
    return 0 ;
}
```

The *showbits( )* Function

We have used this function quite often in this chapter. Now we have sufficient knowledge of bitwise operators and will be able to understand it. The function is given below followed by a brief explanation.

```
void showbits ( unsigned char  n )
{
    int  i ;
    unsigned char  k, andmask ;
    for ( i = 7 ; i >= 0 ; i-- )
    {
```

```
        andmask = 1 << i ;
        k = n & andmask ;
        k == 0 ? printf ( "0" ) : printf ( "1" ) ;
    }
}
```

All that is being done in this function is, using an AND operator and a variable **andmask**, we are checking the status of individual bits of **n**. If the bit is OFF, we print a 0, otherwise we print a 1.

First time through the loop, the variable **andmask** will contain the value 10000000, which is obtained by left-shifting 1 by seven places. If the variable **n'**s most significant bit (leftmost bit) is 0, then **k** would contain a value 0, otherwise it would contain a non-zero value. If **k** contains 0, then **printf( )** will print out 0, otherwise it will print out 1.

In the second go-around of the loop, the value of **i** is decremented and hence the value of **andmask** changes, which will now be 01000000. This checks whether the next most significant bit is 1 or 0, and prints it out accordingly. The same operation is repeated for all bits in the number.

Bitwise Compound Assignment Operators

Consider the following bitwise operations:

```
unsigned char a = 0xFA, b = 0xA7, c = 0xFF, d = 0xA3, e = 0x43 ;
a = a << 1 ;
b = b >> 2 ;
c = c | 0x2A ;
d = d & 0x4A ;
e = e ^ 0x21 ;
```

These operations can be written more elegantly and in a compact fashion as shown below.

```
unsigned char a = 0xFA, b = 0xA7, c = 0xFF, d = 0xA3, e = 0x43 ;
a <<= 1 ;
b >>= 2 ;
c |= 0x2A ;
d &= 0x4A ;
e ^= 0x21 ;
```

The operators **<<=**, **>>=**, **|=**, **&=** and **^=** are called bitwise compound assignment operators. Note that there does not exist an operator **~=**. This is because ~ is a unary operator and needs only one operand.

Programs

Problem 21.1

The information about colors is to be stored in bits of an **unsigned char** variable called **color**. Bit numbers 0 to 6, each represent 7 colors of a rainbow, i.e., bit 0 represents violet, 1 represents indigo, and so on. Write a program that asks the user to enter a number and based on this number it reports which colors in the rainbow do the number represents.

Program

```
/* To determine the color */
# include <stdio.h>
# define _BV(x)  ( 1 << x )
void showbits ( unsigned char  n );
int main( )
{
    unsigned char color, i ;
    int c ;
    char *rbcolors[ ] = { "Violet", "Indigo", "Blue", "Green",
                          "Yellow", "Orange", "Red" } ;
    printf ( "\nEnter any number: " ) ;
    scanf ( "%d", &c ) ;
    color = ( unsigned char ) c ;
    printf ( "Colors represented are:\n" ) ;
    for ( i = 0 ; i <= 6 ; i++ )
    {
        if ( ( color & _BV ( i ) ) == _BV ( i ) )
            printf ( "%s\n", rbcolors[ i ] ) ;
    }
    return 0 ;
}
```

Output

```
Enter any number: 3
```

```
Colors represented are:
Violet
Indigo
```

Problem 21.2

The time field in a structure is 2 bytes long. Distribution of different bits which account for hours, minutes and seconds is given in Figure 21.6. Define a function that would receive the 2-byte time and print the equivalent hours, minutes and seconds.

15	14	13	12	11	10	9	8	7	6	5	4	3	2	1	0
H	H	H	H	H	M	M	M	M	M	M	S	S	S	S	S

Figure 21.6 Bit-distribution for time value.

Program

```
/* Program to display hour, minute, and seconds */
# include <stdio.h>
void display ( unsigned short int time ) ;
int main( )
{
    unsigned short int  time ;
    puts ( "Enter any number less than 24446: " ) ;
    scanf ( "%hu", &time ) ;
    display ( time ) ;
    return 0 ;
}
void display ( unsigned short int  tm )
{
    unsigned short int  hours, minutes, seconds, temp ;
    hours = tm >> 11 ;
    temp = tm << 5 ;
    minutes = temp >> 10 ;
    temp = tm << 11 ;
    seconds = ( temp >> 11 ) * 2 ;
    printf ( "For Time = %hu\n", tm ) ;
    printf ( "Hours = %hu\n", hours ) ;
```

```
    printf ( "Minutes = %hu\n", minutes ) ;
    printf ( "Seconds = %hu\n", seconds ) ;
}
```

Output

```
Enter any number less than 24446:
15500
For Time = 15500
Hours = 7
Minutes = 36
Seconds = 24
```

Exercises

[A] Attempt the following questions:

(a) In an inter-college competition, various sports like cricket, basketball, football, hockey, lawn tennis, table tennis, carom and chess are played between different colleges. The information regarding the games won by a particular college is stored in bit numbers 0, 1, 2, 3, 4, 5, 6, 7 and 8 of an integer variable **game**. The college that wins in 5 or more than 5 games is awarded the Champion of Champions trophy. If a number representing the bit pattern mentioned above is entered through the keyboard, then write a program to find out whether the college won the Champion of the Champions trophy or not, along with the names of the games won by the college.

(b) An animal could be a canine (dog, wolf, fox, etc.), a feline (cat, lynx, jaguar, etc.), a cetacean (whale, narwhal, etc.) or a marsupial (koala, wombat, etc.). The information whether a particular animal is canine, feline, cetacean, or marsupial is stored in bit number 0, 1, 2 and 3, respectively of an integer variable **type**. Bit number 4 of the variable **type** stores the information about whether the animal is Carnivore or Herbivore.

For the following animal, complete the program to determine whether the animal is an herbivore or a carnivore. Also determine whether the animal is a canine, feline, cetacean or a marsupial.

```
struct animal
```

```
{
    char name[ 30 ] ; int type ;
}
struct animal a = { "OCELOT", 18 } ;
```

(c) In order to save disk space, information about student is stored in an integer variable. Bit numbers 0 to 3 indicate whether the student is a I[st] year, IInd year, IIIrd year or IVth year student respectively. Bits 4 to 7 indicate whether the student's stream is Mechanical, Chemical, Electronics or CS. Rest of the bits store room number. Such data for 4 students is stored in the following array:

```
int data[ ] = { 273, 548, 786, 1096 } ;
```

Write a program that uses this data and displays the information about the student.

(d) What will be the output of the following program?

```
# include <stdio.h>
int main( )
{
    int i = 32, j = 65, k, l, m, n, o, p ;
    k = i | 35 ;   l = ~k ;   m = i & j ;
    n = j ^ 32 ;   o = j << 2 ;   p = i >> 5 ;
    printf ( "k = %d l = %d m = %d\n", k, l, m ) ;
    printf ( "n = %d o = %d p = %d\n", n, o, p ) ;
    return 0 ;
}
```

[B] Answer the following questions:

(a) What is hexadecimal equivalent of each of the following binary numbers?

01011010	11000011
1010101001110101	1111000001011010

(b) Rewrite the following expressions using bitwise compound assignment operators:

a = a | 3   a = a & 0x48   b = b ^ 0x22   c = c << 2

(c) Consider an unsigned integer in which rightmost bit is numbered as 0. Write a function **checkbits (x, p, n)** which returns true if all "n" bits starting from position "p" are turned on, false otherwise. For example, **checkbits (x, 4, 3)** will return true if bits 4, 3 and 2 are 1 in number **x**.

(d) Write a program to scan an 8-bit number into a variable and check whether its 3rd, 6th and 7th bit is on.

(e) Write a program to receive an unsigned 16-bit integer and then exchange the contents of its 2 bytes using bitwise operators.

(f) Write a program to receive an 8-bit number into a variable and then exchange its higher 4 bits with lower 4 bits.

(g) Write a program to receive an 8-bit number into a variable and then set its odd bits to 1.

(h) Write a program to receive an 8-bit number into a variable and then check if its 3rd and 5th bit are on. If these bits are found to be on then put them off.

(i) Write a program to receive an 8-bit number into a variable and then check if its 3rd and 5th bit are off. If these bits are found to be off then put them on.

(j) Rewrite the **showbits( )** function used in this chapter using the **_BV** macro.

KanNotes

- Bit = Binary Digit = Basic unit of information
- A bit can take a value 0 or 1
- Units :

  4 bits = Nibble 8 bits = Byte 16 bits = Word
  32 bits = Dword 64 bits = Qword
- 4 popular Numbering systems :

  1) Binary - 0, 1 2) Octal - 0...7
  3) Decimal - 0...9 4) Hexadecimal - 0...9, A...F
- PC/Laptop understand only Binary numbering system

  C/C++ understand Octal, Decimal, Hexadecimal numbering systems

- Always try to convert Binary into Hexadecimal instead of Decimal, as while converting to Hex a nibble can be replaced by its equivalent Hex digit

- Bitwise Operations :

  Set a bit to a value 0/1 → Write operation
  Check whether bit is 1 (on) or 0 (off) → Read operation

- Bitwise operators purpose :

  ~ - Converts 0s to 1s and 1s to 0s. Useful in constructing masks
  << >> - shift out desired number of bits from left or right
  & - Check whether a bit is on / off. Put off a particular bit
  | - Put on a particular bit
  ^ - Toggle a bit

- <<= >>= &= |= ^= - Bitwise compound assignment operators

- a = a << 5 ; is same as a <<= 5 ;

- Except ~ all other bitwise operators are binary operators

- Remember :

  Anything ANDed with 0 is 0
  Anything ORed with 1 is 1
  1 XORed with 1 is 0

- printf ("%#x", var) ; prints the hexadecimal output preceded by 0x

- _BV(3) macro prepares a mask with value 00001000

- _BV(4) macro prepares a mask with value 00010000

- The _BV macro can be defined as #define _BV(x) (1 << x)

22 Miscellaneous Features

"Features that separate men from boys..."

Strictly speaking, you do not need miscellaneous features. But you should not avoid them. This is because, once you know how to use them, you are well on your way to becoming a star C programmer. This chapter puts you on that way...

Contents

The topics discussed in this chapter were either too large or far too removed from the mainstream C programming for inclusion in the earlier chapters. These topics provide certain useful programming features, and could prove to be of immense help in certain programming strategies. These include enumerated data types, the **typedef** keyword, typecasting, bit fields, function pointers, functions with variable number of arguments and unions. Let us understand them one by one.

Enumerated Data Type

The enumerated data type gives us an opportunity to invent our own data type and define what values the variable of this data type can take. This can help in making the program listings more readable, which can be an advantage when a program gets complicated or when more than one programmer would be working on it. Using enumerated data type can also help us reduce programming errors.

As an example, one could invent a data type called **mar_status** which can have four possible values—single, married, divorced or widowed. The **enum** declaration of **mar_status** and definition of variable of type **mar_status** is given below.

```
enum mar_status
{
    single, married, divorced, widowed
} ;
enum mar_status person1, person2 ;
```

Now we can give values to these variables.

```
person1 = married ;
person2 = divorced ;
```

Remember, we can't use values that aren't in the original declaration.

Thus, the following expression would cause an error:

```
person1 = unknown ;
```

Internally, the compiler treats the enumerators as integers. Each value on the list of permissible values corresponds to an integer, starting with 0. Thus, in our example, single is stored as 0, married is stored as 1, divorced as 2 and widowed as 3.

This way of assigning numbers can be overridden by the programmer by initializing the enumerators to different integer values as shown below.

```
enum mar_status
{
    single = 100, married = 200, divorced = 300, widowed = 400
} ;
```

Uses of Enumerated Data Type

Enumerated variables are usually used to clarify the operation of a program. For example, if we need to use employee departments in a payroll program, it makes the listing easier to read if we use values like Assembly, Manufacturing, Accounts rather than the integer values 0, 1, 2, etc. The following program illustrates the point I am trying to make:

```
# include <stdio.h>
# include <string.h>
int main( )
{
    enum department
    {
        assembly, manufacturing, accounts, stores
    } ;
    struct employee
    {
        char name[ 30 ] ; int age ; enum department dept ;
    } ;
    struct employee e ;
    strcpy ( e.name, "Lothar Mattheus" ) ;
    e.age = 28 ;
    e.dept = manufacturing ;
    printf ( "Name = %s\n", e.name ) ;
    printf ( "Age = %d\n", e.age ) ;
    printf ( "Department = %d\n", e.dept ) ;
    if ( e.dept == accounts )
        printf ( "%s is an accounant\n", e.name ) ;
    else
        printf ( "%s is not an accounant\n", e.name ) ;
    return 0 ;
}
```

And here is the output of the program...

```
Name = Lothar Mattheus
Age = 28
Department = 1
Lothar Mattheus is not an accountant
```

Let us now dissect the program. We first defined the data type **enum department** and specified the four possible values, namely, assembly, manufacturing, accounts and stores. Then we defined a variable **dept** of the type **enum department** in a structure. The structure **employee** has two other elements containing employee information.

The program first assigns values to the variables in the structure. The statement,

```
e.dept = manufacturing ;
```

assigns the value manufacturing to **e.dept** variable. This is much more informative to anyone reading the program than a statement like,

```
e.dept = 1 ;
```

The next part of the program shows an important weakness of using **enum** variables... there is no way to use the enumerated values directly in input/output functions like **scanf( )** and **printf( )**.

The **printf( )** function is not smart enough to perform the translation; the department is printed out as 1 and not manufacturing. Of course, we can write a function to print the correct enumerated values, using a **switch** statement, but that would reduce the clarity of the program. Even with this limitation, however, there are many situations in which enumerated variables are God sent!

Are Enums Necessary?

Can we not achieve the same convenience and readability by using macros like

```
# define ASSEMBLY 0
# define MANUFACTURING 1
# define ACCCOUNTS 2
# define STORES 3
```

We can, but macros have a serious limitation—they have a global scope, whereas, scope of enum can either be global (if declared outside all functions) or local (if declared inside a function).

Renaming Data Types with *typedef*

There is one more technique, which, in some situations, can help to clarify the source code of a C program. This technique is to make use of the **typedef** declaration. Its purpose is to redefine the name of an existing variable type.

For example, consider the following statement in which the type **unsigned long int** is given a new name **UTI**:

```
typedef unsigned long int UTI ;
```

Now we can declare variables of the type **unsigned long int** by writing,

```
UTI var1, var2 ;
```

instead of

```
unsigned long int var1, var2 ;
```

Thus, **typedef** provides a nice shortcut. Usually, uppercase letters are used for the new name to make it clear that we are dealing with a renamed data type.

While the increase in readability is probably not great in this example, it can be significant when the name of a particular data type is long and unwieldy, as it often is with structure declarations. For example, consider the following structure declaration:

```
struct employee
{
    char name[ 30 ] ; int age ; float bs ;
} ;
struct employee e ;
```

This structure declaration can be made handier to use when renamed using **typedef** as shown below.

```
struct employee
{
    char name[ 30 ] ; int age ; float bs ;
```

```
} ;
typedef struct employee EMP ;
EMP e1, e2 ;
```

Thus, by reducing the length and apparent complexity of data types, **typedef** can help to clarify source listing and save time and energy spent in understanding a program.

The above **typedef** can also be written as

```
typedef struct employee
{
    char name[ 30 ] ; int age ; float bs ;
} EMP ;
EMP e1, e2 ;
```

typedef can also be used to rename pointer data types as shown below.

```
struct employee
{
    char name[ 30 ] ; int age ; float bs ;
}
typedef struct employee * PEMP ;
PEMP p ;
p -> age = 32 ;
```

Typecasting

Sometimes we are required to force the compiler to explicitly convert the value of an expression to a particular data type. This would be clear from the following example:

```
# include <stdio.h>
int main( )
{
    float a, b ;
    int x = 6, y = 4 ;
    a = x / y ;
    printf ( "Value of a = %f\n", a ) ;
    b = ( float ) x / y ;
    printf ( "Value of b = %f\n", b ) ;
    return 0 ;
}
```

And here is the output...

```
Value of a = 1.000000
Value of b = 1.500000
```

Value of **a** turns out to be 1.000000 and not 1.5. This is because, 6 and 4 are both integers and hence **6 / 4** yields an integer, 1. This 1 when stored in **a** is converted to 1.000000. But what if we do not want the quotient to be truncated? One solution is to make either **x** or **y** as **float**. Let us say that other requirements of the program do not permit us to do this. In such a case what do we do? Use typecasting. This consists of putting a pair of parentheses around the name of the target data type. In this program we used,

```
b = ( float ) x / y ;
```

The expression (**float**) causes the variable **x** to be converted from type **int** to type **float** before being used in the division operation.

Bit Fields

Suppose we want to store the following data about an employee. Each employee can:

(a) Be male or female
(b) Be single, married, divorced or widowed
(c) Have one of the eight different hobbies
(d) Can choose from any of the fifteen different schemes proposed by the company to pursue his/her hobby.

This means we need 1 bit to store gender, 2 to store marital status, 3 for hobby, and 4 for scheme (with one value used for those who are not desirous of availing any of the schemes). Thus, we need 10 bits altogether to store this data. So why waste multiple integers when 10 bits will do? In such cases we can use 'bit fields' to store several values in a single integer. The following program shows how to use bit fields.

```
# include <stdio.h>
# define MALE 0 ;
# define FEMALE 1 ;
# define SINGLE 0 ;
# define MARRIED 1 ;
# define DIVORCED 2 ;
# define WIDOWED 3 ;
```

```
int main( )
{
    struct employee
    {
        unsigned gender : 1 ;  unsigned mar_status : 2 ;
        unsigned hobby : 3 ;   unsigned scheme : 4 ;
    } ;
    struct employee e ;
    e.gender = MALE ;
    e.mar_status = DIVORCED ;
    e.hobby = 5 ;
    e.scheme = 9 ;
    printf ( "Gender = %d\n", e.gender ) ;
    printf ( "Marital status = %d\n", e.mar_status ) ;
    printf ( "Bytes occupied by e = %d\n", sizeof ( e ) ) ;
    return 0 ;
}
```

And here is the output...

```
Gender = 0
Marital status = 2
Bytes occupied by e = 2
```

Observe the declaration of **struct employee**. The colon (:) in the declaration tells the compiler that we are talking about bit fields and the number after it tells how many bits to allot for the field. Once we have established a bit field, we can reference it just like any other structure element.

Pointers to Functions

Like variables, functions are also stored in memory. So, they also have addresses. So, if we store the address of a function in a variable it would be a function pointer. Function pointers provide one more way to invoke functions. Let us see how this can be done.

```
# include <stdio.h>
void display( ) ;
int main( )
{
    void ( *ptr )( ) ;
    ptr = display ; /* assign address of function */
```

```
    printf ( "Address of function display is %u\n", ptr ) ;
    ( *ptr )( ) ; /* invokes the function display( ) */
    display( ) ; /* usual way of invoking a function */
    return 0 ;
}
void display( )
{
    printf ( "Long live excellence!!\n" ) ;
}
```

The output of the program would be:

```
Address of function display is 4198924
Long live excellence!!
Long live excellence!!
```

Note that, to obtain the address of a function, all that we must do is mention the name of the function. This is similar to mentioning the name of the array to get its base address.

We have assigned the address of **display( )** to **ptr**. The declaration of **ptr** states that it is a pointer to a function that receives nothing and returns nothing. To call the function using **ptr**, we are just required to write the statement,

```
( *ptr )( ) ;    /* or simply, ptr( ) ; */
```

There are two possible uses of function pointers:

(a) In implementing callback mechanisms used popularly in Windows programming.

(a) In binding functions dynamically, at run-time in C++ programming.

The callback mechanism is discussed in Chapter 24. Dynamic binding is explained in detail in the book "Let Us C++" or "Test Your C++ Skills" by Yashavant Kanetkar.

Functions Returning Pointers

A function can even return a pointer. This must be explicitly mentioned in the prototype declaration as well as in the function definition. The following program illustrates this:

```
int *fun( ) ;
int main( )
```

```
{
    int *p ;
    p = fun( ) ;
    return 0 ;
}
int *fun( )
{
    static int i = 20 ;
    return ( &i ) ;
}
```

This program just indicates how an integer pointer can be returned from a function. Beyond that, it does not serve any useful purpose. This concept can be put to use while handling strings. For example, a function can copy one string into another and return the pointer to the target string. Try defining this function as an exercise.

Functions with Variable Number of Arguments

Functions like **printf( )** can receive different number of arguments during different calls. How can we define such functions? Well, this can be done using three macros **va_start**, **va_arg** and **va_list**. These macros are defined in the file "**stdarg.h**".

These macros provide a method for accessing the arguments of the function when a function takes a fixed number of arguments followed by a variable number of arguments. The fixed number of arguments are accessed in the normal way, whereas the optional arguments are accessed using these macros. Out of these macros, **va_start** is used to initialize a pointer to the beginning of the list of optional arguments. On the other hand, the macro **va_arg** is used to advance the pointer to the next argument.

Let us put these concepts into action in a program. Suppose we wish to define a function **findmax( )** which can find out the maximum value from a set of values, irrespective of the number of values passed to it. Here is how we can do it...

```
# include <stdio.h>
# include <stdarg.h>
int findmax ( int, ... ) ;
int main( )
{
```

```
    int max ;
    max = findmax ( 5, 23, 15, 1, 92, 50 ) ;
    printf ( "maximum = %d\n", max ) ;
    max = findmax ( 3, 100, 300, 29 ) ;
    printf ( "maximum = %d\n", max ) ;
    return 0 ;
}
int findmax ( int tot_num, ... )
{
    int max, count, num ;
    va_list ptr ;
    va_start ( ptr, tot_num ) ;
    max = va_arg ( ptr, int ) ;
    for ( count = 1 ; count < tot_num ; count++ )
    {
        num = va_arg ( ptr, int ) ;
        if ( num > max )
            max = num ;
    }
    return ( max ) ;
}
```

Note how the **findmax( )** function has been declared. The ellipses (...) indicate that the number of arguments after the first argument would be different in different function calls.

Here we are making two calls to **findmax( )**, first time to find maximum out of 5 values and second time to find maximum out of 3 values. Note that for each call the first argument is the count of arguments that follow the first argument. The value of the first argument passed to **findmax( )** is collected in the variable **tot_num**. **findmax( )** begins with a declaration of a pointer **ptr** of the type **va_list**. Observe the next statement carefully.

```
va_start ( ptr, tot_num ) ;
```

This statement sets up **ptr** such that it points to the first variable argument in the list. If we are considering the first call to **findmax( )**, **ptr** would now point to 23. The statement **max = va_arg (ptr, int)** would assign the integer being pointed to by **ptr** to **max**. Thus, 23 would be assigned to **max**, and **ptr** would now start pointing to the next argument, i.e., 15. The rest of the program is fairly straightforward. We just keep picking up successive numbers in the list and keep comparing them with the latest value in **max**, till all the arguments in the list have been scanned. The final value in **max** is then returned to **main( )**.

Unions

Unions are derived data types that enable us to treat the same space in memory as several different variables. Let us look at a simple program that illustrates this.

```
/* Demo of union at work */
# include <stdio.h>
int main( )
{
    union u
    {
        short int i ; char ch[ 2 ] ;
    } ;
    union u key ;
    key.i = 512 ;
    printf ( "key.i = %d\n", key.i ) ;
    printf ( "key.ch[ 0 ] = %d\n", key.ch[ 0 ] ) ;
    printf ( "key.ch[ 1 ] = %d\n", key.ch[ 1 ] ) ;
    return 0 ;
}
```

And here is the output...

```
key2.i = 512
key2.ch[ 0 ] = 0
key2.ch[ 1 ] = 2
```

To begin with, we have declared a data type **union a**. Then we have defined variable **key of** this type. Next, the union elements are printed. Like structure elements, union elements too are accessed using the '**.**' operator. To understand the output of the program we first need to understand how **key** looks like. This is shown in Figure 22.1.

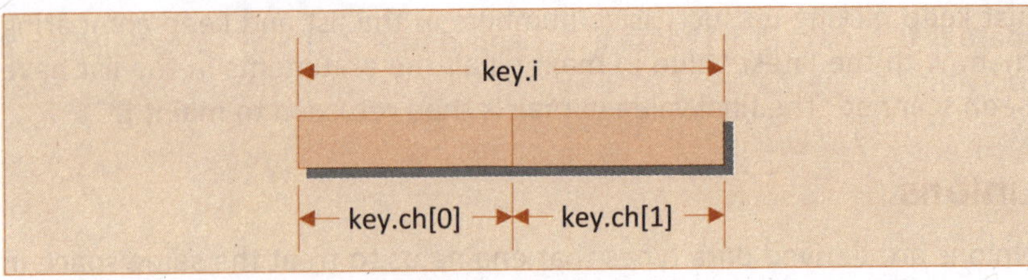

Figure 22.1 Layout of a union in memory.

As you can see, **key** occupies 2 bytes in memory. The same memory locations used by **key.i** are also being used by **key.ch[0]** and **key.ch[1]**. What purpose does this serve? Well, now we can access the 2 bytes taken together by using **key.i**, or the same 2 bytes individually by using **key.ch[0]** and **key.ch[1]**.

Let us now understand the output of the program. Binary equivalent of 512 is 00000010 00000000. So output of union elements **key.ch[0]** and **key.ch[1]** should have been 2 and 0 respectively. But the output is exactly the opposite. Why is it so? Because, in CPUs that follow little-endian architecture (Intel CPUs, for example), when a 2-byte number is stored in memory, the low byte is stored before the high byte. It means, 512 would be stored in memory as 00000000 00000010. These converted to decimal turn out to be 0 and 2. In CPUs with big-endian architecture this reversal of bytes does not happen.

One last thing. We cannot assign different values to the different union elements at the same time. That is, if we assign a value to **key.i**, it gets automatically assigned to **key.ch[0]** and **key.ch[1]**. Vice versa, if we assign a value to **key.ch[0]** or **key.ch[1]**, it is bound to get assigned to **key.i**.

Before we move on to the next section, let us reiterate that a union provides a way to look at the same data in several different ways. For example, suppose we declare a union as shown below.

```
union b
{
    double d ; float f[ 2 ] ; short int i[ 4 ] ; char ch[ 8 ] ;
} ;
union b data ;
```

In what different ways can the data be accessed from it? Sometimes, as a complete set of 8 bytes (**data.d**), sometimes as two sets of 4 bytes each (**data.f[0]** and **data.f[1]**), sometimes as four sets of 2 bytes each (**data.i[0]**, **data.i[1]**, **data.i[2]** and **data.[3]**) and sometimes as 8 individual bytes (**data.ch[0]**, **data.ch[1]... data.ch[7]**).

Also note that there can exist a union, each of whose elements is of different size. In such a case, the size of the union variable will be equal to the size of the longest element in the union.

Utility of Unions

Suppose we wish to store information about employees in an organization. The items of information are as shown below.

```
Name, Grade, Age
If Grade = HSK (Highly Skilled) - hobby name, credit card number
If Grade = SSK (Semi Skilled) - vehicle number, distance from company
```

Since this is dissimilar information, we can gather it together using a structure as shown below.

```
struct employee
{
    char n[ 20 ] ; char grade[ 4 ] ; int age ; char hobby[ 10 ] ;
    int crcardno ; char vehno[ 10 ] ; int dist ;
} ;
struct employee e ;
```

Though grammatically this structure declaration is correct, it suffers from a disadvantage. For any employee, depending upon his/her grade, either the elements hobby and credit card number or the elements vehicle number and distance would get used. Both sets of elements would never get used. This would lead to wastage of memory with every structure variable that we create, since every structure variable would have all the four fields apart from name, grade and age.

This can be avoided by creating a **union** between these sets of elements as shown below.

```
struct info1
{
    char hobby[ 10 ] ; int crcardno ;
} ;
struct info2
{
    char vehno[ 10 ] ; int dist ;
```

```
};
union info
{
    struct info1 a ; struct info2 b ;
};
struct employee
{
    char n[ 20 ] ; char grade[ 4 ] ; int age ; union info f ;
};
struct employee e ;
```

The *volatile* Qualifier

When we define variables in a function the compiler may optimize the code that uses the variable. That is, the compiler may compile the code in a manner that will run in the most efficient way. The compiler achieves this by using a CPU register to store the variable's value rather than storing it in stack.

However, if we declare the variable as volatile, then it serves as a warning to the compiler that it should not *optimize* the code containing this variable. In such a case whenever we use the variable its value would be loaded from memory into register, operations would be performed on it and the result would be written back to the memory location allocated for the variable.

We can declare a volatile variable as:

```
volatile float temperature ;
```

We may want to prevent optimization when the variable is not within the control of the program and is likely to get altered from outside the program, typically by an embedded system.

P</> Programs

Problem 22.1

Define three functions—**fun1( )**, **fun2( )** and **fun3( )**. Each function should receive two integers and return a float. Store the addresses of these functions in an array. Call these functions using the addresses stored in the array.

Program

```
/* Call function using an array of function pointers */
# include <stdio.h>
float fun1 ( int, int ) ;
float fun2 ( int, int ) ;
float fun3 ( int, int ) ;
float fun1 ( int i, int j )
{
    printf ( "In fun1\n" ) ;  return 1.0f ;
}
float fun2 ( int i, int j )
{
    printf ( "In fun2\n" ) ;  return 2.0f ;
}
float fun3 ( int i, int j )
{
    printf ( "In fun3\n" ) ;  return 3.0f ;
}
int main( )
{
    float ( *ptr[ 3 ] ) ( int, int ) ;
    float f ;  int i ;
    ptr[ 0 ] = fun1 ;  ptr[ 1 ] = fun2 ;  ptr[ 2 ] = fun3 ;
    for ( i = 0 ; i < 3 ; i++ )
    {
        f = ( *ptr[ i ] )( 100, i ) ;
        printf ( "%f\n", f ) ;
    }
    return 0 ;
}
```

Output

```
In fun1
1.000000
In fun2
2.000000
In fun3
3.000000
```

Problem 22.2

Define a function which can find average of the arguments passed to it. Note that in different calls the function may receive different number of arguments.

Program

```
# include <stdio.h>
# include <stdarg.h>
int findavg ( int, ... ) ;
int main( )
{
    int avg ;
    avg = findavg ( 5, 23, 15, 1, 92, 50 ) ;
    printf ( "avg = %d\n", avg ) ;
    avg = findavg ( 3, 100, 30, 29 ) ;
    printf ( "avg = %d\n", avg ) ;
    return 0 ;
}
int findavg ( int tot_num, ... )
{
    int avg, i, num, sum ;
    va_list ptr ;
    va_start ( ptr, tot_num ) ;
    sum = 0 ;
    for ( i = 1 ; i <= tot_num ; i++ )
    {
        num = va_arg ( ptr, int ) ;
        sum = sum + num ;
    }
    return ( sum / tot_num ) ;
}
```

Output

```
avg = 36
avg = 53
```

Exercises

[A] What will be the output of the following programs?

(a)
```
# include <stdio.h>
int main( )
{
    enum status { pass, fail, atkt } ;
    enum status stud1, stud2, stud3 ;
    stud1 = pass ;
    stud2 = fail ;
    stud3 = atkt ;
    printf ( "%d %d %d\n", stud1, stud2, stud3 ) ;
    return 0 ;
}
```

(b)
```
# include <stdio.h>
int main( )
{
    printf ( "%f\n", ( float ) ( ( int ) 3.5 / 2 ) ) ;
    printf ( "%d\n", ( int ) ( ( ( float ) 3 / 2 ) * 3 ) ) ;
    return 0 ;
}
```

[B] Point out the error, if any, in the following programs:

(a)
```
# include <stdio.h>
int main( )
{
    typedef struct patient
    {
        char name[ 20 ] ; int age ;
        int systolic_bp ; int diastolic_bp ;
    } ptt ;
    ptt p1 = { "anil", 23, 110, 220 } ;
    printf ( "%s %d\n", p1.name, p1.age ) ;
    printf ( "%d %d\n", p1.systolic_bp, p1.diastolic_bp ) ;
    return 0 ;
}
```

(b)
```
# include <stdio.h>
void show( ) ;
int main( )
```

```
{
    void ( *s )( ) ;
    s = show ;
    ( *s )( ) ;
    s( ) ;
    return 0 ;
}
void show( )
{
    printf ( "don't show off. It won't pay in the long run\n" ) ;
}
```

(c)
```
# include <stdio.h>
void show ( int, float ) ;
int main( )
{
    void ( *s )( int, float ) ;
    s = show ;
    ( *s )( 10, 3.14 ) ;
    return 0 ;
}
void show ( int i, float f )
{
    printf ( "%d %f\n", i, f ) ;
}
```

[C] Attempt the following questions:

(a) Write a program, which stores information about a date in a structure containing three members—day, month and year. Using bit fields, the day number should get stored in first 5 bits of day, the month number in 4 bits of month and year in 12 bits of year. Write a program to read date of joining of 10 employees and display them in ascending order of year.

(b) Write a program to read and store information about insurance policy holder. The information contains details like gender, whether the holder is minor/major, policy name and duration of the policy. Make use of bit-fields to store this information.

KanNotes

- We can write programs without using miscellaneous features like union, enum, etc. But this is not advisable.
- Often, we are required to handle an ordered listing of items. Example, colors like red, green, blue or marital status like married, unmarried or divorced. Instead of handling these as integers, enums offer a better way.
- Usage of enums :

```
enum color { red, green, blue } ;
enum color windowcolor, buttoncolor ;
windowcolor = green ; buttoncolor = blue ;
printf ( "%d %d", windowcolor , buttoncolor ) ;
```

- A typedef declaration can be used to redefine the name of an existing data type as in

```
typedef unsigned long int ULI ;
ULI var1, var2 ;
```

- Usually, uppercase letters are used for the new type name to make it clear that we are dealing with a renamed data type
- typecasting can be used to forcibly convert the value of an expression to a particular data type
- Multiple items of information can be stored in a byte using bit fields

```
struct employee
{
    unsigned gender : 1 ; unsigned mar_stat : 2 ;
} ;
```

The number after colon (:) indicates the number of bits to allot for the field

- void *p() ; - Prototype of a function p( ) that receives nothing and returns a void *

- void (*p)( ) ; - p is pointer to a function that receives nothing and returns nothing
- float * (*p)(int, float) ; - Pointer to a function that receives int & float and returns a float *
- Usage of function pointer :

```
void ( *p )( ) ;
p = display ;        /* stores address of display function in p */
( *p )( ) ;          /* first way to call display() */
p( ) ;               /* one more way to call display() */
```

- We can define a function that receives a variable number of arguments using macros va_list, va_start, va_arg.
- Size of a structure is sum of sizes of its elements. Elements are accessed using the . operator
- Size of union variable is size of biggest element of the union. Elements are accessed using the . operator
- Utility of union - Permits access to same memory locations in multiple ways
- Usage :

```
union a
{
    int i ; char ch[ 4 ] ;
} ;
union a z ;
z.i = 512 ;
printf ( "%d %d %d %d %d", z.i, z.ch[0], z.ch[1] , z.ch[2], z.ch[3] ) ;
```

- If a number is ABCD then in little endian architecture it is stored as DCBA
- Little Endian - Low byte is stored first. Big Endian - High byte is stored first. Endianness is a matter of convenience. So, both are good.

23 Security Programming

"Unlock the power of Security..."

Understanding security programming in C equips you with the tools to protect your applications and data from threats. With this knowledge, you'll be able to implement SHA256 checksums, verify authenticity, encrypt and decrypt data using AES, and ensure non-repudiation through digital signing. This chapter guides you through these crucial security techniques...

Contents

In the digital age, ensuring the security of data is paramount. This chapter delves into the foundational aspects of security programming in C. From verifying file integrity to encrypting sensitive data, this chapter equips you with the knowledge and tools necessary to safeguard digital information against various threats.

Daily Tryst with Security

Security is an integral part of our daily digital interactions, ensuring the safety and integrity of our sensitive information. Here are a few examples where we encounter security in our digital interactions:

(a) When making payments using a credit card, encryption protocols like SSL/TLS protect our card details from unauthorized access.

(b) While doing online banking through a bank's website, multi-factor authentication and secure sessions are used to prevent fraud and keep our financial transactions confidential.

(c) Online trading of stocks necessitates secure platforms to protect not only our investments but also our personal data from cyber threats.

(d) Filing Income Tax returns involves submitting sensitive financial information, which is safeguarded by encryption and secure authentication methods to prevent identity theft and data breaches.

(e) Connecting remotely to an office machine utilizes VPNs and secure login methods to protect corporate data and maintain the confidentiality of our work activities.

Importance of Security

Security has become very important due to several key reasons:

(a) **Connectivity**: With the ubiquity of internet access, our devices are constantly connected, making them susceptible to various cyber threats. Ensuring secure connectivity is essential to protect our personal and professional information from unauthorized access.

(b) **Distributed Computing**: Modern computing relies heavily on distributed systems, where data and processing are spread across multiple locations. This increases the complexity of securing data as it moves across different networks and systems, making robust security measures critical to maintain data integrity and confidentiality.

(c) **Digital Data**: In today's world, digital data is one of the most valuable assets. From personal information and financial records to corporate secrets and intellectual property, protecting this data from breaches and cyber-attacks is essential to maintain trust, privacy, and the overall functioning of our digital economy.

These factors underscore the importance of implementing comprehensive security strategies to safeguard our digital lives.

Four Aspects of Security

From the examples of security given above, four critical aspects of security can be identified. They are as follows:

(a) **Integrity:** Integrity in security programming ensures that data has not been altered, corrupted or tampered with during storage or transmission.

(b) **Authenticity:** Authenticity verifies the identity of users or systems, ensuring that data originates from a trusted source.

(c) **Confidentiality:** Confidentiality protects sensitive information from unauthorized access, ensuring that only intended recipients can access the data.

(d) **Non-repudiation:** Non-repudiation provides proof of the origin and integrity of data, ensuring that a party cannot deny sending a message or performing a transaction.

Every application may not need to implement every one of these aspects. Also, some applications may implement multiple aspects. Let us now see how we can implement them programmatically. We will be using OpenSSL library to implement them. It can be downloaded using the following shell commands:

```
$ sudo apt update
$ sudo apt install openssl
```

Data Integrity

Data integrity can be achieved using algorithms known as hashing algorithms. Examples of these algorithms include MD5 (Message Digest version 5), SHA256 (Secure Hash Algorithm that generates hash value of

256 bits), SHA384 (384 bits), and SHA512 (512 bits). These algorithms compute a unique hash value for a given input data, which is often referred to as a message digest, fingerprint or checksum. The process of generating this hash value is known as hashing. One of the key properties of hashing is that two distinct inputs will always produce different hash values, ensuring the uniqueness of the hash. This process is also known as one-way transformation or one-way hash, as it is computationally infeasible to reverse the hash value back to the original input data.

Computing a message digest involves three key steps: initialization, updating, and finalization. During the initialization step, a context is created and the specific hashing algorithm to be used (such as SHA256) is specified. In the updating phase, the input data, or text, is incrementally added to the context. This step can involve multiple updates as more data becomes available. Finally, in the finalization step, the computation of the message digest is completed, resulting in a fixed-size hash value.

Given below is a program to compute the hash value of a string "How green was my valley".

```
#include <string.h>
#include <openssl/evp.h>
void getSHA256 ( char *source, unsigned char *csum ) ;
int main( )
{
    char input[ ] = "How green was my valley!" ;
    unsigned char chksum[ 32 ] ;
    int i ;
    getSHA256 ( input, chksum ) ;
    for ( i = 0 ; i < 32 ; i++ )
        printf ( "%02x", chksum[ i ] ) ;
    return 0 ;
}
void getSHA256 ( char *source, unsigned char *csum )
{
    EVP_MD_CTX *mdctx ;
    const EVP_MD *md ;
    unsigned int md_len ;
    OpenSSL_add_all_digests( ) ;
    md = EVP_get_digestbyname ( "SHA256" ) ;
```

```
    mdctx = EVP_MD_CTX_new( ) ;
    EVP_MD_CTX_init ( mdctx ) ;
    EVP_DigestInit_ex ( mdctx, md, NULL ) ;
    EVP_DigestUpdate ( mdctx, source, strlen ( source ) ) ;
    EVP_DigestFinal_ex ( mdctx, csum, &md_len ) ;
    EVP_MD_CTX_free ( mdctx ) ;
}
```

To compile and execute the program use the following shell commands:

```
$gcc Sha256OfString.c -lcrypto
$ ./a.out
```

On execution, we get the following 32-byte hash value for our string:

```
56f6eb54bbab0dc1512f3960004dd39bca516a3258fc77c0fd3c2f9b29ad8
a1e
```

Let us now try to understand the program.

From **main( )** we are passing the string "How green was my valley" to **getSHA256( )**. This function stores the resulting hash value in the array **chksum[ ]**, which is then printed out in **main( )** in hexadecimal format.

In OpenSSL, the **EVP_** prefix in function names refers to Envelope. The Envelope based API provides a high-level interface to various cryptographic algorithms, making it easier to work with cryptographic operations in a uniform way. For example, we can use the same set of functions for different algorithms of same type (such as MD5, SHA256, etc.) without having to worry about the specific implementation details.

In **getSHA256( )** function we have called several OpenSSL functions. The purpose of each of these functions is mentioned below.

OpenSSL_add_all_digests( ):

This line initializes all the available digest algorithms in the OpenSSL library. This is necessary to ensure that the specific digest algorithm we want to use (SHA256 in this case) is available for use.

md = EVP_get_digestbyname ("SHA256"):

Here, we retrieve the message digest method for SHA-256. This function looks up the digest algorithm by its name and returns a pointer to an **EVP_MD** structure, which contains information about the digest algorithm.

mdctx = EVP_MD_CTX_new( ):

This line creates a new digest context. The context is used to hold information about the state of the digest computation.

EVP_MD_CTX_init (mdctx):

This initializes the newly created digest context, preparing it for use in the digest operations that follow.

EVP_DigestInit_ex (mdctx, md, NULL):

Here, we initialize the digest operation using the SHA-256 algorithm. This sets up the context to use SHA-256 for the hash computation. NULL indicates that we are going to use the default cryptographic engine provided by OpenSSL.

EVP_DigestUpdate(mdctx, source, strlen (source)):

This function updates the digest context with the data to be hashed. It processes the input data (**source** in this case) and updates the context with the partial hash state. The **strlen (source)** function provides the length of the input string.

EVP_DigestFinal_ex (mdctx, csum, &md_len):

This function finalizes the digest computation. It calculates the final hash value based on all the data provided to the context so far and stores the result in the **csum** array. The length of the computed hash is stored in **md_len**.

EVP_MD_CTX_free (mdctx):

Finally, this line frees the digest context. It releases any resources that were allocated for the context during the hash computation process.

SHA256 of A File

It is possible to compute the SHA256 checksum of a file containing text or binary data. The following program illustrates how this can be done.

```
#include <stdio.h>
#include <string.h>
#include <openssl/evp.h>
void getSHA256OfFile ( char *source, unsigned char *csum ) ;
int main( )
{
```

```
    char fname[ ] = "humor.txt" ;
    unsigned char chksum[ 32 ] ;
    int i ;
    getSHA256OfFile ( fname, chksum ) ;
    for ( i = 0 ; i < 32 ; i++ )
        printf ( "%02x", chksum[ i ] ) ;
    return 0 ;
}
void getSHA256OfFile ( char *source, unsigned char *csum )
{
    BIO *bio_in ;
    const EVP_MD *md ;
    EVP_MD_CTX *mdctx ;
    unsigned char buf[ 512 ] ;
    int len ;
    unsigned int md_len ;
    bio_in = BIO_new_file ( source, "r" ) ;
    if ( bio_in == NULL )
    {
        printf ( "Cannot open file" ) ;
        exit ( 1 ) ;
    }
    OpenSSL_add_all_digests( ) ;
    md = EVP_get_digestbyname ( "SHA256" ) ;
    mdctx = EVP_MD_CTX_new( ) ;
    EVP_MD_CTX_init ( mdctx ) ;
    EVP_DigestInit_ex ( mdctx, md, NULL ) ;
    while ( ( len = BIO_read ( bio_in, buf, sizeof ( buf ) ) ) > 0 )
        EVP_DigestUpdate ( mdctx, buf, len ) ;
    EVP_DigestFinal ( mdctx, csum, &md_len ) ;
    EVP_MD_CTX_free ( mdctx ) ;
    BIO_free ( bio_in ) ;
}
```

The function **getSHA256OfFile( )** begins by creating a new **BIO** (Basic Input Output) file object using **BIO_new_file( )** to open the specified file (**source**) in read mode ("r"). If the file cannot be opened, it prints an error message and exits the program. Note the reason why we are using BIO functions over normal FILE I/O functions. BIOs provide a unified API for different types of I/O operations. Whether we are dealing with files, memory buffers, or network sockets, we can use the same set of functions to handle the I/O operations.

Rest of the working of getSHA256OfFile( ) is almost same as what we learnt in getSHA256( ) in previous section. The only piece of code that is different is the **while** loop.

```
unsigned char buf [ 512 ] ;
int len;
while ( ( len = BIO_read ( bio_in, buf, sizeof ( buf ) ) ) >0 )
    EVP_DigestUpdate ( mdctx, buf, len ) ;
```

This loop reads chunks of data from the file using **BIO_read( )** and updates the digest context with each chunk of data. **buf** is a buffer used to temporarily store data read from the file, and **len** is the length of data read. **EVP_DigestUpdate( )** processes the data and updates the digest context with the partial hash state. Thus, through the loop we can process large files to obtain their SHA256 checksum.

Often along with the files that are made available for downloading from server, their checksum is also published. So, once we download the file, we can compute its checksum (using the above program) and then compare this checksum with the checksum provided by the server. If they match in all 32 bytes, we can be sure that the downloaded file is an exact replica of the file on the server. If not, it means that the two files are different and hence data integrity has been violated.

Authenticity

We can use the SHA256 checksum to check whether the user of an application/website is an authentic user or not. For this when the user does a "sign-up" and enters his login name and password, the server stores the login name and SHA256 checksum of password in a database on server. When the user does a "sign-in" and enters the login name and password, from the server the SHA256 checksum stored against the login name is retrieved from the server database. Next, the SHA256 checksum of the entered password is computed. Then the retrieved checksum is compared with the computed checksum. If there is an exact match then the user is an authentic user, otherwise not.

We can implement this authentication scheme with some simplification. Instead of storing the login name and SHA256 checksum of password in a database on server, we will store it in a text file locally. During "sign-in" we will read this SHA256 checksum from the local file. Both these programs are given below.

```
// Program 1 - Create user during "sign-up"
#include <string.h>
#include <stdio.h>
#include <openssl/evp.h>
void getSHA256 ( char *source, unsigned char *csum ) ;
int main( )
{
    struct Credentials
    {
        unsigned char loginName[ 15 ] ;
        unsigned char sha256OfPw[ 32 ] ;
    } ;
    struct Credentials user = { 0 } ;
    char pw[ 15 ] ;
    FILE *fp ;
    printf ( "Loginname: " ) ;
    scanf ( "%15s", user.loginName ) ;
    printf ( "Password: " ) ;
    scanf ( "%15s", pw ) ;
    int i ;
    getSHA256 ( pw, user.sha256OfPw ) ;
    fp = fopen ( "userData.txt", "wb" ) ;
    fwrite ( &user, sizeof ( user ), 1, fp ) ;
    fclose ( fp ) ;
    for ( i = 0; i < 32; i++)
        printf ( "%02x", user.sha256OfPw[ i ] ) ;
    return 0 ;
}
void getSHA256 ( char *source, unsigned char *csum )
{
    EVP_MD_CTX *mdctx ;
    const EVP_MD *md ;
    unsigned int md_len ;
    OpenSSL_add_all_digests( ) ;
    md = EVP_get_digestbyname ( "SHA256" ) ;
    mdctx = EVP_MD_CTX_new( ) ;
    EVP_MD_CTX_init ( mdctx ) ;
    EVP_DigestInit_ex ( mdctx, md, NULL ) ;
    EVP_DigestUpdate ( mdctx, source, strlen ( source ) ) ;
```

```
    EVP_DigestFinal_ex ( mdctx, csum, &md_len ) ;
    EVP_MD_CTX_free ( mdctx ) ;
}
```

```
// Program 2: Validate user during "sign-in"
#include <string.h>
#include <stdio.h>
#include <openssl/evp.h>
void getSHA256 ( char *source, unsigned char *csum ) ;
int main( )
{
    struct Credentials
    {
        unsigned char loginName[ 15 ] ;
        unsigned char sha256OfPw[ 32 ] ;
    } ;
    struct Credentials userCredKb = { 0 } ;
    struct Credentials userCredFile ;
    char pw[ 15 ] ;
    FILE *fp ;
    printf ( "Loginname: " ) ;
    scanf ( "%15s", userCredKb.loginName ) ;
    printf ( "Password: " ) ;
    scanf ( "%15s", pw ) ;
    int i ;
    getSHA256 ( pw, userCredKb.sha256OfPw ) ;
    fp = fopen ( "userData.txt", "rb" ) ;
    fread ( &userCredFile, sizeof ( userCredFile ), 1, fp ) ;
    fclose ( fp ) ;
    for ( i = 0 ; i < 32 ; i++ )
    {
        if ( userCredKb.sha256OfPw[ i ] != userCredFile.sha256OfPw[ i ] )
        {
            printf ( "Illegal user" ) ;
            return 1 ;
        }
    }
    printf ( "Legal user" ) ;
    return 0 ;
}
```

```
void getSHA256 ( char *source, unsigned char *csum )
{
    EVP_MD_CTX *mdctx ;
    const EVP_MD *md ;
    unsigned int md_len ;
    OpenSSL_add_all_digests( ) ;
    md = EVP_get_digestbyname ( "SHA256" ) ;
    mdctx = EVP_MD_CTX_new( ) ;
    EVP_MD_CTX_init ( mdctx ) ;
    EVP_DigestInit_ex ( mdctx, md, NULL ) ;
    EVP_DigestUpdate ( mdctx, source, strlen ( source ) ) ;
    EVP_DigestFinal_ex ( mdctx, csum, &md_len ) ;
    EVP_MD_CTX_free ( mdctx ) ;
}
```

Today in practise instead of Basic Authentication demonstrated above, Two-factor Authentication (2FA) is used. In this scheme after validating the login name and password, authenticity is checked using one of the following methods:

(a) One-time password (OTP)
(b) Fingerprint recognition
(c) Face recognition
(d) Pattern recognition
(e) Security question

Implementation of these schemes is quite involved and beyond the scope of this book.

In the above schemes authenticity of user is being checked by the server. For user to feel assured, the user should also be able to check the authenticity of the server. For instance, while carrying out financial transactions on a bank's web site, the user should be able to find out whether he is transacting with a legitimate financial institution or not. This is done using Digital Certificates.

Confidentiality

Confidentiality is about keeping data private and inaccessible to unauthorized parties. Confidentiality is crucial in scenarios like credit card transactions, where personal and financial information must be safeguarded against eavesdropping. This is typically achieved through encryption algorithms like AES (Advanced Encryption Standard), which encrypt the data into an unreadable format for unauthorized users. AES is a virtually impenetrable algorithm, extremely secure and widely used worldwide.

AES is a symmetric encryption technique to secure data. Here "symmetric" means that for encryption and decryption same key is used. In addition to key, AES also uses an Initialization Vector (IV) for encryption and decryption. The primary purpose of the IV is to ensure that even if the same plaintext is encrypted multiple times, the ciphertext will be different each time. This prevents attackers from inferring patterns based on repeated ciphertexts. This makes the encryption process unique and unpredictable.

Let us now see how a file "humor.txt" can be encrypted using a key and IV. The program for this is given below.

```
#include <openssl/evp.h>
#include <openssl/aes.h>
#include <openssl/rand.h>
#include <openssl/bio.h>
#include <openssl/err.h>
#include <string.h>
#include <stdlib.h>
#include <stdio.h>
void encryptFile ( const char *in, const char *out, unsigned char *key,
unsigned char *iv ) ;
int main( )
{
    unsigned char key[ 32 ] ;  // 32 bytes = 256 bits
    unsigned char iv[ 16] ;
    RAND_bytes ( key, sizeof ( key ) ) ;
    RAND_bytes ( iv, sizeof ( iv ) ) ;
    BIO *bio_out = BIO_new_file ( "key.bin", "wb" ) ;
    BIO_write ( bio_out, key, sizeof ( key ) ) ;
    BIO_free ( bio_out ) ;
    bio_out = BIO_new_file ( "iv.bin", "wb" ) ;
    BIO_write ( bio_out, iv, sizeof ( iv ) ) ;
    BIO_free ( bio_out ) ;
    encryptFile ( "humor.txt", "encrypted.bin", key, iv ) ;
    printf ( "File encrypted successfully!\n" ) ;
    return 0 ;
}
```

```
void encryptFile ( const char *in, const char *out, unsigned char *key,
unsigned char *iv )
{
    BIO *bio_in = BIO_new_file ( in, "rb" ) ;
    BIO *bio_out = BIO_new_file ( out, "wb" ) ;
    EVP_CIPHER_CTX *ctx ;
    ctx = EVP_CIPHER_CTX_new( ) ;
    EVP_EncryptInit_ex ( ctx, EVP_aes_256_cbc( ), NULL, key, iv ) ;
    unsigned char inbuf[ 1024 ] ;
    unsigned char outbuf[ 1024 + EVP_MAX_BLOCK_LENGTH ] ;
    int inlen, outlen ;
    while ( ( inlen = BIO_read ( bio_in, inbuf, sizeof ( inbuf ) ) ) > 0 )
    {
        EVP_EncryptUpdate ( ctx, outbuf, &outlen, inbuf, inlen ) ;
        BIO_write ( bio_out, outbuf, outlen ) ;
    }
    EVP_EncryptFinal_ex ( ctx, outbuf, &outlen ) ;
    BIO_write ( bio_out, outbuf, outlen ) ;
    EVP_CIPHER_CTX_free ( ctx ) ;
    BIO_free ( bio_in ) ;
    BIO_free ( bio_out ) ;
}
```

In **main( )** we have generated a key and IV of size 32 and 16 bytes respectively by generating random values of unsigned chars using the **RAND_bytes( )** function of OpenSSL library. We have then written the generated key and IV into files "key.bin" and "iv.bin". Lastly we have called **encryptFile( )** to encrypt a file "humor.txt" into "encrypted.bin" using the generated key and IV.

In **encryptFile( )** we first created a new cipher context, and then initialized the AES-256-CBC (Cipher Block Chaining) encryption operation with the provided key and IV. The NULL passed to **EVP_EncryptInit_ex( )** indicates that we are going to use the default cryptographic engine provided by OpenSSL.

Then in the **while** loop we have read the input file in chunks, encrypted the chunk and then written the encrypted chunk into the output file. Once control goes outside the loop **EVP_EncryptFinal_ex( )** finalizes the encryption, processing any remaining data that was buffered and not yet processed by **EVP_EncryptUpdate( )**.

Note that in block ciphers like AES, data must be encrypted in fixed-size blocks of 128-bit. If our data does not perfectly fit into these blocks, padding is added to the data to make it fit. The **EVP_EncryptFinal_ex( )** function adds any necessary padding to the final block of data. If we do not call it, the final block might not be correctly sized, resulting in incomplete encryption and potential data corruption during decryption.

Let us now do the reverse process, i.e. decrypt the "encrypted.bin" file by reading the key and IV from "key.bin" and "iv.bin". Here is the program...

```
#include <openssl/evp.h>
#include <openssl/aes.h>
#include <openssl/rand.h>
#include <openssl/bio.h>
#include <openssl/err.h>
#include <string.h>
#include <stdlib.h>
#include <stdio.h>
void decryptFile ( const char *in, const char *out, unsigned char *key,
unsigned char *iv ) ;
int main( )
{
    unsigned char key[ 32 ] ;
    unsigned char iv[ 16 ] ;
    BIO *bio_in = BIO_new_file ( "key.bin", "rb" ) ;
    BIO_read ( bio_in, key, sizeof ( key ) ) ;
    BIO_free ( bio_in ) ;
    bio_in = BIO_new_file ( "iv.bin", "rb" ) ;
    BIO_read ( bio_in, iv, sizeof ( iv ) ) ;
    BIO_free ( bio_in ) ;
    decryptFile ( "encrypted.bin", "decrypted_humor.txt", key, iv ) ;
    printf ( "File decrypted successfully!\n" ) ;
    return 0 ;
}
void decryptFile ( const char *in, const char *out, unsigned char *key,
unsigned char *iv )
{
    BIO *bio_in = BIO_new_file ( in, "rb" ) ;
    BIO *bio_out = BIO_new_file ( out, "wb" ) ;
    EVP_CIPHER_CTX *ctx ;
    unsigned char inbuf[1024 + EVP_MAX_BLOCK_LENGTH] ;
```

```
    unsigned char outbuf[1024] ;
    int inlen, outlen ;
    ctx = EVP_CIPHER_CTX_new( ) ;
    EVP_DecryptInit_ex ( ctx, EVP_aes_256_cbc( ), NULL, key, iv ) ;
    while ( ( inlen = BIO_read ( bio_in, inbuf, sizeof ( inbuf ) ) ) > 0 )
    {
        EVP_DecryptUpdate ( ctx, outbuf, &outlen, inbuf, inlen ) ;
        BIO_write ( bio_out, outbuf, outlen ) ;
    }
    EVP_DecryptFinal_ex ( ctx, outbuf, &outlen ) ;
    BIO_write ( bio_out, outbuf, outlen ) ;
    EVP_CIPHER_CTX_free ( ctx ) ;
    BIO_free ( bio_in ) ;
    BIO_free ( bio_out ) ;
}
```

The program reads the encryption key and IV from "key.bin" and "iv.bin" files, respectively, then calls **decryptFile( )** to decrypt the contents of "encrypted.bin" and write the decrypted data to "decrypted_humor.txt". The **decryptFile( )** function initializes a BIO for reading the encrypted file and another BIO for writing the decrypted output. It creates and initializes an EVP_CIPHER_CTX context for AES-256-CBC decryption using the provided key and IV. The function reads encrypted data in chunks, decrypts it using **EVP_DecryptUpdate( )**, and writes the decrypted data to the output file. Finally, it finalizes the decryption with **EVP_DecryptFinal_ex( )**, ensuring any remaining data is decrypted and written out, and then cleans up the BIO and context resources.

Non-repudiation

Non-repudiation prevents individuals from denying their actions. This section demonstrates how to use digital signatures to provide undeniable proof of the origin and integrity of a document. To achieve this, we need a pair of keys—a public key and a private key. As their names suggest, the public key can be shared openly with anyone, whereas its corresponding private key must be kept secret. The idea of key pairs was conceived by Rivest-Shamir-Adleman (RSA) and is widely used for two purposes:

(a) Encryption – A symmetric key encrypted using a public key can be decrypted only using its corresponding private key. Since the key used for encryption is different than the one used for decryption, this process is called asymmetric encryption. Contrast this with the method discussed in "Confidentiality" section above which used symmetric encryption (same key used for encryption and decryption). Note that RSA is being used for encryption / decryption of symmetric key and not for data (file) encryption and decryption.

Note that symmetric encryption is faster than asymmetric encryption. So, symmetric encryption is used for file encryption/decryption, whereas asymmetric encryption is used for sharing the key used for symmetric encryption.

(b) Non-repudiation – Data signed using a private key can be verified by anyone using the corresponding public key.

In this section we will concentrate on non-repudiation and not on symmetric key encryption/decryption.

The private and public keys are usually stored in Privacy-Enhanced Mail (.PEM) files. These files are Base64 encoded, and the key is usually encapsulated between "-----BEGIN" and "-----END" lines.

The following OpenSSL commands can be used to generate private and public keys.

```
# Generate a private key, store it in private_key.pem file
$ openssl genpkey -algorithm RSA -out private_key.pem

# Extract the public key, store it in public_key.pem file
$ openssl rsa -pubout -in private_key.pem -out public_key.pem
```

The key generation relies on the mathematical properties of large prime numbers. The size of private and public keys is 2048 bits (256 bytes) by default. However, if you open the two PEM files you will observe that the private key appears to be bigger than the public key. This is because the private key file contains all the information needed to generate the public key.

Let us now develop two programs. The first one will sign a file "humor.txt" using a private key stored in "private_key.pem" and the second one will verify the signature using the corresponding public key stored in "public_key.pem". This mechanism ensures that the signer cannot deny having signed the document, providing a robust non-repudiation solution. Here is the first program.

```
#include <openssl/evp.h>
#include <openssl/pem.h>
#include <openssl/err.h>
#include <openssl/bio.h>
#include <string.h>
#include <stdlib.h>
#include <stdio.h>
void signFile ( const char *in, const char *out, const char *keyFile ) ;
int main ( )
{
    signFile ( "humor.txt", "signature.bin", "private_key.pem" ) ;
    printf ( "File signed successfully!\n" ) ;
    return 0 ;
}
void signFile ( const char *in, const char *out, const char *keyFile )
{
    BIO *bio_in, *bio_out, *bio_key ;
    EVP_PKEY *privateKey ;
    EVP_MD_CTX *mdctx ;
    unsigned char buffer[1024] ;
    int len ;
    long unsigned int sig_len ;
    unsigned char *sig ;

    OpenSSL_add_all_algorithms( ) ;
    bio_in = BIO_new_file ( in, "rb" ) ;
    bio_out = BIO_new_file ( out, "wb" ) ;
    bio_key = BIO_new_file ( keyFile, "rb" ) ;

    privateKey = PEM_read_bio_PrivateKey ( bio_key, NULL, NULL,
                    NULL ) ;
    mdctx = EVP_MD_CTX_new( ) ;
    EVP_DigestSignInit ( mdctx, NULL, EVP_sha256( ), NULL, privateKey );
    while ( ( len = BIO_read ( bio_in, buffer, sizeof ( buffer ) ) ) > 0 )
        EVP_DigestSignUpdate ( mdctx, buffer, len ) ;

    EVP_DigestSignFinal ( mdctx, NULL, &sig_len ) ;
    sig = ( unsigned char * ) malloc ( sig_len ) ;
    EVP_DigestSignFinal ( mdctx, sig, &sig_len ) ;
    BIO_write ( bio_out, sig, sig_len ) ;
    free ( sig ) ;
```

```
    EVP_MD_CTX_free ( mdctx ) ;
    EVP_PKEY_free ( privateKey ) ;
    BIO_free ( bio_in ) ;
    BIO_free ( bio_out ) ;
    BIO_free ( bio_key ) ;
}
```

The program reads the contents of "humor.txt", computes the SHA256 checksum of the content, and then signs this digest using the private key stored in "private_key.pem". The generated signature is then written to "signature.bin". The signing process involves encrypting the hash with the private key. Thus, the signature stored in "signature.bin" is essentially an encrypted version of the hash and is unique to both the file content and the private key.

The different steps performed in the **signFile( )** function are outlined below:

(a) Initial Setup: The function begins by initializing OpenSSL's algorithms with **OpenSSL_add_all_algorithms( )**. It then opens the input file ("humor.txt"), the output file ("signature.bin"), and the private key file ("private_key.pem") using BIO functions.

(b) Reading the Private Key: The private key is read from "private_key.pem" using **PEM_read_bio_PrivateKey( )** which returns an **EVP_PKEY** structure containing the private key. The NULLs passed to this function instructs it to used standard mechanisms provided by OpenSSL.

(c) Initializing the Digest Context: An **EVP_MD_CTX** structure is created to hold the message digest context. **EVP_DigestSignInit( )** initializes this context for signing the SHA256 checksum using the private key.

(d) Reading and Hashing the Input File: The input file is read in chunks (using a buffer of size 1024 bytes), and each chunk is fed into the digest context using **EVP_DigestSignUpdate( )**. This updates the SHA256 checksum with the content of the file.

(e) Determining the Signature Length: The first call to **EVP_DigestSignFinal( )** with a NULL signature pointer is used to obtain the length of the signature **(sig_len)**. This is necessary because the size of the signature depends on the key and the digest algorithm used.

(f) Allocating Memory for the Signature: Memory is allocated for the signature based on the length obtained in the previous step.

(g) Generating the Signature: The second call to **EVP_DigestSignFinal( )** actually generates the signature and stores it in the allocated memory.

(h) Writing the Signature to the Output File: The signature is written to "signature.bin" using **BIO_write( )**.

(i) Cleanup: The allocated memory for the signature, the digest context, private key, and BIO structures are freed to release resources.

Let us now go to the next step, i.e. verifying the signature. This can be done using the program given below:

```
#include <openssl/evp.h>
#include <openssl/pem.h>
#include <openssl/err.h>
#include <openssl/bio.h>
#include <string.h>
#include <stdlib.h>
#include <stdio.h>
int verifyFile ( const char *inFile, const char *sigFile,
                 const char *keyFile ) ;
int main( )
{
    int result ;
    result = verifyFile ( "humor.txt", "signature.bin", "public_key.pem" ) ;
    if ( result == 1 )
        printf ( "Signature verified successfully!\n" ) ;
    else
        printf ( "Signature verification failed.\n" ) ;
    return 0 ;
}
int verifyFile ( const char *inFile, const char *sigFile, const char *keyFile)
{
    BIO *bio_in, *bio_sig, *bio_key ;
    EVP_PKEY *publicKey ;
    EVP_MD_CTX *mdctx ;
    unsigned char buffer[ 1024 ] ;
    int len ;
```

```
    unsigned char sig[ 256 ] ;
    int result ;

    OpenSSL_add_all_algorithms( ) ;
    bio_in = BIO_new_file ( inFile, "rb" ) ;
    bio_sig = BIO_new_file ( sigFile, "rb" ) ;
    bio_key = BIO_new_file ( keyFile, "rb" ) ;

    publicKey = PEM_read_bio_PUBKEY ( bio_key, NULL, NULL, NULL ) ;
    mdctx = EVP_MD_CTX_new( ) ;
    EVP_DigestVerifyInit ( mdctx, NULL, EVP_sha256( ), NULL,
                            publicKey ) ;
    while ( ( len = BIO_read ( bio_in, buffer, sizeof ( buffer ) ) ) > 0 )
        EVP_DigestVerifyUpdate ( mdctx, buffer, len ) ;

    len = BIO_read ( bio_sig, sig, sizeof ( sig ) ) ;
    result = EVP_DigestVerifyFinal ( mdctx, sig, len ) ;
    EVP_MD_CTX_free ( mdctx ) ;
    EVP_PKEY_free ( publicKey ) ;
    BIO_free ( bio_in ) ;
    BIO_free ( bio_sig ) ;
    BIO_free ( bio_key ) ;
    return result ;
}
```

The **verifyFile( )** function reads the content of "humor.txt", and obtains its SHA256 checksum. Next, it reads the digital signature from "signature.bin", and verifies the signature using the public key from "public_key.pem". The different steps performed in the **verifyFile( )** function are outlined below:

(a) Initial Setup: The **OpenSSL_add_all_algorithms( )** function initializes OpenSSL algorithms. Next, the input file ("humor.txt"), the signature file ("signature.bin"), and the public key file (public_key.pem) are opened using BIO functions.

(b) Reading the Public Key: The public key is read from "public_key.pem" using **PEM_read_bio_PUBKEY( )**, which returns an **EVP_PKEY** structure containing the public key.

(c) Initializing the Digest Context: An **EVP_MD_CTX** structure is created to hold the message digest context. **EVP_DigestVerifyInit( )**

initializes this context for verifying the signed SHA256 checksum using the public key.

(d) Reading and Hashing the Input File: The input file is read in chunks (using a buffer of size 1024 bytes), and each chunk is fed into the digest context using **EVP_DigestSignUpdate( )**. This updates the SHA256 checksum with the content of the file.

(e) Reading the Signature: The signature from "signature.bin" is read into the **sig** buffer.

(f) Verifying the Signature: **EVP_DigestVerifyFinal( )** is called to verify the signature against the computed SHA256 checksum.

(g) Cleanup: The digest context, public key, and BIO structures are freed to release resources.

Digital Signing in Practise

There are multiple options available for signing a document using a digital signature. These are as follows:

(a) USB Dongle: It stores the digital certificate and private key securely.
Usage: The dongle is attached to a USB drive and the software that comes with the dongle is used to sign a document digitally.

(b) Smart card: It stores the digital certificate and private key securely.
Usage: Insert the smart card into the reader and use it to sign documents digitally.

(c) Software-Based Digital Signature: Obtain a digital certificate from a trusted Certificate Authority (CA) and store it on your computer.
Usage: Use software such as Adobe Acrobat, Microsoft Word, or specialized digital signature applications to apply digital signature.

(d) Hardware Security Module (HSM): These are dedicated hardware devices that manage digital keys and perform cryptographic operations.
Usage: Often used by organizations to centrally manage and secure digital keys for signing documents and transactions.

(e) Cloud-Based Digital Signatures: Services like DocuSign, Adobe Sign, and HelloSign offer cloud-based digital signing solutions.
Usage: Users can sign documents from any device with internet access. The service handles key management and applies the digital signatures.

(f) Mobile-Based Signing Solutions: Apps like SignEasy, Adobe Fill & Sign, and others allow users to sign documents directly from their mobile devices.
Usage: These apps may use biometrics (fingerprint, facial recognition) to secure the signing process.

(g) Public Key Infrastructure (PKI) Solutions: Organizations can implement their own PKI solutions to issue and manage digital certificates internally.
Usage: Users can sign documents using the digital certificates issued by the organization's PKI.

(h) Browser-Based Digital Signatures: Browser extensions like CertifyID use the browser's built-in security features.
Usage: Users can sign documents directly within their web browser using their digital certificates.

Each of these digital signing solutions has its own advantages and is suited for different use cases. USB dongles and smart cards offer high security, while cloud-based and software-based solutions provide flexibility and convenience. The choice of method depends on the specific security requirements, convenience needs, and the technological infrastructure of the user or organization.

When signing a document digitally using any of the above methods, the process involves the following steps:

(a) Hashing: The document's content is hashed using a secure hash algorithm like SHA256.

(b) Encryption: The hash is encrypted using the signer's private key, creating a digital signature.

(c) Attachment: The digital signature is attached to the document.

On receiving the document, the following steps are performed:

(a) Hashing: The document's content is hashed again using the same hash algorithm.

(b) Decryption: The attached digital signature is decrypted using the signer's public key.

(c) Comparison: The decrypted hash is compared to the newly computed hash. If they match, the signature is verified, ensuring the document's integrity and authenticity.

Exercises

[A] Match the pairs:

(a) Integrity	(1) Signing, Verification
(b) Authenticity	(2) Encryption / Decryption
(c) Confidentiality	(3) SHA256
(d) Non-repudiation	(4) MD5

[B] Pick the correct choice:

(a) Which of the following techniques will you use if you wish to transmit a file ensuring its confidentiality.

(1) Use asymmetric encryption for encryption/decryption
(2) Use symmetric encryption for encryption/decryption
(3) Use asymmetric encryption for sharing symmetric key, use symmetric encryption/decryption for file
(4) Use symmetric encryption for sharing symmetric key, use asymmetric encryption/decryption for file

(b) We wish to download a file from the server and check whether it has been downloaded correctly or not. Which technique would you employ to achieve this?

(1) Download the file, compute its SHA256 checksum
(2) Download the file, compute its SHA256 checksum, compare this checksum with checksum of file reported on server
(3) Download the file using RSA
(4) Use symmetric encryption while downloading the file

[C] Answer the following questions:

(a) What does EVP in OpenSSL functions signify? Why is it used?

(b) Which are the four aspects of security? Does every secure application need to implement them?

[D] Attempt the following questions:

(a) Obtain MD5 checksum of the following strings and check whether they are same:

"Six slippery snails slid slowly seaward."
"Six silppery snails slid slowly seaward."

(b) Compile any C program into a .EXE or a .out file. Obtain SHA256 checksum of the file.

KanNotes

- Four aspects of security :
  a) Integrity
  b) Authenticity
  c) Confidentiality
  d) Non-repudiation
- Every application may or may not need all four aspects of security
- Message digest, checksum, fingerprint, hash value are synonymous terms
- Message digest of two distinct strings/files will always be distinct
- From a message digest of some data, it is impossible to obtain the data
- There are different message digest algorithms available - MD5, SHA1, SHA256, SHA384, SHA 512
- Message digest is computed in 3 steps – initialization of context, updating of context and finalization of context
- OpenSSL library is widely used in implementing security
- OpenSSL is available in Windows, Linux, and Mac
- SHA256 can be used to implement Integrity and Authenticity
- Confidentiality can be implemented using symmetric encryption done using a single key
- Non-repudiation can be implemented using a pair of private – public key

- To implement non-repudiation, a document can be signed using a private key and verified using a public key
- There are many mechanisms available for signing and verifying a document

24 Interaction With ChatGPT Thro C

"AI... The programmer's magic lamp"

Mastering the ability to interact with ChatGPT through C opens exciting new possibilities in your programming journey. This chapter shows you how to harness these powerful AI tools from your C programs...

Contents

Artificial Intelligence (AI) has become the rage of the day. Multiple AI tools are available that let us write programs, translate text, produce images, create videos etc. The most popular amongst these tools is ChatGPT, created by a company named OpenAI. In this chapter we will see how to interact with ChatGPT through C programs. Before we get down to that, let us understand some terminology commonly used with AI.

AI Terminology

AI refers to the simulation of human intelligence in machines, enabling them to perform tasks that typically require human cognition, such as understanding language, recognizing patterns, and making decisions. Some commonly used terms in relation to AI are given below:

Machine Learning: It is a subset of artificial intelligence that focuses on building algorithms that enable computers to learn from and make decisions based on data without being explicitly programmed.

Deep Learning: It is a specialized branch of machine learning that uses neural networks with many layers to automatically learn and extract complex patterns from large datasets. Deep learning is inspired by the working of the human brain and is particularly effective in handling complex tasks like image recognition, speech synthesis, and natural language processing, where they can uncover intricate relationships within large datasets.

Natural Language Processing (NLP): It is a field of artificial intelligence that focuses on the interaction between computers and humans through natural language. It involves the development of algorithms and models that enable machines to understand, interpret, and generate human language, facilitating tasks such as translation, sentiment analysis, and conversation.

What is ChatGPT?

The name "ChatGPT" breaks down as follows:

Chat: This refers to the conversational aspect of the model. The model is designed to engage in dialogue or "chat" with users, answering questions, providing information, or engaging in conversation on various topics.

G: Stands for Generative. This signifies that the model is a generative model, meaning it generates text based on the input it receives. It doesn't simply retrieve information but creates responses dynamically.

P: Stands for Pre-trained. This indicates that the model has undergone extensive training on a large dataset before it is fine-tuned or used in specific applications. The pre-training phase allows the model to learn language patterns, grammar, facts, and some reasoning abilities.

T: Stands for Transformer. The transformer is a type of deep learning model architecture that is particularly effective for natural language processing tasks. The "T" refers to the underlying architecture that powers the GPT model.

So, "ChatGPT" essentially means a Generative Pre-trained Transformer model that is used for chat or conversational purposes.

The core of ChatGPT is built upon the Transformer architecture, a deep learning model that has revolutionized the way computers understand and generate human language. Trained on vast amounts of text data, ChatGPT aims to achieve seamless and intuitive interactions, enabling users to obtain information, solve problems, and engage in creative tasks with a level of fluency and coherence that closely mirrors natural human communication. Whether it's answering questions, providing recommendations, or assisting in technical tasks, ChatGPT's goal is to enhance human capabilities by providing an accessible, intelligent, and responsive virtual assistant.

Ways to Use ChatGPT

There are two main ways to use ChatGPT: interactively and programmatically. These are discussed below:

(a) **Interactively**: We can use ChatGPT by visiting the OpenAI website at https://chatgpt.com. Here, you can engage in a conversational interface where you type your questions or prompts, and ChatGPT responds in real-time. This method is user-friendly and requires no technical setup, making it ideal for casual use or quick queries.

(b) **Programmatically**: For more advanced users, ChatGPT can be accessed programmatically via the ChatGPT API. This approach allows developers to integrate ChatGPT's capabilities into their own applications, automating interactions and customizing the model's behaviour according to specific needs. By sending HTTP requests to the API endpoint with the necessary parameters and receiving responses in a structured format, developers can leverage ChatGPT to power chatbots, virtual assistants, or any application that requires natural language understanding and generation.

Interactive usage of ChatGPT is free, whereas when we use ChatGPT programmatically, we get a free credit of 18$, beyond which it is a paid service. There is a catch here 18$ is a combination of your interactive use and programmatic use. If your quota of free usage exceeds 18$ credit, you may either subscribe to paid service or open a completely new account at OpenAI with a fresh email address and mobile number.

The First ChatGPT Program

Let us now write our first C program that interacts with ChatGPT. For this we need to make API calls using the HTTPS protocol. This is facilitated by an open-source library called 'curl' or 'libcurl'. Its primary purpose is to provide a flexible and efficient way to interact with web servers and other online resources programmatically. On a Linux-based system, it can be installed using the following commands.

```
$ sudo apt-get update
$ sudo apt-get install libcurl4-openssl-dev
```

Another thing that you need to do before writing the program is to get an API key from OpenAI. The OpenAI API uses an API key for authentication when we make calls to the API. It can be fetched by visiting

$ https://platform.openai.com/api-keys

You need to copy the generated API key and paste it in your program. A sample API key is given below:

sk-proj-AndnR8ixP_icm9CPw7KYFeB3Ah2x4Sh5PJNApwDg1jCzsKGBBGLz9x3jjsT3BlbkFJ8e5PvPljb1w7wswpX7l4eg6rdfvls7V72hE9ShSSFw4afu7ky3XmY5oA

Let us now write a program that asks ChatGPT "What is Pythagoras theorem?"

```
// UsingChatGPT.c
#include <stdio.h>
#include <stdlib.h>
#include <string.h>
```

```
#include <curl/curl.h>
#define API_URL "https://api.openai.com/v1/chat/completions"
#define API_KEY "INSERT YOUR API KEY HERE"

// callback function to handle the response data
int WriteCallback ( void *contents, int size, int nmemb, char *userp )
{
    strcat ( userp, ( char* ) contents ) ;
    return size * nmemb ;
}
int main( )
{
    CURL *curl ;
    CURLcode res ;
    char response[ 10000 ] = { 0 } ; // buffer for the response
    char *post_data = "{\"model\": \"gpt-3.5-turbo\", \"messages\":
   [{\"role\": \"user\", \"content\": \"What is Pythagoras theorem\"}]}" ;
    curl_global_init ( CURL_GLOBAL_DEFAULT ) ;
    curl = curl_easy_init( ) ;
    if ( curl == NULL )
    {
        printf ( "Unable to initialize curl library\n" ) ;
        return -1 ;
    }
    // set the URL for the POST request
    curl_easy_setopt ( curl, CURLOPT_URL, API_URL ) ;

    // set the API key in the header
    struct curl_slist *hdrs = NULL;
    hdrs = curl_slist_append ( hdrs, "Content-Type: application/json" ) ;
    hdrs = curl_slist_append ( hdrs, "Authorization: Bearer " API_KEY ) ;
    curl_easy_setopt ( curl, CURLOPT_HTTPHEADER, hdrs ) ;

    // set the POST data
    curl_easy_setopt ( curl, CURLOPT_POSTFIELDS, post_data ) ;

    // set up the function to capture the response
    curl_easy_setopt ( curl, CURLOPT_WRITEFUNCTION, WriteCallback );

    // set up the variable to hold the response
    curl_easy_setopt ( curl, CURLOPT_WRITEDATA, response ) ;

    // perform the request, res will get the return code
```

```
    res = curl_easy_perform ( curl ) ;

    // check for errors
    if ( res != CURLE_OK )
        printf ( "Failed: %s\n", curl_easy_strerror ( res ) ) ;
    else
        printf ( "Response: %s\n", response ) ;

    // clean up
    curl_slist_free_all ( hdrs ) ;
    curl_easy_cleanup ( curl ) ;
    curl_global_cleanup( ) ;
    return 0 ;
}
```

The program begins with initialization of the curl library by calling **curl_global_init( )**. This function sets up the global environment that libcurl needs to operate, including memory management, threading, and SSL libraries. CURL_GLOBAL_DEFAULT tells libcurl to initialize all necessary subsystems. This function is typically called at the beginning before any other libcurl functions are used. This ensures that the library is properly prepared to handle network operations.

The call to **curl_easy_init( )** initializes a CURL handle initializes a specific CURL easy handle, which is used to manage an individual HTTP request. It prepares a new session, allowing us to set options (like the URL, HTTP method, headers, etc.) and perform the transfer.

There are different types of HTTP requests that can be made using libcurl. While interacting with ChatGPT we need to make a POST request to a URL. When we make a POST request to ChatGPT, it returns a response. To make the HTTP POST request we need to perform the following steps:

(a) Set the URL for POST request (CURLOPT_URL)
(b) Set the necessary custom headers (CURLOPT_HTTPHEADER)
(c) Set the POST data (CURLOPT_POSTFIELDS)
(d) Set the POST method (CURLOPT_WRITEFUNCTION)
(e) Set the response variable (CURLOPT_WRITE_DATA)

All these steps are performed using calls to **curl_easy_setopt( )** with suitable macros like CURLOPT_URL, CURLOPT_HTTPHEADER, etc. While setting the header we have specified "Content-Type" as application/json. This informs the server that the body of the HTTP request contains data in JSON (JavaScript Object Notation) format.

When the server receives this request, it knows to parse and handle the body content as JSON.

The **WriteCallback( )** function gets called by libcurl as soon as it receives chunks of data from the ChatGPT server. Its prototype should match the following signature:

```
int WriteCallback ( void *contents, int size, int nmemb, void *userp ) ;
```

Here **contents** is a pointer to received data, whereas **userp** is a pointer to a user-defined data structure where **WriteCallback( )** will copy the received data. The pointer to user-defined structure (**response** array in our case) is communicated to libcurl by calling **curl_easy_setopt( )** with CURLOPT_WRITE_DATA.

The headers are managed using a singly linked list structure provided by libcurl, where each node in the list contains a string representing a header. The function **curl_slist_append( )** is used to add new headers to this list.

The **post_data** variable contains the payload to be transferred during the POST request. This payload is organized in JSON format of key-value pairs. The JSON data in our program is shown below.


```
{
    "model": "gpt-3.5-turbo",
    "messages": [
            {
                "role": "user",
                "content": "What is Pythagoras theorem"
            }
        ]
}
```


While using this data in a C program, we need to escape every " with a \.

Once all settings have been done, to perform the HTTP request **curl_easy_perform( )** is called. The callback function **WriteCallback( )** is used to capture ChatGPT's response.

Once the response is printed, the function **curl_slist_free_all( )** is used to free a linked list of headers or other string data that was previously created using **curl_slist_append( )**. Resources are released with calls to **curl_easy_cleanup( )** and **curl_global_cleanup( )**.

Before executing the program remember to replace API_KEY with your API key. The commands for compilation and execution are as follows:

```
$ gcc UsingChatGPT.c -lcurl
$./a.out
```

On executing the program, the **response** variable would contain the following data in JSON format:


```
Response: {
  "id": "chatcmpl-A0iWEIjAva4Q4leshpkIQiLR3kUGG",
  "object": "chat.completion",
  "created": 1724734494,
  "model": "gpt-3.5-turbo-0125",
  "choices": [
   {
    "index": 0,
    "message": {
     "role": "assistant",
     "content": "Pythagoras theorem is a fundamental principle in
geometry that states that in a right-angled triangle, the square of the
length of the hypotenuse is equal to the sum of the squares of the
lengths of the other two sides. This theorem is named after the ancient
Greek mathematician Pythagoras, who is credited with discovering the
relationship between the sides of a right-angled triangle.",
     "refusal": null
    },
    "logprobs": null,
    "finish_reason": "stop"
   }
  ],
  "usage": {
   "prompt_tokens": 14,
   "completion_tokens": 142,
   "total_tokens": 156
  },
  "system_fingerprint": null
}
```


In this response the value of "content" key explains ChatGPT's understanding of Pythagoras Theorem.

Text to Speech Conversion

ChatGPT has an ability to convert Speech into text. So, if an audio file "WebService.wav" is submitted to OpenAI API, it can transcribe the audio into text and send the transcribed text as a response. To achieve this, our program should perform the following steps:

(a) Configure the necessary HTTP headers.
(b) Prepare the MIME-formatted form data, including the audio file and model selection.
(c) Send the form data to the API.
(d) Captures and process the response from the API using a callback function.

In the context of using the OpenAI API for speech-to-text conversion, the "form" refers to the structured set of data sent in an HTTP POST request. The form includes various parts, such as the audio file ("WebService.wav") being uploaded, the AI speech recognition model to be used ("Whisper-1") for transcribing and other parameters needed by the API. The "whisper-1" model for transcribing audio into text is known for its accuracy and robustness in handling diverse audio inputs.

When making an HTTP request to upload an audio .wav file, MIME (Multipurpose Internet Mail Extensions) is used to structure the request body. Each part of a MIME message can be assigned a specific content type and encoding, making it possible to handle different types of data in a single transmission. MIME allows the server to correctly interpret and process the audio file as part of the request, typically for purposes like transcription or analysis.

Let us now look at the program that performs the transcription of the audio file "WebService.wav".

```
#include <stdio.h>
#include <stdlib.h>
#include <string.h>
#include <curl/curl.h>
#define API_URL "https://api.openai.com/v1/audio/transcriptions"
#define API_KEY "INSERT YOUR API KEY HERE"
#define AUDIO_FILE "WebService.wav" // replace with your audio file

// callback function to handle the response data
int WriteCallback ( void *contents, int size, int nmemb, char *userp )
{
    strcat ( userp, ( char* ) contents ) ;
```

```
    return size * nmemb ;
}
int main( )
{
    CURL *curl ;
    CURLcode res ;
    char response[ 10000 ] = { 0 } ;

    curl_global_init ( CURL_GLOBAL_DEFAULT ) ;
    curl = curl_easy_init( ) ;
    if ( curl == NULL )
    {
        printf ( "Unable to initialize curl library\n" ) ;
        return -1 ;
    }

    // set the URL for the POST request
    curl_easy_setopt ( curl, CURLOPT_URL, API_URL ) ;
    // set the API key in the header
    struct curl_slist *hdrs = NULL ;
    hdrs = curl_slist_append ( hdrs, "Authorization: Bearer " API_KEY ) ;
    hdrs = curl_slist_append ( hdrs, "Content-Type:
                                    multipart/form-data" ) ;
    curl_easy_setopt ( curl, CURLOPT_HTTPHEADER, hdrs ) ;

    // set up the form for file upload
    curl_mime *form = curl_mime_init ( curl ) ;
    curl_mimepart *field = curl_mime_addpart ( form ) ;

    // add the audio file to the form
    curl_mime_name ( field, "file" ) ;
    curl_mime_filedata ( field, AUDIO_FILE ) ;

    // add the model to the form
    field = curl_mime_addpart ( form ) ;
    curl_mime_name ( field, "model" ) ;
    curl_mime_data ( field, "whisper-1", CURL_ZERO_TERMINATED ) ;

    // add the form to the request
    curl_easy_setopt ( curl, CURLOPT_MIMEPOST, form ) ;

    // set up the function to capture the response
    curl_easy_setopt ( curl, CURLOPT_WRITEFUNCTION, WriteCallback );
    curl_easy_setopt ( curl, CURLOPT_WRITEDATA, response ) ;
```

```
    // perform the request, res will get the return code
    res = curl_easy_perform ( curl ) ;

    // check for errors
    if ( res != CURLE_OK )
        printf ( "Failed: %s\n", curl_easy_strerror ( res ) ) ;
    else
        printf ( "Transcription Response: %s\n", response ) ;

    // clean up
    curl_slist_free_all ( hdrs ) ;
    curl_mime_free ( form ) ;
    curl_easy_cleanup ( curl ) ;
    curl_global_cleanup( ) ;
    return 0 ;
}
```

In this program the procedure for initializing the curl library, setting the HTTP headers with API key is same as the previous program. The call

```
curl_slist_append ( hdrs, "Content-Type: multipart/form-data" ) ;
```

adds a HTTP header indicating that the content type of the data being sent is multipart/form-data. This content type is necessary when we wish to upload files, as it allows the data to be formatted as different parts (e.g., files, fields).

The form data is prepared through the statements:

```
curl_mime *form = curl_mime_init ( curl ) ;
curl_mimepart *field = curl_mime_addpart ( form ) ;
```

The first statement initializes a new **curl_mime** handle, which will be used to create a MIME-formatted data body. The second statement adds a new part to the MIME form. Each part represents a distinct piece of data, such as an uploaded file or a form field. Once this is done, the name of the form field "file" and the actual file "WebService.wav" is set through the statements:

```
curl_mime_name ( field, "file" ) ;
curl_mime_filedata ( field, "WebService.wav" ) ;
```

On similar line model is added to the form through the statements

```
field = curl_mime_addpart ( form ) ;
```

```
curl_mime_name ( field, "model" ) ;
curl_mime_data ( field, "whisper-1", CURL_ZERO_TERMINATED ) ;
```

Lastly, the form data is added to the HTTP request through the statement

```
curl_easy_setopt ( curl, CURLOPT_MIMEPOST, form ) ;
```

This prepares libcurl to send the form data to the server when the request is performed. Rest of the procedure for setting the callback function to capture the response, performing the request and obtaining the response is exactly same as the previous program.

The transcribed text returned as a response is shown below.

```
Transcription Response: {
  "text": "now to make use of the web service that we have created
which is able to implement the subscription feature we need to create a
client which can make use of this web service. For that I will open firstly
the visual studio projects folder from where I would locate currency
service 2 and open the current web service"
}
```

Text to Image Conversion

OpenAI has developed an innovative AI model called DALL·E that generates images from textual descriptions. The word DALL·E is inspired by the surrealist art of Salvador Dalí and the imaginative nature of the animated robot WALL·E. By simply describing a scene, object, or concept in words, users can harness DALL·E to produce unique images that reflect their input, making it an invaluable tool for artists, designers, and content creators. This seamless combination of text-based interaction and image generation opens new possibilities for creative expression and visual storytelling.

Given below is a C program that generates an image for the text prompt "Draw a picture of a monkey sitting on a crocodile's back".

```
#include <stdio.h>
#include <stdlib.h>
#include <string.h>
#include <curl/curl.h>
#define API_URL "https://api.openai.com/v1/images/generations"
```

```
#define API_KEY "INSERT YOUR API KEY HERE"
#define PROMPT "Draw a picture of a monkey sitting on a crocodile's
back"
// callback function to handle the response data
int WriteCallback ( void *contents, int size, int nmemb, char *userp )
{
    strcat ( userp, ( char* ) contents ) ;
    return size * nmemb ;
}
int main( )
{
    CURL *curl ;
    CURLcode res ;
    char response[ 10000 ] = { 0 } ;
    struct curl_slist *hdrs = NULL ;

    curl_global_init ( CURL_GLOBAL_DEFAULT ) ;
    curl = curl_easy_init( ) ;
    if ( curl == NULL )
    {
        printf ( "Unable to initialize curl library\n" ) ;
        return -1 ;
    }

    // set the API URL
    curl_easy_setopt ( curl, CURLOPT_URL, API_URL ) ;

    // set the headers
    hdrs = curl_slist_append ( hdrs, "Authorization: Bearer " API_KEY ) ;
    hdrs = curl_slist_append ( hdrs, "Content-Type: application/json" ) ;
    curl_easy_setopt ( curl, CURLOPT_HTTPHEADER, hdrs ) ;

    // create the POST data in JSON format
    char *post_data = "{\"prompt\":\"" PROMPT "\", \"n\":1,
                        \"size\":\"1024x1024\"}" ;

    // set the POST data
    curl_easy_setopt ( curl, CURLOPT_POSTFIELDS, post_data ) ;

    // set the callback function to handle the response
    curl_easy_setopt ( curl, CURLOPT_WRITEFUNCTION, WriteCallback );
    curl_easy_setopt ( curl, CURLOPT_WRITEDATA, response ) ;

    // perform the request
```

```
    res = curl_easy_perform ( curl ) ;
    if ( res != CURLE_OK )
        printf ( "Failed: %s\n", curl_easy_strerror ( res ) ) ;
    else
        printf ( "Response: %s\n", response ) ;

    // clean up
    curl_slist_free_all ( hdrs ) ;
    curl_easy_cleanup ( curl ) ;
    curl_global_cleanup( ) ;
    return 0 ;
}
```

Except for the API endpoint and the POST data being sent in the HTTP request, rest of the program is same as the first program in this chapter. Let us dissect the POST data set up in the variable **post_data.**

```
char *post_data = "{\"prompt\":\"" PROMPT "\", \"n\":1,
                   \"size\":\"1024x1024\"}" ;
```

The **post_data** variable essentially instructs the API about what image to generate, how many images to create **("n": 1)**, and the desired size (**"size": "1024x1024"**) of the output image. These values are specified in JSON format of key:value pairs. The backslashes (\) are used to escape the double quotes within the string.

On executing this program, it produces the following output:


```
Response: {
 "created": 1724923356,
 "data": [
  {
   "url":
"https://oaidalleapiprodscus.blob.core.windows.net/private/org-DXVRyJfL4rz5iWtSnZUTknx9/user-tPfz0FfLPbZWrmHnYwDSzGJ0/img-ygYxD0pHXRLfIKMMgXf39CRY.png?st=2024-08-29T08%3A22%3A36Z&se=2024-08-29T10%3A22%3A36Z&sp=r&sv=2024-08-04&sr=b&rscd=inline&rsct=image/png&skoid=d505667d-d6c1-4a0a-bac7-5c84a87759f8&sktid=a48cca56-e6da-484e-a814-9c849652bcb3&skt=2024-08-28T23%3A19%3A06Z&ske=2024-08-29T23%3A19%3A06Z&sks=b&skv=2024-08-04&sig=N5bFcyFo79zTSquKOMdwCINXSAylrgPZdoPXkL%2BmcMo%3D"
```

```
  }
 ]
}
```

From this output copy the URL "https://oaidalleapiprodscus.... Mo%3D" and paste it in a browser. On doing this you should get the following image. Make sure that you grab this image within an hour. This is because OpenAI preserves your image only for an hour.

The quality and the details of the image can be improved by using a more descriptive prompt. The better you describe the image, better will be the output.

ChatGPT Endpoints

To engage in a conversation with ChatGPT we made a POST request to the URL https://api.openai.com/v1/chat/completions. Similarly, to transcript a wav file we made a POST request to the URL https://api.openai.com/v1/audio/transcriptions. These URLs are often referred to as ChatGPT API endpoints. Thus, an endpoint is a specific URL path provided by the OpenAI API that allows developers to interact with different features of ChatGPT. By making requests to these endpoints, developers can perform tasks such as generating text, creating images, converting speech to text, or moderating content, all by communicating with ChatGPT's underlying models. Each endpoint is designed for a particular function, making it easier to integrate AI capabilities into various applications. Given below is a list of some of the primary endpoints and their purposes:

(a) /v1/completions - Generates text based on a given prompt
(b) /v1/chat/completions - Engages in a conversation with ChatGPT
(c) /v1/edits - Edits a given text based on user instructions
(d) /v1/images/generations - Creates images from text descriptions
(e) /v1/embeddings - Generates vector representations of text for tasks like similarity or clustering
(f) /v1/audio/transcriptions - Converts audio files into text
(g) /v1/audio/translations - Translates audio files into English

While making a POST request to an URL there are some 'required' and some 'optional' parameters that we must pass in the request body. Details of these parameters are available in ChatGPT API documentation available at https://platform.openai.com/docs/api-reference.

Exercises

[A] Answer the following questions:

(a) Arrange the following steps involved in making a HTTP request in correct sequence:

(1) Set the response variable
(2) Set the POST method
(3) Set the URL for POST request
(4) Set the POST data
(5) Set the necessary custom headers

(b) How does ChatGPT API authenticate a user request made through a HTTP call?

(c) Which are the ways to interact with ChatGPT?

[B] Attempt the following questions:

(a) Write a program to convert a given text into an audio file. Use the following information to make the HTTP request.

Endpoint - https://api.openai.com/v1/audio/speech

model - string containing Text to Speech model name tts-1 or tts-1-hd input - string containing the text to generate audio for (maximum length is 4096 characters)

voice - string containing the voice to use when generating the audio. Supported voices are alloy, echo, fable, onyx, nova, and shimmer

(b) Write a program to generate 4 images of birds flying in the sky with a computer's mouse in their beak. Use the following information to make the HTTP request.

Endpoint - https://api.openai.com/v1/images/generations

prompt - string describing the image to be drawn by the model

input - string containing the text to generate audio for (maximum length is 4096 characters)

n - Number of images to be drawn

size - Size of the image

(c) Write a program to analyse a given sentence with a view to detect the mood of the sentence. For example, the mode of the sentence "I am so impressed by your performance" is "admiration and appreciation". Use the following information to make the HTTP request.

Endpoint - https://api.openai.com/v1/chat/completions

model - string containing the model name gpt-3.5-turbo

messages - A list of messages comprising the conversation

KanNotes

- AI simulates human intelligence in machines
- Machine learning involves building algorithms that learn from data and make decisions
- Deep learning uses neural networks to learn and extract complex patterns from large datasets
- Natural Language Processing permits interaction with computers through natural language

- ChatGPT stands for Chat based Generative Pre-trained Transformer
- ChatGPT can be used interactively as well as programmatically
- To use ChatGPT programmatically we need to obtain an API Key for authenticating our HTTP requests
- curl library is needed to make HTTP calls from a C program
- A sequence of steps must be carried out to build the HTTP request while using curl library
- HTTP response from ChatGPT is in JSON format
- DALL·E model lets us generate images from text prompts

25 Interview FAQs

"It's good to know how much you know..."

All that you learnt in this book would be put to test, when you attend an interview for a programmer's position in a software company. You may know the answer to the question, but the way it is presented is what makes all the difference. This chapter will guide you through those "expected" answers for typical C interview questions...

In the interview room you would be tested for three skills—Knowledge, Problem Solving Skills and Social Skills. You might be led to believe that in the interview room what matters is your personality, how smartly you answer questions, how are your mannerisms, etc. In fact, the truth is much farther than that. All of these in my estimate have only 10% importance. Much more weightage is given to your knowledge and problem-solving skills. If you are found good in these areas, then only the interview panel would be even interested in checking your social skills. With this in mind, I have given below questions that are very commonly asked in the interview rooms.

Question 1

What is a Programming Paradigm?

Answer

Programming paradigm means the principle that is used for organizing programs. There are two major Programming Paradigms, namely, Structured Programming and Object-Oriented Programming (OOP). C language uses the Structured Programming Paradigm, whereas, C++, C#, VB.NET or Java make use of OOP. OOP has lots of advantages to offer. But even while using this organizing principle you would still need a good hold over the language elements of C and the basic programming skills.

Question 2

Is it true that Operating Systems like Windows, Linux and UNIX are written in C?

Answer

Major parts of popular operating systems like Windows, UNIX, Linux and Android are written in C. This is because even today when it comes to performance (speed of execution) nothing beats C. Also, the functions exposed by the Operating System API can be easily called through any language.

Moreover, if one is to extend the operating system to work with new devices one needs to write Device Driver programs. These programs are exclusively written in C.

Question 3

What do you mean by scope of a variable? What are the different types of scopes that a variable can have?

Answer

Scope indicates the region over which the variable's declaration has an effect. The four kinds of scopes are—file, function, block and prototype.

Question 4

Which of the following statement is a declaration and which is a definition?

```
extern int i ;
int j ;
```

Answer

First is declaration, second is definition.

Question 5

What are the differences between a declaration and a definition?

Answer

There are two differences between a declaration and a definition:

In the definition of a variable space is reserved for the variable and some initial value is given to it, whereas a declaration only identifies the type of the variable. Thus, definition is the place where the variable is created or assigned storage, whereas declaration refers to places where the nature of the variable is stated but no storage is allocated.

Secondly, redefinition is an error, whereas, redeclaration is not an error.

Question 6

Is it true that a global variable may have several declarations, but only one definition? [Yes/No]

Answer

Yes

Question 7

Is it true that a function may have several declarations, but only one definition? [Yes/No]

Answer

Yes

Question 8

When we mention the prototype of a function are we defining the function or declaring it?

Answer

We are declaring it. When the function, along with the statements belonging to it is mentioned, we are defining the function.

Question 9

Some books suggest that the following definitions should be preceded by the word *static*. Is it correct?

```
int a[ ] = { 2, 3, 4, 12, 32 } ;
struct emp e = { "sandy", 23 } ;
```

Answer

Pre-ANSI C compilers had such a requirement. Compilers which conform to ANSI C standard do not have such a requirement.

Question 10

If you are to share the variables or functions across several source files, how would you ensure that all definitions and declarations are consistent?

Answer

The best arrangement is to place each definition in a relevant '.c' file. Then, put an external declaration in a header file ('.h' file) and use **#include** to bring in the declaration wherever needed. The '.c' file which contains the definition should also include the header file, so that the compiler can check that the definition matches the declaration.

Question 11

Global variables are available to all functions. Does there exist a mechanism by way of which I can make it available to some and not to others?

Answer

No. The only way this can be achieved is to define the variable locally in **main( )** instead of defining it globally and then passing it to the functions which need it.

Question 12

What are the different types of linkages?

Answer

There are three different types of linkages—external, internal and none. External linkage means global, non-static variables and functions, internal linkage means static variables and functions with file scope, and no linkage means local variables.

Question 13

What is **size_t** ?

Answer

It is the type of the result of the **sizeof** operator. **size_t** is used to express the size of something or the number of characters in something. For example, it is the type that you pass to **malloc( )** to indicate how many bytes you wish to allocate. Or it is the type returned by **strlen( )** to indicate the number of characters in a string.

Each implementation chooses a type like **unsigned int** or **unsigned long** (or something else) to be its **size_t**, depending on what makes most sense. Each implementation publishes its own choice of **size_t** in several header files like 'stdio.h', 'stdlib.h', etc. In most implementations **size_t** is defined as:

```
typedef unsigned int  size_t ;
```

This means that on this implementation **size_t** is an **unsigned int**. Other implementations may make other choices.

What is important is that you should not worry about what **size_t** looks like for a particular implementation; all you should care about is that it is the *right* type for representing object sizes and count.

Question 14

What is more efficient, a **switch** statement or an **if-else** chain?

Answer

As far as efficiency is concerned there would hardly be any difference, if at all. If the cases in a **switch** are sparsely distributed the compiler may internally use the equivalent of an **if-else** chain instead of a compact jump table. However, one should use **switch** where one can. It is definitely a cleaner way to program and certainly is not any less efficient than the **if-else** chain.

Question 15

Can we use a **switch** statement to switch on strings?

Answer

No. The cases in a **switch** must either have integer constants or constant expressions that evaluate to integer constants.

Question 16

In which order do the Relational, Arithmetic, Logical and Assignment operators get evaluated in C?

Answer

Arithmetic, Relational, Logical, Assignment

Question 17

How come that the C standard says that the expression

```
j = i++ * i++ ;
```

is undefined, whereas, the expression

```
j = i++ && i++ ;
```

is perfectly legal?

Answer

According to the C standard an object's stored value can be modified only once (by evaluation of expression) between two sequence points. A sequence point occurs:

- At the end of full expression (expression which is not a sub-expression in a larger expression)
- At the &&, || and ?: operators
- At a function call (after the evaluation of all arguments, just before the actual call)

Since in the first expression **i** is getting modified twice between two sequence points the expression is undefined. Also, the second expression is legal because a sequence point is occurring at **&&**, and **i** is getting modified once before and once after this sequence point.

Question 18

If **a[i] = i++** is undefined, then by the same reason **i = i + 1** should also be undefined. But it is not so. Why?

Answer

The standard says that if an object is to get modified within an expression, then all accesses to it within the same expression must be for computing the value to be stored in the object. The expression **a[i] = i++** is disallowed because one of the accesses of **i** (the one in **a[i]**) has nothing to do with the value that ends up being stored in **i**. In this case the compiler may not know whether the access should take place before or after the incremented value is stored. Since there is no good way to define it, the standard declares it as undefined. As against this, the expression **i = i + 1** is allowed because **i** is accessed to determine **i**'s final value.

Question 19

Will the expression ***p++ = c** be disallowed by the compiler?

Answer

No. Because here even though the value of **p** is accessed twice it is used to modify two different objects **p** and ***p**.

Question 20

Why should you use functions in your C program?

Answer

There are two reasons for using functions:

(a) Writing functions avoids rewriting the same code over and over. Suppose you have a section of code in your program that calculates area of a triangle. If later in the program you want to calculate the area of a different triangle, you will not like it if you are required to write the same instructions all over again. Instead, you would prefer to jump to a 'section of code' that calculates area and then jump back to the place from where you left off. This section of code is nothing but a function.

(b) By using functions, it becomes easier to write programs and keep track of what they are doing. If the operation of a program can be divided into separate activities, and each activity placed in a different function, then each could be written and checked independently. Separating the code into modular functions also makes the program easier to design and understand.

Question 21

In what form are the library functions provided?

Answer

Library functions are never provided in source code form. They are always made available in object code form obtained after compilation.

Question 22

What is the type of the variable **b** in the following declaration?

```
#define FLOATPTR float *
FLOATPTR a, b ;
```

Answer

float and not a pointer to a **float**, since on expansion the declaration becomes:

```
float *a, b ;
```

Question 23

Is it necessary that the header files should have a .h extension?

Answer

No. However, traditionally they have been given a .h extension to identify them as something different from the .c program files.

Question 24

What do the header files usually contain?

Answer

Header files contain Preprocessor directives like **#define**, **structure**, **union** and **enum** declarations, **typedef** declarations, global variable declarations and external function declarations. You should not write the actual code (i.e., function bodies) or global variable definition (that is defining or initializing instances) in header files. The **#include** directive should be used to pull in header files, not other '.c' files.

Question 25

Will it result into an error if a header file is included twice? [Yes/No]

Answer

Yes, unless the header file has taken care to ensure that if already included it doesn't get included again.

Question 26

How can a header file ensure that it does not get included more than once?

Answer

All declarations must be written in the manner shown below. Assume that the name of the header file is '**funcs.h**'.

```
/* funcs.h */
#ifndef _FUNCS
#define _FUNCS
/* all declarations would go here */
#endif
```

Now if we include this file twice as shown below, it will get included only once.

```
#include "funcs.h"
#include "funcs.h"
int main( )
{
    /* some code */
    return 0 ;
}
```

Question 27

On using **#include** where do the header files get searched?

Answer

If **#include**d using < > syntax, the files get searched in the predefined include path. It is possible to change the predefined include path. If **#include**d with the " " syntax, in addition to the predefined include path, the files also get searched in the current directory (usually the directory from which you invoked the compiler).

Question 28

Can you combine the following two statements into one?

```
char *p ;
p = ( char * ) malloc ( 100 ) ;
```

Answer

```
char *p = ( char * ) malloc ( 100 ) ;
```

Note that the typecasting operation can be dropped completely if this program is built using gcc compiler.

Question 29

Are the expressions ***ptr++** and **++*ptr** same?

Answer

No. ***ptr++** increments the pointer and not the value pointed by it, whereas **++*ptr** increments the value being pointed to by **ptr** and not **ptr**.

Question 30

Can you write another expression which does the same job as **++*ptr** does?

Answer

```
( *ptr )++
```

Question 31

What would be the equivalent pointer expression for referring the array element **a[i][j][k][l]**?

Answer

```
* ( * ( * ( * ( a + i ) + j ) + k ) + l )
```

Question 32

Where can one think of using pointers?

Answer

At lot of places, some of which are:

- Accessing array or string elements
- In passing big objects like arrays, strings and structures to functions
- Dynamic memory allocation
- Call by reference
- Implementing linked lists, trees, graphs and many other data structures

Question 33

How will you declare an array of three function pointers where each function receives two **int**s and returns a **float**?

Answer

```
float ( *arr[ 3 ] ) ( int, int ) ;
```

Question 34

Is the NULL pointer same as an uninitialized pointer? [Yes/No]

Answer

No. An uninitialized pointer (often called a wild pointer) contains some garbage address. A pointer that contains NULL indicates that it is a valid pointer but it is not pointing to anything right now.

Question 35

In which header file is the NULL macro defined?

Answer

In files "**stdio.h**" and "**stddef.h**".

Question 36

Is there any difference between the following two statements?

```
char  *p = 0 ;
char  *t = NULL ;
```

Answer

No. NULL is **#define**d as 0 in the 'stdio.h' file. Thus, both **p** and **t** are null pointers.

Question 37

What is a null pointer?

Answer

For each pointer type (like say a **char** pointer) C defines a special pointer value, which is guaranteed not to point to any object or function of that type. Usually, the null pointer constant used for representing a null pointer is the integer 0.

Question 38

What is the difference between a null pointer, a NULL macro, the ASCII NUL character and a null string?

Answer

A null pointer is a pointer, which does not point anywhere.

A NULL macro is used to represent the null pointer in source code. It has a value 0 associated with it.

The ASCII NUL character has all its bits as 0 but does not have any relationship with the null pointer.

The null string is just another name for an empty string "".

Question 39

Is there any difference in the following two statements?

```
char *ch = "Nagpur" ;
char ch[ ] = "Nagpur" ;
```

Answer

Yes. In the first statement, the character pointer **ch** stores the address of the string "Nagpur". The pointer **ch** can be made to point to some other character string (or even nowhere). The second statement, on the other hand, specifies that space for 7 characters be allocated and that the name of the location is **ch**. Thus, it specifies the size as well as initial values of the characters in array **ch**.

Question 40

When are *char* **a[ ]** and *char* ***a** treated as same by the compiler?

Answer

When using them as formal parameters while defining a function.

Question 41

What is the difference in the following declarations?

```
char *p = "Samuel" ;
char a[ ] = "Samuel" ;
```

Answer

Here **a** is an array big enough to hold Samuel and the '\0' following the it. Individual characters within the array can be changed but the address of the array will remain constant.

On the other hand, **p** is a pointer, initialized to point to a string constant. The pointer **p** may be modified to point to another string, but if you attempt to modify the string at which **p** is pointing the result is undefined.

Question 42

While handling a string, do we always have to process it character- by-character or there exists a method to process the entire string as one unit?

Answer

A string can be processed only on a character-by-character basis.

Question 43

What is the similarity between a structure, union and an enumeration?

Answer

All of them let you define new data types.

Question 44

Can a structure contain a pointer to itself?

Answer

Yes. Such structures are known as self-referential structures. They are commonly used in declaration of a node while implementing a data structure like linked list or binary tree.

Question 45

How are structure passing and returning implemented by the compiler?

Answer

When structures are passed as arguments to functions, the entire structure is pushed on the stack. For big structures this is an extra overhead. This overhead can be avoided by passing pointers to structures instead of actual structures. To return structures a hidden argument generated by the compiler is passed to the function. This argument points to a location where the returned structure is copied.

Question 46

What is the difference between a structure and a union?

Answer

A union is essentially a structure in which all the fields overlay each other. At a time only one field can be used. We can write to one field and read from another.

Question 47

What is the difference between an enumeration and a set of preprocessor **#defines**?

Answer

There is hardly any difference between the two, except that a **#define** has a global effect (throughout the file), whereas, an enumeration can have an effect local to the block, if desired. Some advantages of enumerations are that the numeric values are automatically assigned, whereas, in **#define** we must explicitly define them. A disadvantage of enumeration is that we have no control over the size of enumeration variable.

Question 48

Is there an easy way to print enumeration values symbolically?

Answer

No. You can write a small function (one per enumeration) to map an enumeration constant to a string, either by using a **switch** statement or by searching an array.

Question 49

What is the use of bit fields in a structure declaration?

Answer

Bit fields are used to save space in structures having several binary flags or other small fields. Note that the colon notation for specifying the size of a field in bits is valid only in structures (and in unions); you cannot use this mechanism to specify the size of arbitrary variables.

Question 50

Can we have an array of bit fields? [Yes/No]

Answer

No.

Question 51

Can we specify variable field width in **scanf( )**'s format string? [Yes/No]

Answer

No. In **scanf( )** a * in format string after a **%** sign is used for suppression of assignment. That is, the current input field is scanned but not stored.

Question 52

Out of **fgets( )** and **gets( )** which function is safe to use?

Answer

fgets( ), because unlike **fgets( )**, **gets( )** cannot be told the size of the buffer into which the string supplied will be stored. As a result, there is always a possibility of buffer overflow.

Question 53

To which numbering system can the binary number 1011011111000101 be easily converted to?

Answer

Hexadecimal, since each 4-digit binary represents one hexadecimal digit.

Question 54

Which bitwise operator is suitable for checking whether a particular bit is on or off?

Answer

The **&** operator.

Question 55

Which bitwise operator is suitable for turning off a particular bit in a number?

Answer

The **&** operator.

Question 56

Which bitwise operator is suitable for putting on a particular bit in a number?

Answer

The **|** operator.

Question 57

What is the type of **compare** in the following code segment?

```
typedef int ( *ptrtofun ) ( char *, char * ) ;
ptrtofun  compare ;
```

Answer

It is a pointer to function that receives two character pointers and returns an integer.

Question 58

What are the advantages of using **typedef** in a program?

Answer

There are three main reasons for using **typedef**s:

- It makes writing of complicated declarations a lot easier. This helps in eliminating a lot of clutter in the program.
- It helps in achieving portability in programs. If we use **typedef**s for data types that are machine-dependent, only the **typedef**s need change when the program is moved to a new machine platform.
- It helps in providing a better documentation for a program. For example, a node of a doubly linked list is better understood as **ptrtolist** rather than just a pointer to a complicated structure.

Question 59

What does the following prototype indicate?

```
void strcpy ( char  *target, const char  *source )
```

Answer

We can modify the pointers **source** as well as **target**. However, the object to which **source** is pointing cannot be modified.

Question 60

What does the following prototype indicate?

```
const char *change ( char *, int )
```

Answer

The function **change( )** receives a **char** pointer and an **int**, and returns a pointer to a constant **char**.

Question 61

What do you mean by **const** correctness?

Answer

A program is 'const correct' if it never changes (a more common term is mutates) a constant object.

Question 62

What is the difference in the following declarations?

```
const char  *s ;
char const  *s ;
```

Answer

There is no difference.

Question 63

To **free( )** we only pass the pointer to the block of memory that we want to deallocate. Then how does **free( )** know how many bytes it should deallocate?

Answer

In most implementations of **malloc( )** the number of bytes allocated is stored adjacent to the allocated block. Hence, it is simple for **free( )** to know how many bytes to deallocate.

Question 64

Suppose we use **realloc( )** to increase the allocated space for a 20-integer array to a 40-integer array. Will it increase the array space at the same location at which the array is present or will it try to find a different place for the bigger array?

Answer

Both. If the first strategy fails then it adopts the second. If the first is successful it returns the same pointer that you passed to it otherwise it returns a different pointer for the newly allocated space.

Question 65

When reallocating memory if any other pointers point into the same piece of memory, do we have to readjust these other pointers or do they get readjusted automatically?

Answer

If **realloc( )** expands allocated memory at the same place then there is no need of readjustment of other pointers. However, if it allocates a new region somewhere else, the programmer has to readjust the other pointers.

Question 66

What's the difference between **malloc( )** and **calloc( )** functions?

Answer

As against **malloc( )**, **calloc( )** needs two arguments, the number of elements to be allocated and the size of each element. For example,

```
p = ( int * ) calloc ( 10, sizeof ( int ) ) ;
```

will allocate space for a 10-integer array. Additionally, **calloc( )** will also set each of this element with a value 0. Thus, the above call to **calloc( )** is equivalent to:

```
p = ( int * ) malloc ( 10 * sizeof ( int ) ) ;
memset ( p, 0, 10 * sizeof ( int ) ) ;
```

Question 67

Which function should be used to free the memory allocated by **calloc( )**?

Answer

The same that we use with **malloc( )**, i.e., **free( )**.

Question 68

How much maximum memory can we allocate in a single call to **malloc( )**?

Answer

The largest possible block that can be allocated using **malloc( )** depends upon the host system—particularly the size of physical memory and the OS implementation.

Theoretically, the largest number of bytes that can be allocated should be the maximum value that can be held in **size_t** which is implementation dependent. For TC/TC++ compilers the maximum number of bytes that can be allocated is equal to 64 KB.

Question 69

What is difference between Dynamic memory allocation and Static memory allocation?

Answer

In Static memory allocation during compilation arrangements are made to facilitate memory allocation. Actual allocation is done during execution time. In Dynamic memory allocation no arrangement is done at compilation time. Memory allocation is done at execution time.

Question 70

Which header file should be included to dynamically allocate memory using functions like **malloc( )** and **calloc( )**?

Answer

stdlib.h

Question 71

When we dynamically allocate memory is there any way to free memory during run time?

Answer

Yes. Memory can be freed using **free( )** function.

Question 72

Is it necessary to cast the address returned by **malloc( )**?

Answer

It is necessary to do the typecasting if you are using TC / TC++ / Visual Studio compilers. If you are using gcc there is no need to typecast the returned address. Note that ANSI C defines an implicit type conversion between **void** pointer types (the one returned by **malloc( )**) and other pointer types.

Question 73

Mention any variable argument-list function that you have used and its prototype.

Answer

```
int printf ( const char *format, ... ) ;
```

Question 74

How can **%f** be used for both **float** and **double** arguments in **printf( )**?

Answer

In variable length arguments lists, types **char** and **short int** are promoted to **int**, and **float** is promoted to **double**.

Question 75

Can we pass a variable argument list to a function at run-time? [Yes/No]

Answer

No. Every actual argument list must be completely known at compile time. In that sense it is not truly a variable argument list.

Question 76

How can a called function determine the number of arguments that have been passed to it?

Answer

It cannot. Any function that takes a variable number of arguments must be able to determine the number of arguments from the arguments themselves. For example, the **printf( )** function does this by looking for format specifiers **(%)** in the format string. This is the reason such functions fail badly if there is a mismatch in the format specifiers and the argument list.

If all the arguments passed are of same type, we can pass a sentinel value like -1 or 0 or a NULL pointer at the end of the variable argument list. Alternately, we can also pass the count of number of variable arguments.

Question 77

Input / output function prototypes and macros are defined in which header file?

Answer

stdio.h

Question 78

What are **stdin**, **stdout** and **stderr**?

Answer

Standard input, standard output and standard error streams.

26 The Next Level

"It's good to know how much you know..."

There are C programmers and then there are 'good' C programmers. Board the train which will help you make the transition from a C programmer to a 'good' C programmer...

Contents

In the previous 23 chapters I have tried to explain different features of C language. The more thoroughly you know them, stronger programming foundation you would have. Once you are done with them, read this chapter which contains topics that would take a good C programmer to the next level.

New Data Types

A few new data types have been introduced in C99. These include **long long**, **bool** and **complex**. We have already seen **long long** in Chapter 11. The following program demonstrates the working of **bool** and **complex** types.

```
#include <stdio.h>
#include <stdbool.h>
#include <complex.h>
int main( )
{
    bool married = true ;
    bool divorced = false ;
    printf ( "%d %d\n", married, divorced ) ;
    complex c = 3 + 2 * I ;
    printf ( "Real part = %.2f\n", creal ( c ) ) ;
    printf ( "Imaginary part = %.2f\n", cimag ( c ) ) ;
    return 0 ;
}
```

Use of **bool** and **complex** types is straight-forward. What is surprising is to use them we must include the files 'stdbool.h' and 'complex.h'. This has something to do with history of C.

Since in C89 bool and complex types were absent, programmers created home-brewed bool and complex types using typedef, #define, enum, structure etc. Since plenty of code was written that included these home-brewed types in various shapes and forms, the C language committee introduced these new types through reserved identifiers (those which begin with _) **_Bool** and **_Complex**. But, since the obvious choice of type name was still bool and complex they provided typedefs to these obvious names in files 'stdbool.h' and 'complex.h'.

What is *size_t*?

Often in situations where size of an object (in bytes) is to be received or returned by functions, its type is mentioned as **size_t**. Prototypes of few such functions are given below.

```
void *malloc ( size_t  n ) ;
void *memcpy ( void  *s1, void const  *s2, size_t  n ) ;
size_t strlen ( char const  *s ) ;
```

For a 32-bit compiler **size_t** is a typedef for **unsigned int**, and for a 64-bit compiler it is typedef for **unsigned long long** as shown below:

```
typedef unsigned int size_t ;  // for 32-bit compiler
typedef unsigned long long size_t ;  // for 64-bit compiler
```

These typedefs have been done in many header files like <stddef.h>, <stdio.h>, <stdlib.h>, <string.h>, <time.h>, and <wchar.h>.

Since **size_t** data type is never negative, it is often also used as type of a loop counter variable whose value should be greater than or equal to 0.

Problem with *gets( )*

When strings are to be received as input from keyboard using library function **gets( )** there is always a possibility of reading strings bigger than the space reserved for them. Here is an example...

```
char  city[ 8 ] ;
puts ( "Enter city name" ) ;
gets ( city ) ;  /* receive city from keyboard */
```

On execution of this code snippet, if we submit a string 'California', the string variable **city** would overflow as 'California' would need space to accommodate 11 characters, whereas, we reserved space for only 8 characters.

This overflow might turn out to be dangerous as we are exceeding the bounds of the string. This can be avoided by using **fgets( )** to read a string from keyboard as shown below.

```
#include <stdio.h>
int main( )
```

```
{
    char city[ 8 ] ;
    puts ( "Enter city name: " ) ;
    fgets ( city, 7, stdin ) ;
    puts ( city ) ;
    return 0 ;
}
```

Now if we supply "California" from keyboard, "Califor\0" would be stored in **city**.

It is wrongly believed that with **scanf( )** also we would run into a similar problem. With **scanf( )** this problem can be avoided as shown below.

```
char city[ 8 ] ;
puts ("Enter city name: " ) ;
scanf ( "%8s", city ) ;
puts ( city ) ;
```

Microsoft provides functions like **scanf_s( )** and **gets_s( )** (standing for safe versions of **scanf( )** and **gets( )**) to get a similar effect. However, these are non-standard functions and may not work with all compilers.

Wide Characters

If we are to write programs for international distribution then to represent a character in different international languages, we should wide character type rather than a simple char. Wide character constant begin with the letter L as in L'A', L'3' and L'+'. A wide character string is written as L"Oh my God!".

The type of wide characters is **wchar_t**. It is a **typedef** of some integer type present in 'stddef.h'. Its size is compiler dependent and may be 8, 16, or 32 bits wide, signed or unsigned. The choice depends on what encodings are expected to be processed on a particular platform. Following program shows how to use wide characters:

```
#include <stdio.h>
#include <wchar.h>
#include <locale.h>
int main( )
{
```

```
    setlocale ( LC_ALL, "" ) ;
    wchar_t ch = L'अ' ;
    wchar_t str[ ] = { 2309, 2310, 2311, 2312, 2313, 2314, 2315 } ;
    wchar_t strinhex[ ] = { 0x905, 0x0906, 0x0907, 0x0908, 0x0909 } ;
    wprintf ( L"%lu\n", sizeof ( ch ) ) ;
    wprintf ( L"%lc\n", ch ) ;
    wprintf ( L"%ls\r\n", str ) ;
    wprintf ( L"%ls\r\n", strinhex ) ;
    return 0 ;
}
```

Here is the output of the program...

```
4
अ
अआइईउऊऋ
अआइईउ
```

Three important points to note here are as follows:

(a) Size of **wchar_t** for the implementation on which I executed this program is 4 bytes. You may get a different answer.

(b) A program's locale defines its character set, date and time formatting conventions, monetary conventions, decimal formatting conventions, etc. The default locale of a C program is C (also known as POSIX) which is ASCII-only. We need to add a call to the function **setlocale (LC_ALL, "")** to set the locale. This indicates that all parts of the locale should be set according to the environment variables.

(c) In Unicode every character is assigned an integer value called code point. Code points for characters **अ आ इ ई उ ऊ ऋ** of Devanagari script are 2309, 2310, 2311, 2312, 2313, 2314, 2315.

Stringizing Macro

If we are to convert a macro argument into a string, it can be done using a # token as shown below:

```
#define STR(x)  #x
```

If we use this macro as follows

```
char fname[ ] = STR( Sameer ) ;
```

on preprocessing, it would expand to

```
char fname[ ] "Sameer" ;
```

When would a need arise to use this type of stringizing macro? Well, imagine a situation where we want to use a format string "%15s%20s" in **printf( )** at several places in the program. Additionally, we want the flexibility of replacing 15 and 20 with other suitable widths by making minimal changes in the program. This can be achieved as shown in the following program:

```
#include <stdio.h>
#define FNW 15
#define LNW 20
#define STR( x ) #x
#define XSTR( x ) STR( x )
int main( )
{
    char fname[ ] = "Sameer" ;
    char lname[ ] = "Joshi" ;
    printf ( "%"XSTR( FNW )"s""%"XSTR( LNW )"s", fname, lname ) ;
}
```

Note that firstly **XSTR(FNW)** is expanded to **STR(15)** and then **STR(15)** is expanded to "15". This is because, if a macro expansion contains a # or ## (discussed in the next section), the expansion happens after all other macros have been expanded.

Token Pasting Macro

Every instruction in a C program consists of multiple tokens. These include keywords, constants, variables, strings and operators. It is possible to paste these tokens using the ## token pasting operator in a #define. For example, consider the following macro:

```
#define PASTE(x, y) x##y
```

If we use this macro through the statement

```
printf ( "%d" PASTE ( 25, 50 ) ;
```

it will output 2550.

From this output it is evident that on encountering the ## operator, the preprocessor simply concatenates x and y after replacing them with the arguments 25 and 50. The token pasting operator is useful in two situations. These are discussed below.

Logging

Often a C program has statements that logs the different events that take place during execution of the program. If something goes wrong during execution of the program, then the logs can be examined to get information about the behavior of the code and would help track down systematically what is wrong with the program.

It is a common practice to log the date and time of an event. Instead of adding the code to display the date and time in each statement that logs an event, it can be achieved using the ## operator as shown below:

```
#include <stdio.h>
#include<time.h>
#define LOG( fmt, args...)  time ( &t ) ; \
                printf ( "\nDebug: %s" fmt, ctime(&t), ##args )
int main( )
{
   time_t t ;
   LOG( "%lu %lu", sizeof ( int ), sizeof ( float ) ) ;
   LOG( "Radius = %d Area = %f", 10, 3.14 * 10 * 10 ) ;
   return 0 ;
}
```

On execution, this program prints the following output:

```
Debug: Fri May 19 09:34:51 2023
4 4
Debug: Fri May 19 09:34:51 2023
Radius = 10 Area = 314.000000
```

Creating Generic Type

If we are to maintain a linked list of integers and a linked list of doubles, then we will have to declare following two structures to represent nodes of each linked list.

```
struct LinkedList_int
{
    int data ;
    struct LinkedList_int *next ;
};
struct LinkedList_double
{
    double data ;
    struct LinkedList_dobule *next ;
};
int main( )
{
    struct LinkedList_int  ll1 ;
    struct LinkedList_double  ll2 ;
    return 0 ;
}
```

Instead of this, we can use the ## operator and rely on the preprocessor to create the two structure declarations. This is demonstrated in the following program:

```
#define LL(T) struct LinkedList_##T {\
                        T data ; \
                        struct LinkedList_##T *next ; \
                      }
int main( )
{
    LL( int ) l1 ;
    LL( double ) l2 ;
}
```

Type Generic Macro

C++ and Java have a feature called function overloading that allows us to use same function name for multiple functions if the arguments of these functions differ in number, order or type. As a result, we can define three functions by the name **abs( )**. Based on the type of argument (int/float/double) the compiler would bind the call to this function to appropriate function definition. This avoids defining functions like **abs( )**, **fabs( )** and **labs( )**, which we would be required to do in C programming.

C language does not have the function overloading feature. However, a similar effect can be obtained using type generic macros as shown below.

```
#include <stdlib.h>
#include <stdio.h>
#include <math.h>
#define ABS(T) _Generic((T), float: fabs, long: labs, default : abs )(T)
int main( )
{
    float f = ABS(-1.5708f) ;
    long l = ABS(-314L) ;
    int i = ABS(-25) ;
    printf ( "%f %ld %d\n", f, l, i ) ;
}
```

On preprocessing, based on the type of argument used for the **ABS** macro, it is replaced by **fabs**, **labs** or **abs**.

Predefined Macros

Some macros are predefined by the implementation and can be used anywhere in the program. Following program shows how to use some of the common macros defined by the C Standard.

```
#include <stdio.h>
int main( )
{
    printf ( __DATE__ ) ;
    printf ( "\n"__TIME__ ) ;
    printf ( "\n%d", __LINE__ ) ;
    printf ( "\n%d", __STDC__ ) ;
}
```

On execution, the program produces the following output:

```
May 19 2023
10:35:36
6
1
```

From the output it is evident that __DATE__ and __TIME__ reports the current date and time. __LINE__ yields the line number of the line in source code and __STDC__ yields 1 if the implementation conforms to C standard. __DATE__, __TIME__, __FILE__ (expands to current file source filename) and __LINE__ can be used in logging events during program execution.

Storage Classes Revisited

In Chapter 11 we learnt about storage classes auto, register, static and extern. To keep things simple, that chapter obscured a few facts. It is time to come clean on that. Before we begin our discussion on storage classes let us understand the meanings of 'Translation unit', 'Scope' and 'Linkage'.

Translation Unit

We know that during preprocessing our source code is expanded based on the preprocessor directives that we have used. This expanded source code is called a 'translation unit'. In professional development the program is split into several files, so the preprocessor creates several translation units. Compiler compiles each translation unit into an object file. All these object files are then linked together by the linker to create a final executable file.

Scope

Scope determines the portion of the program in which the variable or a function can be used. It is also known as availability or visibility. There are four possible scopes:

(a) **Function prototype scope**: Function prototype scope is most restrictive and it ends at the end of prototype declaration of the function. This is the most restrictive as it ends at the end of prototype declaration of the function.

(b) **Block scope**: Formal arguments of a function and the variables defined inside a function have block scope and they are available to statements within that function.

(c) **Function scope**: The labels used with a **goto** statement have function scope. That is why **goto** cannot be used to take the control outside a function.

(d) **File scope**: The variables defined outside all functions and the functions defined in a file have file scope. They are available to all statements in that translation unit.

Linkage

We should be able to control whether variables and functions defined in one translation unit should be visible (be available) to the linker while processing other translation units. This is done by specifying the linkage of the variables and functions. C language supports 3 possible linkages:

(a) **No linkage**: This linkage refers only to elements that have addresses at link/load time; thus, local variables defined inside a function have no linkage.

(b) **Internal linkage**: Internal linkage can be specified using **static** keyword. If a variable or function in a translation unit has an internal linkage, then it is only visible to the linker within that translation unit.

(c) **External linkage**: The external linkage can be specified using the **extern** keyword. If a variable or function has external linkage, the linker can also see it when processing other translation units.

By default, the following entities would have external linkage:

(a) All functions
(b) Variables that are defined outside all functions

Storage Classes of Variables

Variables are stored in memory. Storage classes associated with them determine their 'storage duration' or 'lifetime'. There are two possible lifetimes—static and automatic. Thus, strictly speaking there are only two storage classes—static and automatic. Variables that have static storage class exist throughout the execution of the program. Unlike this, variables that have automatic storage class are allocated new storage when control reaches the block in which they are defined and die when control goes out of the block. Since such variables come and go automatically when control reaches and exit from the block, they are called automatic variables.

C language provides 4 storage class specifiers—**auto**, **register**, **static**, **extern**. Of these, the last two can be used with functions too. When used with a variable they determine:

(a) Where the variable would be stored
(b) What will be its default initial value
(c) What will be the scope (visibility) of the variable
(d) What will be the life of the variable

We have already covered these properties in Chapter 11. But let me present them in a new light based on whether the variable is defined—as function parameter, or inside a function or outside all functions. We would also examine how a function behaves, when a storage class specifier is applied to it.

Variable defined as a Function Parameter

(a) Variable defined as a function parameter can either have no storage class specifier or register storage class specifier.

(b) Its default value is the one received by it when the function is called.

(c) It has no linkage, so it is available only to statements within the function.

(d) It has automatic lifetime, so it dies when control returns from the function.

Variable defined outside all Functions

(a) Variable defined outside all function cannot use **auto** or **register** storage class specifier. It can only use **static**, **extern** or no specifier.

(b) Variable declared with **extern** storage class specifier is a declaration, so no storage is allocated for it in memory. (However, if we use **extern int i = 5 ;**, then it is a definition.) Variable defined with **static** or no storage class specifier is stored in memory.

(c) Variable defined with **extern** storage is a declaration, so no question of its default initial value. Variable defined with **static** or no storage class specifier has a default initial value of 0.

(d) Variable defined with **extern** storage class specifier or no specifier has external linkage, i.e., it is available in other translation units. Variable defined with **static** storage class specifier has internal linkage, i.e., it is visible only within that file (translation unit).

(e) Variable defined with **extern**, **static** or no storage class specifier has static lifetime, i.e., it lives throughout the execution of the program.

Variable defined inside a Function

(a) Variable defined inside a function can use **auto**, **register**, **static** or **extern** storage class specifier.

(b) Variable defined with **auto**, **static** or no storage class specifier is stored in memory. Variable defined with **register** storage class specifier is stored in CPU register if it is available. Variable with **extern** storage class specifier is merely a declaration and no storage is allocated for it.

(c) Variable defined with **auto**, **register** or no storage class specifier has a garbage default initial value. Variable defined with **static** storage class specifier has a default value of 0.

(d) Variable defined with **auto**, **register** or **static** storage class specifier has no linkage and hence is visible only within the function. Variable defined with **extern** storage class specifier has external linkage and hence is visible in other translation unit.

(e) Variable defined with the **auto** or **register** specifier have automatic lifetime. Variable defined with **static** or **extern** storage class specifier has static lifetime, i.e., it lives throughout the execution of the program.

Storage Class Specifier for a Function

(a) Storage class specifiers **auto** and **register** cannot be used with a function.

(b) A function is stored in memory.

(c) Unlike variables, a function does not have a default initial value.

(d) A function defined with **static** storage class specifier has internal linkage, so it is visible within the translation unit in which it is defined. A function defined with **extern** storage class specifier or no specifier has external linkage, so it is visible to other translation units too.

(e) A function defined with **static, extern** or no storage class specifier has static lifetime, i.e., it lives throughout the execution of the program.

A Final Word

(a) An **extern** declaration can be used to make a definition in another source file visible.

(b) An **extern** declaration can be used to make a variable visible before its definition in the same source file.

(c) An **extern** declaration is valid so long as the variable it refers to is defined only once outside all functions in any translation unit.

(d) Local variables and function arguments have no linkage. So, all variable definitions bind to different objects. For example, in the following function **num** has no linkage, hence the two **num** variables are bound to two different entities.

```
int fun( )
{
    int num = 10 ;
    {
        int num = 20 ;
    }
}
```

(e) If we declare a variable to have internal linkage in a header file, each translation unit you include this file in will get its own copy of that variable.

Passing 2-D Array to a Function

If we wish to pass 2-D arrays of different sizes to a function to get them displayed, it can be done as shown in the following program:

```
#include <stdio.h>
void display ( int rows, int cols, int arr[ rows ][ cols ] ) ;
int main( )
{
    int arr1[ 3 ][ 5 ] = {
                            1, 2, 3, 4, 5,
                            6, 7, 8, 9, 10,
```

```
                        11, 12, 13, 14, 15
                    } ;
    int arr2[ 2 ][ 4 ] = {
                        1, 2, 3, 4,
                        6, 7, 8, 9
                    } ;
    display ( 3, 5, arr1 ) ;
    display ( 2, 4, arr2 ) ;
    return 0 ;
}
void display ( int rows, int cols, int arr[ rows ][ cols ] )
{
    int i, j ;
    for ( i = 0 ; i < rows ; i++ )
    {
        for ( j = 0 ; j < cols ; j++ )
            printf ( "%d\t", arr[ i ][ j ] ) ;
        printf ( "\n" ) ;
    }
}
```

Note that the order of passing arguments to **display( )** is important. Since **rows** and **cols** are being used in the definition of **arr**, they must be passed before passing the array. While defining the array in **display( )**, all but the first dimension must be mentioned. So if we want, we can merely define it as **int arr [ ][cols]** or even as **int (*arr)[cols]**.

Callback Mechanism

Usually, we call library functions to do our mundane jobs. But sometimes the library functions call back our user-defined function. A good example of this is the **qsort( )** library function. This is a generic sorting function which can sort integers, floats, longs or even objects of user-defined types. How can the same **qsort( )** function deal with multiple standard data types and user-defined types. Well, the magic happens through function pointers.

Consider the calls to **qsort( )** function shown below:

```
int iarr[ ] = { 23, 43, 21, 55, 23, 67, 18, 29, 37, 87 } ;
float farr[ ] = { 1.2, 5.3, .21, 5.8, 2.9, 1.23, 6.7, 8.11 } ;
```

```
qsort ( iarr, sizeof ( iarr ), sizeof ( int ), icmp ) ;
qsort ( farr, sizeof ( farr ), sizeof ( float ), fcmp ) ;
```

First 3 parameters in calls to **qsort( )** are simple to understand—base address of the array, number of elements in the array and number of bytes occupied by individual element of the array. These parameters help **qsort( )** to work on different data types. The fourth parameter is pointer to a comparison function. Ultimately, while sorting **qsort( )** will have to compare two quantities to decide whether one is less that the other. **qsort( )** doesn't decide this. Instead it expects us to define this comparison function and pass its address to **qsort( )**. **qsort( )** collects the address of the function in a function pointer and uses it to call the comparison function whenever it is time to compare two quantities.

With this background information about **qsort( )**, examine the program given below which sorts an array of integers and an array of floats using the same **qsort( )** function. Note that we must define two comparison functions—one that compares two **int**s and another that compares two **float**s.

```
#include <stdio.h>
#include <stdlib.h>
int icmp ( const void *, const void * ) ;
int fcmp ( const void *, const void * ) ;
int main( )
{
    int iarr[ ] = { 23, 43, 21, 55, 23, 67, 18, 29, 37, 87 } ;
    float farr[ ] = { 1.2, 5.3, .21, 5.8, 2.9, 1.23, 6.7, 8.11 } ;
    int i, sz ;
    sz = sizeof ( iarr ) / sizeof ( iarr[ 0 ] ) ;
    qsort ( iarr, sz, sizeof ( int ), icmp ) ;
    for ( i = 0 ; i < sz ; i++ )
        printf ( "%d ", iarr[ i ] ) ;
    printf ( "\n" ) ;
    sz = sizeof ( farr ) / sizeof ( farr[ 0 ] ) ;
    qsort ( farr, sz, sizeof ( float ), fcmp ) ;
    for ( i = 0 ; i < sz ; i++ )
        printf ( "%.2f ", farr[ i ] ) ;
    return 0 ;
}
```

```
int icmp ( const void *p, const void *q )
{
    const int *pint ;
    const int *qint ;
    pint = ( int * ) p ;
    qint = ( int * ) q ;
    if ( *pint > *qint )
        return 1 ;
    else if ( *pint < *qint )
        return -1 ;
    else
        return 0 ;
}
int fcmp ( const void *p, const void *q )
{
    const float *pfloat ;
    const float *qfloat ;
    pfloat = ( float * ) p ;
    qfloat = ( float * ) q ;
    if ( *pfloat > *qfloat )
        return 1 ;
    else if ( *pfloat < *qfloat )
        return -1 ;
    else
        return 0 ;
}
```

Here is the output of the program...

```
18 21 23 23 29 37 43 55 67 87
0.21 1.20 1.23 2.90 5.30 5.80 6.70 8.11
```

Now you can try your hand at defining a structure to represent a date and then using it to sort 10 dates in reverse chronological order using **qsort( )** function.

Some Interesting Limits

Did it ever occur to you as to how many maximum nested parentheses can be used in an expression or how many nested loops or function calls are we allowed to make? Well, we usually believe that there may not be an upper limit on these, because rarely are these limits tested in a practical program. However, limits do exist. Following table shows some of these interesting limits.

Item	Max limit
Nested ( ) in an expression	63
Nested blocks { }	127
Cases in a switch statement	1023
Parameters in one function definition	127
Arguments in one function call	127
* in pointer declaration	12
External variables/functions in 1 translation unit	4095
#defines in one preprocessing translation unit	4095
Parameters in one macro definition	127
Arguments in one macro invocation	127
Nested #ifdef, #ifndef, #if	63
Characters in a string literal	4095
Bytes in an object	65535
Members in a single structure or union	1023
Levels of nested structure or union definitions	63
Enumeration constants in a single enumeration	1023

Figure 24.1 Some interesting limits.

Unit Testing

A unit is the smallest testable part of any software. In C, a unit is typically an individual function. Unit testing is a process that validates that each unit of the program is working as per the design. To perform unit testing we need to write small programs called unit tests. We can write unit tests ourselves, but it is usually beneficial to use a unit-testing framework like CUnit, Unity, CppUnit, etc. We will use the CUnit framework here. For this we need to install CUnit on our machine. If it is a Linux machine, we can do this using the following command:

```
$ sudo apt-get install libcunit1 libcunit1-doc libcunit1-dev
```

To install CUnit on a Windows machine, we need to carry out following steps:

(a) Open Windows PowerShell in administrator mode by right-clicking the PowerShell prompt and selecting 'Run as administrator.'

(b) Install Windows Subsystem for Linux (WSL) which enables you to execute Linux commands directly on Windows. Do this using the following command:

```
C:\> wsl –install
```

(c) Execute wsl by right-clicking the wsl icon and selecting 'Run as administrator.'

(d) Update the package list using the apt-get package management tool:

```
$ sudo apt-get update
```

(e) Install gcc (if not already installed) using the following command:

```
$ sudo apt install gcc
```

(f) Install CUnit using the following command:

```
$ sudo apt-get install libcunit1 libcunit1-doc libcunit1-dev
```

Once CUnit is installed we are ready to create a program that creates and runs unit tests. Let me first show you the program.

```
#include <stdio.h>
#include <CUnit/CUnit.h>
#include <CUnit/Basic.h>

int factorial ( int n )
{
  if ( n == 0 )
    return 1 ;
  else
    return n * factorial ( n - 1 ) ;
}

void test_factorial( )
{
  CU_ASSERT_EQUAL( factorial ( 0 ), 1 ) ;
  CU_ASSERT_EQUAL( factorial ( 1 ), 1 ) ;
```

```
    CU_ASSERT_EQUAL( factorial ( 10 ), 3628800 ) ;
}

int main( )
{
    // Initialize the CUnit test registry
    if ( CU_initialize_registry( ) != CUE_SUCCESS )
        return CU_get_error( ) ;

    // Create a suite for the factorial tests
    CU_pSuite suite = CU_add_suite ( "Factorial Suite", NULL, NULL ) ;
    if ( suite == NULL )
    {
        CU_cleanup_registry( ) ;
        return CU_get_error( ) ;
    }

    // Add the test case to the suite
    if ( CU_add_test ( suite, "Test Factorial", test_factorial ) == NULL )
    {
        CU_cleanup_registry( ) ;
        return CU_get_error( ) ;
    }

    // Set output verbosity
    CU_basic_set_mode ( CU_BRM_VERBOSE ) ;

    // Run all tests using the basic interface
    CU_basic_run_tests( ) ;

    // Clean up resources
    CU_cleanup_registry( ) ;
    return CU_get_error( ) ;
}
```

Here we are intending to test the **factorial( )** function. For this we have to write the boiler-plate code shown in **main( )**. From **main( )** we have called a function **test_factorial( )**. This is the one that calls **factorial( )** function by passing different values to it. The value returned by the

factorial( ) function is tested against the second parameter of test assertion macro **CU_ASSERT_EQUAL**. This macro is the language of unit tests. If a test fails the current function is aborted, otherwise, the program continues normally. The success or failure of these assertions is tracked by the CUnit framework, and displayed when a test run is complete. We can compile and execute the program as follows:

```
$ gcc -o factorial factorial.c -lcunit
$ ./factorial.out
```

This is the output that we get:

```
CUnit - A unit testing framework for C - Version 2.1-3
http://cunit.sourceforge.net/

Suite: Factorial Suite
 Test: Test Factorial Function ...passed

Run Summary:    Type  Total    Ran  Passed   Failed   Inactive
              suites      1      1     n/a        0          0
               tests      1      1       1        0          0
             asserts      4      4       4        0        n/a

Elapsed time =    0.000 seconds
```

From the above output we can see that the **factorial( )** function has passed all the 4 tests.

Coding Style

Good coding style avoids unnecessary errors and repetitive code and overall makes you a better programmer. This is the last section of this book. I intend to expand this section significantly in future editions. I would love to receive inputs from readers on stuff that they would want to see in this section. Please feel free to send in your suggestions to kanetkar@kicit.com. As a precursor to what you may expect in future editions, I would present here one example.

Consider the following code:

```
do
```

```
{
    // some statements here
} while ( 0 ) ;
```

This loop guarantees that, no matter what, statements in the loop get executed 'only once'. And if we are sure about this, then why should we bother to put the statements in a loop? Well, consider this code:

```
int fun( )
{
    char *p, *q, *r ;
    p = malloc ( .. ) ;
    ..
    if ( some condition )
    {
        free ( p ) ;
        return 1 ;
    }
    ..
    q = malloc ( .. ) ;
    ..
    if ( some other condition )
    {
        free ( p ) ;
        free ( q ) ;
        return 2 ;
    }
    ..
    r = malloc ( .. ) ;
    ..
    if ( yet another condition )
    {
        free ( p ) ;
        free ( q ) ;
        free ( r ) ;
        return 3 ;
    }
    return 0 ;
}
```

In my opinion this is bad code for two reasons:

(a) There are multiple exit points from the function. Code which has multiple exit points is difficult to understand and difficult to maintain.

(b) Before every **return** there are repetitive calls to **free( )** function to prevent memory leaks.

Both these disadvantages can be overcome by putting the above code in a **do-while** loop as shown below.

```
int fun( )
{
    char *p, *q, *r ;
    p = q = r = NULL ;
    do
    {
        p = malloc ( .. ) ;
        ..
        if ( some condition )
            break ;
        ..
        q = malloc ( .. ) ;
        ..
        if ( some other condition )
            break ;
        ..
        r = malloc ( .. ) ;
        ..
        if ( yet another condition )
            break ;
        return 0 ;
    } while ( 0 ) ;
    free ( p ) ;
    free ( q ) ;
    free ( r ) ;
    return 1 ;
}
```

The **do-while** loop permits us to use **break**s to reach the **free( )** calls, which are now done only at one place. Note that **p, q, r** have been initialized to NULL so that they do not contain garbage address and we do not end up calling **free( )** for a garbage address.

Using C++ Functions from a C program

There are many successful products in the market which were initially developed in C. But as time elapsed and new languages like C++ came into existence, to take advantage of the new features of C++ some modules are developed in C++. However, either due to the size of C code or due to the time and cost involved in its conversion from C to C++ the older modules continue to exist as C code. If these modules are to make use of the new C++ modules, then there must be a way to do this. Let me show you with an example how this is done. Suppose a C++ module contains the following code:

```
/* function.cpp */
#include <iostream>
#include <vector>
#include "function.h"
using namespace std ;
int fun ( int x, int y, int z )
{
    cout << x << " " << y << " " << z << endl ;
    vector<int> v ;
    v.push_back ( x ) ;
    v.push_back ( y ) ;
    v.push_back ( z ) ;
    return x * x ;
}
```

As you can notice, it defines a function **fun( )** that uses C++ features like **cout** and **vector** and returns an **int**. This code is present in a '.CPP' file. If we wish to call **fun( )** from C code we can do so as shown below.

```
/* driver.c */
#include <stdio.h>
#include "function.h"
int main( )
{
    int num ;
    num = fun ( 10, 20, 30 ) ;
```

```
    printf ( "Returned value = %d\n", num ) ;
    return 0 ;
}
```

Looks simple? Well, it works because of the connecting piece which declares the prototype of **fun( )** in "function.h" shown below. Note that this file is included in 'driver.c' as well as 'function.cpp'.

```
/* function.h */
#ifdef __cplusplus
    extern "C"
    {
#endif

int fun ( int, int, int ) ;

#ifdef __cplusplus
    }
#endif
```

The **__cplusplus** macro tests whether the program is being compiled by a C compiler or a C++ compiler. For C compiler **__cplusplus** would not stand defined, whereas for C++ compiler it would stand defined. So, in 'driver.c' the prototype would remain

```
int fun ( int, int, int ) ;
```

In 'function.cpp' the prototype becomes:

```
extern "C" { int fun ( int, int, int ) ; }
```

The { } are used in 'function.h' to apply **extern "C"** to a bunch of function prototypes, if present. By declaring the function as extern "C" we are telling the C++ compiler not to mangle the name of function **fun( )**. Mangling means giving a function a new name based on its current name and its parameters. By default, the C++ compiler mangles function names. It does this to support a concept called function overloading in C++, where multiple functions may have same name. C compiler doesn't do name mangling since there is no concept of function overloading in C.

Now we need to compile 'driver.c' using C compiler and 'function.cpp' using C++ compiler. On compilation two object code files—'driver.obj' and 'function.obj' would get created. We then need to link these two files to produce an executable file. These steps are given below:

```
c:\mydir> cl  /c driver.c
c:\mydir> cl  /c function.cpp
c:\mydir> link  driver.obj  function.obj  /OUT: "Final.exe"
```

cl is a Microsoft tool that comes with Visual Studio Community to compile the program at command-line. The **/c** option ensures that **cl** does compilation, creates object code and stops. Note that though we are using **cl** to compile both the programs, based on the extension '.c' or '.cpp', it suitably invokes the C or C++ compiler. While linking **/OUT** switch lets us name the exe file where the executable code would be stored. We have used the filename 'Final.exe'. On executing 'Final.exe' we get the following output:

```
c:\mydir>Final.exe
10  20  30
Returned value = 100
```

Remember to create the files 'driver.c', 'function.cpp' and 'function.h' in the same directory, which in my case was 'mydir'.

Instead of the **cl** tool if we are to compile and link the programs in Linux world, we can do so using the following commands:

```
$ gcc -c  driver.c
$ g++ -c function.cpp
$ g++ driver.o  function.o  -o Final.out
$ ./Final.out
10  20  30
Returned value = 100
```

Using C++ Classes from a C program

In the last section we saw how to call a C++ function from a C program. If we are to call a member function of a class from a C program, we must write a wrapper function in C++ for the member function to be called. We can then call this wrapper function from our C program.

Suppose we have a **Trial** class containing a **message( )** method as shown below:

```
/* trial.h */
/* Class declaration */
class Trial
{
    public :
        void message( ) ;
} ;
```

```
/* trial.cpp */
/* Class definition */
#include <iostream>
using namespace std ;
#include "trial.h"
void Trial :: message( )
{
    cout << "It worked!" ;
}
```

Obviously we cannot call **message( )** directly from a C program as C doesn't understand classes. So, we need to define a wrapper function as shown below:

```
/* wrapper.cpp */
#include "wrapper.h"
#include "trial.h"
void wrapper( )
{
    Trial t ;
    t.message( ) ;
}
```

The glue that connects our C program to the C++ wrapper is the file 'wrapper.h' given below:

```
/* wrapper.h */
#ifdef __cplusplus
extern "C" {
#endif
void wrapper( ) ;
```

```
#ifdef __cplusplus
}
#endif
```

Finally, we need to call the **wrapper( )** function from **main( )** as shown below:

```
/* driver.c */
#include "wrapper.h"
int main( )
{
    wrapper( ) ;
    return 0 ;
}
```

The compilation, linking and execution steps are as under:

```
c:\prog> cl /c driver.c
c:\prog> cl /c trial.cpp
c:\prog> cl /c wrapper.cpp
c:\prog> link *.obj /OUT: "Final.exe"
c:\prog> Final.exe
It worked!
```

You can try the same example in Linux as an exercise.

With that we come to the end of this chapter. I will await suggestions from you at kanetkar@kicit.com about what more I can include in this chapter in future editions.

A Compilation And Execution

"Tools offer convenience..."

In principle, you do not need an IDE to create, compile, assemble and debug C programs. It is like saying, well, you do not need an airplane to crisscross India, you can do it in a bullock-cart. Modern times need modern solutions. IDE is the solution for modern times. This chapter shows how to use it...

To understand C language and gain confidence in working with it you would be required to type programs in this book and then instruct the machine to execute them. To type any program, you need another program called Editor. Once the program has been typed it needs to be converted to machine language (0s and 1s) before the machine can execute it. To carry out this conversion we need another program called Compiler. Compiler vendors provide an Integrated Development Environment (IDE) which consists of an Editor as well as the Compiler. These IDEs and its online alternatives are discussed in this appendix.

IDEs

There are several IDEs available, each targeted towards different processor and operating system combinations. Given below is a brief description of the popular IDEs along with the links from where they can be downloaded.

Turbo C/C++ under Windows

If you wish to use Turbo C/C++ it is available at

https://www.developerinsider.in/download-turbo-c-for-windows-7-8-8-1-and-windows-10-32-64-bit-full-screen/

It is very easy to install and it works for Windows 7, 8, 8.1 and Windows 10 (32/64 bit) with full/window screen mode.

NetBeans under Windows

NetBeans is not a compiler. It is merely an IDE. Its Windows version can be downloaded from

http://www.netbeans.org

For developing C programs using NetBeans under Windows, you would also have to install Cygwin software. Cygwin comes with GCC compiler. It is available at

https://www.cygwin.com/

There is a nice tutorial available at the following link should you face any difficulty in setting up Cygwin and NetBeans:

https://www.wikihow.com/Run-C/C%2B%2B-Program-in-Netbeans-on-Windows

NetBeans under Linux

If you propose to use NetBeans under Linux you will not need Cygwin as with most Linux installations (like say, Ubuntu) GCC compiler comes preinstalled. So, you need to just download and install NetBeans for Linux environment.

Visual Studio under Windows

If you wish to use Visual Studio Community it is available at

https://www.visualstudio.com/vs/express/

You are free to use any of the IDEs mentioned above for compiling programs in this book. If you wish to know my personal choice, I would prefer NetBeans + Cygwin or Visual Studio Community Edition. All the IDEs are easy to use and are available free of cost.

Online Compilers

With ubiquitous availability of Internet, if you wish, you can completely avoid installation of IDE on your machine. Using a browser, you can connect to any of the following to type, compile and execute your programs:

https://www.onlinegdb.com/
https://www.tutorialspoint.com/compile_c_online.php
The limitation of using online compilers is that you need a steady Internet connection while you are using them. Most of these compilers compile our program using the gcc compiler.

Compilation and Execution Steps in IDE

The compilation and execution process with each of the IDEs mentioned in the previous section are a bit different. So, for your benefit I am giving below these steps for each IDE.

Compilation and Execution using Turbo C++

Carry out the following steps to compile and execute programs using Turbo C++:

(a) Start Turbo C++ from Start | All Programs | Turbo C++.

(b) Click 'Start Turbo C++' from the dialog that appears.

(c) Select File | New from menu.

(d) Type the program.

(e) Save the program using F2 under a proper name (say Program1.c).

(f) Use Ctrl + F9 to compile and execute the program.

(g) Use Alt + F5 to view the output.

Compilation and Execution using NetBeans

Carry out the following steps to compile and execute programs using NetBeans:

(a) Start NetBeans from Start | All Programs | NetBeans.

(b) Select File | New Project... from the File menu. Select Project Category as C/C++ and Project Type as C/C++ Application from the dialog that pops up. Click Next button.

(c) Type a suitable project name (say Program1) in Project Name Textbox. Click Finish.

(d) Type the program.

(e) Save the program using Ctrl + S.

(f) Use F6 to compile and execute the program.

Compilation and Execution using Visual Studio Community

Carry out the following steps to compile and execute programs using Visual Studio Community:

(a) Start Visual Studio Community from Start | All Programs | Microsoft Visual C++ Community.

(b) Select File | New Project... from the File menu. Select Project Type as C++ Console Application. Type a suitable project name (say Program1) in Project name Textbox. Choose suitable location where you wish to create the project folder. Click Create.

(c) Type the program.

(d) Save the program using Ctrl + S.

(e) Use Ctrl + F5 to compile and execute the program.

Compilation and Execution at Linux Command-line

C programs can be compiled and executed even at command-line, i.e., without using any IDE. Many programmers prefer this mode. In such cases we need to use an editor like Vim to type the program and the GCC compiler to compile it. In such as case you need to follow the following steps to compile and execute your program.

(a) Type the program and save it under a suitable name, 'hello.c'.

(b) At the command prompt switch to the directory containing 'hello.c' using the **cd** command.

(c) Compile the program using GCC compiler as shown below.

```
$ gcc hello.c
```

(d) On successful compilation, GCC produces a file named 'a.out'. This file contains the machine language code of the program which can now be executed.

(e) Execute the program using the following command:

```
$ ./a.out
```

Compilation and Execution Using Online Compilers

While using the online compilers you must remember to choose the language (C in our case) from the dropdown. Next, we must type our program and click the Run/Execute button. When we do so our typed program is sent to the web server where it is compiled and executed. The output created on execution is then sent back and displayed in the browser. If any errors are found in the program during compilation they are also relayed back and displayed in the browser.

In the past online compilers had a limitation that you could run only single file programs using them. This has been overcome now. For example, in www.onlinegdb.com you can create a multi-file project easily. For this you must first login using your google account and then click on the menu item 'Create New Project' from the left column in the browser window. This will create a skeleton file by the name 'main.c'. In this file you can type **main( )**. Then either use Ctrl M or by clicking the 'New File' icon in the top toolbar you can add a new file with a suitable name. We can add multiple files in this manner. Then run the project as usual by clicking on the 'Run' button.

Onlinegdb.com also has provisions to supply command-line arguments, debug a program using the debugger, create folders and store multiple files in it. From the point of view of security, online compiler is not a preferred choice for serious software development in C. Nevertheless, a good option with zero installation and configuration headaches when you are learning C.

B Precedence Table

"Preferential treatments..."

Whether we like it, or we don't, we live in an unequal world. Somebody gets a priority over somebody else. C programming is no different. With 45 operators in place, somebody has to get a priority over others. This chapter shows the exact order of their priority...

Description	Operator	Associativity
Postfix increment / decrement	++ --	Left to Right
Function call	( )	Left to Right
Array subscripting	[ ]	Left to Right
Structure / Union member access	.	Left to Right
Structure / Union member access	->	Left to Right
Prefix increment / decrement	++ --	Right to left
Unary plus and minus	+ -	Right to Left
Logical not, Bitwise not	! ~	Right to left
Typecast	(type)	Right to Left
Value of address (dereference)	*	Right to left
Address of	&	Right to left
Size in bytes	sizeof	Right to left
Multiplication, Division, Modulus	* / %	Left to right
Addition, Subtraction	+ -	Left to right
Bitwise left shift, Bitwise right shift	<< >>	Left to right
Less than, Less than or equal to	< <=	Left to right
Greater than, Greater than or equal to	> >=	Left to right
Equal to, Not equal to	== !=	Left to right
Bitwise AND	&	Left to right
Bitwise XOR	^	Left to right
Bitwise OR	|	Left to right
Logical AND	&&	Left to right
Logical OR	||	Left to right
Conditional	? :	Right to left

Continued...

Continued...

Assignment	=	Right to left
	+= -=	Right to left
	*= /= %=	Right to left
	<<= >>=	Right to left
	&= ^= |=	Right to left
Comma	,	Left to Right

Figure B.1. Precedence and Associativity of operators.

Note the following important points about precedence and associativity table shown in Figure B.1:

(a) Precedence and associativity of operators is pre-decided. We cannot *change* them.

(b) The table lists the C operators in decreasing order of their precedence, i.e., postfix increment/decrement operators have the highest precedence, whereas comma operator has the lowest precedence.

(c) If several operators occur within the same group (box) they enjoy equal priority. For example, **<**, **<=**, **>** and **>=** belong to the same box, hence have equal priority.

(d) The comma used in a function call is different from the comma operator (often called sequential-evaluation operator).

(e) When several operators of same precedence appear in an expression, evaluation proceeds according to associativity of operators.

(f) If an expression includes more than one *****, **+**, **&**, **|**, or **^** operator then the direction of evaluation does not affect the results.

For example, in the expression **a = 3 * 5 + 6 * 7**, whether **3 * 5** is done first and **6 * 7** is done next, or the other way round, does not affect the result of the expression. Same is the case with following expressions:

```
b = 3 + 5 + 6 + 7 ;
c = 23 | 43 | 56 ;
d = a & b & c ;
```

Since the order of operations is not defined by the language, the compiler is free to evaluate such expressions in any order.

(g) Different compilers may give different results for the following expressions:

```
int i = 3, j ;
j = ++i * ++i ;
```

Some compiler may evaluate this expression as **4 * 5** and others may evaluate it as **5 * 5**. Both are correct in their own way, since the standard is silent about how evaluation should proceed in such situations.

(h) A sequence point is a point in a program's execution at which it is guaranteed that all side effects of previous evaluations will have been performed.

(i) Only the &&, ||, ? :, ( ) and , operators constitute sequence points, and therefore guarantee a particular order of evaluation for their operands. For example, in the expression

```
a = I <= 45 && j > 50
```

I <= 45 is guaranteed to be evaluated before **j > 50**.

C

Chasing The Bugs

"Wading through the choppy waters ..."

There are only two types of C programmers. Those who face problems while creating a program and those who do not. The second variety is the one who never wrote any program. This chapter is for the first variety. It highlights some of the common mistakes that every C programmer makes...

There is no shortage of horror stories about programs that took twenty times to 'debug' as they did to 'write'. Many a time programs must be rewritten all over again because the bugs present in them could not be located. So how do we chase the bugs away? No sure-shot way for that. I thought if I made a list of more common programming mistakes, it might be of help. They are not arranged in any particular order. But I think it is surely a great help!

Bug 1

Omitting the ampersand before the variables used in **scanf( )**. For example,

```
int choice ;
scanf ( "%d", choice ) ;
scanf ( " %d ", &choice ) ;
```

Here, the **&** before the variable choice is missing. Another common mistake with **scanf( )** is to give blanks either just before the format string or immediately after the format string as in the second **scanf( )** above. Note that this is not a mistake, but till you don't understand **scanf( )** thoroughly, this is going to cause trouble. Safety is in eliminating the blanks.

Bug 2

Using the operator = instead of the operator ==. For example, the following **while** loop becomes an infinite loop since every time, instead of checking the value of **i** against 10, it assigns the value 10 to **i**. As 10 is a non-zero value the condition will always be treated as true, forming an infinite loop.

```
int i = 10 ;
while ( i = 10 )
{
    printf ( "got to get out" ) ;
    i++ ;
}
```

Bug 3

Ending a loop with a semicolon. Observe the following program:

```
int j = 1 ;
```

```
while ( j <= 100 ) ;
{
    printf ( "\nUpdate or perish!" ) ;
    j++ ;
}
```

Here, inadvertently, we have fallen in an infinite loop. Cause is the semicolon after **while**. This semicolon is treated as a null statement by the compiler as shown below.

```
while ( j <= 100 )
    ;
```

This is an infinite loop since the null statement keeps getting executed indefinitely as **j** never gets incremented.

Bug 4

Omitting the **break** statement at the end of a **case** in a **switch** statement. Remember that, if a **break** is not included at the end of a **case**, then execution will continue into the next **case.**

```
int ch = 1 ;
switch ( ch )
{
    case 1 :
        printf ( "\nGoodbye" ) ;
    case 2 :
        printf ( "\nLieutenant" ) ;
}
```

Here, since there is no **break** after **printf( )** in **case 1**, the control runs into **case 2** and executes the second **printf( )** as well. However, this sometimes turns out to be a blessing in disguise. Especially, when we want same set of statements to get executed for multiple cases.

Bug 5

Using **continue** in a **switch**. It is a common error to believe that the way the keyword **break** is used with loops and a **switch**; similarly, the keyword **continue** can also be used with them. Remember that **continue** works only with loops, never with a **switch**.

Bug 6

A mismatch in the number, type and order of actual and formal arguments. Consider the following call:

```
yr = romanise ( year, 1000, 'm' ) ;
```

Here, three arguments are being passed to **romanise( )** in the order **int**, **int** and **char**. When **romanise( )** receives these arguments into formal arguments, they must be received in the same order. A careless mismatch might give strange results.

Bug 7

Omitting provisions for returning a non-integer value from a function. If we make the following function call,

```
area = area_circle ( 1.5 ) ;
```

then, while defining **area_circle( )** function later in the program, care should be taken to make it capable of returning a floating-point value. Note that unless otherwise mentioned, the compiler would assume that this function returns a value of the type **int**.

Bug 8

Inserting a semicolon at the end of a macro definition. This might create a problem as shown below.

```
# define UPPER 25 ;
```

would lead to a syntax error if used in an expression, such as:

```
if ( counter == UPPER )
```

This is because on preprocessing, the **if** statement would take the form

```
if ( counter == 25 ; )
```

Bug 9

Omitting parentheses around a macro expansion. Consider the following macro:

```
# define SQR(x) x * x
```

If we use this macro as,

```
int a ;
a = 25 / SQR ( 5 ) ;
```

we expect the value of **a** to be 1, whereas it turns out to be 25. This is because, on preprocessing, the statement takes the form

```
a = 25 / 5 * 5 ;
```

Bug 10

Leaving a blank space between the macro template and the macro expansion.

```
# define ABS  (a) ( a = 0  ? a : -a )
```

Here, the space between **ABS** and **(a)** makes the preprocessor believe that you want to expand **ABS** into **(a)**, which is certainly not what you want.

Bug 11

Using an expression that has side effects in a macro. Consider the following macro:

```
# define SUM ( a ) ( a + a )
int  w, b = 5 ;
w = SUM( b++ ) ;
```

On preprocessing, the macro would be expanded to,

```
w = ( b++ ) + ( b++ ) ;
```

Thus, contrary to expectation, **b** will get incremented twice.

Bug 12

Confusing a character constant and a character string. In the statements

```
ch = 'z' ;  dh = "z" ;
```

a single character is assigned to **ch**, whereas a pointer to the character string "z" is assigned to **dh**.

Note that their declarations should be,

```
char  ch ;  char  *dh ;
```

Bug 13

Forgetting the bounds of an array.

```
int num[ 50 ], i ;
for ( i = 1 ; i <= 50 ; i++ )
    num[ i ] = i * i ;
```

Here, array **num** has no such element as **num[50]**, since array counting begins with 0 and not 1. Compiler would not give a warning if our program exceeds the bounds. If not taken care of, in extreme cases, the above code might even hang the computer.

Bug 14

Forgetting to reserve an extra location in a string for the null terminator. Remember each string ends with a '\0', therefore its dimension should be declared big enough to hold the normal characters as well as the '\0'. For example, dimension of the array **word[ ]** should be 9, if a string "Jamboree" is to be stored in it.

Bug 15

Confusing the precedence of various operators.

```
char ch ;
FILE *fp ;
fp = fopen ( "text.c", "r" ) ;
while ( ch = fgetc ( fp ) != EOF )
    putch ( ch ) ;
fclose ( fp ) ;
```

Here, the value returned by **fgetc( )** will be first compared with EOF, since **!=** has a higher priority than =. As a result, the value that is assigned to **ch** will be the true/false result of the test—1 if the value returned by **getc( )** is not equal to **EOF**, and 0 otherwise. The correct form of the above **while** would be,

```
while ( ( ch = getc ( fp ) ) != EOF )
    putch ( ch ) ;
```

Bug 16

Confusing the operator **->** with the operator **.** while referring to a structure element. On the left of **.** operator a structure variable should occur, whereas, on the left of -> operator a pointer to a structure should occur. Following example demonstrates this:

```
struct emp
{
    char name[ 35 ] ;
    int age ;
} ;
struct emp e = { "Dubhashi", 40 } ;
struct emp *p ;
printf ( "\n%d", e.age ) ;
p = &e ;
printf ( "\n%d",p->age ) ;
```

Bug 17

Exceeding the range of integers and chars. Consider the following code snippet:

```
char ch ;
for ( ch = 0 ; ch <= 255 ; ch++ )
    printf ( "\n%c %d", ch, ch ) ;
```

This is an indefinite loop. Reason is, **ch** has been declared as a **char** and its valid range is -128 to +127. So, when **ch** tries to become 128 (through **ch++**), the range is exceeded. As a result, the -128, gets assigned to **ch**. So, the condition is satisfied and the control remains within the loop.

Bug 18

Forgetting to parenthesize to enforce precedence. Consider the following code snippet:

```
char ch ;
FILE *fs ;
fs = fopen ( "Trial.txt", "r" ) ;
while ( ( ch = getc ( fs ) ) != EOF )
    printf ( "%c", ch ) ;
```

If we do not parenthesize the expression **ch = getc (fs)** then character returned by **getc( )** would first be compared with **EOF** and the result of the comparison (0 or 1) would be stored in **ch**. By parenthesizing the expression we are ensuring that the character returned by **getc( )** is first assigned to **ch** and then contents of **ch** are compared with **EOF**.

Bug 19

Forgetting to check whether the file opened for writing has been opened successfully. Consider the following code snippet:

```
FILE *ft ;
ft = fopen ( "Trial.txt", "w" ) ;
if ( ft == NULL )
    printf ( "\nUnable to open file" ) ;
```

If the file that we are opening for writing does not exist, a new file gets created. But this attempt to create a new file may fail for several reasons like, insufficient space, inadequate writing permissions, etc. So, it is a good idea to always check whether a file is opened successfully, even if it is being opened for writing.

D ASCII Chart

"The bread & butter for any programmer..."

When it is time to represent an A in memory, whether I press it or you press it from keyboard, the same binary should get used. This calls for a standard way of representing it. This chapter shows which is that standard...

There are 256 distinct characters used by PCs and Laptops. They can be grouped as shown in Figure D.1.

Character Type	No. of Characters
Capital letters	26
Small-case Letters	26
Digits	10
Special Symbols	32
Control Character	34
Graphics Character	128

Total = 256

Figure D.1 ASCII character set.

This 256-character set is listed in the following pages. Out of the 128 graphic characters the ones that can be used for drawing single-line and double-line boxes are shown in Figure D.2.

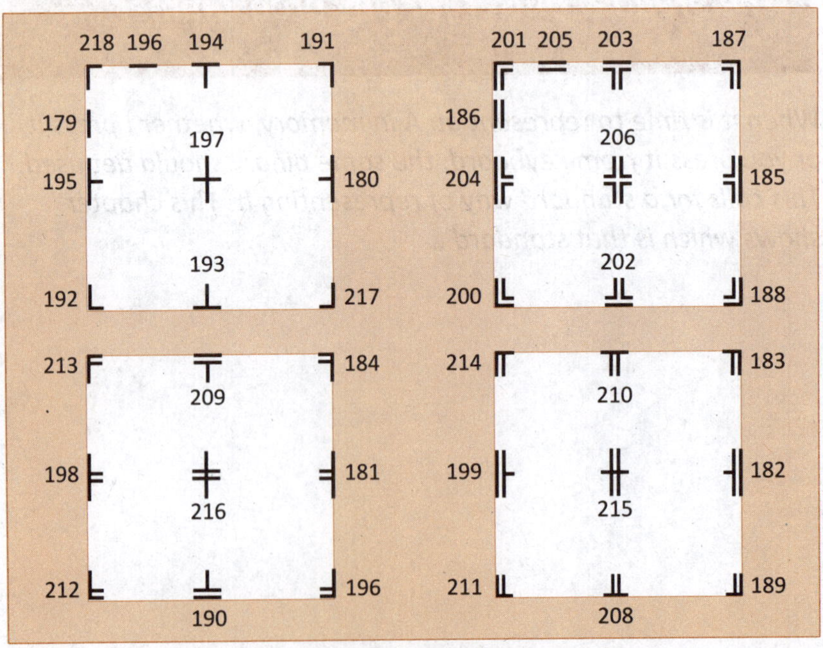

Figure D.2 Characters for single-line and double-line boxes.

Value	Char	Value	Char	Value	Char	Value	Char	Value	Char	Value	Char
0		22	▬	44	,	66	B	88	X	110	n
1	☺	23	↨	45	-	67	C	89	Y	111	o
2	☻	24	↑	46	.	68	D	90	Z	112	p
3	♥	25	↓	47	/	69	E	91	[	113	q
4	♦	26	→	48	0	70	F	92	\	114	r
5	♣	27	←	49	1	71	G	93	]	115	s
6	♠	28	∟	50	2	72	H	94	^	116	t
7	•	29	↔	51	3	73	I	95	_	117	u
8	◘	30	▲	52	4	74	J	96	`	118	v
9	○	31	▼	53	5	75	K	97	a	119	w
10	◙	32		54	6	76	L	98	b	120	x
11	♂	33	!	55	7	77	M	99	c	121	y
12	♀	34	"	56	8	78	N	100	d	122	z
13	♪	35	#	57	9	79	O	101	e	123	{
14	♫	36	$	58	:	80	P	102	f	124	|
15	☼	37	%	59	;	81	Q	103	g	125	}
16	►	38	&	60	<	82	R	104	h	126	~
17	◄	39	'	61	=	83	S	105	i	127	⌂
18	↕	40	(	62	>	84	T	106	j	128	Ç
19	‼	41	)	63	?	85	U	107	k	129	ü
20	¶	42	*	64	@	86	V	108	l	130	é
21	§	43	+	65	A	87	W	109	m	131	â

Value	Char	Value	Char	Value	Char	Value	Char	Value	Char	Value	Char
132	ä	154	Ü	176	░	198	╞	220	▄	242	≥
133	à	155	¢	177	▒	199	╟	221	▌	243	≤
134	å	156	£	178	▓	200	╚	222	▐	244	⌠
135	c	157	¥	179	│	201	╔	223	▀	245	⌡
136	ê	158	₧	180	┤	202	╩	224	α	246	÷
137	ë	159	ƒ	181	╡	203	╦	225	ß	247	≈
138	è	160	á	182	╢	204	╠	226	Γ	248	°
139	ï	161	í	183	╖	205	═	227	π	249	•
140	î	162	ó	184	╕	206	╬	228	Σ	250	·
141	ì	163	ú	185	╣	207	╧	229	σ	251	√
142	Ä	164	ñ	186	║	208	╨	230	µ	252	η
143	Å	165	Ñ	187	╗	209	╤	231	τ	253	^{2}
144	É	166	ª	188	╝	210	╥	232	Φ	254	■
145	æ	167	º	189	╜	211	╙	233	Θ	255	
146	Æ	168	¿	190	╛	212	╘	234	Ω		
147	ô	169	⌐	191	┐	213	╒	235	δ		
148	ö	170	¬	192	└	214	╓	236	∞		
149	ò	171	½	193	┴	215	╫	237	ø		
150	û	172	¼	194	┬	216	╪	238	∈		
151	ù	173	¡	195	├	217	┘	239	∩		
152	ÿ	174	«	196	─	218	┌	240	≡		
153	Ö	175	»	197	┼	219	█	241	±		

E Periodic Tests, Course Tests

"When confident, get tested..."

You should never take a test, when you are not prepared. You should never give up an opportunity to get tested, when you are fully prepared and confident. This chapter will help you check your strengths and weaknesses, once you are prepared and confident...

Periodic Test I
(Based on Chapters 1 to 7)

Time: 90 Minutes Maximum Marks: 40

[A] Fill in the blanks: [5 Marks, 1 Mark each]

(1) The expression **i++** is same as ______.

(2) _____ type of values cannot be checked using **switch-case**.

(3) Every instruction in a C program must end with a ______.

(4) The size of an **int** data type is ______ bytes.

(5) Statements written in _______ loop get executed for once even if the condition is false.

[B] State True or False: [5 Marks, 1 Mark each]

(1) The statement **for (; ;)** is a valid statement.

(2) The **else** clause in an **if – else if – else** statement goes to work if all the **if**s fail.

(3) The ^ operator is used for performing exponentiation operations in C.

(4) C allows only one variable on the left-hand side of = operator.

(5) Conditional operators cannot be nested.

[C] What would be the output of the following programs? [5 Marks, 1 Mark each]

(a)
```
# include <stdio.h>
int main( )
{
    int x = 5, y, z ;
    y =  x++ ;
    z = x--  ;
    printf ( "%d %d %d", x, y, z ) ;
    return 0 ;
}
```

(b)
```
# include <stdio.h>
int main( )
```

```
{
    int i = 65 ;
    char ch = i ;
    printf ( "%d %c", ch, i ) ;
    return 0 ;
}
```

(c)
```
# include <stdio.h>
int main( )
{
    int i, j ;
    for ( i = 1 ; i <= 2 ; i++ )
    {
        for ( j = 1 ; j <= 2 ; j++ )
        {
            if ( i == j )
                break ;
            printf ( "%d %d", i, j ) ;
        }
    }
    return 0 ;
}
```

(d)
```
# include <stdio.h>
int main( )
{
    int x = 3, i = 1 ;
    while ( i <=2 )
    {
        printf ( "%d ", x *= x + 4 ) ;
        i++ ;
    }
    return 0 ;
}
```

(e)
```
# include <stdio.h>
int main( )
{
    int a, b = 5 ;
    a = !b ;
    b = !a ;
    printf ( "%d %d", a, b ) ;
    return 0 ;
```

```
}
```

[D] Point out the error, if any, in the following programs:
[5 Marks, 1 Mark each]

(a)
```
# include <stdio.h>
int main( )
{
    int i = 10, j = 20 ;
    if ( i = 5) && if ( j = 10 )
        printf ( "Those who can't teach, preach" ) ;
    return 0 ;
}
```

(b)
```
# include <stdio.h>
int main( )
{
    int x = 10 ;
    if ( x >= 2 ) then
        printf ( "\n%d", x ) ;
    return 0 ;
}
```

(c)
```
# include <stdio.h>
int main( )
{
    int x = 0, y = 5, z = 10, a ;
    a = x > 1 ? y > 1 : z > 1 ? 100 : 200 : 300 ;
    printf ( "%d" , a ) ;
    return 0 ;
}
```

(d)
```
# include <stdio.h>
int main( )
{
    int x = 0, y = 5, z ;
    float a = 1.5, b = 2.2, c ;
    z = x || b ;
    c = a && b ;
    printf ( "%d %f", z, c ) ;
    return 0 ;
}
```

(e)
```
# include <stdio.h>
```

```
int main( )
{
    int a = 10, b = 5, c ;
    c += a *= b ;
    printf ( "%d %d %d" , a, b, c ) ;
}
```

[E] Attempt the following questions: **[20 Marks, 5 Marks each]**

(1) Write a program to calculate the sum of the following series:

1! 2! + 2! 3! + 3! 4! + 4! 5! + ... + 9! 10!

(2) Write a program to enter the numbers till the user wants and at the end it should display the count of positive, negative and zeros entered.

(3) Write a program to find the range of a set of numbers that are input through the keyboard. Range is the difference between the smallest and biggest number in the list.

(4) If three integers are entered through the keyboard, write a program to determine whether they form a Pythagorean triplet or not.

Periodic Test II
(Based on Chapters 8 to 12)

Time: 90 Minutes — Maximum Marks: 40

[A] Fill in the blanks: [5 Marks, 1 Mark each]

(1) ___ and ___ are pointer operators.

(2) ________ are variables, which hold addresses of other variables.

(3) _____ is called an 'address of' operator.

(4) The preprocessor directive that is used to give convenient names to difficult formulae is called ________.

(5) For a call by reference, you should pass ________ of variables to the called function.

[B] State True or False: [5 Marks, 1 Mark each]

(1) A function can return more than one value at a time.

(2) A fresh set of variables are created every time a function gets called.

(3) All types of pointers are 4 bytes long.

(4) Any function can be made a recursive function.

(5) The correct build order is Preprocessing – Compilation – Assembling – Linking.

[C] Answer the following questions: [10 Marks, 2 Marks each]

(1) Why are addresses of functions stored in the stack?

(2) How do you decide whether a variable should be passed by value or by reference?

(3) Size of a pointer is not dependent on whose address is stored in it. Justify.

(4) What different types of integer variables can be created in C? Which format specifier is used with each type in **printf( )**?

(5) A recursive call should always be subjected to an if. Why? Explain with an example.

[D] Attempt the following questions: [20 Marks, 5 Marks each]

(1) Define a function that receives 4 integers and returns sum, product and average of these integers.

(2) Define a recursive function which prints the prime factors of the number that it receives when called from **main( )**.

(3) Define macros for calculating area of circle, circumference of circle, volume of a cone and volume of sphere.

(4) Write a program that prints sizes of all types of chars, ints and reals.

Periodic Test III
(Based on Chapters 13 to 17)

Time: 90 Minutes Maximum Marks: 40

[A] Fill in the blanks: [5 Marks, 1 Mark each]

(1) Mentioning name of an array yields _______ of the array.

(2) C permits us to exceed ________ and ________ bounds of an array.

(3) Size of an array is _____ of sizes of individual elements of an array.

(4) Array elements are always counted from _____ onwards.

(5) A structure is usually a collection of ________ elements.

[B] State True or False: [5 Marks, 1 Mark each]

(1) If an array size is big its elements may get stored in non-adjacent locations.

(2) All strings end with a '\0'.

(3) Using **#pragma pack** you can control the layout of structure elements in memory.

(4) Elements of 2-D array are stored in the form of rows and columns in memory.

(5) 3-D array is a collection of several 1-D arrays.

[C] Answer the following questions: [10 Marks, 2 Marks each]

(1) What is likely to happen if the bounds of an array are exceeded?

(2) When you prefer a structure over an array to store similar elements? Explain with an example.

(3) What is the limitation of an array of pointers to strings? How can it be overcome?

(4) In a two-dimensional array **a[4][4]**, why do expressions **a** and ***a** yield same base address?

(5) How will you allocate space for a **float** array whose size is received from the keyboard?

[D] Attempt the following questions: [20 Marks, 5 Marks each]

(1) Write a function that receives as parameters, a 1-D array, its size and an integer and returns number of times the integer occurs in the array.

(2) Create an array of pointers containing names of 10 cities. Write a program that sorts the cities in reverse alphabetical order and prints this reversed list.

(3) Declare a structure called **student** containing his name, age and address. Create and initialize three structure variables. Define a function to which these variables are passed. The function should convert the names into uppercase. Print the resultant structure variables.

(4) Write a program that checks and reports whether sum of elements in the ith row of a 5 x 5 array is equal to sum of elements in i^{th} column.

Periodic Test IV
(Based on Chapters 18 to 22)

Time: 90 Minutes Maximum Marks: 40

[A] Fill in the blanks: [5 Marks, 1 Mark each]

(1) 0xAABB | 0xBBAA evaluates to ________.

(2) The values of an **enum** are stored as ________.

(3) An existing data type can be given a new name using the ________ keyword.

(4) The ________ operator can be used to eliminate 3 least significant bits from a character.

(5) The ________ operator is used to invert the bits in a byte.

[B] State True or False: [5 Marks, 1 Mark each]

(1) To check whether a particular bit in a byte is on or off, the bitwise | operator is useful.

(2) It is possible to create a union of structures.

(3) The callback mechanism can be implemented using function pointers.

(4) On evaluating the expression **a ^ 5** value of **a** would change.

(5) Bitwise operators can work on **floats** and **doubles**.

[C] Answer the following questions: [10 Marks, 2 Marks each]

(1) What is the utility of <<, >>, & and | bitwise operators?

(2) Define the **BV** macro. How would the following expressions involving the **BV** macro be expanded by the preprocessor?

```
int a = _BV ( 5 ) ;
int b = ~ _BV ( 5 ) ;
```

(3) In the following expression what does **p** signify?

```
long ( *p[ 3 ] ) ( int, float ) ;
```

(4) Suggest a suitable **printf( )** that can be used to print the grocery items and their prices in the following format:

Tomato Sauce	: Rs. 225.50
Liril Soap	: Rs. 55.45
Pen Refill	: Rs. 8.95

(5) When it is useful to make use of a union? What is the size of a union variable? How can the elements of a union variable be accessed?

[D] Attempt the following: [20 Marks, 5 Marks each]

(1) Write a program to multiply two integers using bitwise operators.

(2) Write a program to count number of words in a given text file.

(3) Write a program that receives a set of numbers as command- line arguments and prints their average.

(4) Write a program to check whether contents of the two files are same by comparing them on a byte-by-byte basis.

Course Test I
(Based on all Chapters)

Time: 150 Minutes **Maximum Marks: 70**

[A] Fill in the blanks: **[5 Marks, 1 Mark each]**

(1) A function that calls itself is known as a ______ function.

(2) Preprocessor directives always begin with _____.

(3) The expression **a[i][j]** in pointer notation is ______.

(4) A string always ends with the character ______.

(5) The keywords used to implement a case control instruction are _______, ______ and _______.

[B] Match the following pairs: **[5 Marks, 1/2 Mark each]**

Shifts bits to left	? :
Convert a bit to 0	++j
Compound assignment operator	%
Put on a bit	^
Type cast operator	==
Toggle bits	&
Pre-increment operator	*=
Comparison operator	|
Modulus operator	<<
Conditional operator	a = (int) b

[C] Answer the following questions: **[30 Marks, 3 Mark each]**

(1) Dynamically allocate space for a 3-D array of dimensions 3 x 5 x 4. Set up each elements of this array with a value 10. Report an error, if enough memory space is not available.

(2) Create an array of pointers to strings for storing names of 5 persons. What is the limitation of this array?

(3) Create a data structure for storing following data:

Name of the fruit
Color of the fruit
Diameter of the fruit

Price of the fruit
Weight of the fruit

(4) If a function is to be called, is it necessary to mention its prototype declaration? If yes, why?

(5) For a file being pointed to by **FILE *fp**, write function calls for carrying out the following operations?

- Set pointer at 5th position from beginning of file.
- Set pointer at 20th position from current position.
- Set pointer at 15th position before end of file.

(6) Suppose there is a user-defined file called 'myfunctions.h'.

- Write a statement to include this file in you program?
- What provision will you make in 'myfunctions.h' to prevent it from getting included twice?

(7) What do **argc** and **argv** represent with regards to command-line arguments?

(8) How will you redefine the types **unsigned long int** to **ULI** and **int **** to **DOUBLEPTR**? What is the scope of a **typedef** statement?

(9) Point out errors, in any, in the following code snippet:

```
int a ;
float b ;
char ch ;
scanf ( "%d %f %c", a, b, ch ) ;
printf ( "%d %f %c", &a, &b, &ch ) ;
```

(10) What will be the output of the following code snippet?

```
int a = 10 , b = 20 , c= 0 ;
if ( a && b || c )
    printf ( "Hello" ) ;
else
    printf( "Hi" ) ;

if ( !a && !b )
    printf ( "Good Morning!!" ) ;
else
```

```
printf( "Good Evening" ) ;
```

[D] Attempt the following questions: [30 Marks, 6 Marks each]

(1) Write a program that defines a function called **isalnum( )**. The function should receive a string and check if all characters in it are alphabets or digits. If so, it should return a true, otherwise false. Call this function for the following strings:

"ABCD1234"
"Nagpur – 440010"

(2) Define an enumeration to represent colors red, green, yellow, magenta and brown. Create two variables **Apple** and **Banana** of this **enum** type and assign colors red and yellow to them respectively. Print these color values and indicate what output will they produce.

(3) Define a function called **showbits(**) which displays all the bits of an **unsigned char** that it receives. Call this function for values 45 and 30. Indicate what output will **showbits( )** produce for these values?

(4) Write a program to generate and print all unique combinations of numbers 1, 2, 3 and 4.

(5) Define an iterative function and a recursive function to print first ten terms of a Fibonacci series. Which of these two functions will run faster and why?

Course Test II
(Based on all Chapters)

Time: 150 Minutes | Maximum Marks: 70

[A] State True or False: [5 Marks, 1 Mark each]

(1) Any function can be made a recursive function.

(2) Macro expansion directive can be used to replace a complicated formula with a convenient template.

(3) In the expression, *** (* (a + i) + j)**, the variable **a** must be a 2-D array.

(4) A char array may not end with '\0', but a string must.

(5) In the expression,

b = (int *) a ;

(int *) represents a typecast operation.

[B] Match the following pairs: [5 Marks, 1/2 Mark each]

Shifts bits to right	j ++
Quotient	? :
Remainder	*
Check bit 1 or 0	&
Post-Increment	->
Ternary operators	Size of
Value at address	/
Address of	bitwise &
Member access	%
Unary operator	>>

[C] Answer the following questions: [30 Marks, 3 Marks each]

(1) Create a data structure for storing the following data:

Name of document – Leaflet / Flier / Brochure
Number of colors – 1 / 2 / 4 / 5
Size – Small / Medium / Big
Type of paper – Maplitho / Bond / Artcard
Number of copies

Type of printing – Positive / Negative

(2) For storing names of months in a year, which out of array of strings and array of pointers to strings is preferable, and why?

(3) Consider the following structure:

```
struct Flower
{
    char name[ 20 ] ;
    int color ;
    int no_of_petals ;
} ;
struct Flower f[ 3 ] ;
```

Write statements to receive values into array **f[ ]** and print them on the screen.

(4) Given two matrices $\mathbf{A}_{3 \times 3}$ and $\mathbf{B}_{3 \times 3}$, define a function that checks whether matrix A is transpose of matrix B.

(5) What is the difference between function declaration and function definition? Which of the two—function redefinition or function redeclaration is an error, and Why?

(6) Write a code snippet to carry out the following operations:

- Open a file 'records.dat' in read binary mode.
- Skip first 200 bytes from the beginning of the file.
- Read next 20 bytes into an array **arr[ ]**.

(7) While using command-line arguments, is it necessary to use variables **argc** and **argv**? Write statements to print the name of the executable file and the first and second argument passed to the program?

(8) Once a type has been given a new name using **typedef**, can you use the previous type? Can the effect of **typedef** be also obtained using a macro? If yes, how?

(9) What is the difference between the following declarations?

```
int *p[ 4 ] ;
int ( *q )[ 4 ] ;
```

(10) What is the difference between a structure and a union as regards:

- Sharing of memory locations

- Size
- Accessing elements

[D] Attempt the following questions: [30 Marks, 6 Marks each]

(1) Consider the following statements:

```
int a = 20 ;
int *p ;
p = &a ;
```

Write statements only using **p** to:

- set a value 45 in **a**.
- multiply **a** with 40 and store the result in **a**
- print current value of **a**

Also write statements to perform the following operations:

- Increment **p**
- After incrementation, what will be present in **p** if variable **a** is at location 4004?
- Does incrementing **p** cause a memory leak?

(2) Write a program that defines a function called **isalpha( )**. The function should receive a string and check if all characters in it are alphabets. If so, it should return a true, otherwise false. Call this function for the following strings:

"NambyPamby"
"Mumbai – 400010"

(3) Define an enumeration to represent marital status of a person—single, married, divorced. Create two variables **he** and **she** of this **enum** type and assign to them values single and married respectively. Print these values and indicate what output will they produce.

(4) Define functions **countzeros( )** and **countones( )** which count number of 0s and 1s in an **unsigned char** that they receive. Call both these functions for values 101 and 111. Indicate what values will these functions return?

(5) Write a program to find maximum out of three given numbers in a single statement. What are the pros and cons of using this statement?

Index

"Random access begins..."

Some people like help, some people do not. But everybody likes "quick" help. This index will help you jump to that quick help...

!

A

B

C

D

E

F

N

O

P

R

S

T

U

V

W

C LANGUAGE INSTANT REFERENCE CARD

(Page 1)

DATA TYPES

DATA TYPE	RANGE	BYTES	FORMAT SPECIFIER
signed char	-128 to +127	1	%c
unsigned char	0 to 255	1	%c
short signed int	-32768 to +32767	2	%hd
short unsigned int	0 to 65535	2	%hu
signed int	-2147483648 to +2147483647	4	%d
unsigned int	0 to 4294967295	4	%u
long signed int	-2147483648 to +2147483647	4	%ld
long unsigned int	0 to 4294967295	4	%lu
long long signed int	-9223372036854775808 to 9223372036854775807	8	%lld
long long unsigned int	0 to 18446744073709551615	8	%llu
float	-3.4e38 to +3.4e38	4	%f
double	-1.7e308 to +1.7e308	8	%lf
long double	-1.7e4932 to +1.7e4932	10	%Lf

STATEMENT SUMMARY

STATEMENT	DESCRIPTION

if (expr)
statement1 ;
else
statement2 ;
	If expr is TRUE, then executes statement1, otherwise statement2.else is optional. If absent statement2 will not be present.

;	No effect. satisfies statement requirement in do, for, and while
while (expr) statement ;	Executes statement as long as expr is TRUE, statement might not be executed if expr is FALSE the first time it is evaluated.
for (e1 ; e2 ; e3) statement ;	Evaluates expression el once; then repeatedly evaluates e2, statement, and e3 (in that order) until e2 is FALSE. The statement might not be executed if e2, is FALSE on first evaluation.
do statement ; while (expr) ;	Executes statement until expr is FALSE ; statement is executed at least once.
break ;	Terminates execution of for, while, do, or switch.
continue ;	Skips statements that follow in a do, for, or, while; then continues executing the loop.

switch (iexpr)
{
case const1 :
statement1 ; break ;
case const2 :
statement2 ; break ;
default :
statement3 ; break ;
}
	iexpr is evaluated and then compared against integer constant expressions const1, const2, etc. If a match is found, then the statements that follow the case (up to the break) will be executed; if no match is found, then the statements in the default case (if supplied) will be executed; iexpr must be an integer-valued expression.

goto label ;	Branches to statement preceded by label, which must be in same function as the goto..
return ;	Returns from function back to caller; no value returned.
return expr ;	Returns from function back to caller with value of expr.

C LANGUAGE INSTANT REFERENCE CARD

(Page 2)

STORAGE CLASSES

STORAGE CLASS	STORAGE	DEFAULT VALUE	SCOPE	LIFE
Automatic	Memory	Garbage	Local to the block	Till control remains in the block in which var is defined
Register	CPU Registers	Garbage	Local to the block	Till control remains in the block in which var is defined
Static	Memory	Zero	Local to the block	Variable persists between different function calls
External	Memory	Zero	Global	Till execution of the program doesn't end

POINTERS

A pointer is a variable which stores address of another variable or function.

A pointer variable can be declared as follows:

```
/* numptr points to a float */
float *numptr ;
*sptr = 'c' ; /* store 'c' into location pointed to by sptr */

/*pointer to struct complex */
struct complex *cp ;
/* if the real part of the complex struct pointed to by cp is 0.0.*/
if ( cp - > real = = 0.0 )

/* fptr is pointer to function returning an int */
int (*fptr)( ) ;
```

FUNCTIONS

Function is declared and defined as follows:

```
ret_type name ( type arg1, type arg2,...) ; /* declaration */
ret_type name ( type arg1, type arg2,...)   /* definition */
{
    localvar_declartions ;
    statements ;
    return value ;
}
```

ret_type the return type for the function and can be void if the function returns no value or omitted if it returns an int.

A function is called as follows:

```
name ( arg1, arg2, ... ) ;
```

ARRAYS

A single- dimensional array aname of n elements of a specified type and with specified type and with specified initial values (optional) is declared with:

```
type aname[ n ] = { val1, val2, ... } ;
```

If complete list of initial values is specified, n can be omitted. Char arrays can be initialized by a string of chars in double quotes. Valid subscripts of the array range from 0 through n-1.

Multi-dimensional arrays are declared as:

```
type aname[ n1 ][ n2 ]... = { init_list } ;
```

Values listed in the initialization list are assigned in 'dimension order' (i.e., as if last dimension were increasing first). Here are some examples:

```
char name[ ] = "Anil" ; /* char array */
/* array of char pointers */
char *days[ ] = { "Sun", "Mon", "Tue" } ;
/* 2 x 4 array of ints */
int mat[ 2 ][ 4 ] = { { 2, 4, 5, 8 }, { -5, 0, 4, 7 } } ;
struct emp e[ 100 ] ; /* array of structs */
```

STRUCTURES

A structure sname of specified elements is declared with a statement of the form:

```
struct sname
{
    element_declaration ; element_declaration ;
} ;
struct sname variable_list ;
```

Each element_declaration is a type followed by one or more member names. If structure declaration and variable list definition are combined then sname is optional.

Elements of a structure are accessed using either . Operator or - > operator. If structure elements are to be accessed using a structure variable use the . operator is used and if they are to be accessed using a structure pointer then - > operator is used. For example:

```
struct emp { char n[ 20 ] ; int age ; } ;
struct emp e1 = { "Anil", 30 }, *e2 = &e1 ;
printf ( "%s%d\n", e1.n, e1.age ) ;
printf ( "%s%d\n", e2 ->n, e2->age ) ;
```

UNIONS

A union permits us to access the same locations in memory in more than one way. For example:

```
union a { int I ; char ch[ 4 ] ; } ;
union a z ;
```

The 4 bytes occupied by this union can be accessed as a 4-byte entity through z.i and as individual bytes through z.ch[0], z.ch[1], ...

typedef

typedef is used to give a new name to data type. For example, in the following code struct employee has been renamed as EMP.

```
struct employee { char name[ 20 ] ; int age ; } ;
typedef struct employee EMP ;
EMP e1, e2, e3 ;
```

OTHER TITLES OF INTEREST

Python Simplified with **Generative AI**
ISBN: 9789365899337

Web Data Mining with **Python**
ISBN: 9789355513632

Python Apps on **Visual Studio Code**
ISBN: 9789355519504

A Journey to **Core Python**
ISBN: 9789355511249

Edge Computing with **Python**
ISBN: 9789355512000

Data Analysis with **Python**
ISBN: 9789355510655

Image Processing Masterclass with **Python**
ISBN: 9789389898644

Python Machine Learning Projects
ISBN: 9789389898262

Python Internals for **Developers**
ISBN: 9789391392024

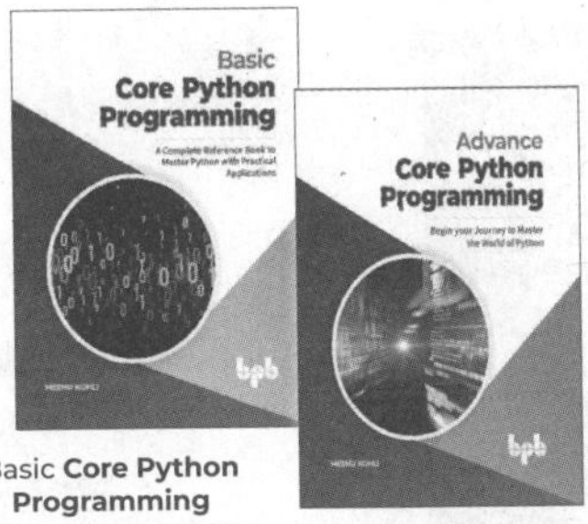

Basic **Core Python Programming**
ISBN: 9789390684953

Advance **Core Python Programming**
ISBN: 9789390684069

Internals of **Python 3.x**
ISBN: 9789391030940

Building Modern GUIs with **tkinter & Python**
ISBN: 9789355518569

Selenium & Appium with **Python**
ISBN: 9789355518354

Learn Penetration Testing with **Python 3.x**
ISBN: 9789390684915

Python GUI with **PyQt**
ISBN: 9789355515575

OTHER TITLES OF INTEREST

Digital Image Processing Using **Python**
ISBN: 9789365898910

Fun with **Python**
ISBN: 9789365893816

Python Programming for **Students**
ISBN: 9789355516084

Basics of **Python Programming** – 2nd Edi.
ISBN: 9789355516404

Mastering Python 3 Programming
ISBN: 9789355517128

Ultimate Data Science Programming in **Python**
ISBN: 9789365895667

Learn Python Generative AI
ISBN: 9789355518972

Python Fundamentals for **Data Analytics**
ISBN: 9789365892314

Comprehensive Data Structures & **Algorithms** in **C++**
ISBN : 9789365898576
By:
S. K. Srivastava
Deepali Srivastava

Ultimate Python Programming
ISBN : 9789355516558
By:
Deepali Srivastava